The Open Space of Democracy

Red

Leap

Desert Quartet

An Unspoken Hunger

Refuge

Earthly Messengers

Coyote's Canyon

Between Cattails

Pieces of White Shell

The Secret Language of Snow

FINDING

BEAUTY

IN A

BROKEN

WORLD

FINDING BEAUTY IN A BROKEN WORLD

...

Terry Tempest Williams

PANTHEON BOOKS, NEW YORK

Pantheon Books and colophon are registered trademarks of Random House, Inc.

Grateful acknowledgment is made to the following for permission to reprint
previously published material: Dow Jones & Company, Inc.: Excerpt from
"Great Plains Rodent Gets Comfy New Life As International Pet—but the
Humble Prairied Dog Now Faces a Ban in Japan Along with Foes at Home" by
Thaddeus Herrick and Phred Dvorak (*The Wall Street Journal*, April 17, 2003),
copyright © 2003 by Dow Jones & Company, Inc. All rights reserved. Reprinted
by permission of Dow Jones & Company, Inc., administered by Copyright
Clearance Center. • Houghton Mifflin Harcourt Publishing Company: Excerpt
from "Choruses from 'The Rock' " from *Collected Poems 1909–1962* by T. S.
Eliot, copyright © 1936 by Houghton Mifflin Harcourt Publishing Company
and renewed 1964 by T. S. Eliot. Reprinted by permission of Houghton Mifflin
Harcourt Publishing Company. • Eric Miller: Excerpt from "Birding with
Roger Tory Peterson" by Eric Miller (*Brick: A Literary Journal*, Spring 1997).
Reprinted by permission of Eric Miller. • *USA Today:* Excerpt from
"Monkeypox Sickens 29 People in USA: Exotic Virus Thought to Have Been
Spread by Pet Prairie Dogs" by Anita Manning (*USA Today*, June 9, 2003).
Reprinted by permission of *USA Today*, a division of Gannett Co., Inc.,
administered by Copyright Clearance Center.

Library of Congress Cataloging-in-Publication Data

Williams, Terry Tempest.
Finding beauty in a broken world / Terry Tempest Williams.
p.   cm.
Includes bibliographical references.
ISBN: 978-0-375-42078-8
1. Aesthetics.   I. Title.
BH39.W554 2008   814'.54—dc22   2008007196

www.pantheonbooks.com

This book is printed on paper containing 20 percent recycled fiber, primarily
PCW (post-consumer waste).

Printed in the United States of America
First Edition
2   4   6   8   9   7   5   3   1

For
Carl Brandt

with my love

These fragments I have shored against my ruins.

T. S. ELIOT, *The Waste Land*

INTERSTICES

These fragments I have shored against my ruins—
The cosmos works by harmony of tensions, like the lyre and bow
And so it was I entered the broken world
Turning shadow into transient beauty—
Once upon a time, we knew the world from birth

FINDING
BEAUTY
IN A
BROKEN
WORLD

We watched the towers collapse. We watched America choose war. The peace in our own hearts shattered.

How to pick up the pieces?
What to do with these pieces?

I was desperate to retrieve the poetry I had lost.

Standing on a rocky point in Maine, looking east toward the horizon at dusk, I faced the ocean. *"Give me one wild word."* It was all I asked of the sea.

The tide was out. The mudflats exposed. A gull picked up a large white clam, hovered high above the rocks, then dropped it. The clam broke open, and the gull swooped down to eat the fleshy animal inside.

"Give me one wild word to follow . . ."

And the word the sea rolled back to me was "m o s a i c."

Ravenna is the town in Italy where the west arm of Rome and the east arm of Constantinople clasped hands and agreed on a new capital of the Roman Empire in 402 AD. It was a pragmatic decision made by a shift in power, the decline of Rome and the rise of Byzantium. A spiritual history of evolving pagan and Christian perspectives can be read in a dazzling narrative of cut stones and glass.

Eloquence is spoken through the labor of hands, anonymous hands of forgotten centuries. With eyes looking up, artisans rolled gold tesserae between their fingers in thought, as they searched for the precise placement in domes and apses where light could converse with glass. Jeweled ceilings become lavish tales. I want to understand these stories told through fragments. I am an apprentice in a mosaic workshop.

Her name is Luciana. She is my teacher. Her work is unsigned, anonymous. Like the mosaicists before her who created the ancient mosaics that adorn the sacred interiors of this quiet town, she conducts the workshop in the traditional manner outlined centuries ago.

The tools required: a hammer and a hardie. The hardie is similar to a chisel and is embedded in a tree stump for stability. A piece of marble, glass, or stone, desiring to be cut, is held between the forefinger and thumb of the left hand, placed perpendicular on the hardie. The hammer that bears two cutting edges, gracefully curved, is raised in the right hand. With a quick blow, a tessera is born, the essential cube in the creation of a mosaic.

Her name is Luciana. She is a mosaicist in the town of Ravenna. She has no belief in invention or innovation. "It has all been done before," she says. "There are rules."

1. *The play of light is the first rule of mosaic.*

2. *The surface of mosaics is irregular, even angled, to increase the dance of light on the tesserae.*

3. *Tesserae are irregular, rough, individualized, unique.*

4. *If you are creating a horizontal line, place tesserae vertically.*

5. *If you are creating a vertical line, place tesserae horizontally.*

6. *The line in mosaic is supreme; the flow of the line is what matters so the eye is never disturbed or interrupted.*

7. *The background is very important in emphasizing the mosaic pattern. There must always be at least one line of tesserae that outlines the pattern. Sometimes there will be as many as three lines defining the pattern as part of the background.*

8. *There is a perfection in imperfection. The interstices or gaps between the tesserae speak their own language in mosaics.*

9. *Many colors are used to create one color from afar. Different hues of the same color were always used in ancient mosaics.*

10. *The distance from which the mosaic is viewed is important to the design, color, and execution of the mosaic.*

11. *The play of light is the first and last rule of mosaic.*

Luciana will tell you that once you learn the rules of ancient mosaics, only then can you break them. She places a gold piece of glass between her finger and thumb on the hardie and holds the hammer at the base of its wooden handle. *Ting*—she strikes the gold smalti into the exact shape she desires.

"You can learn this technique in fifteen minutes," she says. "It will take you a lifetime to master it."

A mosaic is a conversation between what is broken.

The very language of tesserae tells us that this harmony is only achievable through the breaking and then rediscovery of the mosaic fragments.

NATASCIA FESTA, Nittola

You will see that the vibration, the movement, the tremor, the shimmering of that lapidary colour, of that colour of stone or enamel tessera is obtained also by staggering the connection between one tessera and another, by not putting them at the same level, often by making one protrude in respect to the one next to it so as to obtain effects of marginal refraction that give a value of vibration to the entire colour.

GIULIO CARLO ARGAN, *Mosaico d'amicizid fra i popoli*

A mosaic is a conversation that takes place on surfaces.
A mosaic is a conversation with light, with color, with form.
A mosaic is a conversation with time.

The first mosaics were made in Mesopotamia, twenty-five hundred years before Christ. They were decorative embellishments, terracotta or mother of pearl. And then they died out before they could develop as an art form.

Mosaic reappeared in ninth-century Greece, this time as floor decoration. Geometric designs rendered through pebbles were a cheaper alternative to carpets. Two centuries later, floor mosaics became figurative, with colored pebbles creating the shadowed subtleties of lions and stags in a hunt. Dionysus riding on the back of a cheetah was depicted in a pebble mosaic discovered in Pella, Macedonia. The God of Fertility is given not only stature but grace in exquisite detail through the shading of pebbles, thousands of pebbles picked, placed, and permanently secured to the concrete surfaces.

Pebbles gave way to cut stone, which allowed greater control and mastery. Stone cut in small cubes, called tesserae, became the preferred medium of mosaic. This decorative form became widespread in Greece, Turkey, and Egypt. Some of the finest examples of mosaics were the elaborate floors and walls unearthed in the excavations of Pompeii, buried under volcanic ash from the eruption of Vesuvius in 79 AD.

A mosaic located in Pompeii, which celebrates the flora and fauna of the Nile River, is a wildly rich execution of life in foreign lands. Romans occupied Egypt in 30 BC and were charmed by the beauty of what they found. Hippopotami, crocodiles, cobras, wolves, mallards, ibis, and all manner of aquatic plants are created in a highly stylized mosaic.

Mosaics become the narratives of a newly conquered world.

Exotica from the natural world became popular motifs in mosaics in the early centuries before Christ. Dolphins, leaping fish, octopus, lobsters surrounding playful cherubs and cupids became emblematic of the figurative imagery that followed the spread of Rome.

The "Unswept Floor" mosaics in Hellenistic Greece were a trompe l'oeil, amusing as well as beautiful with the creation of gastronomic pleasures painted in stone on the floors. This tradition of hospitality or "xenia"—baskets of fruits, the preparation of fowl and wine, even a mouse biting into a nut creating crumbs on the mosaic pavement of a white background—honored a sense of generosity in the spirit of abundance. The floors always looked as if there had been a feastful party the night before.

Mosaics celebrated seasonal change and embellished the shrines of the gods of fertility, harvest, and renewal with sensual displays of body and earth.

The evolution from a pagan world to a Christian one transformed the florid, mythological stories to a more one-dimensional form where the message became more important than the medium. The Sun God Apollo was transformed into the Son of God. Symbolic representation was emphasized over the extravagant catalog of creation. Depth disappeared in the flat style of belief.

Under the Christian emperor Constantine, mosaics were lifted from the floor to ceilings of worship. Glass replaced stone; light shimmered as Truth in the Houses of God.

Bits of cut glass became the property of prayer as Roman churches, austere on the outside, were encrusted with the brilliance of mosaic on the inside. A particular glass called smalti was made specifically for this kind of embellishment. Durable, with the increased ability to reflect light, and with colors so varied it brought nuance to the work of the most imaginative mosaicists. A golden age of mosaic was born.

Mosaics became everyman's Bible; one didn't have to rely on words, only the shimmering stories told through images above, meant to overwhelm the viewer as one would be in the presence of God. The humble entered an interior space, immediately transported to the Kingdom of Heaven in all its spiritual brilliance.

Standing beneath the storied ceiling of the Church of San Vitale, I am overwhelmed. Dolphins wrap around each other in oceanic garlands that frame the portraits of apostles standing in fields of wildflowers with a bestiary of birds and animals. It is a litany of both religious and secular history. The Empress Theodora and her court, alongside the Emperor Justinian and his retinue, create a procession of power equal to that of the gods.

Begun by the Goths, this chapel was built with Roman technology, including a Roman dome and finished under the Byzantines' architectural genius and consecrated in May, 547 AD. Its transformation from an austere place of worship to one of the greatest examples of Byzantine mosaics in all its florid expressions, solidifies that San Vitale's core inspiration was found not in Italy but in the exotic luxuriousness of the East.

I think of the anonymous workers, their eyes raised to the ceilings, the relentless strain on their necks and backs, their hands drawing from the plates of colored tesserae as they worked from the spectacular heights of primitive scaffoldings. I imagine both the concentration and the wandering of minds as they labored over time in the repetitive trance of craft.

My eyes focus on the tongues of red mosaic flames rising from gray boulders. Moses is removing his sandals before he approaches the burning bush. He rises to receive the law from the hand of God reaching out from a bank of storm clouds.

The tablets he receives, the Ten Commandments, he will shatter into fragments. Mosaic Law.

Upon the mosaic ceilings of the Church of San Vitale, the stories of both the Old and New Testaments are arranged and rearranged. *"An eye for an eye"* is replaced by *"Do unto others as you would have them do unto you."* Moses is searching for truth and delivers it through stone tablets. Jesus Christ is sharing the truth as he delivers his Sermon on the Mount. Both men serve their God within a landscape where lilies and the expanding and intertwining tails of peacocks and dolphins remind us we live within a varied world.

The meticulously patterned landscape of San Vitale is, at once, an ethos and an ecosystem created one tessera at a time. I can only raise my head and look upward. The ceilings, walls, arches, and cupola shimmer and shine like the morning sun striking the expectant wicks of a thousand gilded grasses in the prairie.

Luciana invites us to pick a pattern from those displayed around the studio. They are details from the famed mosaic-covered ceilings and walls of the basilicas, baptisteries, and tombs found within the city. We will become familiar with their names: San Vitale; the Mausoleum of Galla Placidia; Sant'Apollinare Nuovo; Sant'Apollinare in Classe; and the Neonian baptistry, the so-called Mausoleum of Theodoric.

We wander among Byzantine motifs: doves drinking from a fountain; garlands made of olive leaves; geometric patterns; deer; long-legged birds; poppies; lilies; and the faces of emperors and empresses.

I chose three white lilies against a backdrop of blue-green and turquoise. Luciana tells me there are many lilies to be found in the mosaics of Ravenna. This particular detail is found in the mosaics of Sant'Apollinare Nuovo.

Sant'Apollinare Nuovo is cold inside and deeply quiet. The procession of martyrs and saints stuns, one after another, men on one side of the church, women on the other. They are standing straight, staring, glittering and gleaming with late-afternoon light. The white mosaics that make up their robes are formed from the rough face of the tesserae; hence without a sheen, they give the appearance of cotton or linen. The background of vibrant greens and turquoises conveyed through the lilies and shrubs celebrate the lush foliage, alongside the red-petaled poppies, create a grounding of faith inside the basilica.

I step back.

> The strange figures in the great mosaic panorama look down, with coloured cheeks and staring eyes, lifelike enough to speak to you and answer your wonderment. . . . What it is these long slim seraphs express I cannot quite say, but they have an odd, knowing, sidelong look out of the narrow ovals of their eyes which, though not without sweetness, would certainly make me murmur

I sit down on a bench and watch light.

After we have settled on our design, we place a sheet of wax paper over the picture of the mosaic we have chosen and trace each tessera exactly, one by one, paying attention to the gaps and interstices, with a black felt-tip marker. Upon completion of our outlines, we turn the tracing paper over and, with a second piece of tracing paper, trace what we have just done, this time in reverse, with a black water-soluble pen. We transfer this outline onto a bed of wet lime by pressing the pattern with the palm of our hand. The design is now printed on the lime, which has been generously spread on a piece of wood or particle board to serve as the basis for our mosaics.

We now have a step-by-step pattern to begin our mosaics, placing each tessera or glass cube in its designated niche.

This is known as the "direct method" of creating mosaics on temporary stucco, perfected in the workshops of Ravenna, where exquisite copies have been made through the ages.

Outside the patio of Luciana's studio, Mateo, a baker's son, mixes the lime with a little sand and water until it is the consistency of whipping cream. The layer is then smoothed and leveled with a trowel over the wooden base.

One by one, we receive our lime canvas, so to speak, and place our design on the wet stucco. I watch the black ink bleed on to the lime. Mateo carefully pulls off the wax paper, throws it away, and then hands me my lime base. I place the board on an easel with a copy of the color picture or "cartoon" of the lilies nearby so I can replicate the intricate color scheme of the tesserae as accurately as possible.

We are ready to begin to set the tesserae. But first, Luciana tells us, we must cut them.

Luciana has provided each of us with a plate of marble rectangles about two inches by one inch. She briskly shows us how to cut stone, very matter-of-factly. "You put the hardie between your legs. You hold the marble between your first finger and thumb. You place it on the hardie here. You hold the hammer at its base like this, and then you deliver a quick, straight blow." She looks up at us, "Keep your wrist stiff." As she stands up and removes herself from the hardie, she says, "That's it. Now practice."

Cut. Cut. Cut again. The marble pieces just get smaller and smaller. One rectangle becomes two squares. Two squares turn into four into eight into sixteen cubes. Whatever size we need, we cut. If only it were that simple.

For the rest of the afternoon, with the hardie between my legs and a hammer in hand, I cut stone. For hours, I cut stone remembering my own desert country of red rock and sand.

We arrive at the studio the next morning to find that bowls of colored tesserae (in my case, white, gold, green, dark green, turquoise, and cobalt blue) have magically appeared at our work space. There are over three thousand different colors to work with at the Mosaic Studio. They have roughly been cut to size, but we must still tailor them to their rightful positions on the lime outline.

It looks so simple, like child's play. Luciana tells us to first outline the pattern.

"One of the rules of mosaic," she says. "Remember, mosaic is an art, not a craft."

I take the white marble tesserae and begin placing them one by one around the shape of each lily. To match the design, I must cut and refine many of them to fit the shapes I have drawn from the cartoon. The marble is hard and stubborn, and it takes many tries with the hammer and hardie. The sense of satisfaction that comes when the desired shape is reached is akin to finding the right puzzle piece that fits perfectly into the emerging picture. The irregular pieces are then pushed into the soft lime bed like model teeth in a yielding gum.

Next, we are told to put in the first row of background tesserae following the outline we have just created. I cut dark blue tesserae made of glass. The glass tesserae are much more fragile and temperamental than marble or stone or terra-cotta bricks. Small shears occur. Some of the tesserae shatter. I put on safety glasses and cut another and another until I get the feel of the glass cubes between my fingers. Size and shape vary as I try to mirror the tesserae of the lilies with the tesserae outlining them.

"Allora . . ." Luciana says to me, impatient. She picks up the bowl of gold tesserae, the same gold pieces made for generations by the Orsoni family in Venice and the glassmakers before them who made the gold smalti for centuries in stone kilns. On the tiny island of Murano, the scalding liquid gold was drawn out on long wooden ladles from the mouths of the ovens, then poured into flat pancake molds known as "glass pizzas."

These are the same gold tesserae, now cut in squares, responsible for the shimmering backgrounds that have dazzled and enchanted spiritual pilgrims through the ages as they looked up and read the stories of Creation on the Basilica de San Marco in Venice or stood in the Cathedral of Santa Maria Assunta on the island of Torcello, surrounded by wetlands.

The square of gold smalti Luciana holds in her hand is the same gold that dazzles the viewer of these mosaics, the spiritual iconography set in glass relief in these houses of worship designed in the fourth through ninth centuries throughout the Roman Empire to the days of Constantinople.

Luciana stands next to me and cuts several gold tesserae and shows me the line to follow to make the stems of lilies. She encourages me to break up the gold with tesserae made of yellow sandstone.

"It makes it more interesting to vary the textures," she says. "Never use too much of any one color, not even gold. In mosaic, it is the tension that ties one tesserae to another."

I cut and set the lines of gold.

"These no good," Luciana says, pulling out three tesserae from my mosaic with her long tweezers. "They interrupt my eyes." She asks me to move and sits down in my seat and instantly begins cutting more tesserae and placing them where they should be. Her large, dark eyes flash from the cartoon to the board of lime. Luciana works quickly, instinctively, and within seconds, has calmed the agitated space I had created with a more timid monochromatic color scheme.

"See here," she says, running her finger across the arching line just above the first lily on the left. "You must pay attention to what the ancient mosaicists did with color. It may not make sense to you, but stand back and squint."

I follow her instructions. It's true; what appears illogical or abrupt close up, blends from afar. A chartreuse tessera that jars my eye when it's close becomes a glint of light on the dark green stem. It's as though sunlight has entered the room.

The lilies I am replicating in the studio, I find in their native habitat in the basilica. They flourish at the feet of one of the martyrs on the right panel in the middle of the procession. The lilies are a floral trinity. With my neck cranked as far back as it will go, I see the chartreuse tesserae I struggled with earlier in the day. The placement of the tesserae is not perfect, but they are perfect in their overall effect. From this distance, they provide geographic relief to an otherwise flat motif of one-dimensional figures. The stamens set in gold are glistening. I had hardly paid them any attention in my own reproduction.

The lilies are joined with poppies in accentuating the floral background of the saints. Palms set against the glow of gold tesserae stand behind the figures, creating the sensibilities and supporting grace of the natural world. It is an extravagant honoring of the Savior both as a child and as a man. Each man and woman in their long line of devotion bears gifts, a crown of jewels, respectfully held in a repetition of patterns as though one can hear within the intentional interstices of the tesserae the recitation of sacred texts, the long lines inherent in any litany of belief.

Back at the workshop, I sit down and finish the upper right hand corner of the lilies, cutting tesserae in the shapes of triangles, a new skill I have achieved in the last few days. My eye is more acute in recognizing patterns that serve the whole. I am learning to watch and study.

I am also learning to trust the motion that comes through color and interstices, not in the controlled, static placement of each cube but in the joy of odd arrangements and unpredictable moves of choice.

I believe in the beauty of all things common.

Lilies. Stone. Cut glass.

I believe in the beauty of all things broken.

On my way back to the little flat where I am staying, I make another visit to the basilica of Sant'Apollinare Nuovo. It is the end of the day, and no one is here. Late-afternoon light strikes the mosaics of the Royal Palace of Theodoric, but what captures my imagination are the hands wrapped around the white mosaic columns: three disembodied hands and a hand with a jeweled bracelet on its forearm. Who is hiding behind these columns? Why are we shown only their arms? Whomever they belong to are hidden behind the elaborate stone curtains beneath gold mosaic arches. These hands are a sign from the past, a signature left in mosaic by the Arian Christians, viewed as heretics by what became the Orthodox church. The irony is that they are the ones who survived.

I went back for the disembodied arms with the hands clasped in prayer, but they were gone. My eyes searched the table in the Arezzo market. I should have bought them. Fifteen euros. Clearly, it wasn't about the money. Something had frightened me. I turned around and asked the outdoor vendor, who was sitting on a stool against the stucco wall, if he still had them. He shook his head. In a quick exchange of Italian, he told me they had just been sold. Who to? He couldn't remember.

Something had stopped me. This was the impulse I had to trust. Who knew what these broken arms with devoted hands held? Could I in good conscience have lived with them severed from their source, never knowing the face that looked down upon them, much less the body of flesh-painted plaster to which they belonged? No doubt these were fragments of a saint perched on an abandoned altar, perhaps stolen. One never knows the power of such things.

No. I walked away. Now, wandering through the outdoor market, I wondered who had them.

Do I dare to admit that my own hands are those locked in that perpetual gesture of pleading and desire—a disembodied hand clutching a pencil in prayer.

Writers break black letters out of lead and line them up on white sheets of paper and ask others to read the sentences we have created for ourselves.

In Italy, cypress trees speak of vertical time in a layered landscape. There is nothing here that has not been tampered with and tempered by human history. It is a deeply foreign sensibility to my mind permanently placed in the desert of the American West. There is nothing I desire here but those disembodied arms with hands in perpetual prayer. This is what I know as a writer devoted to words. It is all I know in the loneliness of waiting for the right line to appear.

A mosaic is a conversation between what is broken.

His name is Marco de Luca. He is a mosaicist in the town of Ravenna. Unlike the artists before him who created ancient mosaics that embellished the sacred interiors of this quiet town, his work adorns galleries, not ceilings.

De Luca builds geological landscapes with cubes. Each tessera that he cuts with his hammer and hardie becomes a tiny block of earth, a drop of water, or a shimmering note in the composition of light. You stand before his mosaic constructions and witness a stratigraphy of stones, sediments that have been laid down through time, one tessera speaking to the next, some side by side, others turned, akimbo.

Tension builds through size and compression. Some tesserae are orderly, square and small. They create lines like sentences of four-sided words:

> *moon wake over wave blue*
> *rose fish deep sand seen near*
> *cube swim gold next rock face*
> *leaf fell fall land dirt held*

Other tesserae are bold in their displacement because irregular size and shape break up the narrative. Other tesserae are thin like a series of feathers and fan out like an extended wing, defying the simple fact that they are rock; they are glass.

Some tesserae appear as ill-fated figures, slighted and slated to fall like dominos but are kept from a fatal landing by the upright shoulders of neighbors who can bear the weight.

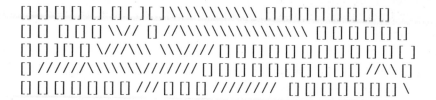

```
[] [] [] [] [] [] [ ] [ ] \\\\\\\\\\ [] [] [] [] [] [] [] []
[] [] [] [] [] \\// [] //\\\\\\\\\\\\\\\\\ [] [] [] [] [] []
[] [] ] [] [] \//\\ \\\//// [] [] [] [] [] [] [] [] [] [] [] [ ]
[] //////\\\\\\//////// [] [] [] [] [] [] [] [] [] [] //\\ []
[] [] [] [] [] [] [] /// [] [] [] //////// [] [] [] [] [] [] [] \
```

And still others are large, intentional breaks in form like a rockfall in the desert. It is motion suspended, stopped, noted. And then there are those that flow through the landscape like water, completely fluid in their meanderings.

My eyes scan a monochromatic plain. I am stopped by a voice of red, one red tessera in a choral reading of beiges, browns, and taupes. Line by line, de Luca creates an organic text akin to the placement of words in a letter press. The mosaics become vigorous in their calm composure. Architectural. Sculptural. Geographic relief is realized through shadow and light.

What you see from a distance is not what you see up close.

His name is Marco de Luca, and he can bend stone with his eyes.

We meet by chance. He invites me to his studio. He leans against the white stucco wall. He is tall. He is dark. His intensity is unnerving.

He walks over to a turnstile loaded with stones, where bowls of smalti are also found. He brings a wooden box over to me.

"Hold out your hands." He places a dozen glass cubes into my open palms.

He puts the box down and then picks up a pitcher and pours water over the glass squares in my cupped hands. The colors begin to speak. Dazzling rich hues: red, maroon, purple, brown, black, gold.

"These are ancient tesserae from the Church of San Vitale that are over fifteen hundred years old," he says. "They fell from the ceiling during the war and were in the safe keeping of an old restorer who gathered them up and kept them in this box. Before he died, he gave them to me."

He puts some in his own hands and pours water over them, as well. He holds them up to my ear. "Listen," he says.

Marco de Luca spent much of his twenties on scaffolding as an apprentice to some of the great Italian restorers of ancient mosaics in Ravenna.

"Seeing the mosaic ceilings up close and not at a distance was a revelation for me," he says. "For example, I was able to see how three red tesserae followed by three green tesserae create a gray line of shadow from afar. Mosaic exists in relationship to surface and light. I spent hours, days, years, observing, studying the mosaics as I restored them."

After the Academy of Fine Arts, Marco de Luca became a successful painter, known for his bold colors and quick strokes. The creation on canvas was immediate. But in time, his paintings held no meaning for him. He became despondent. Years passed. He rediscovered mosaic.

His time cutting stones, placing stones deliberately in a bed of cement, became much more meditative, more conscious.

"I realized the depth of my apprenticeship with the masters and how it had prepared me to reenter this sacred practice as an individual artist. Mosaic became the way I perceived the world: Break it up and re-create a unity. Part of the nature of man is to recompose a unity that has been broken. In mosaic, I re-create an order out of shards."

He speaks of the challenge of "combining the technical skills with emotion, to give stone the impression of lightness and transparency."

De Luca explains the method. Our eyes are convex, not flat, so curved surfaces like the niche in a church provide "a place to rest our eyes." He pauses. "I call this an embrace. In mosaics, it is in the curve that light is reflected—for me, this translates into a spiritual space."

He shows me one of his mosaics, entitled *Nicchia*. It is 73 cm x 52 cm. It is a niche that indeed holds light in the monochromatic hues of whites, beiges, browns, and grays. The longer one looks, the more one sees as a turquoise tesserae appears, along with irregular triangles of flint and a glint of gold here and there. I can become lost in this place of worship. How is it that stones can create a window of light?

"Seeing an object is really about listening." He cradles his hands close to his mouth to explain.

"Art, by its nature, is expressive and creates this emotional reaction in the public. When my eyes are turned outward and inward at the same time, this is where I find my depth."

"The public is used to figurative mosaics, representational mosaics, mosaics as paintings." He shakes his head. "I wanted to find the essential features of mosaic. I wanted to express my language of desire, making use of tesserae to express my emotion."

I watched him become frustrated. "No. This is not what I mean to say exactly." He puts his hands together as if in prayer and rests his chin on them. "Mosaic is a metaphor for my language of desire."

He looked at me. "You learn the rules. You learn the discipline. And then you break the rules to find your freedom."

Marco de Luca pulls out a tray of gold. "Gold is light. These tesserae are over fifty years old. I collect them and use them sparingly. They have great character; they are less uniform, less perfect. Today's gold is much more superficial. I love how the ancient ones understood gold as light, a form of truth."

He puts the tray back into the closet.

"You may write, Marco de Luca is a thief. He has tried to steal from all the arts of antiquities: Roman floors, Byzantine ceilings. The foundation of my art as a mosaicist lies with the knowledge created by the ancient mosaicists." He shakes the glass cubes from San Vitale. "Here. Hear. We create the future through a rearrangement of forms, what we have learned from the past."

De Luca has created a forest of trees, free-standing mosaic trees, that move from light to dark, using variations of gold to green smalti as tesserae. He placed them on plazas throughout Ravenna. With a height of 272 centimeters, these lyrical expressions of cypress trees with their gold elliptical shapes, supported on black wrought iron trunks, create shadows, hence, shade for light-weary park dwellers. I marvel at how the conversation between colors creates a semblance of leaf and the transparency of canopy.

"I love to walk the cobblestone streets near San Vitale after it rains," he says. "I love to look at the reflections, the subtlety of colors. In this way, I study the subtlety of individual tesserae. I like the natural materials better than glass. There is an endless variety in stones—sandstones, limestones, marble." He spins his turnstile of rocks. "You cut them, you find a vein, you exploit each property of stone, and you uncover what makes it special. To retain the skin of the materials is important, but at the same time, you can get into its very soul. This is what I mean by listening to the stones."

"Out of randomness, you create order. I express something very deep and then deny it immediately."

"I want each mosaic to have maximum liberty to be itself."

It is raining. I slip into the Mausoleum of Galla Placidia for shelter. It is like entering a jewel box lit from within. The entire interior of this small tomb once believed to house the body of the Empress Galla Placidia around 450 AD is breathtakingly seeded with mosaics.

The corrosive eyes of time have not stared these ancient walls down. Each tessera sparkles from the security of its intended niche, as if to say there are places in the world where beauty remains hidden and miraculously intact. This is transcendent space where one leaves one world and enters another, exactly what one would desire for a resting place.

The mausoleum is shaped like a cross. You enter through a narrow hallway with a curved ceiling. I think of Marco de Luca seeing curved space as an embrace. Looking up, you find yourself standing beneath the brilliance of a night sky, a dazzling deep blue background of mosaics that holds an ordered constellation of stars that literally twinkle silver and gold as incoming light dances across the surface of the glass tesserae. Small white-petaled flowers hang delicately between the stars. Red, yellow, and silver-crossed mandalas create the vision of other orbs floating freely in the universe. The mosaic ceiling shimmers even under the cover of clouds. With the doors open, it is as though the face of each glass cube is emanating light.

Those who entered this place of reverence on a rainy day centuries ago, would find only flickering light through the fire of a torch. The ceiling of stars would become celestial, creating the night sky.

This space is now lit by fourteen small windows covered with slabs of alabaster, which were presented by Victor Emmanuel III in 1908. Each century leaves its mark. Geometric motifs that appear more contemporary than primitive, cover the arches in vibrant colors of red, blue, yellow, turquoise, and green. I recognize the details re-created in the workshop by various students: doves drinking from a fountain; the swastika motif in blocks of pastels; geometric lines in green, yellow, and blue.

Red laurels wind up the sides of the mausoleum toward the cupola, where the four arms of the cruciform meet. A Latin cross made of gold tesserae hangs in another background of blue mosaic with an elaboration of more than eight hundred gold stars. A lion, an eagle, a bull, and an angel adorn the four corners, or spandrels, which support the cupola. These animals represent the symbols of the Evangelists (the lion of St. Mark, the eagle of St. John, the bull of St. Luke, and the angel of St. Matthew). No image is random in the pagan-Christian mind of mosaicists.

To stand in the center of this room is to stand in the center of the cross. Each of the three arms holds a sarcophagus whose contents remains mysterious. One is most likely the body of Galla Placidia herself. The others, perhaps emperors, her son and her husband. Galla Placidia had his body brought back to Ravenna from Constantinople. No one knows for certain where these Roman emperors and empresses were finally laid to rest. One local told me that in the late sixteenth century, some curious boys lit a candle and stuck it in one of the marble tombs to see who was inside but the body was so badly burned from a previous fire it was impossible to tell the identity, leaving only a few splinters of bone and a scorched skull.

Fragments. The left side of an angel. I returned to the market. This time, as I wandered through the maze of narrow streets crowded with antiques and a steady stream of visitors, what captured my eye in the great market was a wing. A wing once attached to the left side of an angel. The wing had been carved out of wood and painted in primary colors. Now faded, with the tips of its feathers worn, it rested on the corner of a table beneath the rafters of the portico, where pigeons roost for the night. It was another broken appendage, and I wondered what power these fragments held, why I was drawn to them, how they had survived through the centuries and why.

Outside Dante's tomb, there is an artist who draws the anatomy of angels. Her pencil illustrations show the hollow bones protruding from the spines of seraphs exactly the same way the ulna and radius of a bird's wing appear, with the feathers radiating out like fingers. To see the precision of these drawings in the context of medical illustrations brings angels back to Earth as creatures of flesh and bones. Biology. It is a tweak of perception, a suspension of disbelief, that renders angels as real, much more than a puff of hope hovering over us in times of need.

Who will give up this world?

The catalog of forms is endless.

No one sees everything.

I am looking for a way to vocalize, perform, act out, address the commonly felt crises of my time. These are spiritual exercises.

I went back for the disembodied arms with the hands clasped in prayer, but they were gone.

Fragmentation and breaking up is indeed the essence of the twentieth century.

We are now living in the twenty-first century.

We have no compass to reorient ourselves.

Memory is redundant.

didn't we plant the seeds?
weren't we necessary to the earth?

There is an old saying that when you change your life, you also change your ideas.

I used to believe that truth was found only below the surface of things. Underground. I was a disciple of depth. What was hidden was what I desired.

But something changed.

It's the dismemberment of a territory—

I am interested now in what my eyes can see, what my fingers can touch, what my hand can know by moving slowly across flesh, or fur, or feathers, or stone.

I trust what I see.
The surface of things is what we see.

I trust what I touch.
The surface of things is what we touch.

*There, the last blue tesserae is in place—*I tweak it a bit to the right with my tweezers, wipe off the excess lime with the tip of my finger, and leave a larger gap between the two cubes, replicating what was done in the original. Finished. The mosaic is complete. I move the hardie aside, get up from my stool, and take a detached look at my small floral detail from Sant'Apollinare Nuovo. I feel as if I am looking line by line at a crudely constructed paragraph pulled from an exquisite narrative of sacred Byzantine text. I have translated the text poorly. It bears all the mistakes of an earnest amateur; nevertheless, I accept its primitive beauty.

We carry our mosaics outside. Even as apprentices, we take pleasure in small accomplishments. The light strikes our mosaics. They shimmer and shine. I am especially delighted with the golden glare coming from the stems of the lilies, accentuated by the tiny pieces of rough sandstone, a dramatic pause in the line of shine.

Luciana gathers us together and shows us how to proceed with the next step. We watch her stir a foul-smelling concoction which we learn is rabbit glue. This is the preferred adhesive, used in the past as well. She shows us the plastic bag of amber crystals that are brought to a simmering point in the double boiler.

"Be aware if you do this outside," she cautions. "Dogs and cats will come running with their noses looking for rabbits." It is a stench of sizzling, liquid death that brings tears to the eyes, not out of grief but revulsion.

"Get over it," she says. "Breathe through your mouth."

Luciana stirs the glue one more time with a brush and then paints the face of the mosaic she has been working on with the glue. The rabbit binder seeps into all the crevices that will hold the tesserae in place.

Next, she brings out a roll of hospital gauze and cuts a piece perfectly sized for the mosaic in front of her. Luciana then places the gauze over the glue and brushes it with another layer of rabbit glue. All of this is to ensure that the tesserae is firmly in its desired position. When the glue is completely dry, the mosaic is literally "ripped" from the wet lime base, which was only meant as a temporary binder.

Each of us brushes the rabbit glue onto our mosaics, covers its face with gauze, and adds another brush of glue, making certain the cloth covering is smooth and secure. We then leave our mosaics to dry under the Italian sun.

Inside the studio, we watch Mateo change the binder from lime to cement, which we will do to our own mosaics after the glue has dried. Mateo pulls the mosaic from the wooden board with his spatula, then cuts off the excess gauze with a knife.

Mateo pours a thin layer of cement into the bottom of a boxed frame chosen to accommodate the size of the mosaic. He smooths the cement with his trowel. On the reverse side of the mosaic, he pours another layer of cement, which gathers in all the interstices. We gasp, believing the mosaic is ruined. Mateo smiles as he is used to this reaction from novices, and proceeds to place the mosaic in the bed of wet cement. He arranges the mosaic quickly and thoughtfully so it is perfectly centered. He then fills the rest of the boxed frame with grout, which is largely a mixture of sand that surrounds the edges of the design, serving as a neutral background for the mosaic.

After the cement dries, the gauze covering is removed, and we clean the mosaic by pouring pitchers of hot water over its face and vigorously scrubbing off all the glue with a small hand brush like those used for cleaning floors. As I wash down my lilies, I am amazed at how durable and strong the tesserae are. Each cube comes alive as if a silenced voice is now speaking.

We bring our mosaics back to our individual work spaces and begin the laborious process of cleaning each tesserae like a dentist cleans teeth. In fact, we use dental tools. In between each tesserae, instead of removing the build-up of tartar and plaque, we scrape and scrape and chisel away any lime mortar and excess cement.

Our dreams of perfection are interrupted by Luciana's gruff voice, "Enough; now it is time to see the beauty, the imperfect beauty."

I came to this workshop in Ravenna because of a word, "mosaic," unaware of the landscape I was entering. I came to the mosaic workshop in Ravenna to learn a new language with my hands.

People talk about medium. What is your medium? My medium as a writer has been dirt, clay, sand—what I could touch, hold, stand on, and stand for—Earth. My medium has been Earth. Earth in correspondence with my mind.

Here in the village of Ravenna, a continent away from where I live, I am indeed learning a new language, but it is very different from the one I imagined.

I now look to my hands.

"Mosaic is a way to organize your life." Luciana gives us her last instructions. "Making mosaics is a way of thinking about the world."

Luciana's final words: *Mosaics are created out of community.*

The cosmos works
by harmony of tensions,
like the lyre and bow.

HERACLITUS, Fragments

The play of light is the first rule of mosaic.

It is the wind whose sigh animates the prairie as eyes scan the horizon. Many eyes. There is a hissing of grasses, a flurry of blackbirds rising and falling to the soft contours of the land. In the golden light of late afternoon, a small town is on alert.

The line in mosaic is supreme; the flow of the line is what matters so the eye is never disturbed or interrupted.

The residents of this town are always on alert, even as they go about their lives. Their survival depends on a community of eyes and ears that belong to hundreds, thousands of individuals. They study the horizon.

The distance from which the mosaic is viewed is important to the design, color, and execution of the mosaic.

This is a prairie dog town.

A calmness is enforced by moving light.

Prairie dogs find their distinct origins in the Pleistocene era. They embody two million years of evolving intelligence. Historically, prairie dog towns followed the bison, aerating the soil after thundering hooves.

Prairie dog towns seemed to s p r e a d as far as the h o r i z o n.

The largest prairie dog town on record, in Texas, measured 250 miles long, 100 miles wide, and contained an estimated 400 million prairie dogs.

Tessera: the basic unit of mosaic.

There are five species of prairie dogs unique to North America: black-tailed, white-tailed, Gunnison's, Mexican, and the Utah prairie dog.

The surface of mosaics is irregular, even angled, to increase the dance of light on the tesserae.

Prairie dog country is an undulating landscape of small hills and holes.

Tesserae are irregular, rough, individualized, unique.

Prairie dogs literally change the land with their hands. If prairie dogs were to turn their front paws over toward the sky, you would see an extra padding of skin to help them with this task.

If you are creating a horizontal line, place tesserae vertically.

Some mounds created from the excavation of burrows can become two feet high and ten feet in diameter. They serve as lookout posts so the prairie dogs can watch for danger.

Each glass tessera is a mirror reflecting light back.

When danger is near, a series of barks occur in a prairie dog chorus, often led by sentinel dogs guarding the periphery of the colony and picked up by dogs standing on the mounds. Word spreads quickly. They scramble and scurry across the desert, disappearing in one of the nearby holes to their burrows below.

Many colors are used to create one color from afar. Different hues from the same color were always used in ancient mosaics.

Prairie dogs have a significant effect on biological diversity in prairie ecosystems. More than 200 species of wildlife have been associated with prairie dog towns, with over 140 species benefiting directly, including bison, pronghorn antelope, burrowing owls, pocket mice, deer mice, ants, black widow spiders, horned larks, and many predators such as rattlesnakes, golden eagles, badgers, bobcats, weasels, foxes, coyotes, and especially black-footed ferrets.

There is a perfection in imperfection. The interstices or gaps between the tesserae speak their own language in mosaic.

Nine vertebrate species may drop in population or disappear completely if prairie dogs are eliminated from the grassland ecosystem. The black-footed ferret has coevolved with prairie dogs so successfully in a predator-prey dance that the decline of the prairie dog is the decline of the ferret. The disappearance of prairie dog towns may be the disappearance of mountain plovers, burrowing owls, ferruginous hawks, golden eagles, swift foxes, horned larks, grasshopper mice, and deer mice, diminishing biological diversity across prairie landscapes.

The background is very important in emphasizing the mosaic pattern. There must always be at least one line of tesserae that outlines the pattern. Sometimes there will be as many as three lines defining the pattern as part of the background.

golden eagle

nighthawk

bat

red-tailed hawk

raven

ferruginous hawk

kestrel

horned lark

magpie

mountain plover

meadowlark

grasshopper

bison

mule deer

pronghorn antelope

black-tailed jackrabbit

long-tailed weasel

cottontail   coyote

bobcat

badger

swift fox

burrowing owl   deer mouse

black-footed ferret

rattlesnake

bullfrog   sagebrush lizard   black widow spider

rabbitbrush red three-awn phlox lambsquarters

ironweed prickly pear scarlet globemallow wild onion

muhly wild barley knotweed starwort saltbush plaintain

prairie sand grass wild indigo winterfat white prickly poppy

needle and thread dropseed arrow feather mullein peppergrass

beardgrass biscuitroot breadroot fescue foxtail barley wire grass

blue grama bent grass bluestem wheatgrass bromegrass buffalo grass

Prairie dogs create diversity.
Destroy them, and you destroy a varied world.

The Utah Prairie Dog is one of the six species identified, world-wide, as most likely to become extinct in the twenty-first century.

NILES ELDREDGE
"A Field Guide to the Sixth Extinction"
The New York Times Magazine,
December 6, 1999

My brother Steve collects skulls. He finds them in the wild, brings them home, and cleans them up, if necessary. He pulls the fur from the bone, scrapes off the muscle, then boils them, letting the remaining flesh fall free.

My brother gave me the skull of a prairie dog. He handed it to me. "What do you notice about this skull that is different from others?"

I held the prairie dog skull in the palm of my hand. I couldn't say.

"The eyes," Steve said. "Look at the enormous space for the eyes."

The dream: I was walking along a dike that held the river in place. It was close to sunset. Up ahead, I saw a small figure that appeared to be standing. It was a prairie dog. It didn't move. Finally, we were facing each other. The prairie dog spoke: "I have a story to tell."

In the American West, one of the predominant myths that still lives is that of the rugged individual.

The prairie dog stands for community. We are fragmenting ourselves by destroying our sense of community. Utah once understood this concept, in the beginning of its statehood. We are forgetting our communal roots as we are developing our communities.

The prairie dog lives because of community.

Prairie dogs are Pleistocene mammals. They have survived the epic changes through time.

Standing on their hind legs in the big wide open: What do they see? What do they smell? What do they hear?

They hear the sound of a truck coming toward their town, the slamming of doors, the voices, the pressure of feet walking toward them. From inside their burrow, they see the well-worn sole of a boot, now the pointed toe of the boot, kicking out the entrance to their burrow, blue Levi's bending down, gloved hands flicking a lighter, the flame, the heat, then the hands shoving something burning inside the entrance, something is burning, they back up further down their tunnel, smoke now curling inside the darkness as the boot is kicking dirt inside, closing their burrow, covering their burrow, tamping the entrance shut. They are scurrying down, down, down, around, they cannot see, what they smell is fear, they cough and wheeze, their eyes are burning, their lungs are tightening, they cannot breathe, they try to run, turn, nowhere to turn, every one of them, trying to escape, to flee, but all exits and entrances of their burrows have been kicked closed. The toxic smoke is chasing them like a snake, an invisible snake herding them toward an agonizing death of suffocation, strangulation, every organ in spasm, until they collapse onto each other's bodies, noses covered in blankets of familiar fur, families young and old, slowly, cruelly, gassed to death.

The truck drives away, the American flag is flapping in the wind, the red, white, and blue banner of the American West that says the rights of private property take precedence over the lives of prairie dogs who are standing in the way of development.

Nearly four hundred Utah prairie dogs disappeared in the summer of 1999 at the Cedar Ridge Golf Course in Cedar City, Utah. It is believed they were murdered, gassed to death. Two federal agents investigated the crime. This is a federal criminal offense. Penalties for killing or attempting to kill the federally protected animals range from fines of up to a hundred thousand dollars to one year in prison. Some say locals know who did it and are glad they did. Other locals are outraged. Nobody is talking. Both sides offered rewards for the offender's arrest. Cedar City is a small town. The killers were never caught.

The Spectrum
July 7, 2006

CEDAR CITY—The Cedar Ridge Golf Course and Paiute Tribe of Utah's prairie dog problems will continue for at least another year.

The golf course and tribe applied for permits allowing them to remove the prairie dogs from their property by relocating some and killing the rest.

Elise Boeke, U.S. Fish and Wildlife Service ecologist, said she received comments from Forest Guardians, a New Mexico–based environmental group, protesting the project.

"We'll have to work through these," she said.

This means no relocation will take place until next year because USFWS can't issue any permits until this issue is resolved, and the trapping season ends in August.

SETBACKS This comes as a huge disappointment for the city and Paiute Tribe.

Paiute Tribe of Utah Chairwoman Lora Tom said she was hoping to do something about the tribe's prairie dog problem soon.

"It is disappointing," she said. "I wish that those groups or individuals who feel that prairie dogs are endangered would look at some of the areas affected by prairie dogs.

"Prairie dogs on the tribal land are restricting land use; they're completely out of control because they're breeding quickly," Tom said.

Mayor Gerald Sherratt agreed it's frustrating to have a group from New Mexico trying to stop actions in Cedar City.

"It's discouraging because our hope was to start trapping this summer," he said. "This will delay us, but I don't think it will stop us. The plan makes sense. I think this is just a glitch; we'll work past it."

But Nicole Rosmarino, Forest Guardians endangered species program director, said the plan is unnecessary and outlines a death sentence for a species on the brink of extinction.

"We strongly, strongly oppose this plan," she said. "We think it's little more than an extermination plan."

PRAIRIE DOG PLAN   Henry Maddux, U.S. Fish and Wildlife Service field supervisor, said a separate Habitat Conservation Plan and Environmental Assessment were necessary for the golf course and tribal lands because the Iron County conservation plan is insufficient for such a large number of dogs.

It only allows for 300 dogs to be relocated each year.

"The numbers at the golf course and Paiute land are so large there's just no way to cover it under the current HCP," he said.

Keith Day, Division of Wildlife Resources wildlife biologist, said according to the DWR's latest count, he estimates there are more than 360 prairie dogs on the golf course alone.

Tom is concerned with the number on Paiute land.

"If you talk with others in this area, they'd also give you an earful of the problems they're having," she said.

It's difficult knowing she'll have to wait even longer now that the USFWS must work through the comments.

"It's been a long process as it is," she said. "We have no other option. We're at a standstill." Day said he already trapped 100 dogs at the golf course under the Iron County HCP this year, yet to golfers, it seems like there are more dogs than ever.

He added if the new HCP is approved, the golf course will come out of the Iron County plan, freeing up more dogs for relocation for everyone involved.

PLAN WITHDRAWAL   Rosmarino said because the current Iron County Habitat Conservation Plan should cover the golf course and Paiute land, adding another plan and removing more dogs would just stack the odds against this threatened species.

"So this plan is unnecessary," she said. "This could all be done under the Iron County HCP."

Forest Guardians and those who support the comments would

like to see the HCP withdrawn, noting the plan is in violation of the Endangered Species Act, National Environmental Policy Act, and Administrative Procedures Act laws.

"What's on the table is unacceptable," Rosmarino said. "There's no getting around it—the picture on this animal is very bleak. The species is on the verge of extinction. It's in real trouble biologically."

Her next biggest concern is relocating the dogs. In the past, relocation has been on "abysmal failure." She's also worried about the relocation site, Wild Pea Hollow, which is located about 28 miles northeast of Cedar City by Bald Hills, not too far east off Minersville Highway.

"We are very pessimistic about the chances of these animals surviving," she said. "The area is dubious at best. Translocation is just another word for extermination because they don't make it."

On the other hand, Maddux said he believes relocation will work in this situation.

"We think translocation still has a role," he says. "In the long run, translocation won't get us where we want to be. Relocating dogs is not a long-term solution to the problem prairie dogs create, but it can be used as a limited tool."

Rosmarino believes the conservation easement, meant to protect the prairie dog habitat, is weak and allows for too many conflicting uses, such as hunting, off-road vehicles, and grazing.

The area is also infested with cheat grass, which will hinder the animals' survival.

Both Day and Maddux have expressed their confidence that Wild Pea Hollow will be sufficient to support the prairie dogs. Maddux said there are colonies on the property now and the dogs do fine.

Day said the county already has done seeding to improve the area. Maddux said prairie dogs like to be able to see and need shorter grass, so grazing is beneficial.

In the end, Rosmarino said she understands the argument for conflicting uses, such as the 6000 golfers who use the course every month, but as development continues, she wonders where to draw the line and where the dogs will go as development grows.

"I think its unreasonable with the species endangered," she said. "It's an important species. I would like to see the golf course have more tolerance."

Rosmarino said if the USFWS meets every demand to remove or relocate dogs, there won't be any left.

"The end of the road is extinction," she said.

In 1979, I wrote a case study of the Utah prairie dog.

I remember visiting the Utah State Legislature that winter, where I interviewed Ivan Matheson, a state senator from Iron County. He was sponsoring Senate Bill 207, "AN ACT ENACTING SECTION 23-13-14, UTAH CODE ANNOTATED 1953; RELATING TO WILDLIFE RESOURCES; PROVIDING FOR COMPENSATION OF PERSONS WHOSE CROPS OR DOMESTIC ANIMALS ARE DAMAGED OR DESTROYED BY PROTECTED WILDLIFE; AND PROVIDING A PROCEDURE FOR ASSESSING THE CAUSE AND AMOUNT OF SUCH DAMAGE."

He believed people had a right to earn a living. "Endangered species should not be protected at the cost of economic disadvantage to man."

"What is the value of a prairie dog?" I remember him asking me. "Would you rather eat prairie dog or beef?"

He believed farmers whose lands had been destroyed by the prairie dogs should be financially compensated by the Utah Division of Wildlife Resources.

The bill did not pass. But it serves as a historical marker showing how helpless farmers and ranchers felt after the enactment of the Endangered Species Act of 1973. It had only been law for six years. It is a soaring law that says the rights and dignity of animals must be considered, that if an animal or plant is endangered or threatened, its life in the context of its habitat takes precedence over development. In the mind of a rural Utahn, especially in Mormon country, where the land is for the taking, this was blasphemy.

After our interview, Senator Matheson handed me a piece of paper. It was a recipe for prairie dog stew.

"My wife thought you would enjoy this," he said.

Perhaps nothing in the grasslands of the American West is as common.

No, let me rewrite this sentence.

Perhaps nothing in the grasslands of the American West was once as common.

Lewis and Clark note in 1804, on their journey west, that this "wild dog of the prairie . . . appears here in infinite numbers." They were so taken by the multitudes of these "barking squirrels" that they captured one (with great difficulty) and carried it all the way back to Washington alive as a present for President Thomas Jefferson. It was later placed on public display in Philadelphia, Pennsylvania.

Ernest Thompson Seton estimated that prairie dogs once numbered an astonishing five billion in North America in the early 1900s.

All of them are sociable creatures.
All of them live in towns and villages.
All of them are vulnerable.

With the scope and scale of World War I, the U.S. government suddenly had to feed massive numbers of troops abroad, so there was a huge push to maximize beef production. To the government's way of thinking, eradicating prairie dogs from the range meant improved conditions for cattle. Killing rodents became a patriotic act.

UNITED STATES DEPARTMENT OF AGRICULTURE YEARBOOK, 1920

To eliminate a crop-production loss of $5,000,000,000 a year, due to rodents, looks like a staggering undertaking. When a leak is detected in a corporation, mill, or factory and a means of prevention is found, it is possible to issue orders putting improved practice into effect . . . Not so in the case of losses caused by rodent pests: you cannot order the rodents to stop eating.

The magnitude of the task is measured by the length and breadth of the whole of the United States, and its execution requires not only action by Federal and State officials, but the voluntary cooperation of hundreds of thousands of people who must be enlisted in the movement . . . Plans and means of organization must be provided, trained and experienced leadership secured, cooperation of great numbers of people effected, legislation enacted, financial support furnished, and special supplies procured and laid down at the point of use . . . The Biological Survey received many urgent appeals for help from the far-western States, the cry being that if the rodents could not be controlled the people would have to abandon their ranches."

[PHOTOGRAPH OF A BIOLOGICAL SURVEY FIELD PARTY DISTRIBUTING POISONED GRAIN TO DESTROY RODENT PESTS IS ACCOMPANIED BY THE FOLLOWING CAPTION:]

Over 132,000 men working afoot and on horseback in cooperative campaigns distributed 1,610 tons of poisoned grain on more than 32,000,000 acres of "infested" range and farm land during the year 1920. The resulting destruction of prairie dogs and ground squirrels effected a saving of $11,000,000.00.

METHODS OF DESTROYING PRAIRIE DOGS

POISONING: Cyanide of Potassium. Kills quickly . . . but is sometimes difficult to administer, chiefly on account of its odor, which is offensive to most animals. Dangerous to man, must be handled with great care. Has been administered in prunes and raisins, mixed with grain, disguised by a coating of molasses, flavored with oil of anise.

POISONING: Strychnine. Best and most satisfactory poison now known for the destruction of prairie dogs. Can be obtained everywhere. Simple. 3 ounces to a bushel of wheat. Can be sprinkled on buttered bread, coated lightly with syrup, after which the bread is cut in small squares and placed around the burrows. One bushel of grain will poison 40 acres at a cost of 12 and a half cents per acre. A man can scatter poison grain over 50 acres or more in a day.

FUMIGATION: Bisulphide of Carbon. Destruction of animals by fumes arising from substances thrown into the burrows. A volatile liquid. Inflammable. Highly explosive. Usual dose for prairie dog: one ounce (a teaspoon). Method of application is exceedingly simple:

pour on absorbent substance such as a lump of horse manure, corn-cob, or even a clod of earth, drop into burrow, close the mouth. Costs 10 cents a pound. A dollar's worth is enough to poison 100 holes."

Since no community can consume its resources faster than they are produced without ultimate disaster and since prairie dogs have been in the grassland community for at least 1,000,000 years, probably occurring in great numbers, it would seem that if prairie dogs were detrimental they would have long ago destroyed the community of which they are a part.

TIM W. CLARK
"Ecological Roles of Prairie Dogs"
Wyoming Range Management, *No. 261 (1968)*

In the 1920s, Utah prairie dogs, *Cynomys parvidens,* numbered more than 95,000 individuals. By the 1960s, distribution of Utah prairie dogs was greatly reduced because of intensive poison control campaigns administered through the Department of Agriculture, indiscriminate shooting, disease, and loss of habitat. It was estimated that only 3,300 Utah prairie dogs remained in 37 separate colonies and that the species would be extinct by the year 2000.

Because of the dramatic decline in numbers and distribution, the Utah prairie dog was classified as an endangered species on June 4, 1973, one of the original listees when the Endangered Species Act was signed into law on December 28, 1973.

In the year 2000, the Utah prairie dog did not become extinct.

According to the 2007 spring count of Utah prairie dogs, there are approximately 10,000 individuals in the state. But this number is misleading. It is not enough to think about prairie dogs in terms of individuals; they are social creatures that need to be seen in social terms. Their health and viability as a species must be viewed in terms of populations or communities. The Fish and Wildlife Service suggests that small populations contain less than 200 prairie dogs. With this standard in mind, there are only nine populations of Utah prairie dogs that are not small, therefore having a reasonable chance at long-term survival. Six out of these nine prairie dog communities are found on private lands, making them vulnerable to elimination through translocation (at best, only 10 percent of prairie dogs relocated from original towns survive) and habitat destruction.

Given Utah prairie dogs' uncertain future, they should be protected alongside America's most imperiled species, such as the California condor, whooping crane, and black-footed ferret.

What is the state of prairie dogs in the Interior West today?

REPORT FROM THE BURROW: FORECAST OF THE PRAIRIE DOG

This report assigns a letter grade to each federal agency and state responsible for managing prairie dogs based on the most accurate and current scientific data. The grading system is a standard 4-point scale similar to those used in American high schools, universities, and colleges. The grades are tallied based on combined performance in the following categories: population, habitat, poisoning policy, shooting policy, monitoring, and conservation activities.

FISH AND WILDLIFE SERVICE: D −

Between 2003 and 2007, the Service rejected citizen petitions to list the Gunnison's and white-tailed prairie dogs under the Endangered Species Act, removed the black-tailed prairie dog from the Endangered Species Act candidate list when it issued a "not warranted" finding, and rejected a petition to upgrade the Utah prairie dog from Threatened to Endangered. The Service acknowledges that the black-tailed has lost 98 percent of its occupied habitat; the Gunnison's, 97 percent; and the white-tailed, at least 92 percent. It further notes that the Utah prairie dog is down to only 10,000 adult individuals. The Service is failing to protect and recover the listed Utah prairie dog. The Service allows shooting of up to 6,000 Utah prairie dogs every year under a rule it has admitted is biologically indefensible. Government agencies recognize that the Fish and Wildlife Service's translocation efforts often result in survival rates of only 5 to 10 percent or even lower. The Fish and Wildlife Service just missed being given an F because it did acknowledge in 2007 that former employee and President Bush appointee, Julie MacDonald, wrongfully tampered with the white-tailed prairie dog decision. Under court order, the Service will reexamine its decision on the Gunnison's prairie dog petition by February 2008. Additionally, the Service overcame significant state and local opposition to do the right thing and reintroduce black-footed ferrets onto private land in Kansas.

BUREAU OF LAND MANAGEMENT: D−

The Bureau controls the oil and gas leasing program for most federal lands and some state and private lands and has leased millions of acres with active prairie dog colonies or potential habitat.

FOREST SERVICE: D

The Forest Service rescinded a 2000 moratorium on poisoning black-tailed prairie dogs in 2004. Since 2004, the Nebraska National Forest and Pawnee National Grassland amended their management plans to allow poisoning. Thunder Basin and Dakota Prairie National Grasslands are developing such amendments.

ARIZONA: C+

Black-tailed prairie dogs (extinct in Arizona), Gunnison's prairie dogs.
Arizona Game and Fish officials have undertaken a black-tailed prairie dog reintroduction plan. Despite a spring seasonal shooting closure for Gunnison's prairie dogs, the state reported an increase in prairie dogs shot between 2002 and 2006—at least 256,290 Gunnison's prairie dogs were shot.

COLORADO: D+

Black-tailed prairie dogs, Gunnison's prairie dogs, white-tailed prairie dogs.
In 1997, the state enacted a five animal bag limit per day rule to prevent contest killings. Wildlife officials enacted a spring shooting closure on public land for all three species in 2006 but rescinded a total ban on black-tailed prairie dog shooting. Colorado approved poisons Rozol and Kaput-D in 2006 and 2007. In 1999, the state legislature enacted a law (SB-111) that makes relocating prairie dogs nearly impossible. State scientists claim that black-tailed prairie dog numbers keep increasing, but their rejection of offered monitoring assistance by independent scientists and long delays in releasing published data call into question the accuracy of this claim.

KANSAS: D —

Black-tailed prairie dogs.

The State legislature has, thus far, failed to repeal antiquated laws from the early 1900s that mandate prairie dog poisoning at the discretion of county commissioners. Commissioners can force private landowners to eradicate prairie dogs against their will and at the landowners' personal expense. The state wildlife and agriculture departments have aided Logan County in its extermination efforts by, for example, approving Rozol. The Fish and Wildlife Service released ferrets on private land at the end of 2007 in Logan, but continued poisoning could prevent their recovery.

MONTANA: D +

Black-tailed prairie dogs, white-tailed prairie dogs.

In 2007, the Montana legislature voted down a proposal to give the Fish, Wildlife and Parks permanent authority to manage its black- and white-tailed prairie dogs. This removed protective status for prairie dogs, nullified several shooting closures across the state, and put conservation plans on indefinite hold. Had this not occurred, Montana may have received a B.

NEW MEXICO: D

Gunnison's prairie dogs, black-tailed prairie dogs.

Oil and gas drilling is wreaking havoc on habitat in the last remaining population strongholds, particularly on federal land but also on private, state, and tribal lands. New Mexico does not allow shooting on state trust lands but does limit shooting on other lands.

NORTH DAKOTA: D —

Black-tailed prairie dogs.

Significant legal and illegal poisoning occurs in the state. The North Dakota Game and Fish Department does not make prairie dog conservation a priority.

OKLAHOMA: C

Black-tailed prairie dogs.

The state does not allow poisoning in counties where the total prairie dog acreage could be reduced below 1000 acres. Oklahoma does not limit shooting.

SOUTH DAKOTA: F

Black-tailed prairie dogs.

South Dakota pressured the Fish and Wildlife Service to remove black-tailed prairie dogs as an ESA Candidate species. In 2004, the governor enacted his "emergency" prairie dog control program. The state spent taxpayer money to poison prairie dogs on private land. The state pressured the Forest Service to poison prairie dogs on the most successful black-footed ferret recovery site in existence, located in the Conata Basin on the Buffalo National Grassland.

TEXAS: D+

Black-tailed prairie dogs.

The state agriculture department distributes poison and recently approved Rozol and Kaput-D for use on prairie dogs. The state enacted a ban on collecting and transporting prairie dogs as part of the pet trade in 2003.

UTAH: D+

Gunnison's prairie dogs, Utah prairie dogs, white-tailed prairie dogs.

The U.S. Fish and Wildlife Service delegates much of its authority of the Utah prairie dog to the Utah Division of Wildlife Resources, which fails to monitor and tolerates shooting of this listed species. The state has a spring seasonal closure on shooting Gunnison's prairie dogs but no restriction on shooting white-tailed prairie dogs, except for the Coyote Basin black-footed ferret recovery site, which is closed to shooting.

WYOMING: D

Black-tailed prairie dogs, white-tailed prairie dogs.

Rampant oil and gas development is now destroying prairie dog habitat throughout the state. The state agriculture department recently approved Rozol for use on prairie dogs. The Wyoming Weed and Pest Control Act of 1973 allows counties to control prairie dogs on private land if damage has been documented to neighboring landowners.

Utah prairie dog towns have created a very contentious situation between ranchers in southern Utah, developers wanting to cash in on the value of these open lands, conservationists who want to protect them, and the federal agencies who must administer the Endangered Species Act. This hostile environment is fueled further by the fact that this is one of the largest and fastest-growing areas in the United States. Eighty-five percent of all Utah prairie dogs live on private lands. Sixty-five percent of those populations live in Iron County. Iron County commissioner Gene Roundy has said, "I think it's a crime against society that a prairie dog can move into your front yard and you can't take care of it."

Whose society?

On my desk, I have the prairie dog skull my brother gave to me. Now, it is obvious, the enormity of the eye sockets. What they see and how fast they see it is their vision of survival.

Prairie dogs are the eyes of the community.

I have other bones bleached by the sun. Some are so weathered and fragile, they have the appearance of honeycombs. Two femurs are about the length of my little finger, and of the two tibia, one is broken in half. Red sand still shakes out of the tiniest pores. Two jaw bones, not related, have beautiful front and bottom incisors. There is a pause, an open space between the front and back teeth. Where the molars begin, they look like tiny Greek columns leaning side by side.

These bones belong to white-tailed prairie dogs. I found them on the desert pavement near the ghost town of Cisco, just off Interstate 70, twenty miles from home. These prairie dogs most likely died from plague, the same illness that murdered the Dark Ages.

What is communicated through bones? A bird bone becomes a whistle. Bones carved create tools like an awl or the handle of a knife. And I have a necklace of frog fetishes crafted from cow bones, each one with a spot of turquoise circling its back. In the desert, I wear this strand with the hope of rain. Bones are the essence of the life they once held.

What is communicated through the voice of a prairie dog?

On the desert pavement around Cisco, the cries of prairie dogs become a steady pulse of alarm translated through the wind. Alarm calls from one prairie dog to another create an audio shorthand, a quick image transmitted based on astute awareness and species differentiation. One alarm call may articulate a coyote on the periphery of their town. Another call with a slightly different arc may identify a dog. They can also differentiate between animals like a deer and a pronghorn or cow.

Biologist Constantine Slobodchikoff, in his twenty years of researching communication patterns among prairie dogs, has proven that they have the most sophisticated animal language decoded so far. Not only do sentinel prairie dogs warn the colony of impending danger from a predator, but they have different calls for different species of predators be it a badger, a red-tailed hawk, or an eagle. They can incorporate descriptive information about the individual predator including size, color, and how fast they are traveling.

Focusing primarily on Gunnison's prairie dogs near Flagstaff, Arizona, he has also found variations within prairie dog speech—call them dialects—that differ from region to region. But studies have shown that they do understand one another. Their use of "language" includes not only nouns, but modifiers, and the ability to coin new words. To date, one hundred words have been identified among Gunnison's prairie dogs. And now, with the use of advanced technology, Dr. Slobodchikoff is in the process of deconstructing prairie dog grammar. "A short chirp, about a tenth of a second is analogous to a sentence or paragraph . . . If we dissect the chirp into a bunch of different time slices, each slice has some specific information on it."

Time slices become words and the assemblage of an idea appears.

But perhaps, most remarkably, Dr. Slobodchikoff has witnessed something he may never be able to explain. During a set of observations involving widely separated Gunnison's prairie dogs from different colonies, he showed each village a European ferret, an animal they have never seen before, and the isolated prairie dogs came up with the same word.

I asked Dr. Slobodchikoff, who speaks four languages himself, if what he has learned from Gunnison's prairie dogs might be applicable to Utah prairie dogs.

Dear Ms. Williams,

I think that the Utah prairie dogs probably have much the same system of communication as we have found with the Gunnison's. One of my PhD students did a comparative study of the alarm calls of all five species of prairie dogs, calling for her when she was wearing either a yellow shirt or a green one. All five species had distinctly different calls for the two colors of shirts. Also, each species had different vocalizations for each color, suggesting that each species has its own language, but the languages differ from one another, much as German, French, and English differ.

We just published a study of black-tailed prairie dogs, showing that they had the same kind of descriptive elements in their alarm calls as the Gunnison's, describing the color of clothes and the size and shape of different humans. We also showed that they could remember when someone shot a gun, and could incorporate this information into their alarm calls, calling in a way that was distinctly different from the alarm calls that they gave to the same person prior to his shooting the gun. So my guess is that each species has a very sophisticated language, and has the cognitive capacity to detect subtle differences among predators and incorporate information about these differences into the alarm calls.

I am hoping that this work will help show that prairie dogs, and all animals, are not just mindless robots that can be disposed of as vermin or property but are sentient beings that should be treated with empathy and respect.

Best regards,
Con Slobodchikoff

Above ground   Above ground   Above ground
        belowground   belowground
                        below

Within colonies, prairie dogs live in territorial family groups called "coteries" or "clans." A typical coterie contains one adult male and three to four adult females, and a typical coterie territory is about one-third of an acre.

Prairie dogs kiss.

The "kiss" is used to distinguish one clan member from another. When they recognize each other, they will participate in elaborate grooming behavior. If there is an intruder, an animal from a different town or coterie, teeth may be bared, territory may be fought for—claimed or reclaimed by dominant males—and in most cases, the outsider flees.

Prairie dogs understand darkness and light. Deeper inside the complex system of burrows, prairie dogs make nests and line them with grasses where they sleep. Gunnison's, Utah, and white-tailed prairie dogs hibernate, but black-tailed and Mexican prairie dogs do not. In northern latitudes, black-tailed prairie dogs sometimes remain underground for several days—or even a few weeks—in inclement weather, but they are not true hibernators like the other species of prairie dogs.

Native grasses comprise 70 to 95 percent of a prairie dog's diet during the summer. A single prairie dog may consume up to two pounds of grasses and forbs per week. Driven by their appetite, prairie dogs literally prune the prairie with their incisors. They prefer short grass to tall so they can see their predators.

With bare patches common around prairie dog burrow entrances, this kind of habitat engineering has an affect on other creatures. In the case of darkling beetles, their movement patterns on naked land are more linear than undulating and they move with greater velocity and speed.

Nevertheless, the hunger of prairie dogs shocks the landscape into greater productivity. Their digging and scratching stimulates the soil, creating more opportunities for seeds to germinate. With heightened water drainage as a result of their tunnels, plants grow. Plant diversity follows. Animal diversity follows the plants. Meadowlarks appear with an appetite for grasshoppers who are chomping on leaves. Grasshopper sparrows appear with the abundance of seeds. Vacant or abandoned prairie dog burrows become the homes of cottontails, kangaroo rats, and deer mice. Burrowing owls with their long spindly legs stand on the mounds of prairie dogs with an eye on the multiplying mice to feed owlets below. A ferruginous hawk soars over the prairie dog town, its eyes focused down, casting a shadow that sends the dogs running like ripples through the grasses. There is a down sweep of air. Talons pierce fur. A prairie dog is taken on the wing as a clean kill is made by the hawk. Rattlesnakes hiss. The webs of black widows quiver. Coyote watches. Badger waits. One successful life inspires another, creating the strength of a grassland community.

Like a fist pushing from below—prairie dog mounds are like mines, like minds create openings for other species to inhabit, to hunt, to hide in.

> *Prairie dogs have been labeled a keystone species based on the assumption that they have a pronounced effect on biological diversity in prairie systems . . . It has been argued that if we save prairie dogs, we save a key component of the prairie ecosystem that includes declining grassland species considered dependent upon prairie dog colonies for survival.*
>
> *. . . Our review indicates that nine vertebrate species may decline or disappear at a local scale, and in several cases at a landscape scale, if prairie dogs are eliminated. The black-footed ferret is apparently so specialized on prairie dogs that it does not persist where prairie dogs are eliminated. In addition, the continued reduction of prairie dog populations could hasten the demise of mountain plovers and burrowing owls, decrease the abundance and distribution of the ferruginous hawk, golden eagle, swift fox, horned lark, grasshopper mouse, and deer mouse, diminishing biological diversity across prairie landscapes.*
>
> NATASHA B. KOTLIAR, BRUCE W. BAKER, APRIL D. WHICKER, AND GLENN PLUMB *"A Critical Review of Assumptions About the Prairie Dog as a Keystone Species."* Environmental Management *24, no. 2 (Sept. 1999), pp. 177–92.*

Prairie dogs are part of a grassland mosaic. Mosaic as a word and a concept has found its place in ecological principles.

One of the earliest references to "mosaic" can be found in William S. Cooper's paper, "The Climax Forest of Isle Royale, Lake Superior, and Its Development," published in *Botanical Gazette* on January 13, 1913.

Cooper writes, "The climax forest is a complex of windfall areas of differing ages, the youngest made up of dense clumps of small trees, and the oldest containing a few mature trees with little or no young growth beneath, those of a single group being approximately even-aged. This *mosaic* or patchwork changes continually in a manner that may almost be called kaleidoscopic when long periods of time are considered. The forest as a whole, however, remains the same, the changes in various parts balancing each other . . ."

By the 1980s, the word "mosaic" was widely used as a term to describe varying types of plants within a given community. "The shifting mosaic" was a concept employed in 1986 by Richard T. T. Forman, from Harvard University, in his text *Landscape Ecology*. He writes, "*Mosaic changes* have been studied within an ecosystem, where patches are different stages of a successional sequence. Despite the presence of disturbances and progressive transformations in the patches, the ecosystem as a whole may be in steady state . . ."

A picture emerges of a green mosaic of varied hues, tones, and textures, a forest with multiaged and multilayered patches of trees, shrubs, wildflowers, and grasses.

The most frequent use of "mosaic" as a metaphor is in fire ecology. Mosaic becomes the image of change through disturbance. A fire burns in the forest or prairie and activates diverse patches of new vegetation. In E. A. Johnson's article, "Wildfires in the Western Canadian Boreal Forest: Landscape Patterns and Ecosystem Management," published in *The Journal of Vegetation Science*, 1998, he writes, "The *landscape mosaic* created by wildfire is generally one of small, younger patches embedded within a matrix of older forest."

In their paper, "Effects of a Fire-Created Landscape Mosaic on Ecosystem Processes in Yellowstone National Park, Wyoming," M. G. Turner and D. B. Tinker write that "the 1988 fires in Yellowstone National Park produced a complex *mosaic* of early successional stands in response to variation in fire intensity and prefire serotiny in lodgepole pine."

Diversity of species and age, disturbances from fire, all create a mosaic of change within the natural world. From a raven's point of view, mosaic is a story told on the ground through color, pattern, and form.

The play of light is the first and last rule of mosaic.

The possibility of metaphor is disappearing.

JEAN BAUDRILLARD, The Transparency of Evil

The banner on the front page of the *Rocky Mountain News* this morning reads, "Little Help for Prairie Dogs." In Colorado, 98 percent of the prairie dog population is gone, as Denver's Front Range is being developed from Boulder to Colorado Springs. The U.S. Fish and Wildlife Service wants to list the black-tailed prairie dog as threatened, but they say they have no money to enforce it. Conservationists argue that it cost the agency just as much time and money removing the black-tailed prairie dog from the candidates lists as it would have cost to list it.

Meanwhile, developers of subdivisions and shopping malls are quickly and steadily buying up the land comprised of prairie dog towns as fast as they can—building immediately before any protective measures on behalf of prairie dogs are in place which would make further development against the law.

Developers hire companies such as Dog Gone to remove prairie dogs from their sites. These businesses are called "dog suckers." Their employees come to the prairie dog towns, stick a high-powered suction hose down into the burrows, and vacuum the prairie dogs up into the back of an enclosed truck complete with padded walls, then release the dogs outside of town or, more often than not, sell them, ironically, as food for the black-tailed ferrets being captively bred for reintroduction into the wild.

THE WALL STREET JOURNAL
Thursday, April 17, 2003
Reported by Thaddeus Herrick and Phred Dvorak

LUBBOCK, Texas—Linda Watson plunged her bare hand down a hole in the dirt, plucked a six-week old, black-tailed prairie dog from his high-plains burrow and assigned him a new role in life: pet.

For six months, the prairie dog was bottle-fed and allowed to roam about the house of his harvester, Ms. Watson. Then he was neutered by a local vet and sold for $50 to a Japanese broker, who ferried the rodent across the Pacific in a quilt-covered carrying case she stored beneath her economy-class seat on Delta Airlines.

Now Siva, as he is affectionately known, sits in an apartment in Yokohama, Japan, in a cage beside the bed of Sayumi Tashiro, a 34-year old Japanese office worker. Ms. Tashiro paid $250 for Siva, and provides him a wheel for exercise, prairie-dog pellets for dinner and much-appreciated attention when she returns home from work at the end of the day. "He loves being petted," Ms. Tashiro said, as Siva on a recent evening stood on his hind legs, then toppled over on his back for a tummy rub.

The most social member of the squirrel family, prairie dogs are increasingly popular pets. Several thousand are sold as pets each year in the U.S., although they aren't legal in 18 states. And some 15,000 are exported annually to markets stretching from Bangkok to Brussels. The bulk of them go to Japan, where they fetch as much as $300, three times their price in the U.S. . . .

USA TODAY
Monday, June 9, 2003
Reported by Anita Manning
"Exotic Virus Thought to Have Been Spread by Pet Prairie Dogs"

Health officials across the Midwest are trying to contain an outbreak of a rare virus, a cousin of smallpox that has spread from pet prairie dogs to people in three states.

Monkeypox, which has never been detected in the Western Hemisphere, is thought to have been carried into the USA by exotic animals. The infected prairie dogs have been traced to a Milwaukee animal distributor who got them, along with a Gambian giant rat that was sick at the time of purchase, from a northern Illinois animal dealer. Officials say it is possible the Gambian rat was the source of the virus. . . .

The Centers for Disease Control and Prevention confirmed Sunday that the virus is monkeypox, which occurs sporadically in rainforest regions of West and Central Africa. . . .

Until all the animals are tracked down, said Stephen Ostroff of the CDC, "the risk is out there for individuals that may have been in contact with these prairie dogs."

Health officials don't know where the prairie dogs have been sent, in part because no documentation of their movement is required. Pet stores keep records of sales, but some were sold at swap meets, and it is possible that they have been shipped "far and wide," Ostroff said.

David Crawford of Rocky Mountain Animal Defense, an animal welfare group that opposes the selling of prairie dogs, said 10,000 were taken from the wild in Texas last year and sold as pets, mainly in Japan.

There is a lion with his mouth open. I walk through and enter TOTE-EM-IN, a roadside attraction off Carolina Beach Road in Wilmington, North Carolina. The interstate zoo boasts of having "over 100 exotic animals in a Dr. Doolittle atmosphere where you can 'talk with the animals.' "

The list is impressive: alligators, snapping turtles, painted turtles, box turtles, cottonmouth, king snakes, corn snakes, green rat snakes, copperheads, spur-thighed tortoise, squirrel monkey, weeper capuchin, mandrill, jaguar, binturong, peccary, palm civets, kinkajou, python, black leopard, golden spider monkeys, black spider monkeys, Himalayan bear, Siberian tiger, Bennett's wallaby, Sitka deer, Patagonian cavy, zebra, camels, aoudads, prairie dogs—my eye stops at a hometown species.

"Where are your prairie dogs?" I ask the woman behind the counter of the gift shop inside.

"Out in back," she says. "We have two of our own and took two others in that belonged to someone else. We tried to slowly introduce them to one another, but it didn't work out."

"What do you mean?" I ask.

"I mean there are a lot of people that love prairie dogs, but they are more than they can handle; they are wild after all. Some college students had them in their apartment, and the prairie dogs got out and made new tunnels in the heating-duct system between apartments and escaped. They eventually found them and brought them in to us, and they didn't get along with ours," she pauses. "It didn't work out—two of the prairie dogs died."

The woman is Sherrie Brewer, she and her husband, Jerry Brewer, run TOTE-EM-IN Zoo, bought it several years ago from George Tregembo, who started the zoo in 1952. Sherrie has kind eyes. Bucket in hand, she is on her way to feed the animals. "Come on out," she says. "I'll take you to the prairie dogs."

Wearing an orange knitted cap and a camouflage jacket, she pours the bucket into a yellow wheelbarrow, then lifts the wheelbarrow and steers it down the gravel aisle with cages on either side.

We walk past the squirrel monkeys and two black panthers that are pacing back and forth.

Sherrie stops at a hay-lined cage on wheels, six feet tall, maybe four feet wide, and makes kissing sounds with her lips.

"Where you at, little guy? You're hidden real good now, aren't you."

We wait.

"It doesn't say much for us that we've spread ourselves so far that we've ruined all their natural habitat and this is where these animals end up, does it?" Sherry adds.

The guinea hens are crying for more food. Peacocks in the background are yelling, "Halp! Halp!"

"There he is," she says. "Hi, little guy."

We bend down, and I see a prairie dog peeking out from the garbage can that is turned on its side, covered with hay. He scurries back in.

"How old do you think he is?"

"Probably two years."

We wait a few more minutes.

He comes out again, walks toward me, sniffing, stands upright, nose twitching, tail ticking like a fast metronome. A tractor comes toward the cart; the prairie dog runs back into the can and turns his back.

"I'll leave you alone. If you need anything, I'll be over by the cats." Sherrie walks over to the man driving the tractor and begins another conversation.

In time, the prairie dog comes back out and climbs the side of the cage, his fingers with long black nails grasping the chain links. I move closer and crouch down, eye to eye. This is the closest I have ever been to a prairie dog; it is also the only one I have seen in captivity.

My first impulse is to offer him something, anything. Without thinking, I click my tongue and offer my finger which he takes. He just keeps staring. Eyes. His eyes. Black unwavering eyes.

The characteristic mask is faded, a slight dusting of brown against beige. The black tip on his tail gives the species away. This is not a Utah prairie dog but a black-tailed prairie dog, indigenous to the Great Plains.

Suddenly, he jumps down and begins chewing on hay, holding a piece in both hands. He is the color of dry grasses in the prairie, perfectly camouflaged, even in the hay.

Another visitor arrives, "How's my boy? How's my little boy, my little prairie dog boy?"

The prairie dog climbs back up the cage, and the man, who is obviously a regular, begins to scratch his stomach.

"Yes, that feels good, doesn't it, what a good boy, what a sweet boy, yes, yes; you don't get your belly rubbed every day, do you, oh yeah, yeah; that's my sweet prairie dog boy."

The prairie dog puts his cheek against the chain link and closes his eyes as the man continues to rub his stomach.

"I come here a lot," the man says.

When does a prairie dog become a varmint?

Varment, Varmint: *var' ment (rare usage before 1825)*
1. An animal of a noxious or objectionable kind (*collective* vermin) 2. An objectionable or troublesome person or persons.

The Varmint Militia was founded in the 1990s to "defend farmers from the true invaders: prairie dogs." Julie Jargon, a journalist in Colorado, bears witness: *One of the shooters is dressed in camouflage gear that has insignias of both the Varmint Hunters Association, dedicated to the shooting of small animals for sport, and the National Rifle Association.*

The owner of a ranch in Colorado had called for the Varmint Militia's services to kill the prairie dogs on his land.

The shooter sets up his bench, takes out his high-powered rifle, in this case, a Savage rifle with a .22 caliber bullet, loads the chamber, cocks the gun, looks through his scope, scans the horizon for dogs, holds his breath to keep the gun steady, then pulls the trigger. BAM! Almost 200 yards away, all one can see is dust. He puts down his gun and takes a look through his binoculars.

"Got him in the head," he says. "You can tell when you hit 'em in the head because their legs kick."

The landowner is pleased.

The shooter takes a walk, crosses under the barbed-wire fence separating the ranch from the neighboring party, and finds his kill. He drops down and touches the dead prairie dog. A pregnant female. There are small movements in her belly. Half her face is blown off. Blood glistens beneath the afternoon sun. The shooter stands up and looks around. There are no prairie dogs to be seen or heard.

"We'll wait. They're curious."

Another shooter in Utah likes to do his target practice on Sundays. He calls his shooting activities the "First United Church of the Latter-Day Splat Puppies."

Formalized prairie dog shoots are organized around the Interior West. It's a free-for-all for hunters who want to test their marksmanship skills with long-range rifles. Kills made from 200 to 250 yards are highly prized. This kind of shooting enlists its own kind of "aficionados" who see themselves as part of "The Red Mist Society" of varmint hunters. Prairie dogs are the perfect moving targets. They are affectionately known among this community as "pop-guts," which is what happens to the animals' stomachs when they are shot, their bodies exploding in a bloody spray.

One of the most notorious of these prairie dog killing contests was staged in Nucla, a small depressed mining town located on the western slope of Colorado. The first gathering was sponsored by the Ten Ring Gun Club. They called it "The 1990 Nucla Top Dog World Championship."

More than one hundred hunters showed up. There was a one-hundred-dollar entry fee. Each hunter was allowed fifty shots a day. It was a carnival-like atmosphere, "lots of beer, lots of food, lots of dogs . . . A good time was had by all."

By the end of the weekend, over three thousand prairie dogs had been slaughtered, their bodies left to rot.

> *It appears, in fact, that if I am bound to do no injury to my fellow-creatures, this is less because they are rational than because they are sentient beings; and this quality, being common to man and beasts, ought to entitle the latter to the privilege of not being wantonly ill-treated by the former.*
>
> J. J. ROUSSEAU

What is a Rodenator?

The Colorado Wildlife Commission approved the use of an explosive device known as the Rodenator to destroy prairie dog burrows. This "bunker buster" ignites a mixture of propane and oxygen. The ensuing explosion can break animals' bones, burn their bodies, crush their internal organs, and cause suffocation. Despite the inherent cruelty involved, it is currently legal for anyone in Colorado to use this horrific tool to maim and kill any animals unfortunate enough to be in prairie dog burrows, including foxes and rabbits. It is a dangerous device for users and a cruel and indiscriminate tool when it is used to demolish burrows.

MEMO FROM THE PRAIRIE DOG COALITION,
PRAIRIE PRESERVATION ALLIANCE,
AND ROCKY MOUNTAIN ANIMAL DEFENSE, 2006

An ethic, ecologically, is a limitation on freedom of action in the struggle for existence. An ethic, philosophically, is a differentiation of social from antisocial conduct. These are two definitions of one thing. The thing has its origin in the tendency of interdependent individuals or groups to evolve modes of cooperation. The ecologist calls these symbioses. Politics and economics are advanced symbioses in which the original free-for-all competition has been replaced, in part, by cooperative mechanisms with an ethical content.

The complexity of cooperative mechanisms has increased with population density, and with the efficiency of tools. It was simpler, for example, to define the antisocial uses of sticks and stones in the days of the mastodons than of bullets and billboards in the age of motors.

The first ethics dealt with the relation between individuals; the Mosaic Decalogue is an example. Later accretions dealt with the relation between the individual and society. The Golden Rule tries to integrate the individual to society; democracy to integrate social organization to the individual.

There is as yet no ethic dealing with man's relation to land and to the animals and plants which grow upon it. Land, like Odysseus's' slave-girls, is still property. The land-relation is still strictly economic, entailing privileges but not obligations.

ALDO LEOPOLD
Sand County Almanac, *1949*

One day a shovel unearths a day of its own.

A terrible beauty is born.

Everything that happens to us, everything that we say or hear, everything we see with our own eyes or we articulate with our tongue, everything that enters through our ears, everything we are witness to (and for which we are therefore partly responsible) must find a recipient outside ourselves . . . Everything must be told to someone.

At night, putting your ear to the ground, you can sometimes hear a door slam.

How many millions lost their homes to clear the ground?

How many homeless
Wandering, improvisatory
As new deserts move up

The sight made us all very silent

We've got to go underground therefore, like seed, so that something new something different, may come forth. It isn't time that's required it's a new way of looking at things.

Night-season. I think that is a lovely phrase.

W e are living amid a sixth extinction," writes Niles Eldredge, a curator at the American Museum of Natural History, "one that, according to the Harvard biologist E. O. Wilson, is costing the Earth some 30,000 species a year. Biologists estimate that there are at least 10 million species on Earth right now. At this rate, the vast majority of the species on Earth today will be gone by the next millennium."

Who cares?

Only if we understand can we care. Only if we care will we help. Only if we help shall they be saved.

JANE GOODALL

The prairie dog is not a charismatic species, not a grizzly bear or wolf or whale. It is a rodent. A pest. A pop-gut. Prairie dogs are the Department of Agriculture's public enemy number one. In the agency's own words, "The prairie dogs have multiplied until they have become one of the most pernicious enemies to agriculture." The pernicious prairie dog. We have gassed them, poisoned them, and used them as targets. They are expendable, despised, a lowly caste of animals; call them "the untouchables."

The issues circling the Utah prairie dog are the same issues shaping politics and culture in the American West. How do we view progress?

What is our definition of development? What is sustainable development? What kind of world do we want to create? What kind of world are we creating?

Is economics the only standard by which we measure society's values? Or is it possible to adopt another ethical structure that extends our notion of community to include compassion toward other species?

How do we wish to live and with whom?

7 February 02

Dearest Jacob:

You asked me as we were walking in the short-grass prairie this weekend, why Steinbeck mattered to me, why *To a God Unknown* in particular has had such an impact on my thinking and consequently, my writing. I told you I would write you a letter.

I first came across this small novel in 1980. It was placed in my hands by an Indian scholar from Hyberdad named Professor Sharma, who was studying American Literature. When I asked him to pick one book after all his research that he felt best represented American letters, he said without hesitation, *To a God Unknown* by John Steinbeck. I had never heard of this work of Steinbeck's and thought I knew all of his books and had read most of them.

To a God Unknown was written in 1933. Franklin Delano Roosevelt was inaugurated as the 32nd president of the United States; American banks were closed by presidential order; Adolf Hitler was appointed Germany's chancellor; the first concentration camps were erected by the Nazis in Germany; Federico Garcia Lorca published *Blood Wedding;* Carl Jung had just published *Modern Man in Search of a Soul;* and in Utah, Philo Farnsworth was developing electronic television. America was deep into the Depression.

In these days of dustbowls and nationalism, John Steinbeck created an allegory, a myth about our relationship to the American landscape and what it means to find home. I love this novel because it is a story about a family in relationship to place and one man's obsession with paying homage to a tree.

Who is the god to whom we shall offer sacrifice?

The story begins with Joseph visiting his dying father, John Wayne, in Pittsford, Vermont. He is torn. Does he stay with his father until death or does he travel west? He has dreams of the land that awaits him in California. As he shares his divided heart with his father, "John Wayne nodded and nodded, and pulled his shawl close about his shoulders. "I see," he mused, "It's not just a little restlessness. Maybe I can find you later." And then decisively: "Come to me, Joseph. Put your hand here—no, here . . ." He bowed his white head, "May the blessing of God and my blessing rest on this child. May he live in the light of the Face. May he love his life." He paused for a moment. "Now, Joseph, you may go to the West. You are finished here with me."

Joseph knows that when he finds the land that is his, he will feel his father's spirit. He finally arrives in northern California, near Monterey. Looking west over the golden hills of grass, he sees a magnificent oak tree. He recognizes the presence of his elder. "My father is that tree!" He has found his home, "for his father and this new land were one."

In time, his three brothers join him. The Wayne family expands with the farm. Wives are taken. Children are born. But Joseph never forgets his debt to his father or to the land. And so, each night before going to sleep, he talks with the tree, calls him "Sir," brings offerings of fresh milk taken from his cows, lays a sow's ear against its bark, or pours the blood of firstborns around its roots. He sits often in the arms of this tree and listens.

Joseph's brother, Burton, a Christian, hides and watches. One evening, he confronts him.

"You think you have been secret, but I have watched you. I've seen you make offerings to the tree. I've seen the pagan growth in you, and I come to warn you . . . You have left God, and his wrath will strike you down." He paused . . . "Joseph," he begged, "come to the barn and pray with me. Christ will receive you back. Let us cut down the tree."

Joseph told Burton "Save yourself . . . Don't interfere . . . keep to your own."

That night, under the cover of darkness, Joseph's brother girdled the tree at the base, then covered it with soil. The tree dies. Joseph's soul is wrenched as he realizes his ties to the land have been severed.

I hear D. H. Lawrence's words, "This is what is wrong with us, we are bleeding at the roots."

Joseph returns to his sacred grove on the edges of his farm and lies on the black rock that has become his altar. He opens the vessels of his wrist with his knife. He watches "the bright blood cascading over the moss, and he heard the shouting of the wind around the grove . . . He lay on his side . . . and looked down the long black mountain range of his body. Then his body grew huge and light. It arose into the sky and out of it came the streaking rain. "I should have known," he whispered. "I am the rain . . ." He felt the driving rain, and heard it whipping down, pattering on the ground. He saw his hills grow dark with moisture. Then a lancing pain shot through the heart of the world. "I am the land," he said ". . . the grass will grow out of me in a little while."

This is the story that lives inside me and drives my own hand across the page. It is not my wrist that bleeds, but my words. Blood. Bloodwork. Perhaps this is the act of writing, of conservation, of trying to make peace with our own contradictory nature. We love the land. We are destroying the land. We are eroding and evolving, at once.

John Steinbeck wrote in his journal in 1932, "This story has grown since I started it. From a novel about people, it has become a novel about the world . . . The new eye is being opened here in the west—the new seeing."

Our kinship with Earth must be maintained; otherwise, we will find ourselves trapped in the center of our own paved-over souls with no way out.

I cannot help but think of the prairie dogs we watched last week under that arching roof of sky. I cannot stop thinking about the community they inspire even at their own peril; coyote, badger, rattlesnake, red-tail hawk, ferruginous hawk, and bald eagle. I cannot help but feel hopeful as I watched their resolve as they stand their ground as bulldozers raze their towns, one after another, their homeland shrinking acre by acre as our own species develops another strip mall and housing project named after the very thing they destroy, "Refuge at Comanche Flats."

And I love that a small group of friends have bought land together in Baca County, Colorado, Nicole Rosmarino, among them, as a refuge for displaced prairie dogs.

I will forever see those prairie dogs, thousands of them, standing on their haunches, backlit by a setting sun on the plains of southeastern Colorado, looking like a gathering of monks with their hands pressed together in prayer to a god unknown to us.

My love, Terry

The men in my family wear boots, work boots by day and cowboy boots by night. Their tool of choice is a shovel. As my brother Dan says, "A shovel is part of my arm." How well you shoveled matters in a pipeline construction business. This is the livelihood of our family. The Tempest Company is now in its fourth generation. John Henry Tempest, Sr., was a man who could walk the streets of Salt Lake City and know what was underground. He gave the business to his son, John Henry Tempest, Jr., who passed it on to his sons, John Henry Tempest III and Richard Blackett Tempest, who then sold it to their sons, Stephen Dixon Tempest and Robert Laurence Tempest. It is now in the hands of Robert and his brother, David Clifton Tempest. With boots and shovels are how the Tempest men engage with the land.

A shovel is a way of getting somewhere or finding something. Joe Raso, a laborer, set the standard. He could shovel left-handed and right-handed. It was a known gift. My father would say that if you could shovel as fast as Raso then you could work for The Tempest Company. Many would leave.

My brothers say it is an art to be able to shovel well. Foot-hand-and-eye coordination. Being a girl, I never learned this art. My tool of choice was a pen. I would argue that like a shovel, it, too, is a way of getting somewhere or finding something. Instead of a shovel opening up a piece of ground making way for a ditch or trench, a pen opens up a piece of paper for a story.

I remember watching my brothers Steve and Hank help my father put in a small drainage system so that when the water ran off the roof it wouldn't pool in his garden. Steve had drawn up a plan and purchased some plastic pipe to do the job. He outlined how the system was going to work. Hank began digging a small trench that would house the pipe. Behind Hank, Dad was laying the pipe in the ground. Behind Dad, Steve backfilled the trench.

I watched how easily my brother shoveled dirt over his shoulder and how fast. Back straight, waist bent, handle gripped, foot pressured edge of shovel, shovel engaged with the dirt, dig, lift, and throw dirt over shoulder. His body became a lever, a powerful, efficient machine, his right arm resting on his right thigh to offer maximum stability, strength, and movement. Within a few hours, the trench was dug, the pipe laid, then covered with the lawn tamped back into place. You would never have known mechanical surgery on the backyard had ever taken place.

"People look down on us," my brother Dan said from California. "I don't know how many times I heard people say, 'I'm so glad I'm not at the end of a shovel.'" He paused. "But what they don't realize is the deep satisfaction that comes from knowing a trade, from being able to accomplish something through the physical know-how of your body."

I remember Steve saying, "What I love about this work is seeing what a few good men can accomplish together."

Tools. A shovel in hand. I have watched the men in my family perform surgery on the Earth. Pipelines. Gas lines. Water lines. Sewer lines. The men in my family are responsible for seeing that the circulatory system of our communities works. A contractor has learned a trade like a doctor. A shovel is a scalpel. The Earth doesn't bleed, but it can collapse, cave in, or fill with water. Working with the land depends on the tools in hand and the trained eyes who know how to make things work.

The men in my family wear boots, work boots by day and cowboy boots by night. I rarely see them in anything but Levi's and a long-sleeved shirt. Occasionally, they will appear with a white collarless shirt and sport coat. But that is the exception. Ties are for Sunday and for church, only. The men in my family are most comfortable outside on the job, walking the pipeline, imaging what the substrate is below. Inside, the men in my family are quiet, brooding, intense.

What my brothers know is lodged inside their bodies, their beautiful muscular bodies that are now battered and broken, be it a neck that has been fused or a back that carries a chronic history of pain. Their minds hold the maps of an underground landscape of labyrinths and mazes that direct the oil and gas, sewer and water lifelines for the construction of our species.

It's snowing. My father and I are parked behind Amerigas just off the freeway in Cedar City. The Tempest Company has a job here, and word got out that I was interested in prairie dogs. Steve Harker told Dad they were here and they are. We have rolled down the windows. We are silent.

These prairie dogs are strawberry blond, redder than the ones we saw in Panguitch. It makes sense; here the soil is pink. They're just trying to blend in.

Meadowlarks are singing. Ravens are flying overhead. Guard prairie dogs are chirping. I see only eyes raised above the mounds. They are wary. They should be. This prairie dog town does not sit in the midst of pristine country. There is a corral to the west, a highway to the north, railroad tracks beyond the highway, and the village itself is right in the middle of the Amerigas complex where barbed wire is rolled outside the trucking warehouse.

Dad told me that the last job they had in Panguitch was on Highway 89, a high-pressure natural gas line using eight-foot welded steel pipe with five hundred to seven hundred pounds of pressure. Providing the town with gas. Up until then, Panguitch only had propane.

Another job they just finished involved a distribution line servicing sixteen hundred homes with natural gas inside the town itself.

"The American Southwest is exploding with growth," Dad says. "We're part of the boom."

Parked just to the left of the prairie dog town is a Cat 563C, a crawler trackloader. Many trucks are parked nearby, and there are tire tracks everywhere.

Three Utah prairie dogs appear in a landscape so abused it is hard to even catalog all the remnants of industrial life, not to mention the glare and glint of broken glass strewn across the desert.

Wildlands are becoming farmlands. Farmlands are being put up "for sale" and developed into industrial parks adjacent to highways, railroad tracks, and eventually the Cedar City airport. In this prairie dog town, there is no peace, only the constant noise and stream of traffic with planes overhead.

A few miles east, there is another prairie dog town situated on the median strip of I-15, just off Exit 59. A large sign reads, "Wrong Way." Prairie dogs dart across the freeway, barely escaping speeding cars to return to their families. The median strip is flanked by a half-dozen gas stations: Exxon. Standard. Sinclair. If you get off on Exit 59, you will be greeted by Burger King, McDonald's, Wendy's, Chevron, Texaco, Phillips 66, Arby's, Econo Lodge, Comfort Inn, and Color Country Diesel. A billboard brags, "Southern Utah's Largest Entertainment Center." And there you see more restaurants, more gas stations, and the Wal-Mart Supercenter with neighboring movie theaters.

We are all complicit. A rising population is settling in subdivisions. The land scraped bare. Sad, sorry states of habitation. The prairie dog towns and villages are being displaced. They are prisoners on their own reservations.

A killdeer feigns a broken wing as she tries to divert our attention on the dirt road. Cows are mooing. A train is passing. Airplanes overhead. I wonder who is she trying to distract; there are so many threats to her world. Exhausted, she finally sits down in the middle of a tire track.

We drive south on the dirt road past abandoned prairie dog towns. The entrances to old burrows are now choked with tumbleweeds. Ghost towns. We keep driving. Dad tells me about all the new development slated for this canyon. I look out my window and see more tumbleweeds stacked on top of each other against the barbed wire fences.

We get out and walk the fence line. The museum curator in me can't help but catalog what I see: Starbucks coffee cup, Food Farms corn dog wrapper, deer pellets, bones, Styrofoam cup, underground telephone cable, broken glass, orange twine, plastic pipe, a church flier that reads "Free pizza and a movie following Priesthood Meeting."

"Do you remember Evald Erickson?" my father asks me. "Evald Erickson buried a trailer in his backyard to get away from his wife. He took a Tempest Company backhoe and dug a hole deep enough to set his trailer inside. Then he covered it, digging an entrance to his trailer by hand that appeared like a long, dark burrow."

We were fed these stories every night at dinner. The men became legends crossing raging rivers with ropes in their mouths as they swam pipe from one bank to the other, jumping into unstable trenches to weld pipes together so no natural gas leaks would end in explosions. The mantra in my family was this: "In our business, you don't have to be smart, you have to be aggressive."

My father has a bid to make. We are now walking up a trail in a pinyon-juniper forest. I stumble on two dead coyotes. Their skulls, partially covered with fur, are in a tight grimace. The smell of sage in spring masks the stench of death. They were shot. I find red and white cartridges, fifteen of them in a blue plastic bag that must have been thrown out of a fast-moving vehicle. The cartridges are scattered.

We halt in front of a warning sign noting that this is where the gas pipeline runs. Questar. This is the gas company my family works for.

"This is the beginning of the job," Dad says. "It begins here and goes ten miles south." He looks down at his papers and makes a few notations. "Pretty easy digging." My father's mind is trained to map underground. So are the minds of prairie dogs.

My eyes follow the horizon, looking for the uprisings of prairie dogs, mounds that appear like fists raised to the sky.

If one could chart one's natural autobiography with an animal, my companion species would be the prairie dog. We are both tied to community. We both seek time above- and belowground. And we are both struggling with how to survive in a world we hardly recognize.

As a child, I never forgot the watchful eyes of prairie dogs barely visible from their mounds. I am searching for them now.

My father and I sit on his porch in St. George, Utah, overlooking the Entrada golf course with black lava–strewn hills to the south. We are reading the newspaper. Snow Canyon burns red behind us. It is close to one hundred degrees.

> *UTAH: CEDAR CITY—Conservation groups are suing to stop the federal government's trapping and relocation of hundreds of prairie dogs from a golf course here. The groups say stress is killing 90% of the animals moved elsewhere. Golfers and local officials complain the prairie dogs are digging burrows all over the course and stealing golf balls.*
>
> USA TODAY

He looks up from the paper, "I feel for the owners of the golf course," he says voicing his frustration over the government bureaucracy that The Tempest Company has to deal with when it comes to getting the job done in the midst of prairie dog towns. "It's almost impossible to sort through the various jurisdictions between local, state, and federal interests and regulations."

"How so?" I ask.

"In the town of Panguitch, for example, our foreman notifies me that he is encountering prairie dog colonies. I make a call to the mayor and ask him what we should do. He says, 'Who cares—just dig through them.'

"And then a few miles north, you've got the State of Utah actually gassing prairie dogs alongside Highway 89." He looks at me, "It's true. The Utah Department of Transportation was getting complaints from the traveling public that all they can hear is 'splat-splat-splat' as their cars hit prairie dogs, making the road surface slippery and a bloody mess. UDOT crews bring propane to the site, inject it into prairie dog holes and ignite it, solving the problem. Ask our men; they reported back to me that UDOT torched the entire prairie dog village, killing the whole population. But nobody is supposed to know about it."

"We are talking about Utah prairie dogs, right?"

"Right. And then you've got the Feds, both the Bureau of Land Management and the Fish and Wildlife Service telling us that we can 'take' eight prairie dogs, but the ninth one will cost us $200,000.00. What's going on here? They're either endangered or they're not. It shows how stupid the government is—you've got one agency killing them intentionally, while another is fining private citizens who may kill one accidentally and a local official who says, 'Who cares?' "

He gets up and paces the porch, stoops down in the garden, and pulls a few weeds.

"The serious part in all of this is not the fine, but the delay. Our contracts include twenty miles of eight-inch steel transmission line, plus distribution lines carrying the gas to Panguitch. The bid awarded to us by Questar is good for sixty calendar days. We are anxious to start the job because of the high mountainous terrain for the first eleven miles. We have about a four-month window of opportunity before the weather gets us. Old-timers in Panguitch tell me that the pipeline tie-in site could have a foot of snow by deer hunting season, the third week in October. Our whole project is held up during July and August because the BLM will not issue us a permit to proceed with the pipeline because 'they must study the issue' and the issue is whether or not there are any prairie dogs on the site."

I watch my father become more and more agitated.

"Time passes and I become very apprehensive of the timing problem. I finally issue an ultimatum to Questar Gas that at the end of sixty days, I will withdraw my bid if we cannot proceed soon. Because The Tempest Company is the low bidder, it's to their advantage to solve the situation. An emergency meeting is called and the BLM sends an emissary to Salt Lake to issue us the permit we need to begin the job. Now added to the normal risk of pipelining in high mountain country, we have lost two months of good weather."

He shakes his head.

"When we finally got started, the men heard about the prairie dog rule. Whenever Steve and I would walk up and down the pipeline, our men would constantly joke with us, 'Hey Boss, I'm holding the ninth prairie dog. How about a raise, or can I have next weekend off?' "

"The problem is we've got no leadership," Dad says. "None."

"What kind of leadership are you talking about?" I ask.

"No leadership in the government. For the most part, they're a bunch of nincompoops. It's just a bureacracy with no one accountable." He pauses. "Inherently in every man there is a competitive instinct. You want to tap into that spirit with those who work for you. Ultimately, it's not about the boss; it's about the men. In our business, in the men's minds it's not about the money; it's about the footage. Our men know the records of footage made in a day. It's nothing that's written down, but among the foreman, welders, and operators, the men all know. For example, they know that Bill Yates welded twenty-two hundred feet of two-inch pipe at Mt. Dell Reservoir. They know that George Opolous welded thirty-two hundred feet of six-inch steel pipe toward Taylorsville. They know that Ron Tanner dug four thousand feet of trench in one day with a John Deere 690-D backhoe in Sandy, Utah. A crew starts going double time, racing from pipe joint to pipe joint, breaking their backs to break a record. The records of how fast and how far pipe can be laid become the lore of the company. And the men know these records are in my head, too."

My father turns to me, unsure he is making his point, "You're a writer; read Dostoevsky."

"Excuse me?"

"In *The Brothers Karamazov,* there is a chapter on labor and what men do for their own pride. It shows what men are capable of when they are motivated.

"Men inherently want to work and be part of something larger than themselves. That's what the multinational corporations have taken away from people. It's the compartmentalization of the workforce. They've taken away the whole picture. People today only see a fragment of the pic-ture. They feel insignificant, invisible, not part of a team. They don't feel like they are accomplishing anything real.

"I remember this job we had in Rock Springs, Wyoming. It lasted three months, very tough. A lot of rock. We had to cross I-80, and you couldn't bore the highway, too much rock and too much traffic. The State of Wyoming wouldn't let us cut through the highway; you had to bore beneath the road. The men weren't able to get the job done with all these restrictions and the difficulty of the physical ground. The next thing I hear is that Phil Johanson cut through the road in the middle of the night. The Wyoming officials were irate. It was illegal.

"I later found out that the true story was that Johanson was under so much pressure that he got drunk that night due to all the stress and he passed out in his motel. His men loved him so much, knowing what was at stake, they worked throughout the night and got the job done."

Dad gets very emotional and has a hard time finishing the story.

"His men accomplished the mission even though it was dangerous, stupid, and illegal. I admire that.

"A mythology begins to surround the company—'Oh, you're the company that cut I-80 at midnight.'

"I love this work. I love being outside. It's always exciting. There's a certain swing to pipeline construction—a repetition in efficiency. You put the ditch out there in front, and the men break their backs to fill it."

He gets up.

"I've probably talked too long, but I could go on and on about our men, like the time we were digging a trench in Stockton, Utah. Paul Elkington was the foreman, as tough as any man I know. He worked in the uranium mines in Moab. The terrain was so rugged—comprised of gray shale—that the trench had to be dug by hand up a narrow canyon. The men literally carried the pipe on their backs. Iron pipe—eight inches in diameter. It was so heavy, they had to lift it up on the side of the hill with ropes. It's how it was done in 1920, and it's how it was done in 1970. And not one of those men complained. These men have broken their backs for this work in all kinds of weather. They don't whine and they don't quit. So do you see how frustrating it is for us to hear that we have to shut down our job because of some insignificant little prairie dogs?"

What will we lose if prairie dogs disappear from North America?

In 1950, government agents proposed to get rid of prairie dogs on some parts of the Navajo Reservation in order to protect the roots of sparse desert grasses and thereby maintain some marginal grazing for sheep.

The Navajo elders objected, insisting, "If you kill all the prairie dogs, there will be no one to cry for the rain."

The amused officials assured the Navajo that there was no correlation between rain and prairie dogs and carried out their plan. The outcome was surprising only to the federal officials. The desert near Chilchinbito, Arizona, became a virtual wasteland. Without the ground-turning process of the burrowing animals, the soil became solidly packed, unable to accept rain. Hard pan. The result: fierce runoff whenever it rained. What little vegetation remained was carried away by flash floods and a legacy of erosion.

If you take away all the prairie dogs, there will be no one to cry for the rain.

A coalition of environmental groups, Forest Guardians, Center for Native Ecosystems, The Southern Utah Wilderness Alliance, and the Escalante Wilderness Project, along with concerned individuals, are petitioning the U.S. Fish and Wildlife Service to reclassify the Utah prairie dog from "threatened" to "endangered" status under the Endangered Species Act.

I offer my own opinion to *The New York Times*, on Groundhog Day, 2003, just weeks before we invade Iraq.

. . . As we find ourselves on the eve of war with Iraq, why should we care about the fate of a rodent, an animal many simply see as a "varmint." Why should we as citizens of the United States of America with issues of terrorism, weapons of mass destruction, racism, and a shaky economy care about the status and well-being of an almost invisible animal that spends half of its life underground in the western grasslands of this nation?

Quite simply, because the story of the Utah prairie dog is the story of the range of our compassion. If we can extend our idea of community to include the lowliest of creatures, call them "the untouchables," then we will indeed be closer to a path of peace and tolerance. If we cannot accommodate "the other," the shadow we will see on our own home ground will be the forecast of our own species' extended winter of the soul.

J. M. Coetzee in his book, *The Lives of Animals*, creates a character named Elizabeth Costello, a novelist, who defends the rights of animals before a skeptical university audience. She argues that "there is no limit to the extent to which we can think ourselves into the being of another."

Her response is met by a professor of philosophy, Dr. Thomas O'Hearne: "We may certainly wish for there to be community with animals, but that is not the same thing as living in community with them. It is just a piece of prelapsarian wistfulness."

Most people are not comfortable making a connection between racism and specism or the ill treatment of human beings and the mistreatment of animals. We want to keep our boundaries clean and separate. But isn't that the point, to separate, isolate, and discriminate? We create hierarchies, viewing life from the top down, top being, of course, God, then a ranking of human races, and so our judgments move down "the Great Chain of Being" until we touch rocks. This is the attitude of power, and it hinges on who is in control. Who has power over whom? How does this kind of behavior infiltrate the psyche of a culture? And what are the consequences of *scala naturæ*?

Arrogance is arrogance, and cruelty committed to a person or an animal is cruelty. We would rather not think too much about "what is being done to those outside the sphere of the favored group," yet I believe it is time in the evolution of our imagination to make a strong case for the extension of our empathy toward the Other.

Again, Elizabeth Costello: "Anyone who says that life matters less to animals than it does to us has not held in his hands an animal fighting for its life. The whole of the being of the animal is thrown into that fight, without reserve."

One of the last wild, protected Utah prairie dog towns is located in Bryce Canyon National Park.

I am denied access by the superintendent of Bryce Canyon National Park. I am not allowed in the Utah prairie dog town because I signed on to a lawsuit against the U.S. Fish and Wildlife Service. Alongside the coalition led by the Center for Native Ecosystems, Forest Guardians, Southern Utah Wilderness Alliance, American Lands Alliance, Biodiversity Conservation Alliance, the Ecology Center, and Sinapu, I am asking our government to address the declining population of white-tailed and Utah prairie dogs, to move them from threatened status to an endangered species.

The park service says that because I am a citizen suing the United States government, they cannot allow me to observe the Utah prairie dogs for fear of what I might do, the danger I might represent to this population.

They say that my opinion piece in the *New York Times* on prairie dogs gives them cause not to trust me.

I say I thought we wanted the same thing.

The park ranger behind the desk in the Visitor Center hands me a map of the park for tourists and asks if I have any more questions.

I say I will find a way to be with the prairie dogs.

19 May 2004

Hi TTW:

    I am glad that you will be joining me for my 2004 field season with Utah prairie dogs. Below I list various sorts of information that will be important to you.

1) My family (wife and one son) and one research assistant have been at Bryce Canyon since 08 March 2004. We will finish on 15 July 2004. We are glad that you will join us soon.

2) I suggest that you come with at least the following items of clothing and equipment:

    a) a 10-day supply of laundry: Although Bryce Canyon National Park has a laundromat nearby, doing laundry there is a real drag. So please bring myriad socks, shirts, underwear, etc.

    b) eating and cooking utensils.

    c) raingear suitable for work during prolonged showers.

    d) field or hiking boots, suitable for mud, cold, snow, etc.

    e) some sort of pillow or foam pad to sit on.

    f) a battery-powered transistor radio; a radio really helps you to get through some of those long days in April and May.

    g) a large-brimmed hat or sunvisor; the elevation at Bryce Canyon is approximately 8100 feet, and the sun is intense.

    h) a good pair of binoculars, with at least 7-power magnification; on many days you will be using binoculars nonstop for 10–12 hours; if you do not already have a good pair, buy or borrow; good brands whose prices are usually reasonable include Bushnell, Bausch & Lomb, and Cabela; call me for suggestions if you need more assistance for this critical item. If you have won the lottery recently, you might want to purchase 10x40 binoculars by Leica and Zeiss.

    i) at least two good pairs of long underwear.

    j) several sweaters and a warm outèrcoat.

    k) a good pair of mittens or gloves that will allow you to write.

    l) an accurate wristwatch.

    m) a reliable alarm clock.

    n) shorts, T-shirts, etc., for working in hot days of May and June.

    p) a pair of tight-fitting leather gloves for setting traps.

    q) enthusiasm and a great sense of humor.

3) To color-mark the prairie dogs for identification from a distance, we use a black fur dye that has a nasty habit of getting on clothes as well as prairie dogs. Thus, do not bring any fancy clothing unless you do not mind if it ends up with black spots and blotches.

4) On some days, we will enter the observation towers shortly after dawn and remain there until the last prairie dog goes to bed at dusk. Days of this sort usually are interrupted by trap-checks, setting up experiments with the stuffed badger, etc. During the period of infanticides, however, we just watch, watch, and watch for the entire day.

5) While working with the prairie dogs, plan to work every day, seven days a week—at least during critical periods such as breeding and marking of babies. At less critical times I will make every effort to give you an occasional day off.

6) The best way for you to prepare for working with prairie dogs is to read my book, The Black-Tailed Prairie Dog: Social Life of a Burrowing Mammal *(University of Chicago Press, 1995). The chapters on methods, the anti-predator call, infanticide, and communal nursing should be especially helpful. Bring a copy with you to Utah, because many chapters will become more meaningful as you see for yourself many of the behaviors that I describe in my book.*

7) Our 2004 field season will have five main foci: The breeding season, during which we will try to determine exactly which male(s) copulates with each estrous female; some trapping, detailed observations—this is the only part of the 2004 field season that you will miss.

Infanticide, by which males and females try to kill unweaned young; some trapping to verify parturition, intense observations, grisly discoveries.

Marking of juveniles by litter; serious trapping here, with some observations; to verify paternity, we will also collect blood samples from all juveniles, which are the cutest animals in the world.

Communal nursing; if our circumstantial data are accurate, then females sometimes give milk to offspring of genetically related females following the first emergences of young from their natal burrows; trapping and detailed observations here.

Alarm calling: Both males and females are surrounded by juvenile kin in June, but only females call. Why? Myriad experiments with stuffed badgers will help us solve the silent-male puzzle.

Notice that the list of recommended equipment prepares you for both the North Pole and the Equator, as it should. Bryce Canyon National Park in March and April can be freezing and nasty. But Bryce Canyon in June can be hot and dehydrating. More than once we have had SNOW in June, and on 18 June 1996 we had 6 inches!

Many people have been out in cold weather before, but few have sat still in frigid weather for long periods. In addition to items on the list above, bring anything that you can imagine that might help you to stay warm while sitting in a 4-meter-high tower for 14 consecutive hours while we try to detect and understand infanticide.

If you arrive maximally prepared for Utah as I have outlined, then your experience will be exciting and thoroughly worthwhile. That's a guarantee.

With this e-mail, I am officially saving you a position on the 2004 Prairie Dog Squad. If your circumstances change so that you cannot participate, please notify me immediately so that I can offer somebody else the experience of a lifetime.

Cordially,
John L. Hoogland
P. S. Prairie dog research: It's not a job, it's an ADVENTURE.

31 May 04

6:30 A.M.

John Hoogland pulls up in a gold 1983 Plymouth Reliant with a painted prairie dog on the passenger's door that reads "Prairie Dog Squad." The license plate reads "CYNOMYS." Three graduate students are with him.

"Morning!" he says as he jumps out of the driver's seat and opens up the trunk. "Welcome to Bryce Canyon."

We shake hands as I put my pack in the trunk and get in the backseat.

I am introduced to fellow researchers, Sarah, Alyssa, and Theo. It is too early to remember their full names. It's cold. We drive to the prairie dog town, and John gives us our instructions.

Shaking. Helped set traps with John. I was useless. He told me not to be overwhelmed, that I'll get the routine down soon.

He sent me over to the far tower, which I had to climb. I am certain I will fall. Had to try twice. Finally made it with my pack on—felt like a turtle climbing a twenty-foot tree.

My task is a simple one: observe prairie dog behavior.

Our first assignment for the morning is to note the order of wake-ups. I will record each prairie dog as it rises, what number the dog is and what hole it emerges from.

I am charged with watching for dogs #35, #24, #R31, HWA, #70, and #RR6. John tells me each prairie dog is marked. I am not to worry about the meaning of the numbers or letters; it's John's special system. This is his tenth year of research here at this site in Bryce Canyon National Park.

This is one of the last "protected" Utah prairie dog colonies in the world. There are around 125 individuals living here with a lively population of pups expected next week. I am perched in this rickety tower twenty feet above the ground with binoculars in hand, my notebook and pen ready to record.

There is a makeshift desk made out of plywood next to the cut-out window. In fact, this whole little box on top of metal pipes is made of plywood—the walls, the ceiling, and the floor.

The box that will be my home for fourteen days measures four feet by six feet with large cut-out windows in front, back, and on both sides. The floor has a small hole in one corner; my guess is so you can pee without having to climb down. A nice, pragmatic touch.

Looking ahead toward the colony I am responsible for observing, I see no activity. Only robins chattering.

Here are the basics about Utah prairie dogs:

Length: 12–14 inches in length
Weight: 24–38 ounces
Teeth: twenty-two teeth (two matching pairs of incisors that keep growing, typical of all rodents; a gap between the incisors and small molars in back)
Habitat: sagebrush steppe
Elevation: 5000–9000 feet
Range: Southcentral to southwestern Utah
Behavior: Diurnal; hibernates for several months of each year; females attain sexual maturity as yearlings, but males commonly defer sexual maturity until the second year after birth; at Bryce Canyon National Park, mating occurs in late March and early April; gestation lasts 28–32 days; young born in late April or early May; juveniles first appear above ground in late May or early June, when they are about 5.5 weeks old; Utah prairie dogs live in smaller colonies than black-tailed prairie dogs.
Special Adaptations: long black nails for digging with a pad of extra skin on the front paws; varied vocalizations which are part of a highly sophisticated communications system.

7:50 A.M.

My first sighting: Prairie dog HWA. I have been briefed on her. Her markings are as follows: black head with two black stripes wide apart (hence her name Head Wide Apart).

HWA emerges from Burrow NX. Second sighting: an unmarked dog emerging from Burrow 9J. Third sighting: Dog #24 emerging from Burrow 9J.

Chipping sparrow on ground. Chipmunk foraging. The sun is peering through the ponderosa pines. Diffused light on the Prairie Dog Village.

HWA and #24 are foraging, eating supple spring grasses.

8:10 A.M.

Prairie dog #RR6 is now standing in front of Burrow 6. (RR6 translates to black ring around rear.) John marks each dog in the colony with Nyanzol fur dye.

Enter golden-mantled ground squirrel and a dark-eyed junco.

8:17 A.M.

Prairie Dog #4 emerges from Burrow S22. When you imagine the habitat of a protected colony of Utah prairie dogs, you would not imagine this—to my left is a horse corral where the horses for the park concession are kept. The smell of manure and oats is enough to break concentration. Behind the corral is a road and on the other side of the road is the park maintenance yard. Next to the maintenance vehicles and garages is a gravel pit used for road building and repairs. No wonder the Park biologists refer to this prairie dog town as "the mixing circle colony."

"This place looks like a nuclear disaster," says John. The sun is shining on Prairie Dog #24 highlighting the beautiful golden-orange fur. These prairie dogs are so alert. P Dog #24 stays poised in the burrow, motionless, watching me. A robin has its ear cocked to the ground, listening.

Wind blowing, clear blue sky.
Ponderosa pines swaying.
Tower also swaying.

Sagebrush is the predominant plant in the colony, along with grasses I do not know. I suspect not native due to the proximity of the horse corral.

P Dog HWA is eating blue flax blossoms. Another p dog emerges from Burrow NZ. I cannot read its markings. It stands outside its mound like a beacon, a sentinel, its paws hanging down by its side, long black nails apparent. There is another p dog on the edge of the forest standing perfectly still as it faces the sun.

All the prairie dogs in this colony are standing motionless facing the sun.

My eyes catch a shock of lapis on the ground. With my binoculars, I recognize it as a mountain bluebird. It, too, is foraging.

The prairie dogs are the exact color of the clay-colored soil.

8:45 A.M.

P Dog #21 emerges near Burrow S24. I missed the exact moment, distracted by the chipmunk. Unmarked Prairie Dog at Burrow NW has not moved for one hour. It is simply standing on top of its burrow facing the sun. I cannot even see it breathe.

P Dog #24 is moving, its mouth full of hay and other vegetation. P Dog #35 is also very active. P Dog #24 is depositing vegetation in Burrow 9J. It is 8:55 A.M.

A raven flies overhead.

9:05 A.M.

Unmarked P Dog is still standing in front of Burrow NW. P Dog #24 returns with third load of grass to Burrow 9J.

Mourning doves fly through.

Violet-green swallows soaring beyond my window and above the Prairie Dog Town.

Unmarked P Dog still acting as sentinel on Burrow NW.

Wind whistling through tower. Tower rattling.

John and Sarah on radio see babies. Theo has trapped seven babies.

9:14 A.M.

P Dog #24 in for hay load number five. P Dog HWA is out and about in the far-right quadrant of the Village. Unmarked P Dog is watching, motionless.

9:20 A.M.

P Dog #24 runs from Burrow 9J to Burrow 6. Unmarked P Dog standing sentinel still.

9:27 A.M.

P Dog #24 returns to Burrow 9J with seventh load of grasses

9:30 A.M.

P Dog HWA returns to Burrow NZ.

9:50 A.M.

P Dog HWA now foraging next to a chipping sparrow.

10:00 A.M.

P Dog #RR6 appears in Burrow NZ.

10:05 A.M.

P Dog #35 is seen for the first time. Male. Very large. He stands upright in front of Burrow 9X. He is marked with black stripes on his back.

New p dogs on south side of town:
Collar o
P Dog #29
P Dog #87

The wind is howling, tower shaking.

P Dog #35 is now out foraging.

10:17 A.M.

No prairie dogs in sight. They've all gone underground.

Four hours have passed. Eleven hours to go.

Question: How am I going to do this for two weeks? Time moves sooooo slowly.

The cowboys have returned to the corral with a string of mules.

P Dog #31 has just made an appearance.
P Dog #46 is also a new sighting for me.

10:45 A.M.

P Dog #24 is making another hay run to Burrow 9J.

I can hear John trying to start his car, but the motor won't turn over.

I watch some of the p dogs run into the horse corral. One of the cowboys complains. Sounds travel.

Car starts.

John told me the park has been very difficult to work with. Based on my brief encounter, it is easy to imagine. And I wonder why the bureaucracy of our national parks gets in the way of their mandate to protect and preserve wildlife?

It is chilly for June. We are close to 8100 feet above sea level on the Paunsaugunt Plateau, one of the highest plateaus in the state. It runs northeast to southwest and measures approximately thirty miles in length and twelve miles across. The elevation varies from ninety-two hundred feet on the southern rim to seventy-eight hundred feet in the northeast section of the plateau.

This is also the landscape of bristlecone pines *(Pinus longaeva)*, one of the oldest living species on Earth. Five thousand years old. Beauty created in the extreme, these trees are sometimes called "wind timber" because of their gnarled and twisted stance sculpted through time. Endurance meets the wind meets drought, and bristlecones live, thrive, and survive the millennia.

I have sat among them. They speak in a shrine of exposure.

Silence alone is worthy to be heard.

HENRY DAVID THOREAU
January 21, 1853

From my perch, I can see just an edge of the Pink Cliffs. It looks like a cut in the flesh of the forest. These tablelands fool you. The landscape appears flat until it drops off abruptly into steep cliffs. Below, an erosional fairyland of sandstone spires appears. A thousand candles are lit in pastel shades of pink, orange, and yellow. As many times as I have visited Bryce, I never take its geologic magic for granted.

Beyond the Pink Cliffs, the Grand Staircase makes its descent into the red-rock desert of Utah. This is big, broken country born of faults, tilts, and thrusts, and a history of weathering. For all its stillness and the vast expanse of silence, this is tortured terrain.

I am reading a paper that John wrote entitled "Black-tailed, Gunnison's and Utah Prairie Dogs Reproduce Slowly." It appeared in the *Journal of Mammology* in 2001.

The article maintains that long-term research with marked individuals shows that these three species reproduce slowly because of five factors:

1. Survivorship in the first year is low, less than 60 percent.
2. In all three species, females reproduce only 1 litter per 1 year.
3. There is a low percentage of males in all three species that can copulate as yearlings.
4. The probability of weaning a litter each year is only 43 percent for black-tailed; 82 percent for Gunnison's; and 67 percent for Utah prairie dogs.
5. For the females that do wean a litter, the average size of the litter for all three species is around 3.5 pups.

Alarm calls. All p dogs below in the Village are on high alert, clicking, chirping, all standing upright in the same direction with their backs arched, crying.

I look out and see nothing.

Two minutes pass—a pronghorn antelope walks on the periphery of their town.

NOON

I notice the following graffiti on the plywood walls: "2 more days!" "Sigh—" I will add my own word, "patience."

It is very quiet in the P Dog Town as midday approaches. Chilly. I still have on my down parka and wool gloves. A pair of Townsend's solitaires fly by. I must check my field guide and see if the sparrows I am seeing are chipping or tree sparrows. Wind picks up, tower creaking.

The p dogs are so different when they stand upright versus when they waddle along the ground on all fours. P Dog #35's head is barely visible above the sage.

More alarm calls.

Juncos and golden-mantled ground squirrels foraging for seeds in the Village.

12:27 P.M.

Bluebird on corral fence. With my eyes closed, the p dogs sound like Clark's nutcrackers or jays.

Besides the horse corral, the park maintenance site, and the gravel pit, there is also a dump adjacent to this prairie dog colony.

Cowbirds in corral picking insects off the backs of mules.

I am watching Unmarked P Dog. He has his right paw on the ground, his left paw is open toward the sky. It is hard not to see him as reading the pulse of the Earth.

P Dog #RR6 and P Dog #24 are foraging in the pines. P Dogs #35 and HWA are standing on the periphery giving alert calls.

Over the radio, John and Theo are talking about the babies. John tells me to watch Head Wide Apart at Burrow NZ, where she was this morning at 9:30 A.M.

"She should have a litter in there," he says.

In the last four minutes, John and Theo have seen four new litters.

I am watching—suddenly, in Burrow 9W, where P Dog #RR6 hangs out, three babies pop up! Now they are down. I see three pairs of eyes. In my binoculars they look like tiny pools of deep water.

1:20 P.M.

P Dog #RR6 running across the Village. I now see that she is female. When she stands on her hind legs, I note tiny black nipples.

1:27 P.M.

P Dog #24 is doing another hay run. Robin singing. Unmarked P Dog is back in Burrow NW. P Dog HWA is barking with her head thrown back. In Burrow 9W, two little ones, now three years old, appear to belong to P Dog #RR6, who is circling them.

The three baby prairie dogs are eating the blue flax growing around the burrow. They stand, maybe six inches tall, and reach up to the blue blossoms, pulling down the stem with their tiny paws and nibble.

P Dogs #35 and #24 are touching noses in Burrow NW.

According to John, these babies are thirty-seven to thirty-eight days old, roughly five weeks. Near Burrow 9W, there are four young now standing in a shrub, camouflaged. I believe it is a rabbitbrush. P Dog #RR6 returns to the mound at 9W, and as she does, the four pups disappear underground.

1:30–3:00 P.M.

For an hour and a half, I helped John mark prairie dogs.

Here are the steps:

1. Let p dogs warm in sun so they "bleed" more easily.
2. Bring trap into van; then close door.
3. Open trap and let p dog crawl into what John calls a "marking bag."
4. Weigh them (you put the babies in a plastic sandwich bag to weigh them).
5. Let p dogs move to the cone of the bag.
6. One person holds on to them behind their jowls so they are stabilized.
7. John unzips the marking bag while the other holds the p dog.
8. John cuts p dog's nail on back foot. Artery in nail bleeds. He uses tiny glass tube and "bleeds" the p dog, which amounts to sucking the blood up the tube; then he blows the blood into the vial.
9. John stops the bleeding with a towel.
10. He lifts up sleeve to expose p dog's back.
11. He combs p dogs fur and counts fleas.
12. Then he applies dye (Nyanzol) to p dog with appropriate symbol, i.e., a number or letters.
13. Return p dog to cage/trap.
14. Put back in shade.
15. Carefully return animal to colony.

With the babies, the protocol is a bit different because they are so vulnerable. No sleeve bag is used. You weigh them in a clear baggie with a hole in it so they can breathe. You put on two tiny ear tags and then paint a small number on their back after combing for fleas.

You must wear heavy canvas gloves. The prairie dogs have incredibly strong jaws and can wield a nasty bite.

Working with prairie dogs, I discover that some are feisty; others are docile. John talks to them, which seems to calm them. He is passionate about this work. Second nature.

It's hard not to project human emotions to their behavior. I mention this to John.

He smiles and says, "You mean it's hard not to say that prairie dogs are cute?" He brushes one of the prairie dog's fur. "Three fleas." I write the number three down on the chart as he places each flea in a vial with his tweezers. "It's impossible," he says, "because they *are* cute."

After about an hour of marking prairie dogs in the closed van, John tells me that the head biologist of the park service at Bryce told him that under no circumstances should he let me on this colony, that this edict came down from the superintendent. Perhaps I should consider an alias, something nonthreatening like Betsy Ross.

4:20 P.M.

Wind picking up. Temperature is dropping again. Tower rattling. The clouds are like huge clipper ships with sails floating above the plateau.

To hold an animal, to look into its eyes and have it look back at you; to try to calm its terrified heart; to try to inflict the least amount of pain on this small creature in the name of science, the science that in the end may save its life is to open the door to empathy and cross a new threshold of shared existence.

We are so removed from the lives of wild beings.

Alarm calls. I look up from my notebook. The p dogs have scattered and are all underground. A raven flies by.

4:33 P.M.

P Dogs #35, #70, and #24 are all back up foraging.

5:00 P.M.

Much activity, dogs out and about. Shadows are lengthening. Cooler.

Raising my binoculars, I spot a male western bluebird alongside a mountain bluebird, also male. This is a first for me. I have never seen these two species together. The western has a rusty-red breast with a blue plumage more akin to lapis; whereas the mountain bluebird is closer to turquoise, with a sky blue breast. Both species were extremely vulnerable in the 1960s and '70s, as were robins, due to the wide usage of DDT as a pesticide.

I look at my watch—four more hours.

5:20 P.M.

P Dog #70 running west—robins singing in the ponderosa pines. Unmarked P Dog is standing on Burrow NW.

5:30 P.M.

White-breasted nuthatch is circling the old snag to the right of the tower. Deepening light. Black-capped chickadees appearing on edge of the forest, also chirping.

Not much p dog activity—dogs are either underground or away from Village.

6:30 P.M.

John has alerted us to the fact that we are now on "night watch," which means we need to watch the burrow where each prairie dog retires for the night.

Someone told us a badger was run over last night across from the gravel pit. Roadkill.

6:35 P.M.

HWA is back. She has been gone all day. Pronghorn on the edge of the east woods. Mourning doves flying across Village, cooing. P Dogs #53, #RR6, HWA, and Unmarked are all here. Where is P Dog #24?

6:50 P.M.

Unmarked P Dog disappears in Burrow NW, not a surprise. He is clearly identified with this burrow and stayed close to it all day. HWA returns to Burrow NR. #RR6 returns near NZ. P Dog #53 near 9X, now moves to NZ, now over to 8Z.

It is a challenge to see and record where each prairie dog will "go to bed." You are watching one animal and then another disappears, and you missed it. I'm trying to establish wide vision instead of tunnel vision.

#RR6 is surveying the Village standing in front of mound NZ.

6:55 P.M.

Five Prairie Dogs are out:
Unmarked
#RR6
HWA
#24
#35

Black-chinned hummingbird is at my window, so close, his tiny wings are fanning my face. I try not to breathe.

7:05 P.M.

Intensifying light. The Pink Cliffs on the edge of the plateau are blood-red. I can imagine the sandstone spires as flames below.

#RR6 is standing near 9W in a meditative stance. HWA near burrow NX; she is foraging. Unmarked standing on the mound at NW. P Dog #24 is calling near 9J. P Dog #53 is foraging in the middle of the Village. Babies nowhere to be seen.

RR6 went to bed at 9W.

P Dog #24 went to bed at 9J.

Unmarked went to bed at NW.

HWA disappears into Burrow NX.

P Dog #35 goes to bed at NZ. And so ends my first day as a prairie dog witness on May 31, 2004.

1 June 04

Arrival in perch after setting twelve traps for RR6 and her babies so they can be marked.

P Dog #24 is awake, emerging out of burrow NW. He sits. He stretches. He surveys the landscape.

Good morning, prairie dogs—emerging all at once:

P Dog #35—Burrow NZ
HWA—Burrow NX
#RR6—Burrow 9W

I watch these p dogs rise to the sun, and it's as if their spine is a hydraulic jack as they crank themselves upright one vertebrae at a time.

John talked about how plague was present in 1998 and 2001. The Centers for Disease Control and Prevention (CDC) identified two prairie dog bodies as positive for the disease.

Bryce Canyon National Park gave John permission to dust burrows with a powder insecticide for fleas, and luckily the plague did not persist.

But what happens when John Hoogland is not doing his research in Bryce? Who will be watching? Who will be vigilant, watching and guarding this Utah Prairie Dog Village from the plague?

A pair of mountain bluebirds are picking off insects from inside the prairie dog burrows. They flash cerulean blue on top of the sagebrush they have now adopted as a perch.

Sounds of backhoes and trucks roaring from the National Park Service maintenance lot. Plumes of smoke and machine exhaust foul the air.

Lots of dust is being kicked up by the horses in the corral as the cowboys file out with their string of mules. The prairie dogs in the Village are watching.

Jets overhead.

In *Waiting for God*, Simone Weil writes, "The beauty of the world is the mouth of a labyrinth."

The elaborate system of prairie dog burrows is a labyrinth belowground.

My brother Steve has a dream of creating a labyrinth for Salt Lake City as part of the new Intermountain Healthcare complex. Since his diagnosis with lymphoma last year, he has found the labyrinth to be a walking meditation. He experienced this peace at Commonweal, a cancer retreat center near Point Reyes National Seashore. He believes a labyrinth could offer comfort to both cancer patients and their families, providing both exercise and a calming of the mind.

A labyrinth is different from a maze. There are no tricks to get in or out. There are no dead ends. A labyrinth has one clearly defined path. Walking a labyrinth has helped him to accept the changes he faces.

I think of him as I contemplate time. How much time? I have so much time. Time watching prairie dogs.

Dearest Steve:

I appreciated you reading the radiologist's report to me over the phone. I am struck by how much harsher the language of science is when compared to the direct, soulful exchange you had with the radiologist in person. One was the voice of a clinical report, the other the voice of compassion and concern.

This brings me to the threshold of hope, Steve, not hope in the sense of denial, but hope as Margaret Wheatley defines it, "an orientation of the heart."

I've been reading The Impossible Will Take a Little While *by Paul Loeb. He says, "Nothing cripples the will like isolation." I cannot imagine the isolation you must feel at times, how no one can carry you through this pain and suffering; we can only circle you with our love.*

You would love it here among the prairie dogs. Each night, deer or pronghorn walk through the prairie dog town to great cries of disturbance. Biologists say they can differentiate between the two with their calls. Bryce is beautiful, and I have come to love the ponderosa pines rooted in red sand. My job is to record what I see in this prairie dog town in the midst of the sage flats. At times, I'll be honest, the days can be long, but that is my problem. I think of what you wrote from Commonweal, "Sit still and look for what is looking for you."

Can you share with me not just how you are feeling but what you are feeling? What is this experience, Steve? It's true we went through this with Mother, but it feels so different now, my beautiful brother, my littermate. I have no memory of life without you. Educate me. So that I may be more humbly present with you as your loving sister,

T

8:30 A.M.

Only two dogs are up this morning   P Dog #35 and P Dog #24.

I wonder where HWA, #RR6, and #70 are, also Unmarked P Dog?

Two mule deer, a young buck and doe, appear on the edge of the east woods. They now walk across the meadow, near the upper reaches of the prairie dog colony. There have been no alert calls.

Ah, good morning, Head Wide Apart! She emerges from Burrow 8Z. There is something very tender about HWA. It's as though she is aloof from the other dogs.

Another buck in velvet joins the deer in the meadow. I hear a tin slap and turn to see P Dog #35 caught in one of the traps. A chipmunk nearby chirps and cranks its tail with each cry. Hummingbird buzzes my window.

I climb down the tower and release P Dog #35 from the trap. John wants #RR6 and her babies.

8:45 A.M.

P Dog #35 lays himself flat on the ground and stretches both arms in front of him. He sits up on his haunches and now slowly jacks himself upright and faces the sun. Chipmunk foraging near. P Dog #35 eats flax blossoms. Two male chipping sparrows are foraging next to P Dog #35.

P Dog #35 stands upright and delivers an alert call. Raven flies overhead. P Dogs #35 and #24 are kissing.

P Dog #35 returns to eating flax, purple petals are strewn across the colony.

From this perch, it is easy to see that the golden-mantled ground squirrels are twice as large as the chipmunks. Chipmunks are not only smaller but have more stripes, and the stripes run through their eyes on their pointed little faces. These are least chipmunks, so small they run through the traps set for prairie dogs.

Chipmunks are feisty and animated, and they run with their tails up. Golden-mantled ground squirrels have red shoulders and no stripes on their heads. They are much more mellow and less active than the chipmunks.

P Dog #35 has crawled in and out of three traps and has eaten all the oats without setting any of them off.

8:55 A.M.

After I released P Dog #35, he ran and quickly disappeared into one of the unmarked burrows.

HWA is finally moving off her mound. When p dogs sit on their haunches, they appear immovable, grounded and secure in place.

I see movement in the North Pole, the name John has given the farthest reach of the colony. Two unmarked prairie dogs appear in the lenses of my binoculars.

9:05 A.M.

Another tin slap. A golden-mantled ground squirrel caught in a cage. Another descent down the tower for a quick release.

9:10 A.M.

The four babies are up in 9W, eating purple-blue flax petals. The flowers have opened fully in the morning sun. They close in late afternoon and remain so until well after dawn.

It is difficult to watch these animals get caught in cages. I have to remember that in the case of these Utah prairie dogs, this research is what is going to save their lives. John said that when he got the report back from the CDC that the prairie dogs did in fact have plague, he felt he had been kicked in the stomach.

He was "devastated" and immediately contacted the park service to ask for permission to spray. Luckily, the park service said yes, and it saved the colony.

#RR6 is not that interested in the traps. She just moves around them, acting as though they are not there.

No sign of Unmarked P Dog this morning. He was the last one to "go to bed" last night in Burrow NW.

I hear John talking to Sarah over the radio: "The prairie dogs are over in the corral with the Bobcat pushing around the horse manure."

I look over my shoulder, and there is the minidozer cleaning up with a tribe of prairie dogs following in the machine's wake of dust.

10:05 A.M.

The cardinal rule in the baby encampment: Mark trap first with yellow tape, identifying what burrow baby prairie dog came from, before you transport the cage to John or do *anything*. Otherwise, babies may get put back in wrong burrow. CRITICAL.

Trapping babies is the hardest part of my job. They have to go through the ordeal of being weighed, having blood drawn from their foot, being hurt with the punch of the ear tag, and then enduring the trauma of being handled and painted. All this is the protocol of animal research.

I think about the ethics of wild animals being tagged and collared, the grizzlies and wolves in Yellowstone, the harlequin ducks I saw with tags stapled to their beaks, the whooping cranes I witnessed at Gray's Lake in Idaho years ago, burdened by radio collars dangling around their long, thin necks. Even a raven, now, in Grand Teton National Park, can be seen wearing a silver bracelet around its leg. Tens of thousands of animals in the United States of America are numbered and scanned, then monitored through biological surveillance.

What are we learning that we didn't know? That we couldn't learn simply by observation? If wildlife is tagged, painted, and weighted with transmit-

ters, do the animals become less wild? The background noise of the Bobcat (a small, front end loader) pushing manure in the corral, coupled with
the park service excavation across the road creates a sense of an industrial
zone more than a wildlife sanctuary. What is the mandate of our national
parks? Is there a higher priority placed on maintaining roads and manning
concessions than protecting a safe haven for a threatened species?

Given that this is a "protected" Utah prairie dog colony, rare in all the
world, why couldn't the park service move its maintenance facility, gravel
pit, and horse corral to another site?

If we cannot protect the remaining habitats of prairie dogs, how can we
protect them?

10:45 A.M.

No activity in the Village. Very quiet.

It is a gift to be outside and settle into the rhythms of this place. When do
we have the opportunity to simply observe one square acre of nature for
two weeks without disturbance? To be outside and settle into the native
rhythms is to witness a unity of time and space.

The tower I inhabit is the farthest one from the road.

The view before me is a sage meadow bordered, framed, by ponderosa
pines. The water songs and gurgles of the Brewer's blackbirds are filling
the meadow, with punctuation marks provided by robins and the clicking
of prairie dogs to the south.

Sage, rabbitbrush, bitterbrush, blue flax, yellow western wallflowers, and
Indian paintbrush are here. Also, yarrow. I am unable to identify many
of the grasses growing here, with most being invasive species like cheat
grass due to a history of grazing.

Who inhabits this meadow at night? Owls. Badgers. Coyotes. And I would
love to know what takes place below, what the labyrinth of prairie dog
tunnels, the twists and turns, must look like and what kinds of activities
go on in the privacy of their underground world.

John tells us the burrows and tunnels can be as deep as ten feet and as long as fifty feet, usually around six inches wide. In some places, the tunnel will be wider so the prairie dogs can turn around. Typically, each burrow has two entrances. John tells us over and over, "They are all connected." The entrance mounds can be three to six feet across and a foot high, a perfect viewing platform for the animals. The mounds also create a barrier against breezes, helping regulate air flow within the burrows. As air blows across the mound, air pressure inside drops, creating a force that pulls air in through other entrances. This creates a form of ventilation through the burrows.

I worry. I worry about not being able to see all the traps; I need to know which traps have prairie dogs inside and which ones don't so that no animal overheats, caught inside a trap in the hot afternoon sun. The minute one of the prairie dogs is trapped, we have to set it free if it is not the dog we are looking for, or if it is, we must take it immediately into the shade so John can get the information he needs and then release it quickly back to its niche.

Not one prairie dog is expendable. Not one.

I am learning. I am learning that basic things like where a prairie dog emerges from in the morning and where it retires at dusk convey a wealth of information about an individual.

Many other creatures are intertwined with prairie dog colonies. This is an entire community of beings, not just a town of one particular species.

At noon, I am learning life slow downs. The animals rest, take naps at midday. I can do the same, even in this tower.

#RR6 appears. It is 11:00 A.M. No pups in sight.

Here comes Head Wide Apart, HWA. Her wake-up time: 11:09 A.M. #RR6 is trying to get into Burrow 9W. She's peering into traps, standing up with her arms on them, now scurrying to the second blocked hole. Now she runs to the third blocked hole. John has set the traps well. Now she runs around all of them trying to get back into Burrow 9W.

#RR6 runs to a fourth burrow that is not blocked and disappears.

#RR6 is back up, out of the burrow she disappeared in. She was underground for about ten minutes. Most likely with her litter of pups.

Alarm call made by P Dog #24. Pronghorn walks on edge of Village. All p dogs disappear. I wonder why they do not issue alert calls for deer?

#RR6 is now in front of Burrows 9T and 8Z. You cannot convince me that she is not stressed, that she doesn't perceive something is amiss. She stands up. Sits down. Stands again and turns around. How can an animal's consciousness be denied?

Marc Bekoff, a founder, with Jane Goodall, of Ethologists for the Ethical Treatment of Animals, uses the phrase *"minding animals"* as a way of respecting other species for who they are and the worldview or "umwelt" they possess. As a biologist, he is committed to the investigation and understanding of animal cognitive intelligence and consciousness, asking the question, "What do they feel and why?"

Do we really believe we are the only animals on the Earth with deeply emotional lives?

Minding prairie dogs.

#RR6 goes down again—Burrow 8Z. Clouds pass overhead. Village darkens. #RR6 looks like she is wearing a long coat with black clasps running down the sides. Two rows of long, black nipples hang down.

#RR6 back up, foraging alongside HWA. Still no sign of babies.

Huge black wasp in tower. Huge machine spewing black smoke at dump site next to maintenance facility. My brothers would tell me it is a loader. I should know these things as the daughter of a pipeline contractor.

11:35 A M

#RR6 caught in trap. HWA standing upright looking up at me. I'm out of the tower to take #RR6 over to John to the measurement van.

NOON

Theo is talking to John on the radio, saying that from his tower (which is nearest to the park gravel pit) he can see logging going on by the National Park Service. John and Alyssa come to transfer #RR6 back to her burrow. John says that #RR6 was born under the lone pine, had a litter south last year, but then moved north this year when the area became available due to the predator activities of the goshawk and red fox.

"When a niche opens up, it gets filled," he says.

"By June of last years, 2003, the northern section of our study colony contained hardly any Utah prairie dogs because red foxes, northern goshawks, and golden eagles had captured almost all the adult and juveniles who lived there. They almost wiped out this colony completely."

Theo says he saw a raven take a baby prairie dog behind his tower last week.

"You never know what you are going to see," says John.

12:05 P.M.

HWA just went into Burrow 9T.

Hello, P Dog #24. He is crawling toward an orange plastic cone used to block one of the burrows. He is looking around, now backs up. Tell me they don't recognize change and reasons to be alarmed. Still no babies. HWA is standing on the mound of 8Z.

John is talking about infanticide over the radio to Theo and Alyssa. It occurs usually when prairie dog babies are very young, under two weeks old. P Dog #21 (now known as Jeffrey in reference to Jeffrey Dahmer, the serial killer and cannibal who murdered 17 individuals from 1978–1991) killed five babies this spring. The male prairie dog dragged their bodies aboveground, carried them to the center of Alyssa's area of study (which is between John's tower and the one I am in), and cannibalized their bodies.

Now, with the prairie dog pups entering their fifth and sixth weeks, they are bigger, and therefore less vulnerable to predation by the males.

1:55 P.M.

Red-tailed hawk cries. Alarm calls in the Village. All dogs underground.

Hawk's shadow crosses the meadow.

2:00 P.M.

P Dog #24 out and about. John is bring back #RR6 and putting her back in the shade.

2:07 P.M.

Red-tailed hawk crosses the Village again. And again, all dogs underground.

2:35 P.M.

First baby emerges in burrow next to 9W which is "supposedly" blocked by orange plastic cone.

John tells me that when he dies he wants to be a ghost so "I can enter prairie dog burrows and see where they go and what's going on."

Question: Are these coteries or wards?

Answer: John doesn't use the word "coterie" for Utah prairie dogs. He calls these family groupings a "clan." The "clan" I am watching is the "North Clan."

I ask John about infanticide among prairie dogs. He tells me that within colonies of black-tailed prairie dogs, both males and females kill juveniles. Within Utah prairie dog colonies, however, only males are infanticidal.

"I think it's about food," he says. "I'll kill your babies so my babies will have more to eat. The lactating females lose weight. It's very hard on them, and it may be a practical thing; they need to eat protein to stay strong." He pauses. "There's just so much we don't know."

2:40 P.M.

A western tanager is perched on top of the old snag. Red head, yellow body, black wings.

John and I are now surrounding the second burrow with traps. As we set up the orange plastic cones, he tells me a story of a golden eagle that would sit on top of the old snag. It would watch the Prairie Dog Town with great patience, then drop like dead weight and pounce on a prairie dog before anyone realized what had just happened.

He said that about five or six years ago, there was an eagle everybody called "butter talons" because the eagle would pick up a prairie dog and then drop it. This happened over and over. The eagle just couldn't keep the dogs in its grip.

3:25 P.M.

One pup is caught: its first experience of terror and betrayal. A second pup is just outside the trap. The one inside and the one outside are touching noses. One is frantic, the other puzzled. Sentient beings living in a charged world.

I climb down the tower to retrieve the little dog and carry it over to John's van for measurements.

Big winds—back up in the tower—shake, rattle, and roll!

I look at the watch on the makeshift desk: five more hours inside. Alyssa Taylor, Sarah Druy, and Theo Manno are my colleagues. I finally learned their full names.

Robin singing.

From my perch, I have seen: pronghorn antelope, mule deer, golden-mantled ground squirrel, least chipmunk, red-tailed hawk, raven, tree swallow, violet-green swallow, robin, mountain bluebird, western blue-bird, chipping sparrow, brown-headed cowbird, mourning dove, slate-colored junco, white-breasted nuthatch, western tanager, black-capped chickadee, Townsend's solitaire. Alyssa, Theo, Sarah, and John carrying prairie dog babies back and forth in Tomahawk traps.

Cloud ships are sailing across the plateau once again.

A cloud covers the sun—a change of light, a momentary drop in temper-ature. A change to be noticed, one that marks the natural rhythms of a day in the life of a prairie dog.

Human beings are turtles carrying the self on their backs. The self as home. My home is in this tower. Once in the tower, I throw my pack on the floor and hoist myself into the shelter, lowering my head so I can slip through the square door and stand upright. Each day is a discipline. To stay focused on the task at hand—prairie dog activity among the North Clan.

I watch, record, write, wonder, question, ponder, read, dream, and spec-ulate. It is a worthy form of work, all with a bird's-eye view of a strug-gling community just trying to survive.

P Dog Baby #2 caught in trap. Two down, two to go. Back down the tower to retrieve the little one, much smaller than P Dog Baby #1 and deliver it to John for it's first "checkup," that is how I am seeing the weighing and measurement sequence now.

HWA back. She is standing upright giving an alarm call on the mound of Burrow NZ. I look around and see nothing. She disappears in 9T and reappears, alert and wary.

A pinecone falls. My eyes just happened to witness this as I was watching a pair of swallows fly.

P Dog Baby #3 caught in trap in burrow directly across 9W. Back down to retrieve and deliver. The challenge is to keep the Tomahawk trap with the prairie dog baby inside as level as possible when walking the half mile through the edge of the woods up to John. I also find that if I talk to the prairie dog in a low, calm voice, he or she relaxes more.

Rain clouds advancing. Babies #1, 2, and 3 are returned to Burrow 9W after being weighed, bled, measured, and marked. #RR6 returns to NZ area. No doubt she has missed her babies. P Dog #25 returns to NZ area. Traps and cones are gathered. Today's work on the ground is done.

HWA and P Dog #24 are facing the sun, paws pressed together. #RR6 disappears in unmarked burrow. P Dogs #35 and #24 kiss, then fight. P Dog #35 and HWA kiss.

HWA runs into Burrow NZ at 7:11 P.M., then runs back out at 7:12 P.M.

Wind blows through tower—scent of pine, temperature dropping. Shadows lengthening.

7:17 P.M.

All dogs standing—alarm calls. Buck and doe move across meadow from east woods across Village.

All dogs up—more alarm calls. Deer have crossed over into west woods.

7:21 P.M.

Another buck passes through Village, then two more females. No alert calls.

7:30 P.M.

All dogs still aboveground, foraging, feeding on blue flax.

#RR6 stands on mound at Burrow 9W. She turns in all four directions very slowly with her paws pressed together. Stops. Stands facing the setting sun. Waits. Sun disappears behind ponderosas. She disappears into Burrow 9W at 7:32 P.M.

7:53 P.M.

Coyotes howl in west woods. All dogs freeze. The coyotes create a frenzy of yips and yaps, no doubt, young coyotes high-pitched and manic are practicing their newly found voices.

8:00 P.M.

P Dog #35 to bed in Burrow NZ. I lost track of HWA—didn't see her disappear. Good night, Head Wide Apart. I miss her.

2 June 04

7:10 A.M.

Colder this morning. Gloves on. Stiff.

Wing beats of ravens—four—the mantra that fans the stillness of the high desert.

It is our wedding anniversary. Brooke and I have been married for twenty-nine years. He is working north of Bryce in the Grand Staircase-Escalante National Monument area, seeing if ranchers in Garfield County are interested in selling locally grown beef to restaurants in Salt Lake City. It's part of his sustainable development work along Highway 12. I miss him.

7:45 A.M.—Good morning, #RR6 at 9W.
7:46 A.M.—Good morning, HWA at NX.
7:51 A.M.—Good morning, Unmarked P Dog at NR.
7:53 A.M.—Good morning, P Dog #35 at NZ.

And where are you P Dog #24?

Least chipmunks are scampering every which way in the Village.
Chickadees singing their morning song in the woods.
Chipping sparrows foraging in the Village.

Even from here, I can see a golden-mantled squirrel's pouches are full of seeds. Looks like it has the mumps.

Alarm calls. #RR6 and HWA are standing their ground, putting out the word. Two pronghorn antelope passing through. Elegance on four legs. #RR6 is relentless with her alarm calls. The pronghorn stop; fannies flare white, their manes erect.

John said yesterday that the alarm calls of the prairie dogs can actually deter unwanted visitors.

These prairie dogs are more aggressive and vigilant against pronghorns than mule deer. I have seen this consistently. Why?

No sign of P Dog #24 today. No sign of Unmarked P Dog yesterday. Blue flax continues to open and bloom.

8:50 A.M.

HWA standing on mound—alarm call. I also hear an olive-sided flycatcher: *"quick-three-beers!"* *"quick-three-beers!"* Unmistakable in aspen communities.

9:00 A.M.

No pups up yet.

Hummingbird wings. I hear them but don't see one, most likely broad-tailed humming bird.

Mules kicking metal siding of corral. Annoying. Brings new meaning to the word "ass"—for that matter, "kick ass."

9:07 A.M.

Mule deer, a doe, walks through Village. No alarm calls.
P Dog #35 and HWA emerge both out of Burrow NZ.

9:09 A.M.

Babies up. Today we are trapping for P Dog Baby #4. #RR6 emerges out of Burrow 97 . . . a new entrance. P Dogs #35, HWA, #RR6, all up and active. No sign of P Dog #24 or Unmarked Dog.

Whoops, P Dog #24 is up—from where? I missed him. He is clicking, chirping on mound with HWA.

Pronghorn approaching from the north.

Cowboys in chaps are pushing the horse shit with their long-handled brushes. The smell reaches me on the breeze. They are dressed in turquoise shirts or red shirts with white silk handkerchiefs tied around their necks. The leather chaps they wear places special emphasis on their crotches. Black hats. Wrangler jeans. Boots, of course. These are the show cowboys that are also working cowboys who take the tourists for a ride.

Beyond the mule corral comes the dump truck spewing black smoke again, with its deafening sound, driving up the gravel road. For what? If the prairie dogs are alerting one another, you can't hear them.

9:10 A.M.

Most dogs up—P Dogs #35, HWA, #RR6, #24. No sign of Unmarked Dog. Babies back underground.

"Click, click, click, click, click, click"—their calls sound like a pen tapping on wood. I can see their pink mouths as they continue their chipping, chirping.

P Dog #35 is intensely eating the purple-blue blossoms of the blue flax. He sits solidly on his haunches, holds the flax down with both paws, inhales the flower, strips stem, then moves to the next delicate blossom with five periwinkle blue petals. Imagine a diet comprised of flowers.

I have not noticed the black eyebrows of prairie dogs until this morning. In partial light, the eyebrows can appear as a mask.

P Dog #24 and HWA keep trading places on top of mound 9J.

10:15 A.M.

Babies emerging from Burrow NX. Babies #1 and #2 are kissing. John alerts all of us over the radio that there are five new litters today. Oh, oh, Baby #2 caught in trap—down the tower I go to release her.

10:20 A.M.

While I was out walking around the burrows, I thought I heard a purring coming from Burrow NR. Could those be babies, another litter that has not yet emerged? Yesterday we "processed" fourteen babies, including three of "mine" from the North Clan. "Nine litters counted as of today," John reports on the radio.

With my binoculars, I focus on HWA's eye. Upon first glance, a prairie dog's eye appears black, but in truth, if you look long enough when the light is just right, prairie dogs have brown eyes, a deep amber color with a black iris. The eyes are shaped like pumpkin seeds. Head Wide Apart blinks. Her focus is straight ahead. She has a black eyebrow and below her eye is a faint streak resembling the dark stain of tears.

11:13 A.M.

Babies are emerging from Burrow NX. They are so *cute*—even John says so. . . .

What am I trying to convey with this word, "cute," is that they are adorable, tiny and vulnerable, tough and cocky, much more sure of themselves in this dangerous world than their wee little bodies should be. Prairie dog babies make you laugh as they play and roll over each other in accidental somersaults and startled leaps and jumps when surprised. They kiss and fight and tumble and dig and eat and sleep wrapped around each other with an eye half open for alarm. They are food bundles with personality, unaware of their appeal to hungry predators.

Out of darkness, these pups emerge to a world of light. A stem of blue flax brushes their heads. They look up at the flower petals that shade them from the heat.

#RR6 is back collecting grass and disappears down Burrow NZ.

Golden-mantled squirrel loading its jowls with seeds once again.

Goshawk flies by. All dogs down. Its shadow silences the Village. In my binoculars, I catch its relentless garnet eye.

Dogs back up. P Dog #35 is digging a new mound at 8Z with his own rhythm.

One, two, three, four with front paws
One, two, three, four with back feet

This sequence of digging is repeated while he lies on his belly in the dirt or, in this case, the slope of the mound.

#RR6 is up from Burrow NZ, having taken in her grasses to line the burrow for babies.

"Ten litters," John says over the radio.

John is in the tower next to the road. He wears a white Lawrence of Arabia hat with a sheet of white fabric hanging down his back. His large black wraparound sunglasses are added protection from the sun. Every day he wears a royal blue sweatshirt, and his Levi's are streaked with the black dye he uses with the prairie dogs, as are his fingernails. His hands look more like those of a heavy metal guitarist, rather than first-rate scientist. His work boots are the color of sand like his boyish blond hair.

11:30 A.M.

I am watching Head Wide Apart. There is something about her that touches me deeply. Her small black head that has been dyed for distinction, the black stripes painted far apart. She is a small, lactating female who is calm yet attentive. Her young have just emerged today, two babies so far. She looks directly at me and doesn't run away. And at night, before she retires, she stands beneath the tower and looks up, before she focuses on the setting sun.

It's easy for me to project my own thoughts onto her, but I dare anyone to sit in this tower for two weeks, fourteen hours a day, after you have watched them wake up each morning, forage, kiss, survey, dig, play, fight, copulate, forage some more, kiss, call, then disappear underground for bed, and not be touched by their inquisitive and vibrant character.

If those who poison them, drown them, gas them, and shoot them for sport considered them as sovereign beings with their own evolutionary consciousness and intelligence, would their actions be different?

To regard any animal as something lesser than we are, not equal to our own vitality and adaptation as a species, is to begin a deadly descent into the dark abyss of arrogance where cruelty is nurtured in the corners of certitude. Daily acts of destruction and brutality are committed because we fail to see the dignity of Other.

Madame Head Wide Apart is teaching me about the dignity of Other. With her babies out in front of Burrow NX, she is digging forcefully with her front claws, creating a plume of dirt behind her that is building up the mound like a fortress for protection. The babies are barely visible now.

P Dog #35 has disappeared down Burrow NX where Madame HWA is still digging.

11:45 A.M.

P Dog #35 is out and is following Madame HWA as she forages with an eye always toward her litter. She stands, surveys. She goes down with them. I hear cries and whimpers. She's out, aboveground; they follow her like a billowing train of fur.

These babies in the next day or two will be dyed, hooded, striped, numbered, bled, and pierced. Right now, they are innocent and camouflaged, the color of clay.

Three babies are out, pulling on roots. Madame Head Wide Apart scurries them back into the burrow. She runs to the tower, stops, and looks up, then begins eating more blue flax in the shadows, holding the thread-like stem down with her small paws.

11:50 A.M.

All three babies are back out, tripping over one another, rolling down the burrow, and falling off the mound as they play. They can barely walk. They continue to roll over as they can't quite negotiate sitting yet, either. These babies are the length of human fingers.

#RR6 is sitting on the mound of Burrow 9W with her four babies around her. Her pups are older, larger and more precocious.

#RR6 just walked into one of the traps. Down the tower I go to release her. She loves the oats.

NOON

#RR6 is in the trap again. Down the tower to release her.

1:30 P.M.

Madame Head Wide Apart is a digging machine—front and back. She is digging a trench and in so doing is widening the mouth of the burrow. Her babies in NX are out—just saw one of the babies stand on its hind legs for the first time, then fall over.

1:35 P.M.

Now Madame Head Wide Apart is digging near the mound of NX with the babies near. The babies are wrestling each other, looking like one fur ball rolling down the burrow. She is wary and stands her ground next to an aggressive robin.

In Burrow NJ, two more pups are spotted. It is 1:45 P.M. These look to be the offspring of P Dog #70, a large female in the South Clan.

A junco sends the four babies at NX down the hole. It becomes a game.

The pups emerging from NJ are HUGE. Total bruisers. P Dog #70 is near.

NX babies are kissing each other; one pup puts its head on the other one's lap. Now they are roughhousing like any other siblings in the animal world. On their backs, they stop momentarily, blinded by the sun.

2:00 P.M.

The four little prairie dog pups of Burrow NX hold out their arms to steady themselves as they sit on their haunches in the wind.

From my perch, the babies are perfectly camouflaged with a tint of orange just like the sandstone cliffs of Bryce.

2:15 P.M.

Caught unmarked baby from 9W. This completes the litter of four captured pups belonging to #RR6.

Down the tower, will tag the Tomahawk trap and take it up to John in the van.

3:00 P.M.

On my way back to the tower, I watched a driver of one of the Bryce Canyon National Park maintenance vehicles spit on a prairie dog who was standing on the side of the road.

3:15 P.M.

Sarah and I checked traps all through the woods for prairie dogs. All traps empty. We ran into one of the cowboys.

"That John's a slave driver, ain't he?"

I am too far away to respond. He keeps talking.
"Don't ya'll get any days off?"

"Nope," says Sarah as she quickly checks each trap.

3:35 P.M.

Exhausted. Baby #4 returned and released to 9W. #RR6 seems to relax.

Now, when I take these babies to the van, I think of it as their first checkup, and it's not so painful. We all went through it.

Five more hours. Damn.

The clouds look like falcons with their wings tucked back in a horizontal rush.

I had no idea how verbal and nervous mules are. There cannot be a more hideous sound than "hee-haw."

Today we have tagged and painted over twenty-four babies, twelve litters, maybe more.

Tomorrow is my turn to mark prairie dogs in the van with John, always an intense and claustrophobic experience being cooped up in such a small space in the extreme heat. The payoff is being with the prairie dogs, holding them, talking to them, trying to keep them calm, all the while learning from John as he measures, marks, and identifies them. He is constantly teaching us what he knows, what he has learned and continues to learn each day.

3:45 P.M.

Madame Head Wide Apart and #RR6 are kissing.

The 9W babies look like little charred pieces of wood with their collective markings. Either that or little jailbirds, scientific inmates.

Without the markings, however, it would be almost impossible to distinguish them.

#RR6 is digging out Burrow 9W, widening it just like her cohort, Madame Head Wide Apart.

5:05 P.M.

Took a nap on the floor of the tower.

Before falling asleep, I listen to Shostakovich's Tenth Symphony. Because it was written in 1953, after Stalin's death, I hear it as a raised fist against oppression. The calling of strings is an outpouring of emotion. A lone clarinet. An oboe weeps in sorrow, echoed by a bassoon and then the voice of the flute. A melody emerges in the midst of mass tragedy. And the military cadence continues.

The flute reminds me of the prairie dogs. Or perhaps it is the prairie dog's voice that holds the place of the flutes. There is an ecological orchestration that is ongoing, a symphony of voices, sometimes dissonant, sometimes harmonious, always dynamic.

P Dog #70 returns to Burrow NJ. Her pups are still out.

5:15 P.M.

P Dogs #35, #21, and #70 are standing on the edge of the East Woods, upright, alert.

Another pinecone falls from the same ponderosa as yesterday, at virtually the same time.

A dust devil disperses mules.

5:30 P.M.

One baby prairie dog from 9W is standing behind a rabbitbrush, and it looks like he is wearing black boxers. Am I going mad?

Baby from NJ has wandered all the way from the South Clan to the North Clan. Vulnerable. From my vantage post, no raptors in sight.

5:40 P.M.

Alarm call from an unmarked baby, a member of South Clan. John has said that I need to pay attention to both what is in front of the tower and what is behind. My focus has been north, not south. More ground to cover.

Violet-green swallows preening on one of the branches of the old snag. They nest in the hollow of this dead tree.

7:00 P.M.

Back in tower after taking another p dog to the van. I delivered six dogs to Theo. Dismantled enclosures, picked up cones, and released more dogs caught in traps.

Woodpecker on snag. What species? Lewis's woodpecker. First sighting.

No sign of Madame Head Wide Apart, P Dogs #35 or #24, or Unmarked Dog. P Dogs #BB4, #21, and #10 of the South Clan are all standing. Chickadees flitting about in West Woods. What long, languishing days. Whistling wings—mourning doves fly by—a constant as dusk approaches and good-night calls are made.

3 June 04

7:00 A.M.

Clear, warmer, with cirrus clouds. Yesterday, thirty prairie dog babies were trapped, tagged, weighed, bled, and marked. John is calling this an explosion! A record high for Utah prairie dogs in almost a decade of research.

This morning as we drove into Bryce, he told us he was the first biologist to identify "infanticide" among prairie dogs. He was so shocked he waited seven years before publishing his findings.

Say's phoebe perched on top of trap at Burrow NR.

Good morning, #RR6—W9 at 7:38.
Good morning, #35—NZ at 7:39.
Good morning, HWA—NX at 7:41.

8:07 A.M.

All prairie dogs are standing, their paws pressed together facing the sun.

8:43 A.M.

Alarm calls. Four deer cross meadow.

No signs of P Dog #24 and Unmarked P Dog—whoops, I take that back, Unmarked P Dog is foraging near 8N. Without John's black markings, the prairie dogs that are unmarked are truly camouflaged.

8:50 A.M.

P Dog #24 up.

9:02 A.M.

Babies up at Burrow W9.

9:13 A.M.

Madame Head Wide Apart in trap. Like #RR6, she loves the oats. Down the tower to release her. Brewer's blackbirds in Village.

9:30 A.M.

In a low, quiet voice, I urged Madame Head Wide Apart not to enter the traps for her own safety. She was unusually calm inside the trap, simply enjoying the oats. This is her second season with researchers. I opened the door to the trap, and she immediately ran out returning to Burrow NX. John and I surround her burrow with eight traps to get the babies in for marking. All mouths of the Tomahawk traps are open. The babies will become curious, step inside, set off the mechanism, and the door will close.

10:29 A.M.

Baby #1 caught in trap at Burrow NX. (I have seen four pups this morning pop up and down.) I look away, and suddenly, Baby #1 has jumped out of cage and is on top of the cage! How did that happen? The door is closed. The baby was inside . . . Houdini is reincarnated.

10:45 A.M.

Baby #2 is now caught in trap at Burrow NX. Baby #1 has disappeared completely.

Babies out in Burrow NJ. Another "surrounding" is in place to trap them. I notice that when a prairie dog confronts danger or suddenly is faced with a "surrounding"—an encircling of traps at the entrance to its burrow—it sniffs, checks it out through various sensory means (chirps, barks, touch, and smell), doesn't get too close, and then goes underground.

The Underground—what is hidden from us?

It is impossible not to notice striking personalities and traits within the North Clan. P Dog #35 keeps everyone together, is always kissing; Madame Head Wide Apart is very tender, very sweet, eccentric in her behaviors, like always coming to stand beneath the tower and look up; #RR6 is an explorer, wanders far and wide into the woods and seems the most independent of the group; P Dog #24 is somewhat of a loner and is most connected to P Dog #35 and Unmarked P Dog; Unmarked P Dog is elusive, refuses to be caught, cannot be identified with any one burrow or repetitive behavior. A maverick.

12:45 P.M.

Mourning doves on old snag cooing.

1:00–5:00 P.M.

Tagging, weighing, bleeding, combing, painting babies. Down the tower to John's van and the prairie dog encampment.

Forms must be filled out meticulously. The categories for data are as follows:

Site/Burrow
Right ear tag
Left ear tag
Sex
Weight

Markings
Fleas
Ticks
Scars
  sm
  med
  large
Number of capillary tubes of blood collected
Time of Day
Molt %
Weaning weight—circle here if this is mother's weight at weaning

6:37 P.M.

I return Madame Head Wide Apart and her three babies to Burrow NX. The lactating females, mothers, also need to be weighed and bled. Madame Head Wide Apart has the sweetest demeanor. I don't know how to describe it. Trusting? Her babies carry her same qualities. Each day she stands at the base of my tower, stands where I can see her through the door, on her hind legs and looks up at me. Every day.

She is slight, creating a thin shadow. She weighs maybe seven hundred grams. Her babies weigh somewhere around one hundred grams. Out of her four babies, three are males. We have yet to catch the last of her litter. Will it be a female?

7:10 P.M.

#RR6 stands on her mound, her four babies inside their burrow. She faces the setting sun. Her hands are resting above her belly like an expectant mother, a habit she has failed to break.

7:25 P.M.

#RR6 on Mound 9W—down. Good night, Madame RR6.
HWA foraging near Burrow NX—not interested in retiring.
P Dog # 35—down—Burrow NZ. Good night, sir.
No site of P Dog #24 or Unmarked P Dog or Miss #70.

I love this time of night, especially the rush of wind through the pines. The closure of each day is a benediction of light.

7:30 P.M.

My back aches. Tonight I could barely climb up the tower and get myself back into my perch after the markings. To sit cross-legged in the dark heat of the van for over four hours with the pressure of handling prairie dogs so they don't get hurt takes its toll.

But worth it. To be able to work with these animals and begin to see the different personalities of each prairie dog is a privilege. Some of the little ones have serious strength as they clamp down on your finger with their sharp teeth and refuse to let go!

Back in my perch, hoping baby #4 in Burrow NX and all of P Dog #70's little ones will find their way into their burrows.

No prairie dogs in view. They must all be underground. I missed the exit times.

John is amazing. With each animal, he exudes such enthusiasm. René Dubos defines enthusiasm as "god within."

Here comes Madame Head Wide Apart running in from the far north. I thought she was up close foraging. Apparently not.

Pink light. The old snag is an apartment building with a pair of western bluebirds, violet-green swallows, and five chipmunks (sitting side by side) perched on various branches.

P Dog #R31 just disappeared into Burrow NN.

8:00 P.M.

Alarm calls. Two deer walk back through the Village.

There is Madame #70 retreating to the East Woods. Good night.

And there is Madame Head Wide Apart beneath my tower looking up. *Hello, Madame Head Wide Apart.*

Robin singing twilight hymns.

8:05 P.M.

John decided he wanted to study mammals who live in colonies rather than birds, swallows. Prairie dogs fit both his imagination and research design perfectly.

He met his wife, Judy, when they were seniors at the University of Michigan. Their son, Alex, was born on Groundhog Day, 1988. John smiled when he told me this. "True story," he said.

There is not that much research on prairie dogs because they are very difficult to study. February through April is the breeding season, and it is very cold on the prairie. They are hard to trap; there are many individuals, complex relations within prairie dog towns between coteries and neighboring clans. And then the obvious, most of their time is spent underground, out of view, hidden.

8:17 P.M.

Madame Head Wide Apart returns to Burrow NX and quickly disappears. Good night.

9:00 P.M.

I keep thinking of the prairie dogs I met today, held, talked to. I noticed while John was taking their blood, if I held one of their little paws gently with my fingers, they would calm down. Or if I gave them part of my glove that they could clench their teeth on, their discomfort appeared to lessen.

The business of prairie dogs and my family's business is digging—digging tunnels and trenches underground creating the infrastructure of their respective communities.

Work that is hidden: My father never winced when someone called him a "ditch digger." He was proud of it. "It's honorable work," he has always said. "It is only the ignorant and arrogant who see this essential work as a lowly occupation."

My brothers know right away if their work is good. When the natural gas flows through the pipelines and people's homes are heated, if the sewage system works or the water flows from the tap to the sink, their work is good, done, complete. John Gregory Dunne has said, "Writing is manual labor of the mind: a job, like laying pipe." I wonder. As a writer, you never know if your work has standing or has any practical value in the world.

9:30 P.M.

John just called on the radio, "Fifteen more minutes." It's grown dark, and I didn't even notice. . . .

I can't get #RR6 out of my mind, how at dusk she sits on her haunches facing the setting sun with her palms pressed together—how can this not be seen as worshipful? Sun salutations.

Many of the gestures we are observing are predictable and expected, but many of them are not. Surprise is part of each day. How else could I sit here largely rapt in a four-by-six-foot plywood box on stilts and be mesmerized?

I had no idea. I had no idea of the power of prairie dogs, the force of their personalities and the impact that is theirs on this grassland-sage community on the edge of a ponderosa forest in the high plateaus of Bryce Canyon National Park.

I had no idea of their resiliency in the midst of a damaged landscape—the mules, the maintenance crews and machines, and most devastatingly, the road.

Their watchfulness inspires me.

They are teaching me what it means to live in community.

7:45 A.M.

Madame Head Wide Apart is standing outside Burrow NX surveying. Clear morning. Warm. Today is going to be hot. Theo and I set twelve traps for Unmarked Prairie Dog. Theo is from New Jersey. Confident, tough, and likes to delegate his work.

Last night, he was complaining to John on the radio about one baby who refuses to be caught.

John's reply: "This is just what you want—babies that go over, under, and resist arrest."

7:57 A.M.

#RR6 wakes up beyond Burrow 9X, not in her usual Burrow 9W. Maybe these two burrows are connected. Must be. This is why recording wake-ups is important.

I am watching #RR6. Something about her reminds me of Mimi. How can a prairie dog remind me of my grandmother? Something about the way she stands straight with her head slightly raised and the quality of her mouth. Dignified. Pursed lips when in trouble.

Or maybe its how her arms rest on her belly, paws pointing down. She holds her presence for a long, long time, never wavering. On guard? Or in repose? Could it be her love of light knowing what lies below?

In her book *Animals and Why They Matter*, Mary Midgley argues that the real act of anthropomorphism is to assume animals don't think or feel. She believes in the sentience of Other. To postulate and suppose that we are the only species that has consciousness is the ultimate act of solipsism.

8:12 A.M.

Hummingbird, robin, deer in meadow. Alarm calls. Madame Head Wide Apart is up on her toes calling. Steller's jay also calling. The idea of ensemble is ever present in nature. The blue flax are open, shading the babies.

Set surrounding at Burrow NX for the fourth baby of Madame Head Wide Apart. It will be difficult not to catch the others as well. Unmarked P Dog nowhere to be seen. He is wary and smart.

The prairie dogs in the far north area are unmarked, unstudied—wild. They are so beautiful in this mountain setting of ponderosa pines and sage meadows.

Bryce Canyon is so much more than just the orange and red spires one associates with this park. It is clear, crisp skies, with freezing temperatures even in summer. It is the peaceful presence of ponderosa pines and the disturbing grace of bristlecones. It is the predictability of pronghorn walking the edges of the forest. It is the company of deer at dawn and dusk.

And it is where "prayer dogs" face the last light of day, standing.

9:05 A.M.

Golden-mantled ground squirrel caught in trap. She must have had over one hundred grains of oats in her cheeks. As I opened the cage, out of fear, she dropped at least fifty, before running out. (I counted them.)

This is the third day of trying to trap Unmarked P Dog. He seems to sense what we are doing. We have not seen him for two days.

Another deer, a doe, crossing the meadow. Dozens of violet-green swallows soaring above the Village.

9:10 A.M.

#RR6's babies up. When they hear an alarm call, they stand up, look shocked, and run into the hole.

Madame Head Wide Apart is in the burrow with her babies. Now she stands on the edge of the surrounding and gives one chirp. She looks stressed as she surveys the circle of traps. With good reason.

As I watch these families of prairie dogs, I wonder about the hatred they inspire and the cruelty that ensues.

What is plentiful is discarded.
What is small is discounted.
What is defenseless is violated.

Those who cannot speak are spoken for.

9:50 A.M.

Took down twenty-four traps for Unmarked P Dog. Caught Madame Head Wide Apart in trap again. Second time. Tried to transfer her to adult cage. She walked into the baby trap near Burrow NX, but she leaped out—an act of civil disobedience, in protest of trapping her babies.

Red-shafted flicker foraging along entrance burrows picking up ants.

Whenever I see a flicker, I think of the one who flew into our home at a moment of doubt. I was struggling, wondering if I dared to write what I know in my body, what I have experienced regarding my relationships with animals. Do I tell the truth, that I believe animals can be messengers; would I lose all credibility, appear unstable, insane? I was staring out the window. All at once, a flicker flew into the house through the open door and circled the room. I was startled, pleased, worried. I realized I had to get the flicker out safely. I stood up and in a quiet voice said, "Hello. Welcome. We need to get you back outside." He flew down the hallway and perched on the corner of the framed poster Robert Rauschenberg printed for the Rio Earth Summit in 1992. It is a collage of words from a dream of William S. Burroughs: *"They did not fully understand, the technique in a very short time nearly wrecked the planet."*

The flicker stayed on the frame for some time, his beak pointing down. I went into the next room and opened the door to the balcony. The flicker flew into the room and found its way outside, dropping two tail feathers on the carpet. I held them as evidence.

"Hot already," John says over the radio. "Get ready for a long, stressful danger zone." This is when prairie dogs caught in traps can die from heat

■ 142 ■

stroke and dehydration if not properly attended to. "We must all be vigilant," he says.

"Ten-four," reply Sarah, Theo, and Alyssa.

"Are you with us, Terry?"

"Ten-four," I reply.

10:10 A.M.

Caught Madame Head Wide Apart and successfully transferred her to an adult cage and took her over to Alyssa's shed for shade. She has cut her nose. We apply triple antibiotic cream.

We've also caught the three marked babies and now await the last one.

10:40 A.M.

I wonder if the remaining unmarked baby in Madame Head Wide Apart's litter is aware of what it means to be alone, that its mother and three siblings are gone? Is this baby aware that yesterday its littermates came back with little black heads and two lines across their backs just like their mother?

I wonder.

10:45 A.M.

An AMAZING dust devil—more like a mini-tornado—originating in the corral, building, building, spinning, faster and faster, higher and higher, until dirt and trash were circling above us; a white U.S. mail bin was caught in the whirlwind, then suddenly this crack! We watched a black tarp ripped from the roof of the barn, and, it too, got caught in the centrifugal force, circling like a magic carpet for one hundred yards or so, flying right toward Sarah's tower.

And then the wind stopped; everything dropped to Earth. My tower was barely holding itself together. Sarah lost part of a wall when a piece of plywood unhinged and flew off.

Unmarked prairie dog baby belonging to Madame Head Wide Apart caught. Down the tower. Trap labeled. I carry it over to Alyssa's shed of shade.

I bring back Madame Head Wide Apart and her three babies and release them to Burrow NX.

Alyssa put a dab of Neosporin on HWA's cut nose. We didn't know if this would work or if she would let us do this. But Madame Head Wide Apart put her nose right up to the cage and let Alyssa administer to her.

Alarm calls. Rapid and many. I look up. Red-tailed hawk soaring above the Village.

Watching NX babies digging—they are completely covered in dirt, their black markings barely visible.

Theo and Sarah tried to remove the black tarp that landed in their area, but they radioed in that they couldn't even lift it. Gives new meaning to the force and power of wind.

John said he would grab a couple of cowboys to help.

Before signing off, Theo tells John that the babies he is watching are "playing pretty good at the game of copulation."

"Have you seen it yet, Terry?" asks John.

"Not yet, John, but I'm looking forward to it."

John tells me to note when the young of NX and 9W mix and to watch for communal nursing of juveniles involving Madame Head Wide Apart and Madame #RR6. "Could be anytime."

Red-tail flies over again. The shadow crosses the Village, and all prairie dogs run to the burrows and go underground immediately.

12:50 P.M.

John is out checking all his traps, which he does at twenty- to thirty-minute intervals. He looks more like a motocross participant than a biologist, with his large sun goggles, white Arabian hat, blue sweatshirt, black-stained Levi's, white plastic knee pads, and boots and gloves. He moves from trap to trap with lightning speed.

12:53 P.M.

Steller's jay.

Madame Head Wide Apart's baby is standing on Mound 8Z, a very large wander for such a wee little thing.

12:54 P.M.

Just like John said—#RR6 baby is "play-copulating" with Madame HWA's baby. The two litters are merging.

I call John on the radio and let him know.

The babies have become very adventurous. Every day there are significant changes in their growth and behavior.

I only see one baby in Burrow N1. Two days ago, there were three. And no sign of P Dog #70 for three days now. This is the litter I am watching within the South Clan behind me.

John gives us his own alarm call on the radio. He tells us that water or mud around the mouths of prairie dogs indicates an overheated dog.

He found one. "Slowly pour water over their mouths, if you see this," he says.

John is on his knees tagging two more babies. I saw him running earlier carrying a trap, then dropping to his knees again, grabbing water and pouring it over another overheated prairie dog.

Good news. I saw P Dog #70, first time in three days, but with only one baby.

At 3:15 P.M., we set traps around Burrows NJ, J8, and N1. At 4:45 P.M., we set another group of traps around Burrow N1 in a different configuration. We are trying to get P Dog #70's babies so they can be marked, measured, and weighed.

Back in my perch, watching Madame Head Wide Apart's babies. The largest one stands on the mound as tall as he can be. One of #RR6's babies comes up to him and stands up. They face each other with their paws up like little boxers and start fighting, tip over, grab each other as they roll into a ball straight into the burrow and disappear. They make me laugh.

A lot of prairie dog activity today inside the North Clan—kissing, digging, play-copulating, fighting, roaming, calling, foraging, and standing guard.

Eight new kids on the block, so to speak, out and about.

I have climbed down and back up the tower more than twenty times today, set five surroundings, plus twenty-four traps this morning. It's been a busy day and it has gone by quickly.

I've hardly thought about time.

Each day is different, even though our tasks are similar.

One of the babies in the South Clan was just caught. Most likely, one of Madame #70's pups. From my perch with binoculars, it looks like the acrobat who was jumping from top to top of the cage surroundings.

Down the tower.

6:00 P.M.

Took the pup to John. Dismantled all surroundings and organized traps in pyramid under the pines.

6:50 P.M.

Retrieved and released the last baby of Madame Head Wide Apart to Burrow NX. They all look like little prisoners in striped suits.

Ruby-throated hummingbird visitation at window. Madame Head Wide Apart staring up at me again from the base of the tower. Near sundown. Long shadows are running west to east. The mules are kicking their feeding troughs violating the gathering peace toward dusk. Deer behind me, south.

Madame Head Wide Apart looks like she is sitting on a chair instead of her haunches beneath the tower.

Madame #RR6 is standing upright in front of Burrow 9W facing the sun.

No sign of the males—P Dog #35, #24, or Unmarked P Dog. Also, no sign of Madame #70.

No activity from young at Burrows N1, N1a, or NJ in the South Clan Area. Sunrays fan across the meadow, one is shining on #RR6's face. She doesn't blink.

All dogs underground almost at once. Same expected burrows.

Good night.

Surprise: Unmarked P Dog appears and disappears down Burrow 8Z.

Over the radio, John tells me that Madame Head Wide Apart's weight is 902 grams; her last baby marked weighed 155 grams; and Miss #70's one baby the we have captured so far weighed a whopping 233 grams, huge for a pup.

I remember asking a nurse who assisted a brain surgeon regularly how she would describe the color of the brain. She looked at me, paused, and then said, "You know how clouds at sunset turn pink, then gray—that's the color of a healthy, human brain." Brain clouds are floating across the plateau.

The word "faith" comes to mind.

5 June 04

7:15 A.M.

This seems to be the time each morning that I arrive in my perch.

In the morning, driving to the Village, John goes over the day's work, sets a plan, perhaps tells stories pertinent to our understanding of a particular concern, and then at night, on our way back, we recount the day. During the day, there is no time to socialize because we are all too busy setting up traps and surroundings, checking traps so there are no overheated prairie dogs, transporting dogs, retrieving them, releasing them. I know virtually nothing about my fellow members of John's "Prairie Dog Squad." We are not here for each other; we are here to attend to the prairie dogs. Our job is to pay attention and respond.

As we get out of the car, John turns to us and says, "It always astounds me that animals with a brain the size of a BB can be so complicated."

I am beginning to see prairie dogs differently, being stretched by all I am seeing, learning, perceiving. I am becoming familiar with the North Clan dogs: Madame Head Wide Apart, #RR6, their babies, Madame P Dog #70 and her pups, P Dogs #24, #35, and Unmarked P Dog.

I am awakening to the Village. I love the specificity of these days and all that is unexpected, unknowable, and uncertain. The morning shadows stretch out from the west woods with the sun rising. Beauty creates its own stamina.

Sunrise occurs after seven o'clock, filtered light cresting over the ponderosa.

Wake-ups
Good morning, P Dog #35, Burrow NZ at 7:25 A.M.
Good morning, HWA, Burrow 8Z at 7:35 A.M.
Good morning, #RR6, Burrow 9W at 7:36 A.M.

Madame Head Wide Apart's babies are up at Burrow 8Z after she emerges. There is the little one who loves to stand on the mound, as if in a model's pose.

Another visitation by a hummingbird, broad-tailed hummingbird.

Good morning, P Dog #24, Burrow 9T at 8:08 A.M.
Good morning, Unmarked P Dog, Burrow 9T (unmarked hole to left) at 8:09 A.M.

Juncos, bluebirds, chipmunks on ground, violet-green swallows swarming above the Village.

Rabbitbrush, sage, blue flax shimmering with dew in silver light.

Within the ponderosa pines, there is a mat purple penstemon, yellow evening primrose, and wallflowers.

8:15 A.M.

P Dog #35 with hay in his mouth going down Burrow 8Z.

Chipmunk on top of sage, watching.

Prairie dog's head sticking out of sage.

I must ask John about social learning among the juveniles and kin recognition. He wants us to watch for females late in the day. They will stand before their burrows, and their babies will come to nurse; the mothers will also nurse other babies who come. Communal nursing is more common among black-tailed prairie dogs than Utah prairie dogs—39 percent versus 10 to 15 percent. John has documented five cases this year. Five years ago, he documented sixteen cases. One case last year. Why the decrease in communal nursing?

9:25 A.M.

John and I set up four surroundings at Burrows NJ, J8, N1, N1a and covered them with white canvas to prevent the possibility of overheating.

Madame Head Wide Apart's babies are mingling with Madame #RR6's babies, playing and cavorting around Burrow 8Z.

Baby #3 of Madame #RR6 has roamed very far from 9W. He's now at 9T. #RR6 runs over to him and appears to be disciplining him. She is standing. He rises on his back legs and places his paws around her face. They kiss.

Over the radio, John tells us, "There are enough differences to warrant classification of Utah and white-tailed prairie dogs as separate species." The distinction has been made primarily according to physical location. There has been no interbreeding.

Moonrise occurs after nine o' clock.

10:45 A.M.

Least chipmunk caught in trap, mad as hell. Down tower to release it.

11:00 A.M.

Burrow 9T connected to NW Burrow.

Unmarked P Dog and Madame Head Wide Apart kiss.

12:15 P.M.

Checked surroundings at NJ, J8, N1, N1a—nothing
Hottest day yet.

1:00 P.M.

Checked traps and surroundings—nothing

Suddenly, walking back to the tower, it struck me, what must a prairie dog's point of view be? I am down on my belly. I lower my eyes to meet theirs—sage level with so much sky; how could you not rely on other members of your community? The world is too vast to rely on one set of eyes and too small not to discount what you do see.

2:00 P.M.

Trap check—NJ, J8, N1, N1a—nothing. Scorching hot!

Took a walk to the North Pole—lots of prairie dog activity. Dozens of mounds. I've been watching two prairie dogs for the past week. None are marked.

3:00 P.M.

Trap check—NJ, J8, N1, N1a—nothing yet; perhaps its the heat. One baby coming out of NN. John had me put ten orange cones down on adjoining holes. He also thinks these white covers are interfering with prairie dogs coming to traps.

A breeze—finally—whistling.

3:05 P.M.

Alarm call. Pronghorn running through west woods

Insight sees the insignificant.

Steve sent me the Prairie Dog Memo, sent by the U.S. Fish and Wildlife Service, which is a notice to all employees working on the Panguitch gas line, maybe a hundred miles southwest.

I will wait for a break in the day to read it.

3:46 P.M.

Burrow NA—unmarked baby pops out. We've seen one marked, one unmarked.

4:00 P.M.

Trap check—nothing. Another surrounding set at Burrow NA. Prairie dog bones scattered at mouth of burrow. John says this is common. Prairie dogs will bring out the bones from below in a type of housecleaning behavior.

4:06 P.M.

Sarah informs us on the radio that she just witnessed a prairie dog kill a baby golden-mantled ground squirrel and then eat it.

John is very excited. "I've always wondered why prairie dogs didn't go after other babies if they needed protein instead of just their own—and this one did."

"The thing about working with animals like prairie dogs is they are always teaching you something new," he says.

4:15 P.M.

It feels like a change of weather might be coming . . .

Yesterday, a prairie dog baby died, most likely from overheating. John was heartsick. It was the first baby he has lost in nine years. When he checked the trap, the baby didn't look good, so he ran to his shed and poured water over it to revive the tiny creature. It seemed to work, and he took the baby up to his tower. The animal seemed to recover. Later, he took the baby to the van and put him in the lineup to be marked like everyone else. The baby was spread eagle on its stomach. Sarah said, "This baby looks dead." John told Sarah to give the little dog CPR and on her own initiative began mouth-to-mouth resuscitation. Sarah began to breathe into its tiny mouth and press on its heart with her index finger. It rallied for a moment with a few wee utterances but then died.

Sarah noted that while she was performing CPR on the baby, the other prairie dogs in the cages moved to the entrances and watched, very, very still. John was extremely upset, felt responsible, and had us all use covers today to prevent any more mishaps.

4:30 P.M.

No babies in traps anywhere.

Alyssa says over the radio, "I think all my prairie dogs are at an underground meeting discussing how to boycott the traps."

It was Prairie Dog #R18 who ate the chipmunk. John was so enthused over this sighting but feels guilty about his gruesome delight. Sarah reassures him. "Don't worry about it, John; it's all in the name of science."

4:50 P.M.

I love how these prairie dogs "ratchet" themselves upright as though there is a little hydraulic jack that cranks up their spines, vertebra by vertebra, so they can see better.

Finally, one p dog pup in surrounding at N1. But it is the only marked one, 70X—male. John says to simply watch him; he may lure in his siblings. I sit behind a ponderosa in the East Woods and do exactly that.

5:00 P.M.

A flock of cowbirds, male and female, are walking through the Village with their water-gurgling calls. To hear the sound of water in this arid landscape evokes thirst. I drink at least a gallon of water a day up here in the tower.

There are now dozens of cowbirds in the Prairie Dog Town. Why? I wonder what they are looking for and what they are eating.

Madame #70 appears at the North Clan. Kisses other babies. Alyssa sets traps for four new litters and has trapped only one baby so far. Very active on north side of the tower, no activity on the south side with surroundings.

A complete lineup of all eight prairie dog babies—from east to west. Strong alarm call in the south. P Dog #R31 crying, crying, crying.

Down the tower. I just want to sit on the Earth with the prairie dogs. Madame Head Wide Apart sits near. She stares at me, unwavering. I try to meet her gaze.

There are no bounds to the sympathetic imagination.

I believe in prairie dogs. I hear the echo of Elizabeth Costello's voice, *"I believe in what does not bother to believe in me."*

Underground. On the ground. Aboveground. Below.

What if the burrows of prairie dogs follow the energy paths of the Earth?

6:15 P.M.

To date here are the numbers of babies caught:

2 June: 30.
3 June: 21.
4 June: 15.
5 June: 6.

Dismantle all surrounds—Burrows NJ, J8, N1, N1a. Leave cones in holes.

Bed watch.

Helped Alyssa dismantle traps behind John's tower and at the corral. I dismantled my surroundings: NJ, J8, N1, N1a, NA. Took a newly caught baby, fresh, to the van for its checkup. The baby was very nervous. When I rubbed its little belly from beneath the trap, it calmed right down, rested on my hand (about that size) as I tickled its stomach with my finger.

At no point during the day did I think about how many hours were left. It is simply my day, the privilege and joy of watching, wondering, and learning from prairie dogs.

Time is intimacy. It's that simple.

> *Never postpone gratitude. Ingratitude robs us of enthusiasm.*
>
> *ALBERT SCHWEITZER*

Two things I have come to appreciate about Bryce Canyon: the clouds and the steady voice of wind speaking through the ponderosa. I don't think I've ever heard it stop, not a lull in the day. It is akin to being at the ocean and hearing the constant roar of the surf. No wonder the canyon is chiseled.

Beneath the ponderosa on the forest floor, there is no lush understory like you see in the northwest or northeast. Here it is a bed of needles. Bursting forth are the purple penstemon, yellow wallflowers, and the voluptuous evening primroses that open as the day ages. There is a type of white borage with fuzzy silver frosted leaves that the prairie dogs devour and some type of groundsel, a yellow five-petaled starflower in bunches that I don't recognize.

In the sage and rabbitbrush meadows, it is a blaze of blue flax that the prairie dogs are mad for. They eat the blossoms and stems all day long.

And the next day, there just seems to be more. If these wildflowers are picked, they wilt almost instantly. Left alone, they remain strong and adaptive and generous.

Madame Head Wide Apart is sitting near Burrow 8Z. She looks tired, bent over on her knees with paws hanging down. Her shape is like a little beanbag chair.

She just tried to catch a gnat with her paws. Her feet are crossing each other, and she looks like a fur ball as she moves back and forth on her mound.

You start to notice irregularities. Usually Madame Head Wide Apart is standing, especially this time of day, her slight, slender body stretched to see. She moves more like a weasel than a prairie dog. Very energetic. But today she seems worn out. How could she not be with all her babies and then some?

Madame #RR6 looks very dignified this evening, sitting on her haunches, her paws on her belly.

No males in sight tonight.

Good night #RR6, Burrow 9W at 7:35 P.M.

Flicker foraging for ants in the Village. Hopping on the ground, "dusting," to thwart gnats and other pests from infesting their feathers.

Did not drink enough water today—slight headache.

#RR6 back out. She and Madame Head Wide Apart keep going underground and then popping back up. Each has done this three times.

The light on the rabbitbrush and sage is deep and jewel-like, transforming common shrubs into various shades of jade.

Deer in woods—two deer running to the far north. Bucks in velvet.

#RR6 and HWA down in their usual nursery burrows—8:17 P.M.

> *Words come from ancestry*
> *Deeds from a mastery . . .*
> *In my obscurity*
> *is my value.*
> *That's why the wise*
> *wear their jade under common clothes.*

TAO TE CHING

Hummingbirds out.

Madame Head Wide Apart up, good morning—7:25 A.M.

Good morning, P Dog #35, missed him last night—7:45 A.M.

No babies caught yesterday in Burrows N1, N1a, NJ, J8, or NA. Six babies weighed and marked yesterday. A very strange day. Quiet in the Village.

9:45 A.M.

All surroundings set and covered.

Intense noise from corrals, Bobcat piling horse shit in heap for mules to roll in.

Miss P Dog #70 appeared this morning south in Burrow 91 and disappeared in Burrow N4.

Everybody out and active in the North Clan; babies continue to comingle. Madame Head Wide Apart's babies seem significantly smaller than Madame #RR6's babies.

One of #RR6's babies looks like a little tai chi master, standing up, knees bent, arms to his side, a direct focus forward. He slowly turns with his right foot forward, arms out. Already one can see dominance being established among the young. The largest baby of #RR6 is the most imposing and aggressive. The other juveniles defer to him.

10:20 A.M.

Say's phoebe is perched on sage in the Village.

Two ravens overhead, wing beats heard before birds seen.

Cowboys piling up the shit. No peace in the corrals. Dust. Neurotic mules. These men work hard.

11:00 A.M.

Trap check—nothing.

NOON

Trap check—nothing.

1:00 P.M.

Trap check—nothing.

A very quiet day.

I've been thinking about words, individual words and the language we use when talking about nature, how language shapes perceptions. A word enters my mind: "hypography"—*hi-pah-grah-fee*\ n: 1) any public lands given over to corporate interests at the public's expense; 2) landscape once pristine, now abused by clear cuts, strip mines, toxic waste dumps, or oil and gas development; 3) a state of extreme corruption fueled by bureaucrats.

1:30 P.M.

White-breasted nuthatch in ponderosa pine.

Lots of babies mingling and interacting.

I have not witnessed communal nursing yet. Babies are now six weeks old and coming above ground for almost a week. This morning at 8:45 A.M., I saw Madame #70 on her own home ground with the South Clan. She woke up at Burrow 91, then a few minutes later went down in Burrow N4. We've been wondering when she feeds her babies. They are very large, the biggest of the three litters I am watching.

This is the third day of surrounding her young—N1, N1a, NJ, J8, NA— I wonder how much this is thwarting their foraging and normal routine, hence hurting them?

John is frustrated. He was hoping for two hundred babies this year. So far, we've marked between fifty or sixty with no new litters spotted yesterday. And Alyssa didn't catch a single unmarked yesterday. Neither did I. And so we wait.

1:45 P.M.

Check traps—nothing.

A low insect buzz. I associate this with the pulse of heat in the desert. Wind is constant. Nobody out in the North Clan.

Very quiet, very still, very hot. Even the mules are quiet.

The ponderosa are in constant movement, waving their limber branches in the breeze. Plateau music.

RADIO TALK SHOW

THEO: I think we've got "Tic-Tac-Toe."
SARAH: Yeah!
THEO: I think he's moving into the cage.
JOHN: Give him five more minutes to see if siblings will follow.
THEO: Okay, I think we've got two. I can't see the doors, but they're behaving as though they are in the cage.
JOHN: That's fantastic. The mothers are driving me crazy, pulling off the covers, tearing them up for nesting materials, alert-calling their babies to stay underground—ugghhhh.

Four babies so far—three in Alyssa's area; one in John's area; now, possibly two in Theo's territory.

P Dog #21 and #R31 running about in the South.

Still the undertones of wind in the background.

Check trap—nothing.

From the corner of my eye, I see movement. There is P Dog #35 digging out his home burrow NZ; dirt is flying.

Juncos feeding near surrounding.

Female mountain bluebird perched on branch of the big snag.

Through the square hole in the floor of my tower, I watch P Dog #24 forage below, a hawk's view, talons on its back. I can't help it; I instinctively think like a predator. Why else would I have eyes forward?

RADIO TALK SHOW

RADIO: Oh my god! Runaway mule!
  (A saddled mule runs back to the horse corral without a rider or cowboy.)
RADIO: Sarah, is that you?
JOHN: Wow, this has been a very good check. I've got four babies, one baby in the last six hours and now suddenly, three in the last forty-five minutes.
THEO: I've got three in my shed.
ALYSSA: I've got one.
JOHN: That means we're up to ten for the day—that makes it a great day! Terry, perhaps you can bring a bugle tomorrow and play reveille.

All quiet on the northern front. Nothing moving but the ponderosa and a few juncos kicking up the dust.

Wind—all I've done today is watch, drink water, and pee.

Trap check—nothing.
John thinks they'll be out in the next hour.

RADIO TALK SHOW

THEO: Horses loose.

SARAH: They're freakin' out my dogs.

JOHN: Where are they?

THEO: I'll be darned, there's another one.

SARAH: Who is holding these horses?

THEO: Make that four—there are four horses up here.

SARAH: Are they walking?

THEO: Nope—they're running through the colony up here.

ALYSSA: You guys get all the drama!

JOHN: I see them; the four horses are now down here running through the woods right behind you, Sarah.

SARAH: I see them—I just hope they don't . . .

JOHN: These damn cowboys are driving the horses right through the prairie dog colony, no thought, just incompetence.

TTW: The cowboy with the black hat is riding his white horse through the endangered Prairie Dog Town.

ALYSSA: I know. Isn't he afraid he's going to break his horse's leg; that's what they complain about.

TTW: I can just see Madame Head Wide Apart hiding in her burrow just waiting to grab the horse's ankle and throw it down.

SARAH: Yeah, maybe we can sic P Dog #24 alias Jeffrey Dahmer on one of the horses. That would fill his belly for awhile.

One baby is up in the South Clan Area but not in any of the burrows where we have set up traps and surroundings. He's standing on top of the mound at Burrow N2. The little one is looking toward all the traps. And people don't think prairie dogs are smart?

I feel like such a fool—outsmarted by a creature barely five inches tall and barely two hundred grams!

3:50 P.M.

Baby is now up in NA. I am assuming it is the same one that popped up in Burrow NZ. Sunday has no relevancy here in nature. Say's phoebe perched on white trap covers at Burrow NA.

4:10 P.M.

Madame Head Wide Apart is beneath my tower. We had our daily communion this morning. I sat near her for almost twenty minutes as she went about her business.

She disappears into Burrow 86. I wonder what burrow this is connected to?

Say's phoebe on rabbitbrush by Burrow NZ. It scared one of Madame #70's babies back underground. Female baby of Madame #RR6 is out.

John and Alyssa are leaving their towers to go mark the ten babies. Red admiral butterfly floats by. White-breasted nuthatch circling around ponderosa at Burrow NJ. Steller's jay in same pine as nuthatch.

4:30 P.M.

Check trap—nothing.

I put orange cones, tip down, to close Burrows NZ and N6. John wants to see if that makes any difference. Sarah is now in John's tower. Theo is in Alyssa's tower. They have teamed up because there is so much prairie dog activity in these areas to observe.

Allergies are flaring up in all of us with all this manure blowing around.

5:00 P.M.

Catnap—ten minutes—refreshed.

Five ravens fly by; wind steady and growing.

John says that we will shut down at 6:15 P.M. tonight.

Fourteen babies weighed and marked today. That makes seventy-four total as of 6 June.

7:00 P.M.

All surroundings dismantled: N1, N1a, NJ, J8, NA. And then I helped take down Alyssa's traps. P Dog #35 just ran north. Collar O, one of Alyssa's members, is released.

The smell of skunk is strong.

Long shadows—we are all tired.

Today I was struck by how long and connected the tunnels are from burrow to burrow. Intricate and wide-ranging. It has been evident in the South Clan as we've tried to trap Madame #70's pups. We've got dozens of the burrows blocked, but still they pop up in unexpected places. It's like a game we are playing with them.

I try to imagine what these tunnels must look like below, what it must feel like to move through them, long, dark, and cold. It's like an underground maze. My mind sees Tokyo, the city above and the city below.

I think about the word "assemblage"—a prairie dog colony or village is an assemblage—burrows are an assemblage of tunnels—a book is an assemblage of passages—*everything functions in relationship to other bodies.*

Gilles Deleuze and Felix Guattari speak of rhizomes, roots, tubers, bulbs, functioning on the subterranean level—propagating from the middle, not from the hierarchical trunk of a tree with its linear branches upward and out. *A rhizome ceaselessly establishes connections.* Perhaps prairie dogs are not a keystone species but a rhizome species.

Can one be a rhizome artist? Can one "form a rhizome with the world?"

Who can map the underground?

7:16 P.M.

Madame #RR6 is running toward the West Woods. No babies out. Last night the babies were running all over the Village.

John puts the babies' voices over the radio. They sound more like baby birds than prairie dogs.

7:25 P.M.

Nobody around—no dogs tonight with the exception of Unmarked P Dog.

7:40 P.M.

Good night, Unmarked P Dog.

7:50 P.M.

No Madame Head Wide Apart or #RR6 or P Dogs #24 or #35 or #70. So strange, just when you think you see a pattern, it unravels. Nothing can be taken for granted.

There's #RR6 running back to the North Clan from the West Woods. And Madame Head Wide Apart is back.

Good night, #RR6, down at 8:00 P.M.
Good night, Madame HWA down at Burrow 9J. It is 8:05 P.M.

Sun almost down; breezes have increased; temperature dropping. I put on my down jacket. Ponderosa pines are still dancing.

7 June 04

7:25 A.M.

#RR6 wakes up. This is early for her.

Sun just cresting over the East Woods. Blinding light. I can't see a thing. Very clear day.

On the prairie dog front, I must lure the unmarked babies of Miss #70 into surroundings at Burrows N1, N1a, NJ, J8, NA. One baby marked, two to go. For the past two days, no luck.

I must think like a prairie dog.

It is my turn to mark prairie dog babies this afternoon. So far, 113 babies have been marked. John anticipates around 180.

Madame Head Wide Apart is up, standing on the edge of her preferred mound 8Z. Time: 7:25 A.M. Good morning.

Good morning, P Dog #24 in Burrow NR at 7:30 A.M.
Good morning, P Dog #35 in Burrow NZ at 7:31 A.M.

Today marks one week for me in this tower.

> *Who can be stillness, little by little*
> *make what is troubled grow clear?*
> *Who can be movement, little by little*
> *make what is still grow quick?*
>
> TAO TE CHING

7:35 A.M.

Unmarked P Dog is up—I missed seeing which burrow he emerged from. All the prairie dogs are looking healthy and strong.

Last night, as I was about to leave, I noticed the five least chipmunks all lined up once again on their preferred branch on the big snag again, near the top third of the tree.

Morning shadows move west to east. The light creates a warp through the weft of vegetation. At 8:00 A.M., I'll climb down the tower to set up the surroundings in the South Clan Area.

How strange—an iris in the sage is about to bloom, not a wild iris, but the tall garden variety, perhaps a clue that this meadow was once a homestead, the iris a remnant from a woman's garden. I will anticipate its color.

No wind—the ponderosa are still.

8:16 A.M.

The wind has arrived. All is in motion once again.

Three of Madame Head Wide Apart's babies are out and about in front of Burrow 9T. Morning stretches and play-copulations: joy on four legs.

8:50 A.M.

This is my favorite time of day when all the blue flax are open and blooming like a delicate hand. All flax are facing the sun. The sage flats look as though they have lavender polka dots sprinkled throughout.

John told me to hold off a bit on the surroundings. Madame #70 is still foraging. And as he said, "We know the babies won't even be out for six hours." At least, I'd say, not until three o'clock.

Wicked wind. Tower swaying.

Two prairie dog babies (belonging to #RR6) are getting down low, dragging their bellies on the ground, crawling toward each other. They kiss.

A SNAPSHOT: Baby prairie dogs feasting on the flowers of blue flax; the five-petaled blossoms in hand are being inhaled. They stand upright in bouquets of periwinkle blue on virtually invisible stalks. The sage flats are blinking with the blossoms in the breeze. When the babies are sitting down, the flax tower over their heads, against the back drop of salmon-colored sand.

The babies' tails flare as they play, fight, and pretend to copulate. Something I haven't noticed until now.

Robins are singing.

Sixteen prairie dogs are up and active within the North and South Clans.

I close my eyes. Two images emerge: one man spitting on the prairie dog standing on the side of the road and Sarah pressing her lips against the dying prairie dog baby's lips as she gave him mouth-to-mouth resuscitation.

What moments in our personal histories determine contempt or communion; cruelty or care?

John has missed the funerals of close friends, honors within his department, and trips to Europe, all because he will not leave the prairie dogs March from June.

"I so admire your commitment," I said to him.

"You would do the same thing," he replied.

But I knew in an instant, I would not. There are those rare individuals who surrender themselves to a particular species or study or cause and see the world through the lens of their devotion. John Hoogland and prairie dogs; Jane Goodall and chimpanzees; E. O. Wilson and ants; John and Frank Craighead and the grizzlies of Yellowstone National Park.

In coming to know one animal well, we can come to understand ourselves in more complex terms. We are not so different. We respond to the world around us. Can we imagine the needs of other species, not just our own? Can we allow our imagination to create an empathetic response to Other. Might this be another pathway toward peace?

Science as it reveals biological understanding fosters an ecological awareness that identifies an integrity of interconnected relationships. Humility and respect follows. We recognize this indomitable web of life that plays like a symphony.

9:45 A.M.

Madame #70 is still out in the meadow. The cowboy sitting on the Bobcat is moving shit again inside the corral. The noise disturbance to the prairie dogs is extreme.

All babies are out, running around the Village, mixing, playing, kissing. One week ago, they were underground. Madame #70 enters Burrow 7X on the eastern boundary. She disappears.

10:00 A.M.

Surroundings set: N1, N1a, NJ, J8, NA. Orange cones are stuffed down burrows N2 and N6. I saw the marked baby in Burrow NZ. Two robins mating, circling each other in a ponderosa pine.

Big winds today—chilly.

Flocks of blackbirds fly through at 10:31 A.M.

1:00 P.M.

Check traps—nothing.

P Dogs #70, #21, and #R31 are all madly gathering grasses for nesting material and taking it underground into Burrows 8C and 82.

1:30 P.M.

I set up a new surrounding at Burrow 9L and dismantled J8.

Very strong winds. This is not repetition or redundancy; it is breath. John tells us prairie dogs do not like wind because it hurts their defense system, which is designed to pick up motion.

Alarm calls throughout prairie dog colony.

Tourists move through the woods. Their children walk into the Village to see prairie dog babies. The babies disappear down the burrows.

2:00 P.M.

Theo is coming to create another surrounding to the east of NA where they just popped up. Rascals! We cannot catch them.

3:00 P.M.

Check traps—nothing.

3:45 P.M.

All the covered traps surrounding the burrows look like a circling of covered wagons.

A lull from the wind, but I hear a wave coming from the southwest through the trees—here it comes—loud and hard, the tower now jiggling.

4:15–7:15 P.M.

My turn to mark babies and adults: two adult males were repainted, nine babies (eight males and one female).

I love this time holding the baby prairie dogs, comforting them, letting them chew on my glove, rubbing their paws while John does his work. As he combed their fur, more fleas than usual.

Today I learn that the black-tailed, white-tailed, Utah, and Mexican prairie dogs have fifty chromosomes while Gunnison's prairie dogs have forty. Gunnison's prairie dogs also have a different call, distinctive from those of white-tailed and Utah prairie dogs. The prairie dogs who inhabit the ghost town of Cisco are white-tailed prairie dogs.

Nobody outside my window . . . yet

RADIO TALK SHOW

John "Wetsuit" just stole one of his covers and took it into her burrow. That little thief!

Madame Head Wide Apart is out, now down Burrow 9T at 7:30 P.M. P Dog #35 is running back, then down Burrow NZ at 7:31 P.M. #RR6, too, down Burrow 9W at 7:45 P.M.

Deer walking through Village—all quiet in the colony.

Pygmy nuthatch, yellow-rumped warbler, black-capped chickadee. Big winds continuing. Tower creaking.

Near 8:00 P.M. and Madame Head Wide Apart is back up, simply gazing, solid on her haunches, sitting, now up on her legs facing the last light, her paws pressed together.

<u>8 June 04</u>

Today Venus passes in front of the sun, the first time since 1886. It will swing in front again on 6 June 2012.

> *Heaven and Earth aren't humane . . .*
> *Wise souls aren't humane . . .*
>
> *Heaven and earth*
> *act as bellows:*
>
> *Empty yet structured,*
> *it moves, inexhaustibly giving.*
>
> TAO TE CHING

8:00 A.M.

Good morning, P Dog #35, Burrow NZ at 7:33 A.M.
Good morning, Madame Head Wide Apart, Burrow 9T at 7:35 A.M.
Good morning, P Dog #24, Burrow NW at 7:42 A.M.
Good morning, p dog babies, Burrow 9W at 7:50 A.M.

Steller's jay on tip-top of ponderosa pine, crest blowing in breeze.

P Dog #24 looks like an old man with watery eyes.

The iris I have been waiting to see bloom has been eaten, undoubtedly by deer.

Driver of the maintenance truck rolls down the dirt road again. He is the one who spits on prairie dogs, and each time he drives by now, he pretends he is shooting them.

Haven't seen Madame #RR6 this morning. P Dog #35 is very affectionate with #RR6's babies, kissing them, rubbing noses with them. He disappears down Burrow 9W. I wonder if he is looking for #RR6 as well?

11:45 A.M.

No traps. No babies.

A hard morning. Cold. Windy. No action. Damn, this wind. I pray this tower holds up. A bit disconcerting.

Unmarked baby—OUT—12:07 P.M. at N9. The unmarked babies of Madame #70 have appeared in Burrows NJ, J8, N2, N1a, NA, N2, N7, N9, and 9L.

1:15 P.M.

Two babies of Madame #70 are still up around Burrow N9.

Madame Head Wide Apart's babies and Madame #RR6's babies are relaxing in the the shade. They are lying down on each other, some sitting, their backs curled, paws resting on their little bellies.

We have determined that Madame #70 is using up to ten different burrow entrances. John said that he has documented as many as twenty-nine connecting burrows. John's question is "Why so many connections?"

It seems to me for precisely the reason we are seeing—they won't get trapped, literally and figuratively. The more connecting burrows, the more options the prairie dogs have for escape and retreat.

1:45 P.M.

We stuff Burrow NF with orange cones.

2:10 P.M.

Task completed.

3:00 P.M.

Trap check—nothing.

RADIO TALK SHOW

JOHN: Am I allowed to surrender? All these tunnels are connected.
THEO: Do you really want to surrender to a squirrel?
SARAH: Who was the president who said, "I will not surrender"? I think it was during the War of 1812.
THEO: George Bush.
SARAH: That was good, Theo. Very good.

3:45 P.M.

Western tanager in ponderosa: red head, yellow body, black wings.

Set up surrounding at Burrow N9.

The wind is relentless today. There have been many times when I worried the plywood wall would fly off.

Wind is wearing. The Chinese say it robs you of your chi, energy.

5:00 P.M.

Trap check—nada.

5:45 P.M.

Turkey vulture soaring over the North Pole. Inebriated flight.

Twelve babies trapped today.

7:00 P.M.

Still no sign of Madame #RR6 today. P Dog #35 is grooming her babies, one by one. He is so nurturing and attentive to these pups.

Take down surroundings at Burrows NF and N9.

Wind. Wind. Wind. Did I mention the W–I–N–D?

A male mountain bluebird in the evening light is a brilliant turquoise.

7:50 P.M.

Theo spots this year's first example of communal nursing. He is ecstatic over the radio. "Five babies are suckling on P Dog number 69 now." John is seeing the communal nursing as well. Babies seem to need about ten days aboveground before they start nursing communally. Theo's babies are the oldest.

Very quiet out here in the North Clan.

8:00 P.M.

No sign of Madame Head Wide Apart or #RR6. Or Unmarked P Dog or P Dog #24, Miss #70, R31, or P Dog #21.

Theo is giving us a live account on the radio of the communal nursing, blow by blow, or more accurately, suck by suck.

Skunky, one of the lactating females under Alyssa's watch, has no babies.

John fears they were killed by P Dog #21 alias Jeffrey Dahmer. The reason he suspects this is because she is no longer spending the night in the burrow where she gave birth.

8:05 P.M.

P Dog #R31 down, Burrow 8T at 8:10 P.M.
P Dog #24 up with hay, now down.

8:30 P.M.

John tells us we can go home early. Gorgeous light bathing over the plateau.

<u>9 June 04</u>

Theo and I walked down to the North Pole and set twelve traps. I will check them this morning at 10:00 A.M.

Today we are hoping to finally lure the last two unmarked babies of Madame #70. It has been the focus of my week's work, to no avail. Yesterday, the pups popped up in Burrow N9, unexpectedly.

Sun cresting over the ponderosa forest. I want to note the hours when the blue flax open. Some are already opening—7:30 A.M.

So the unwanting soul
Sees what's hidden,

and the ever-wanting soul
see's only what it wants.

Mystery of all mysteries
The door to the hidden.

Prairie dogs embody mystery—aboveground and below. How can we even begin to perceive their world as they do?

7:45 A.M.

#RR6 appears.

Good morning, Madame #RR6, Burrow 9W at 7:45 A.M.
Good morning, little ones #RR6x, all 4, Burrow 9W at 7:46 A.M.

Good morning, P Dog #24, Burrow north of 9F at 7:48 A.M.
Good morning, Madame Head Wide Apart, Burrow 974 at 7:50 A.M.
Good morning, P Dog #35, Burrow NZ at 7:50 A.M.

Wind picking up, violet-green swallows crisscrossing the sky above the Village.

#RR6 ran north almost immediately upon waking. P Dog #35 stays with her babies and watches over them, grooming them, kissing them, surveying the landscape as sentinel.

Seeing prairie dogs standing in the meadow, alert, attuned to the slightest nuance, they truly are "watch dogs." When the sun shines on their golden fur, they become candles, a presence lit, illuminated on the land.

I try to imagine millions upon millions standing their ground across the Great Plains—I cannot. All I see in my mind's eyes are the quilted squares of agriculture that stretch across the Midwestern prairies.

Four babies of #RR6 are playing near Burrow 35.
Four babies of HWA are playing near Burrow 24.

Both the mothers, Madame Head Wide Apart and Madame #RR6, disappear as soon as they arise, running north through the grasses until I can no longer see them.

The blue flax are shimmering in sunlight; all flowers open at 8:30 A.M.

Everyone is up and accounted for in the North Clan.
Everyone is still asleep or belowground in the South Clan.

We have marked 153 prairie dog babies as of this morning.

John asks Theo when his first litter appeared in his area? Answer: May 27, 2004. He thinks we could break 200.

Theo reports that P Dog #WA5 is engaged in communal nursing twelve to thirteen minutes at a time. She rests and then continues.

"Now that's serious nursing," John says.

In the woods, I hear a western wood pewee.

Theo also reports to John that P Dog #BB2's babies are missing and presumably dead; also one or two are missing from P Dog #98 and one or two babies are missing from P Dog #69.

This morning when the Prairie Dog Squad came to pick me up in the gold 1983 Reliant, John was talking about plague. Plague in prairie dogs is transmitted by fleas. That's why we count the fleas we find on the prairie dogs and bottle them. They pick up the plague after biting animals who have it. Sylvatic plague. *Yersinia pestis.* He told us what the symptoms were in case any of us start to come down with it.

We all looked at each other wondering if he was serious. He was dead serious. I asked if any of his assistants had ever come down with plague.

"Just two." One of his assistants contracted plague when he was working with the East Creek population in Bryce. That whole population of prairie dogs was destroyed.

He tells us about another assistant, Jane Jackson, who was working with him on Gunnison's prairie dogs in the Petrified Forest National Park in Arizona. They did not know or even suspect plague among them. But prairie dogs began dying. John told Jane to dissect the dead animals (this is most likely where she caught it). Then, more dogs started dying. John realized it was plague. Shortly thereafter, Jane came down with the symptoms: a spiking fever, headache. She was in the hospital for five days under an array of antibiotics.

"But I've never had an assistant die."

"How reassuring," Sarah says.

I've watched John blow out the prairie dog's blood from the capillary tubes into tiny bottles. I've seen the blood flow back onto his lips.

"Aren't you at risk?" I ask.

"I'm sure I could be, but I just don't think about it." John abruptly changes the subject and tells us the area we are working in is known by the park service as the Horse Corrals. This is now the only colony in Bryce Canyon National Park that has more than thirty individuals. "These prairie dogs are so vulnerable," he says. "East Creek is completely wiped out, a ghost town."

We stop at the Visitor Center. A stuffed Utah prairie dog stands in a Plexiglas cube in the lobby. Beneath the prairie dog is a sign with a solicitation for money, asking park visitors to help protect this threatened species. The sign implies that these donations go to supporting park research on prairie dogs.

They do not.

9:00 A.M.

Cumulus clouds are moving over us quickly. This damn wind is even making the clouds run.

The prairie dogs stand and look up as a helicopter flies above them.

Unmarked P Dog is just sitting in front of his burrow at NW. Lots of courtship behavior going on among birds—robins, mountain bluebirds, violet-green swallows.

It is the nature of prairie dogs to vanish. They are up; they are down; they reappear. You put your binoculars on them; they are gone. You bring your binocs down, look again for movement, nothing. You scan the landscape: Up. Down. Disappeared. I can imagine, if we come down to that last dark day when the Utah prairie dogs are believed extinct, one clan could simply stay underground and quietly go about their lives without notice in a remote pocket of the wild and bring back its species one precious litter at a time.

Animals have only their silence left with which to confront us.

J. M. COETZEE

I think of the ivory-billed woodpecker. We can hope. No, we can have faith in the resiliency of life if the habitat is maintained, if our greed can be set aside in the name of a greater wealth, a commonwealth.

Why is the North Clan so open and lively in their Village whereas the South Clan is so elusive and secretive? The South Clan is right next to the horse corrals. The North Clan is more protected. Could that be one of the reasons that the South Clan is more wary? More disturbed by the sounds and dust kicked up by the mules?

Plague. I can't stop thinking of the near plague catastrophe that John shared with us and the vulnerability of this particular population.

9:30 A.M.

P Dog #87 emerges from Burrow 7X. She is the one impossible to catch.

To give an idea of how powerful this wind is and its effect on this landscape and the life here, I peeled an orange and left half of it on my desk in the tower for an hour while I set traps. When I returned, it was withered and dry, not a drop of juice to be found.

Wind takes every ounce of moisture with it as it blows through. Dehydration is another cause of weathering. All I have to do is look at my face when I return home from the field. There is a reason hoodoos and spires, arches and windows are found here. The wind wields its sculptor's chisel against stone.

The manure is carried by the wind. The cowboys rake it up each day, and then the Bobcat piles it high for the mules, who love to roll in it. A gust of wind blows, and the dried shit is carried right into our towers to settle.

I wonder what cumulative effect this is having on the prairie dog colony? The noise level heightens. The back-up beeps of backhoes, the diesel engines of trucks, jets, helicopters—this is anything but serene.

I am now watching Alyssa, a caring and capable woman from New Hampshire, check her traps in her Carhartt pants, black pile jacket, and hiking boots. She told me last night that she and her mother will go to Wales in July for a walk on behalf of breast cancer. Her mother is a survivor.

Alyssa has been here in Bryce since April. She is a biology student who previously worked with ferrets in a lab.

Ferrets. Black-footed ferrets. *Mustela nigripes.* Nocturnal. Weasel-like. Predatory companion to the prairie dog. John says that according to the limited information from the 1800s and early 1900s, ferrets have always been rare. But as prairie dogs became scarce, the black-footed ferret fell perilously close to extinction. Now, only a ghost presence haunts the burrows of prairie dogs.

Theo is a big, burly guy from New Jersey who loves fieldwork. He has been here with John since February and has only had one day off. He wears Broncos sweatshirts, hats, baggy khaki shorts that fall below his knees. A bit of a belly with strong calves. He is strong and short with olive skin, dark eyes and hair.

Sarah, like Alyssa, is another strong young woman. Beautiful blue eyes, hair in ponytail beneath hat. Matter-of-fact. No nonsense. No small talk. Smart. Observant. A student at Virginia Tech. She has been here just short of a month.

9:45 A.M.

Madame #70 emerges from Burrow 9L. Babies mixing and mingling in the North Clan. P Dogs #35 and #24 are out with them, playing, grooming, and disciplining them. I'm interested that it is the males who spend time with them during the day. The females disappear and wander north.

Steller's jays calling.

Babies are hunkering down in this extreme wind. They lie flat on the ground like lizards and choose not to go into their burrow.

My eyes are tearing. I can barely see. WRETCHED WIND.

10:00 A.M.

Red-tailed hawk circles over the Village. Dogs scatter—disappear underground.

Pronghorn is walking through the North Pole. Morning light on back, orange and white coloration with black horns, spiked.

Repetition is spiritual.

KIKI SMITH

10:50 A.M.

This is a friggin' joke, this goddamn wind. The tower is going to blow over. I'm going down. Madame Head Wide Apart has returned to her babies. Sarah asked John over the radio if a dust devil had ever injured a prairie dog. John said no, but it's not inconceivable. All adults are back, near their home burrow entrances, no doubt because of this vicious windstorm.

#RR6 is back with her babies as well. The little ones stand next to their mothers and lean into them with their backs arched.

Trap check in Far North—nada.

Scarlet gilia blooming. Yellow wallflower blooming in sage flats.

Trap check in Far North—nada.

Still wind.

Looks like a storm is building in the west—gray, threatening clouds.

Trap check in North Pole—nada.

Walking north in the wildest of the prairie dog colonies, it is very peaceful. The mounds are made of beautiful, rich soil, untrammeled, away from the horses, the manure, the trucks, and gravel pit with its accompanying noise.

And the prairie dogs are elegant in their golden fur coats. They are much more wary.

Bitterbrush in bloom.

There is evidence of an old road where the asphalt has been broken up. Household crockery, rusty cans, wires, glass jars—perhaps an old homestead. I wonder if the prairie dogs' ancestors were here, too?

A strange day—time has wings. I feel as if we have been caught in the vortex of this storm that keeps whirling around us.

Parka, pile jacket, hat, gloves—and it is June.

I could have gone on walking north forever toward the vermillion cliffs, pink sand underfoot in a palette of sage. Wildflowers create an impressionists canvas with blue flax, scarlet gilia, yellow wallflowers. Primary colors are repeated through feathers: western bluebirds and western tanagers. All this on the edge of the ponderosa forest swaying back and forth.

Just inside one of the burrow entrances are hundreds of flax petals. It looks like a lover's bed.

5:00 P.M.

Trap check—eureka! One unmarked baby. Finally, two down, one more to go.

Rain in the north. Virga: wisps of rain not reaching the Earth. Wind whistling hard. Dark clouds gathering. By seven o'clock or eight, the rain may be pouring, and we will have to release prairie dogs in the rain.

Only a few slits and pocket of blue sky remain. Gray. Green. The land is wearing the colors of a park service uniform or visa versa.

Three more hours.

Chipmunks. Cheek-swollen golden mantled squirrels. Bluebirds. Juncos. Robins.

6:00 P.M.

Wind howling.
Tower rocking.
Hands freezing.

Another day with at least a dozen babies. Soon, I'll take down the surrounding and walk back to the North Pole and close the traps up for the night.

Too cold and windy for the prairie dogs to be out. They are smarter than we are. NT prairie dog baby returned to siblings of Miss #70. I made a vow to this little one that I would work on his behalf. The light in his eye was so magnetic. He just kept staring at me. In another rare moment, I could see the contrast of a prairie dog's eye—amber iris and black pupil. They let you in, momentarily. But most of the time, the eye of a prairie dog is unfathomable in its depth, a black hole of both mystery and knowing.

7:00 P.M.

Sun breaking through clouds.

7:15 P.M.

Everyone is saying over the radio, "No dogs out tonight." John says, "Roger."

An early night—fingers numb. Body stiff. The wind hastens our return home.

10 June 04

Sixty degrees this morning. No wind.

John, Alyssa, and I set twelve traps here in the North Clan for Unmarked P Dog. We then walked down to the North Pole and set eighteen more. John wonders why the prairie dogs have not moved north. Instead they initially moved south into the 232 Area, which has been totally trashed by maintenance.

A habitat of disturbances. A habit of disturbances.

Until 1997 and 1998, there were no prairie dogs beyond Lone Pine, which is north of the road. And then the south side of the road was colonized by one female and her daughter.

Madame #70 is six years old, one of the oldest prairie dogs in the colony. Madame #RR6 moved north from Lone Pine this year, which is very unusual. Each dog has its own story, its own personal history, that John has been diligent enough to record. The oldest prairie dog in the colony according to John's data is seven years old.

7:30 A.M.

Good morning, Madame Head Wide Apart. First one up. She stands and gives her alarm call.

> *The root of the noble is in the common,*
> *the high stands on what's below.*
> *Princes and Kings call themselves*
> *"orphans, widowers, beggers,"*
> *to get themselves rooted in the dirt.*

Madame Head Wide Apart has been standing on the edge of her mound issuing her alarm call for ten minutes. I have not heard this cry before. Only her jaw is moving—and the call is very, very faint.

Madame #RR6's babies are out and standing on Mound 9W looking like lit candles in first light.

Violet-green swallows flying overhead of the little ones. They look up as the swallows swoop low for insects. A broad-tailed hummingbird buzzed my head. Must be my red scarf.

8:17 A.M.

P Dog #35 is in trap. Down the tower I go. Madame Head Wide Apart is also in a trap eating her beloved oats. Her babies are on top of the cage trying to paw her. It reminds me of a friend of mine who writes inside a playpen so her children will stay close to her.

Unmarked P Dog is the one not up yet. John says over the radio, "Why am I not surprised?"

A junco also caught in trap. He has just finagled himself out of one of the squares and is free. Flicker foraging in the Village, picking up ants near the burrows.

9:00 A.M.

All babies in the Village are very active. No wind today. No blurred vision. Chickadees calling. The sun is striking the emerald backs of the violet-green swallows, electric.

One of Madame Head Wide Apart's pups is sitting on the mound waiting for Unmarked to come out of his burrow (NW) and play.

No adults around, just babies. No one to give alarm calls. Vulnerable.

9:50 A.M.

Three babies in cages. John says to wait. Cold today, very cold—but no wind. Male and female broad-tailed hummingbirds visit me in the tower.

10:00 A.M.

Traps in North Pole dismantled.

Seven prairie dogs caught today in traps (Madame HWA, P Dogs #35, #21, four babies) all while we were trying to trap Unmarked P Dog, who is nowhere to be seen. He knows.

Last night, I read Steve's Prairie Dog Awareness Memo. The Tempest Company was working with Questar Gas in constructing and burying a 19.7-mile-long natural gas pipeline from Fremont Pass to Panguitch in Garfield County, Utah. Panguitch, a town just north of Cedar City, had no gas distribution system. This pipeline would "promote economic development, safety, health, comfort and convenience for Panguitch residents."

Construction of the gas line would include: clearing and grading, excavation, stringing and bending, welding, coating, lowering, and backfilling, cleanup and restoration, testing, and commissioning.

According to the memo, *"Placement of the natural gas pipeline will impact the Utah prairie dog through temporary displacement and disturbance and through direct mortality as a result of crushing animals or entombing them in their burrows."*

The Fish and Wildlife Service, however, *"believes the impacts described above will not jeopardize the continued existence of the Utah prairie dog."*

An "Incidental Take" clause is found in the document:

"The Service anticipates that a maximum of eight (8) Utah prairie dogs could be directly taken (killed) due to the subject project through crushing or entombing them in their burrows. An undetermined number of animals may be indirectly taken via disturbance from the proposed action. This take level will not significantly impact local or regional Utah prairie dog populations."

But if The Tempest Company "takes" or kills the ninth prairie dog, the fee will be up to two hundred thousand dollars in fines and up to one year in prison.

I can still hear my father railing over this regulation.

"And do tourists get charged two hundred grand for turning prairie dogs into roadkill? We're gettin' screwed once again by the Endangered Species Act."

Steve told me they had to hire "a qualified Bureau biologist" who would oversee, monitor, and document all The Tempest Company's activities and report any violations. All Tempest Company employees had to enroll in a "Prairie Dog Sensitivity Training Course" (Steve sent me the piece of paper that all the men and women on the Panguitch job had to sign when they took the course. There were twenty-one signatures) in which they were informed that *"if Utah prairie dogs are found within the construc-tion site and there is no feasible route around the mounds/burrows, then the Division would be contacted to remove the prairie dogs from the area if such trapping is possible within a reasonable amount of time."* Translation: The job is shut down.

This was the same situation they faced in St. George, Utah, with the desert tortoise, another endangered species.

Steve told me that, at one point on the job, a prairie dog was accidentally run over by one of The Tempest Company trucks. Steve was on site and recognized that the prairie dog's leg had been broken, and it was writhing in pain. He called the U.S. Fish and Wildlife Service and reported the mishap, hoping they would let him shoot the prairie dog and put it out of its misery.

"Instead, the government sent a helicopter to our job in rugged terrain, put the prairie dog in a box, and transported it to Utah State University in Logan."

I remember looking at Steve in disbelief. He smiled.

"And did I also mention you're not allowed to have any firearms or pets while on the job site and no maintenance vehicles can drive over ten miles an hour." Steve said.

What becomes clear to me in reading this document and talking with my family is the hypocrisy within the United States Department of the Interior. You have one set of standards for pipeline contractors and another for park service employees right here in Bryce Canyon National Park.

I do not see any calls being made to remove prairie dogs within the park maintenance facility. I do not see any calls being made to the horse concessionaires for their disturbances. And I would bet more than eight prairie dogs have become casualties to their business operations, not to mention those run over by their trucks, which often exceed ten miles per hour.

The "Terms and Conditions" of this memo are not even close to being met.

I read "Reasonable and Prudent Measure Number Two," Paragraph B:

"Vehicles used to access the project site or equipment used on the project should be parked at least 50 feet from any Utah prairie dog mounds to avoid any adverse impacts to prairie dogs. All construction and maintenance vehicles should stay within the designated rights-of-way within prairie dog colonies. Overnight parking and storage of equipment and materials should be in previously disturbed areas at least 50 feet away from prairie dog colonies."

Fifty feet? How about underfoot? We hold private businesses accountable for obeying the laws of the land. Who holds our government agencies who are supposed to be guardians of our public lands accountable? And what would happen to John Hoogland and his ability to conduct his prairie dog research should he blow the whistle on what's happening here in Bryce?

Again, who cares?

11:30 A.M.

Madame #70's babies are up in Burrow 9L, including the one unmarked baby. A surrounding is set.

The temperature inside prairie dog burrows and tunnels is fairly consistent, around fifty-five degrees Fahrenheit. Cool in the summer. Warm in the winter. This is the equilibrium they find within their home.

NOON

Alyssa and I check traps in the North Pole. We trapped the beautiful orange male that I have been watching for two weeks. His burrow is by the big ponderosa on the forest's edge. He does have ear tags, so it will be interesting to see who he is and where he has come from to recolonize this area.

Now, if we can just catch the last unmarked pup of Miss #70 in the South Clan, I will have completed trapping three litters of prairie dogs. I would also like to see if we could trap the other prairie dog I have been watching in the North Pole so we could get a more complete picture of this migration north.

Of course, there is the elusive Unmarked P Dog of the North Clan. . . .

Over the radio, John just reported a huge prairie dog pup that weighs close to three hundred grams. Alyssa is so excited about this. She has been watching this baby of P Dog RaBr who has been "jumping, leaping, circling everyone." A very spirited pup.

12:50 P.M.

One of the marked babies of Madame #70 has been caught again. John says to wait a few minutes before releasing it to see if it will lure its unmarked sibling.

1:15–1:30 P.M.

Red-tailed hawk interaction: hawk mobbed by Steller's jays and robins. Strong alarm calls from Madame Head Wide Apart. Red-tail cries out, that unmistakable chilling call that echoes through the woods, as it perches in the old snag on the edge of the North Clan. Mobbing cries from jays and robins continue. Hawk shrieks again. Flies. Soars over the Village and then down to the North Pole. Flies back up through the Village and perches once again on the old snag. More mobbing and cries from robins and jays and the prairie dogs themselves. Madame Head Wide Apart stands alone giving the alarm call, fearless, even as the hawk flies over her.

1:30 P.M.

Climb down tower and release the marked p dog pup of Madame #70 from Burrow 9L. Still waiting for the unmarked pup of hers.

Enormous cumulus clouds float above the plateau in the shape of turtles. Always turtles. They are moving so slowly, almost imperceptibly, makes me dizzy. The ground is stable, but the sky is in motion. When do we have the time in our lives to notice these things so fully? I remember when Steve first learned of his diagnosis, we stood in the corner of his library and he said, *"Something had to give. I was working too hard, moving too fast."* I was right there with him, understanding both personally and pre- cisely what he meant. Why must we wait for the body to speak before we hear what we really need? From this peculiar vantage point, my body feels the Earth in rotation as my eyes sense the curvature of the planet simply by the bend in the horizon.

In my binoculars, both Madame Head Wide Apart's nose and P Dog #24's nose are healed. No cuts visible. The Neosporin works.

Chipping sparrow on pine. Still no sign of Unmarked P Dog. As I watch P Dog #24, I feel such respect. He is five years old. Think what he has survived.

I ask John over the radio when he gives the babies numbers. He answers, "Next March." This is when the p dog pups graduate into adults with a yearly marker.

Red-tail still crying in the woods. Its blood-chilling shriek strikes the prairie dogs. They stand upright on alert, then scramble underground. Ripples of fear undulate through the grasses.

The cry of the red-tail is an audible memory. I was thirteen years old. My father and I were hiking early one morning in Flaming Gorge, Utah, in the heart of the Uintah Basin. I heard the cry. Looked up and saw the circling red-tail. It cried again. I cried back. My father kept walking. The red-tail kept circling. I simply stood and looked upward.

2:00 P.M.

On my back, looking up through this stand of ponderosa, I can hear the prairie dogs talking to each other, speaking in the clearing, their voices carrying their messages into the woods. They are the pulse of the plateau. Eyes open. Ears alert. Their voices are a conveyance of unity.

When Albert Schweitzer speaks of a "reverence for life," in these three words, he is acknowledging the profound mystery that exists on the planet and our ethical responsibility toward all beings. Einstein understood this, as well, when he wrote that the mysterious is "the source of all true art and science." Why must the extreme stance of rationalism be the only stance of credibility? And what is the cost to our deeper understanding of the interconnectedness of life?

Day after day, I watch these prairie dogs raise their arms at sunrise and sunset.

Eduardo Galeano tells a story he calls "The Voyage":

> *Oriol Vall, who works with newborns at a hospital in Barcelona, says that the first human gesture is the embrace. After coming into the world,*

at the beginning of their days, babies wave their arms as if seeking someone.

Other doctors, who work with people who have already lived their lives, say that the aged, at the end of their days, die trying to raise their arms.

And that's it, that's all, no matter how hard we strive or how many words we pile on. Everything comes down to this: between two flutterings, with no more explanation, the voyage occurs.

The prairie dogs know—

2:45 P.M.

Second surrounding set around Burrow NF. Unmarked baby in the South Clan popped up there. Afternoon winds are picking up.

> *"Time tells"*
> *We are made of time.*
> *We are its feet and its voice.*
>
> EDUARDO GALEANO

The prairie dogs are the voices of time speaking from the Pleistocene.

3:45 P.M.

Looking at P Dog #35, he is so beautiful, stoic—eyes shaped like a watermelon seed sideways. When the wind blows, it creates cowlicks on his coat, dark fur exposed beneath the honey-colored fur like a blonde with her roots exposed.

John broadcasts another baby's voice squawking through the radio.

P Dog #35 hears the pup's voice resounding from my walkie talkie and looks up at the tower. His head raised, I note the longer fur that hangs from his elbows. His ears resemble the number 3. Dark eyebrows furrowed with worry. The dark markings below the eye look like tear stains. He has a potbelly. He stands, alert. No more baby crying. He returns back to the mound by his burrow and continues to forage. Bluebirds in the Village are also foraging.

4:20 P.M.

Two marked babies caught and released around Burrow NF. Gave each an evening primrose to eat, which they love.

Only one day left in this tower.

These two weeks have settled in my soul and painted a portrait of the dynamic nature of Bryce Canyon, the power and consistency of the winds and its relentless voice within the pines. I have loved watching the weather roll in and out through clouds and the profusion of wildflowers and their ongoing blooming cycle within the sage meadows.

Blue flax
Wallflower
Scarlet gilia
White composites
Yellow composites
Sage
Rabbitbrush
Bitterbrush
Evening primrose
White and blue borage
Purple penstemon
Woodland star
Spring beauty
Indian paintbrush

One of my great pleasures is walking on the soft bed of pine needles and feeling the buoyancy of woodland duff beneath my feet. Bare feet. And the lying down of trees as they fall back into Earth.

The daily tides of deer and pronghorn through the Prairie Dog Village are a wave of predictability alongside the chipmunks, golden-mantled ground squirrels that share the Village with the prairie dogs. Ravens. Red-tails. Mountain bluebirds.

The predators on the periphery are always watching. You may not see them, but you hear them. You see their effect; simply by watching the prairie dogs respond, you can tell whether it is a hawk, an eagle, or coyote.

Theo and John have had a badger in view, perhaps one of the most successful predators of the prairie dogs.

And then there are the songbirds—warblers, vireos, and kinglets—the stringed section of the woodland symphony providing the melody, always in the foreground.

5:20 P.M.

A golden eagle is soaring above the Village. It casts a very large shadow. All dogs down. It soars, then falls into a tuck, down sweep, upsweep, soar. Prairie dogs are easy prey to the powerful clutch of the eagle's talons, a perfect purse of meat to be carried off and devoured. One life feeds another.

But I have also witnessed the tenacity of prairie dogs, felt their tiny jaw and chisel teeth clamp down on my finger with great strength, causing me to yelp, not them.

5:25 P.M.

The red-tail is back, so is the clamoring of jays and robins. They do not want the hawk around. Perhaps they are protecting their own nests and territory. How to coexist? The red-tail also has a nest nearby.

While out walking this morning, I found a great horned owl feather. It shares the niche of the red-tail; one is predator by night, the other by day.

One of the p dog babies is hunkered down into a little ball, the size of a stone. Is this camouflage behavior?

5:30 P.M.

We have marked 11 prairie dog pups today, making the total count of "processed" prairie dog babies, 174 individuals.

Here comes Madame Head Wide Apart running from the North Pole through the sage meadow toward home with the North Clan.

Red-tail overhead.

Trap check in the North Pole—one male, the other prairie dog I had been watching. Turns out these two males are P Dog #R44, a yearling, and P Dog #R07, one of Skunky's pups from last year. John refers to these two prairie dogs as "loners." The question is why did they move to the farthest reach of the colony? What makes these yearlings redistribute themselves, and how will they attract females so they can repopulate the area?

Madame Head Wide Apart is suckling her pups and Madame #RR6's pups. This is the first time I have witnessed "communal nursing."

I radio John. He is ecstatic. We all are. I watch in awe. She hangs her arms down and stands with pups pulling on her tiny black nipples. She is looking straight ahead and then returns her gaze to her babies.

6:30 P.M.

Deer browsing in the North Pole meadow, the same group of three.

A flock of a dozen or more cowbirds are moving through the Village of the North Clan picking up black beetles.

Here is Unmarked P Dog making his late-day appearance. He has outsmarted us once again, refusing to be trapped. The light reflected in his eyes creates a momentary flamed presence in the colony.

Unmarked P Dog looks up at the tower. He turns and faces the wind through the pines and turns his back toward the sun, then turns around again and faces the slant of light.

6:45 P.M.

A rare moment of silence.

Unmarked P Dog still standing, staring at the sun, east. Now his back is in shadow, his face and belly lit. Very wary. Now, slowly, foot by foot, he sniffs his way back to Burrow NW, then quickly disappears.

11 June 04

7:00 A.M.

My last day here in the tower with the prairie dogs of the North Clan.

Using John Hoogland's number system, here are the prairie dogs I have met in these two weeks:

THE NORTH CLAN
ADULTS
   HWA
   RR6
   70
   35
   24
   Unmarked

THE SOUTH CLAN
ADULTS
   70
   21
   R31
   BB4
   Collar o
   87

THE NORTH POLE
ADULTS
   RR4
   R07

THE NORTH CLAN
LITTERS
   HWAx—four pups (HWA)
   RR6x—four pups (RR6)

THE SOUTH CLAN
LITTERS
   70x—3 pups (70)

To have this privilege, the luxury of time with prairie dogs, to simply observe their behavior within their village hour by hour, day by day, has widened my perception. The degree of our awareness is the degree of our aliveness.

We have forgotten the virtue of sitting, watching, observing. Nothing much happens. This is the way of nature. We breathe together. Simply this. For long periods of time, the meadow is still. We watch. We wait. We wonder. Our eyes find a resting place. And then, the slightest of breezes moves the grass. It can be heard as a whispered prayer.

> *The faith and the love and the hope are all in the waiting.*
>
> *T. S. ELIOT*

Much of our world now is a fabrication, a fiction, a manufactured and manipulated time-lapsed piece of filmmaking where a rose no longer unfolds but bursts. Speed is the buzz, the blur, the drug. Life out of focus becomes our way of seeing. We no longer expect clarity. The lenses of perception and perspective have been replaced by speed, motion. We don't know how to stop. The information we value is retrieved, never internalized.

> *Where is the Life we have lost in living?*
> *Where is the wisdom we have lost in knowledge?*
> *Where is the knowledge we have lost in information?*
>
> *T. S. ELIOT*

And what about knowledge gleaned through patience? What about a species who has survived through time by simply paying attention?

Prairie dogs are embodied knowledge.

To be able to witness the embodiment of a different kind of knowing, an intelligence that is not human but prairie dog, is to realize we are just one consciousness among many. Prairie dogs are an awareness, a keen attentiveness, always alert, always echoing back to their fellow prairie dogs what they see, what they hear, what they want known.

They create community for others while maintaining community for themselves.

The gift I have been given has been in the waiting and the natural passage of time. As a speed addict, it has taken time for me to detoxify. But slowly, hour by hour, panic and boredom became awe and wonder. I grew quiet. I began to see, to hear, but perhaps most importantly, I began to feel and believe that I could reconcile myself with another species by simply being present with them.

> *I am life that wants to live in the midst of other life that wants to live.*
>
> *ALBERT SCHWEITZER*

I am leaving this tower and returning home. When I speak with family, the comments are always the same: *"Won't you be glad to get back to the real world."*

This is my question after two weeks of time, *only two weeks*, spent with prairie dogs, "What is real?"

What is real? These prairie dogs and the lives they live and have adapted to in grassland communities over time, deep time?

What is real? A gravel pit adjacent to one of the last remaining protected prairie dog colonies in the world? A corral where cowboys in an honest day's work saddle up horses with prairie dogs under hoof for visitors to ride in Bryce Canyon National Park?

What is real? Two planes slamming into the World Trade Center and the wake of fear that has never stopped in this endless war of terror?

What is real? Forgiveness or revenge and the mounting deaths of thousands of human beings as America wages war in Afghanistan and Iraq?

What is real? Steve's recurrence of lymphoma? A closet full of shoes? Making love? Making money? Making right with the world with the smallest of unseen gestures?

How do we wish to live? And with whom?

Faith McNulty writes in her book, *Must They Die? The Strange Case of the Prairie Dog and the Black-Footed Ferret:*

> *Two or three generations from now there will be few people who have seen a living creature in the wild. Will these future people find this as inexpressibly sad as we do, contemplating it now? Can one miss what one has never had? By definition, one cannot. And yet a person robbed of his inheritance is the poorer whether he knows it or not. The death of the animals will be the end of a long and intimate association. If one consults Genesis, one finds that man's relationship with the animals began shortly after the fifth day, when God gave him dominion over every living thing. Or, if one consults the scientists, one is told that in early times the progenitors of men were indistinguishable from the rest of the animal kingdom, becoming altered and estranged only seven or eight million years ago. Even after that, the relationship remained close.*

What is happening to us?

There are long skeins of time when I feel so confused and lost in this broken world of our own making. I don't know who we have become or what to believe or whom to trust.

In the presence of prairie dogs, I feel calm, safe, and reassured, sensing there is something more enduring than our own minds. I feel a peace that holds my heart, not because I believe this is better than the world we have created. I feel at peace because the memory of wild nature is held within the nucleus of each living cell. Our bodies remember wholeness in the midst of fragmentation.

As I watch chipmunks line up each night on the horizontal branch of an old snag, where swallows rest on the branch above and where wind shatters any notion of stability, I fall into the reverie of patterns.

What is real to me are these prairie dogs facing the sun each morning and evening in the midst of man-made chaos.

What is real to me are the consequences of cruelty.

What is real to me are the concentric circles of compassion and its capacity to bring about change.

What is real to me is the power of our awareness when we are focused on something beyond ourselves. It is a shaft of light shining in a dark corner. Our ability to shift our perceptions and seek creative alternatives to the conundrums of modernity is in direct proportion to our empathy. Can we imagine, witness, and ultimately feel the suffering of another?

> *What was it like? How did it feel? How did you bear it?*
>
> J. M. COETZEE

In the presence of prairie dogs, I am no greater and no lesser than the life around me. We are all blood and bones, muscle and spirit.

As human beings in the twenty-first century, we carry an enormous responsibility for the well-being and health of the other species with whom we share this planet.

We can no longer claim ignorance, nor innocence.

What is real to me is this mosaic of wild beauty.

> *Being Different*
>
> *How much difference between yes and no?*
> *. . . . climbing a tower . . .*
> *Everybody has something to do*
> *I'm the clumsy one, out of place*

I'm the different one,
for my food
is the milk of the mother.

TAO TE CHING

I see Madame Head Wide Apart from my tower, upright, eating the flowers of blue flax in this meadow of sage on a high desert plateau where millennium trees called bristlecone pine stay rooted on the eroding red sands of Bryce Canyon.

> *"Bewilderness"—the place where the mind wanders without certainties.*

<u>12 June 04</u>

8:00 A.M.

Clear sky. Chilly—temperature around forty degrees. I spoke with Steve last night. He is very excited about a sculpture he is designing. He found a beautiful granite pinnacle of stone at Silver Lake up in Big Cottonwood Canyon where they are working. "I imagine it as a point of meditation," he said, "to help me visualize lymphoma leaving my body." He will cut the stone into six sections, placing them vertically between one inch slabs of black granite. "I'll then weld the granite onto a steel triangular post and place it in our backyard." As he describes this work of art, I see a pillar of hope.

Today, I hope to be able to trap the last unmarked pup of Madame #70. As far as trapping Unmarked P Dog, I would just as soon let him remain *au naturel,* even though this is not a responsible attitude as a research assistant. His spirit of intuitive resistance inspires me.

There he is, standing in front of Burrow NR, even as I write on this plywood desk, the unmarked one foraging on the edge of the East Woods. He is nibbling on forget-me-nots in the shadows of the ponderosa. I wonder if Unmarked P Dog is male or female? John thinks it is #R17, a yearling male. Unmarked P Dog is standing right in front of my tower. A white streak of fur runs down the middle of its forehead. I have never noticed this before.

Their eyes are like burrows.
Their burrows are like eyes.
Unfathomable—no way for us to enter.

P Dog #24 just doesn't have the shine the younger dogs do. He's been around awhile, bears scars from fighting and has fathered many.

In the center of the Village, Madame Head Wide Apart, Madame #RR6, Madame #70, P Dog #35, and all the babies are upright, facing the same direction, standing together on alert.

Who am I not seeing on the periphery?

2:00 P.M.

Trap check—surprisingly enough, we caught Madame Head Wide Apart in the South Clan Village. Today is a day for wandering. She loves the oats.

John says over the radio that we have seven or eight babies.

2:45 P.M.

Found a dead golden-mantled ground squirrel in the forest, alive with beetles, impossible to tell cause of death. I placed some flowers on its ravaged body, now more beetle than squirrel.

Madame #RR6 is standing outside her burrow just like a mother expecting to see her children and call them home.

Alert calls from the south.

3:00 P.M.

Blackbirds flocking, leaving the tower to go mark babies.

6:50 P.M.

The last time I will climb up this tower.

I just returned from helping to mark fourteen babies including my last prairie dog baby from Madame #70! A memorable encounter from such a smart one. Wild eyes giving in. We also worked with five adults—one female that was seven years old. John has never known a Utah prairie dog older than seven.

John has three hundred notebooks of prairie dog data. During breeding season, he and his researchers will have up to thirty interaction sheets a day with up to one thousand interactions. The meticulousness of his watch over this colony is remarkable.

I think of Mary Midgley's words, *"When some portion of the biosphere is rather unpopular with the human race—a crocodile, a dandelion, a stony valley, a snowstorm, an odd-shaped flint—there are three sorts of human being who are particularly likely still to see point in it and befriend it. They are poets, scientists and children. Inside each of us, I suggest, representatives of all these groups may be found."*

7:00 P.M.

All babies are down—I miss them already. The evening primroses are closed. A doe is browsing in the meadow. A mountain bluebird flies north. What an extraordinary two weeks—I am grateful.

The Way bears them,

power nurtures them;
Their own being shapes them.
And not one of the ten thousand things

fails to hold the Way sacred
or to obey its power.
Their reverence for the Way
and obedience to its power
are unforced and always natural
For the Way gives them life;
its power nourishes them,
mothers and feeds them,
completes and nurtures them,
looks after them, protects them.

To have without possessing,
do without claiming,
lead without controlling:
this is mysterious power.

TAO TE CHING

Here is my question: What is the Way?

In spite of all the abuses, prejudices, and compromised landscapes, Prayer Dogs have never left. This is their Way. Given half a chance, they will survive us.

We can no longer say, "Let nature take care of itself." Our press on the planet is heavy and relentless. A species in peril will most likely survive now only if we allow it to, if our imaginations can enter into the soul of the animal and we pull back on our own needs and desires to accommodate theirs. What other species now require of us is our attention. Otherwise, we are entering a narrative of disappearing intelligences.

The prairie dogs are a profound intelligence on the planet.

You are most near to God
when underground.

FAZIL ISKANDER

Robin song—twilight hymns.

Madame #RR6 is standing outside her burrow—9W. I admire that she moved north from Lone Tree. Very unusual, adventurous, brave, by my standards, not hers.

Will I see dear Madame Head Wide Apart before I leave?

I want to thank her.

I do not see her.

There she is—at the base of my tower—looking up.

Patience from the Pleistocene. Instinctual knowledge is another kind of intelligence. Kind—another kind—*kind-ness*

What can I give her? I can give her my words.

She looks up.

On my hands and knees on the floor of my perch, leaning out the square cutout door, I meet her gaze.

No words.

I pack my belongings and quietly climb down the tower. She is still there, illuminated. I sit down on the sand, very near to her. Madame Head Wide Apart does not move or seem to mind my presence.

She suddenly stands and faces the sun. We both do.

Clay-colored monks
dressed in discreet robes of fur
stand as sentinels
outside their burrows, watching,
watching as their communities
disappear, one by one,
their hands raised up
in prayer.

Steve passed away on Friday, January 21, 2005.

Before he died, Steve requested that his body remain at home for a period of time as family and friends gathered. He wanted the Tempest children to be able to witness his body after his spirit had moved on. He said to those close, "I want the children to be familiar with death and not fear it."

The children were invited to come to the house. There were eight nieces and nephews ranging from four to fourteen: Hayden, Clare, Mason, Grace, Christian, Sam, Ruby, and Hannah. They stood in the hallway, tentative and frightened, but they loved Steve, and we told them before entering that this was Steve's gift to them, to be able to witness how death is part of life and how the body becomes a shell after the spirit leaves.

The children entered the room where Steve's body lay. They touched his feet; they touched his arms and felt them as cold. They moved closer and lovingly rubbed his forehead. Respectful. Curious. And then, one by one they began to cry, freely and unself-conscious. One of them said, "Steve was my best friend." Another said, "I miss him." Within minutes, the children were sitting on the bed alongside his body telling stories about their uncle. Fear was transformed into comfort, curiosity melted into love, and the silence was no longer uncomfortable.

Mason, eight years old, who lives across the street, quietly said, "I get it now; so this is why Steve collected skulls." And he recounted to his cousins, how Steve had invited him over to his house to help him clean the skull of a badger he had found. "I was afraid of the skull, and Steve said, 'You don't need to be.' "

The children understood.

Even in death, Steve was still giving, still teaching.

I thought about the prairie dog skull he had given me and all of the skulls he had found and shared with family and friends.

Steve with binoculars in hand, bringing them up to his eyes, scanning, focusing, watching deer, watching elk, watching birds, a great gray owl, among them. He walked miles following the pipeline, traversing the wild country he loved.

And I thought about the conversation we had shared a few days earlier about what we thought the afterlife might be. He said, "I'm looking forward to seeing how all this works."

> *We do not serve the weak or the broken. What we serve is the wholeness of each other and the wholeness in life.*
>
> RACHEL NAOMI REMEN

Steve was buried on January 25, 2005. It was a cold winter day. His body rested in a pine box built by his neighbor, and it was transported to the cemetery in the back of a Tempest Company red flatbed truck. The men who worked for him followed the truck that carried his body in a long convoy of Tempest Company trucks. It looked like a red river moving slowly through a white landscape.

The men in my family lifted the casket from the truck and carried it to the gravesite. Friends and family gathered. A large pile of dirt was covered by a discreet green tarp next to the grave. His brothers Hank and Dan immediately pulled the cover off, leaving the dirt that would bury Steve exposed. Dirt has dignity. One by one, Steve's wife, his daughters, my brothers, and I with our father picked up a fistful of Earth and walked over to the coffin and dropped the dirt where Steve's body would lay. I watched the men in my family weep. I watched the men who had worked with Steve weep. These are tough, rugged, beautiful men weathered and weary from decades of beating their bodies against the land. Hot and cold. Day and night. Theirs is labor in the extreme.

I watched and I wondered what the men in my family know that I will never understand because of one simple thing—their tool of choice is a shovel.

When the funeral was over and everyone walked back to their cars and drove home, I turned. What I saw was Johnny McIntosh, longtime Tempest Company foreman, backfilling my brother's grave.

Jean Spence escorts me to the mezzanine of Building One at the American Museum of Natural History in New York. The smell of naphthalene is strong; it is a smell I am familiar with having spent more than a decade at the Utah Museum of Natural History from 1981 through 1996.

I sign in, aligning myself with the tribe of *Cynomys,* and we walk briskly up the metal staircase to what can only be described as a narrow hallway lined with floor-to-ceiling white cabinets.

It is in fact a mammal morgue. The collection holds 280,000 pieces of mammals: bones, skulls, scat samples, study skins, and mummies.

I am handed a printout of all the *Cynomys* that were collected in Utah. Each specimen has a catalog number listed by genus and species, along with identifying information such as whether it is a skin; whether the skull is intact or absent; whether alcohol is present; what country it was found in and then the specific location, in the case of the United States, what county, elevation, and so forth. Twenty-eight specimens of prairie dog are listed in this collection at the American Museum. This afternoon, I will examine all twenty-eight skins and then take a comparative look at all five species of prairie dogs: Utah, Gunnison's; white-tailed, black-tailed, and Mexican.

The fumes from the moth balls are intense, especially in summer heat. The ventilation system is poor.

Jean has given me a large white cardboard tray where I can place the prairie dog skins. I have a magnifying glass and a table to work on. A low hum from the fan can be heard above the buzz of fluorescent lights that create a line of light that extends down the hallway for what looks like a hundred feet.

As I carry the first tray back to the table, I feel like a waitress serving mummies and skulls. As I remove each object, I must replace it with a small yellow card and note that it is a skin, skull, or skeleton.

To be precise, which is what museums demand, I open the first box on the tray.

Box One: #249735
Date: 1896–1899
Cynomys gunnisoni
New Mexico, San Juan County
Chaco Canyon, Pueblo Bonito Ruins
Collector: T. B. T. Hyde—#7168—partial cranium

I open the yellow box as though the contents are jewels. They are bones. The top part of the skull is marked #249735 with black indigo ink. The script itself is a work of art. When I worked here as an intern in 1983, I met the gentleman who had perfected this craft of scientific writing on bones. It requires great precision and care. The notations, which identify each bone, are so tiny, millimeters, they beg for a magnifying glass.

I turn the partial cranium upside down and find more numbers: #64 marked on roof of mouth and inside H #7168.

Six teeth remain in place, four molars on one side, two on the other. Another molar has fallen out and is in the box. Under the magnifying glass, it appears like a tiny three-pronged claw with the tiniest fourth appendage.

It is hard not to see this fragment of bone as an object of art. The beauty of form is as alive in death as it was in life. Bones expose what was hidden, housed in muscle, fat, and fur, tingling with the circulatory wrappings of blood and nerves.

Context: Pueblo Bonito ruin in Chaco Canyon. The Pueblo peoples and prairie dogs were no strangers to each other.

Next specimen: glass cylinder
#249733
Date: 1896–1899
Cynomys gunnisoni
New Mexico: San Juan County
Chaco Canyon, Pueblo Bonito Ruins
Collector: T. B. T. Hyde—#2562

Inside the glass cylinder is the upper jaw with front incisors; dirt from Pueblo Bonito is still attached to bone after more than one hundred years. I recognize the terra-cotta-colored sand. I have been to Pueblo Bonito many times, and placed my hand against the handprints left by the Ancient Ones.

I look at two other specimens, also Gunnison's prairie dogs. Similar jaws from similar areas.

Now, the mummy.

#249747
Date: 1896–1899
Cynomys gunnisoni
New Mexico: San Juan County
Chaco Canyon, Pueblo Bonito Ruins
Collector: T. B. T. Hyde—#5796

Its fur, now hide, is shriveled and tough like the sole of an old shoe. Desiccated. Life is preserved in the desert.

I have seen mummies before. Human mummies were on display during our childhood at Temple Square in Salt Lake City. Indians wrapped in the dried hide of their own skins—weathered, withered, and shriveled—beyond human. We would sneak over to the museum when the LDS general conference was in session. Our parents were more than happy to let us go, knowing we would be rapt for hours.

Those mummies have since been removed from public viewing and, in most cases, returned to the tribes in the name of repatriation. In this instance, the Ute Nation requested proper burials.

I tentatively, respectfully pick up this body—dried in anguish. Its mouth is open in a grotesque scream. Jaw agape. Eyes hollow. I look at it under a suspended magnifying glass. The dried body rattles. A bone has broken out of the torn skin, more akin to the taut covering of a drum than fur. Same with the shoulder. Tiny pinholes appear on the chest with larger holes and tears. The black claws of this Gunnison's prairie dog are clenched like a fist. Exaggerated collar bones. The tail is intact. Vertebrae are still held in place covered by the hide.

When I turn the mummy over on its back, this prairie dog looks more reptilian than mammal. A red thread is wrapped around its right foot.

I turn the mummy again. Its hand is no different than mine. Animal, human—tell me the difference in death?

Remembering mummies housed in the museum at home, I notice that this prairie dog and the human beings I saw look eerily similar.

"Dlǫ́ǫ́," "Little Man"—the name prairie dogs are given by the Navajo, or Diné, who reside in the Four Corners of the American Southwest.

I put the mummy carefully back on my tray.

> Next specimen.
> #123906
> *Cynomys parvidens*
> *Date:* May 3, 1936
> *Sex:* Female adult
> Washington County, Cedar City, Utah
> *Elevation:* 5700'
> *Collector:* W. S. Long

There is a remarkable symmetry of skins in trays.

Black nipples apparent. I cannot help but think of Madame Head Wide Apart. Black eyebrows. Long black whiskers. How to describe the color of fur? Buff? Golden? I ask the biologist sitting next to me, who works at the Smithsonian, how she would explain the color. She looks at the skin and says, "Light sand. A biologist must be consistent in their own color semantics."

I thank her.

Pods of fur. Five skins in tray. Each one is accompanied by its skull in a small brown box. I open one of the boxes—there is a pair of beetle wings alongside the skull and jaw bones.

#140090
Cynomys parvidens
Date: August 1, 1904
Beaver County, Pine Mountain, Utah
Collector: G. P. Engelhardt

This is the oldest Utah prairie dog specimen collected in Utah in the American Museum of Natural History's registry.

It is a beautifully prepared skin. The arms and legs are perfectly out-stretched and in alignment with each other. It looks like it is flying. The body is plump, not flat. The mouth is stitched almost imperceptibly with black thread as is its belly. The cowlicks are visible, just like I witnessed on the prairie dogs in Bryce when the wind would blow. Dark skin exposed, golden fur. The cowlicks become sunbursts at its throat. White tail visible. Golden arms with longer fur. Eyebrows black. The dark tear stains. Coat is brownish red, typical of Pine Mountain's soil near St. George, Utah.

The accompanying skull in the box has been painted with a glaze. It looks like porcelain.

The person who prepared this particular skin was a master. And it is an art, not a science. I remember making study skins at the Teton Science School when I was eighteen. We were preparing deer mice, *Peromyscus*. Our specimens were field mice trapped in the kitchen, kept in the freezer just for this purpose. I remember how surprised I was when I made my cut gently down the belly and folded the fur back over its arms and head like a little cape. We would then sprinkle cornmeal on the inside of the fur to absorb any blood and prepare a body out of cotton, wrap the skin around it, straighten the arms and legs and sew it back up. This is a practice belonging more to the past than the present when mammal surveys were being done, a discipline that routinely is no longer justified: killing in the field.

As I carry trays back and forth from the cabinets to my desk, I note that six prairie dogs study skins look like loaves of bread, so perfect are they in their alignment and symmetry.

These six specimens were also collected by W. S. Long in April 1936.

Some of these skins are in a compromised state, fur coming off, cotton stuffing exposed, skin rubbed raw, even cornmeal spilling out. And in some cases, there has even been beetle damage.

Deterioration is inevitable with collections this large in museums this big when funding is inadequate for the needs at hand.

These collections of mammals and birds, insects and shells are libraries of the Earth. Artifacts of witness. Physical records of life on the planet. Each year they become more and more precious.

#123904
Cynomys parvidens
Date: April, 1936
Collected three miles north of Panguitch, Utah
Elevation: 6600'
Collector: W. S. Long

#123742
Cynomys parvidens
Date: April 7, 1936
Collected three miles northwest of Ruby's Inn
Garfield County, Utah
Collector: W. S. Long

This specimen interests me; it could be an ancestor of the prairie dogs we were working with in Bryce Canyon National Park. The pink sand under the black nails is the same pink sand I saw a few months ago. There is also pink sand on the fur in the corners of its mouth, which makes me think perhaps this prairie dog may have been dehydrated, foaming at the mouth due to heat.

#123743
Cynomys parvidens
Date: April 7, 1936
Collected three miles northwest of Ruby's Inn
Garfield County, Utah
Collector: W. S. Long

This study skin shows white tips on the prairie dog's black nails. Perhaps an older animal. I notice the distinct suture lines on the skull that lead down to the teeth.

Another tray of prairie dogs: These are a different type of study skin, longer, narrower, more like a weasel in presentation than bread. The prairie dogs are raised on their elbows, alert, instead of in a flying posture.

There are seven prairie dogs in this tray.

#28737
Cynomys parvidens
Date: August 25, 1904
Beaver County, Buckskin Valley, Utah
No collector's name

This sorry specimen looks like a flying carpet, complete with ripples, or roadkill without innards. No stuffing, truly a skin.

1904—one hundred years old—one hundred years ago, this Utah prairie dog was alive, part of a village, scurrying between sage, sitting on its haunches surveying the grasslands for predators, standing, stretching, delivering an alarm call.

#140629
Cynomys leucurus
Date: July 23, 1936
Sex: Male juvenile
Rio Blanco County, White River, Colorado
Collector: G. G. Goodwin

White-tailed prairie dog. Hard to tell the difference between this species and the Utah prairie dog. Location is key.

There are two other white-tailed prairie dog specimens from Daggett County, Utah, that were collected on the banks of the Green River.

Specimens #140629, #140630.

Two more specimens in this tray that are Gunnison's prairie dogs, one collected in New Mexico, another in Arizona. They are different subspecies: *Cynomys gunnisoni gunnisoni* and *Cynomys gunnisoni zuniensis*.

The greatest distinction can be seen in the black-tailed prairie dog study skins. They are much bigger and have black tails.

All of the specimens in this tray, *Cynomys ludovicianus ludovicianus*, are from Colorado, Wyoming, Montana, South Dakota, Kansas, and Nebraska—moving into the Great Plains.

The white-tailed, Gunnison's, and Utah prairie dogs are found geographically in the Southwest, a landscape of aridity, sage flats, grasslands, and high plateaus.

There are obviously crossovers and exceptions. I just found a tray of black-tailed prairie dogs, a subspecies now no longer recognized, *Cynomys ludovicianus arizonensis*, which were collected in New Mexico, Arizona, and Texas.

There are no Mexican prairie dogs in the American Museum of Natural History's collection.

One box, in particular, intrigues me: Box #200174. No data. I open it. It is full of bones, random bones, bone fragments from a prairie dog whose location and date of collection has been lost. Call me obsessive-compulsive, but I count each bone as if this act will make up for the unknown, displaced, anonymous prairie dog.

Skull, vertebra, fifteen vertebrae, some still fused as spine, scapula, collar bones, ribs, hip bones, femur, tibia, fibula, ulna, radius, such tiny, numerous bones. Much smaller than toothpicks, more like solid bird bones. Fragments of bone I cannot identify. I count ninety-nine bones in this box and twenty-four black claws.

On my desk, I try to reconstruct this creature and see its sturdy stance through a scaffolding of bones: wind chimes on the prairie near a ghost herd of bison. Give this prairie dog a heart with blood flowing through a mesh of veins, arteries, muscles, tendons, tissues, organs, all systems pulsating with purpose; add a brain, one small brain, and a jolt of electricity that runs through its nervous system—the prairie dog is breathing. Give her a cloak of fur, with eyes alert, nose sniffing, and add whiskers, a voice, that characteristic voice, now calling, arms raising, now standing, the prairie dog alive on hind legs, "Yip-yip-yipping"—the prairie awakened, a community engaged.

The yellowed card reads:

```
Am. Mus. Nat. Hist., Dept. of Vert. Palaeont.
No #174
....................Cynomys............................
..................skull + skeleton........................
..................Epoch........Form'n............Beds.
Loc.................................................Exp........
```

No species, no sex, no location, no date. Only bones.

The skeleton is close to being intact: What comes through this impressionistic attempt at reconstruction is how the gravity of a prairie dog's skeleton settles in the hips. Haunches. They sit. They sit with great stamina, and I see now, they are built for it.

Prairie dogs have a practice of sitting. And it is written in their bones—literally. The back of the skull looks like a woman in meditation, her head slightly bowed, her legs crossed with the spine slightly curved. You see the back of her arms and imagine her hands gently resting on her knees. A script for survival is found in the formation of the prairie dog skull.

I slowly dismantle this prairie dog and put her carefully back in the cardboard box.

What is it about my species that craves order, demands it, practices the organizing and cataloging of data like a religion, but it is not a religion; it is a science.

Or is it?

We place what we find, what we don't know, but believe to be value, in a box. We put what remains in a box.

What remains is what is hard and solid like rock and bone. Anything fluid, soft, or of spirit drains, dissipates, disappears. Eventually, bones will crumble into powder, dust, and be absorbed into dirt. Even rocks are reduced to sand.

I don't want to be remains in a box. I want to be fluid, alive, ephemeral. The evidence of life is preserved through stories. Find the stories. Tell the stories. The order of animals is the organization of narratives. Natural histories create a patterned landscape and a mosaic of nuanced minds.

I hold out one beautiful bone, a tibia and fibula combined creating what appears as a musical bow or lyre. How does this delicacy of form not collapse under the weight of its own creation? Beauty creates a structure of strength.

Shortly after Steve died, I walked down to the Colorado River. A piece of driftwood left on the bank caught my eye. The driftwood was weathered white and measured from the tip of my finger to the bend in my arm. Its shape reminded me of the pictographs painted on canyon walls, the humanlike figures with small heads, broad shoulders, the torso tapering to a point.

I cut three red willow twigs; they were long and thin, over two feet tall. I attached these red spirit lines to the back of the driftwood with a small piece of thread I found in my pocket.

Rabbitbrush caught my eye. I cut a piece the size of my finger and arched it over the head as a halo. The red willow shoots fanned out from the halo like rays of fire.

I had made a doll.

Lastly, I placed a sprig of sage, gray-blue, diagonally across the doll's body. Its fragrance was a jolt of ritual. My doll was complete. The abstract form spoke to me. She said, "Make your brother a bridge of bones."

I looked around the pink sandy beach, still moist from the rain, and improvised. White sticks would do, becoming bones of intention. 1, 2— I picked each stick with care and interest. Some were straight, some gnarled and twisted, others more bark than stick.

3, 4, 5, 6, 7—I counted them out, hunting and gathering my brother's bones that were sticks bleached so they looked like ribs, placing them flat on the sand, one next to the other, vertically set, side by side.

8, 9, 10, 11, 12, 13, 14, 15—they came fast and easily through the river's generosity, gifts left from high water. What had been broken and carried away, I retrieved. I would bend down, pick one stick, then another, and continue making the bone bridge.

16, 17, 18, 19—I saw each stick-bone as a day, a day that my brother had been dead—20, 21, 22, 23, 24, 25, 26, 27, 28, 29, 30, 31—one month to the day, call this stick-bone February 21.

A Buddhist friend told me that Steve's spirit was still in transition here, near, for 49 days—32, 33, 34, 35. I am counting the days, 36, seeing them as bones, my brother's bones. I once wrote that if I can learn to love death, I can begin to find refuge in change—37, 38, 39. Perhaps, this is the time—40, 41, 42, 43, 44, we have been here before, 45, 46, 47. Stephen Dixon Tempest was 47 years old, a beautiful man who, five months prior to his death, stood on a summit in the Wasatch Range, smiled, and said matter-of-factly, *We are all terminal.*

He wanted to live. He died at 47. 48. 49. I am his older sister at 49 years.

49 days.

I am building a bridge of bones across a river of light, golden light, and once on the other side, will you sing your words back to me, my little brother, my lovely, wise brother, a man of construction who welds pipe into art, you gave me these words:

What is a body but a house—
What is a soul but a light—
What is heaven and earth
but the same shared radiance.

The Safe Harbor Agreement came about in the mid-1990s when it became clear that federal agencies and environmental groups had to find ways to work with private land owners. Most endangered species are found on private lands. In the case of the Utah prairie dogs it is 75 percent. On July 21, 1997, fifteen distinguished scientists wrote a letter to the U.S. Fish and Wildlife Service in support of a Safe Harbor Agreement. In 1999, it was adopted by the agency as policy. It has become a promising tool in finding peace on private lands between animals and human beings.

Allen Henrie is a rancher in Garfield County, Utah, not far from Bryce Canyon National Park. He owns a nine hundred-acre cattle ranch. Not long ago, he received a knock on his door. It was Ted Toombs, an ecologist who works for Environmental Defense. They sat down together with another neighbor and talked about Henrie's land and what it might mean to enter into a Safe Harbor Agreement with Utah prairie dogs.

"We had to find a way to pair regulatory assurances with financial incentives," said Toombs, "that would encourage landowners to become responsible stewards and conservationists."

In 1998, the Environmental Defense began involving landowners in Utah prairie dog recovery. "We recognized that many ranchers lacked the money to improve their land. We have been helping them find the funds to restore their range," said Ted Toombs. If Henrie signed a Safe Harbor Agreement with the Fish and Wildlife Service, it meant that he would make land improvements that would benefit both his cows and the prairie dogs, and in so doing, he would not be penalized by the federal regulations regarding prairie dogs. "The Fish and Wildlife Service effectively freezes a landowner's Endangered Species Act responsibilities at their current levels for a particular species if he or she agrees to restore, enhance, or create habitat for that species," Toombs explained.

With the Environmental Defense's help, Henrie would receive funding in part through a private stewardship grant administered by the U.S. Fish and Wildlife Service for improving his land by planting native grasses and implementing "a new prescribed grazing plan" to maintain the restored vegetation. What is particularly remarkable is that Henrie agreed to reintroduce Utah prairie dogs on about a fifth of his land. "This will not be easy, but relocation methods have been improving," said Toombs. And what will happen if one day the Henrie Ranch is more prairie dogs than cows? Henrie negotiated a "direct-take provision," which means if the prairie dogs one day spread beyond his ranch, then he is allowed to request nonlethal trapping.

"It's a win-win situation for everyone," said Ted Toombs. "For the rancher, the land, the cows, and especially, the prairie dogs."

Listening to Ted Toombs talk about "a culture of recovery," one can begin to believe in the power of creative partnerships where landowners, state and federal agencies, and conservationists are working together on behalf of the health and restoration of Utah prairie dogs.

But critics of the Safe Harbor Agreement worry it undermines the integrity of the Endangered Species Act, especially Section 9, which prohibits take (including killing, harm, and harassment of listed species), by granting private landowners enrolled in this program immunity from federal regulations.

On April 18, 2005, Allen Henrie applied to the Fish and Wildlife Services for an Enhancement of Survival Permit for the Utah prairie dog *"pursuant to section 10 (a)1 (A) of the Endangered Species Act of 1973 (U.S.C. 1531 et seg.), as amended. This permit application includes a Safe Harbor Agreement between the Applicant, the Utah Division of Wildlife Resources, and the Service. And so, for the next 15 years, as agreed upon, Mr. Allen Henrie's land is a safe harbor for Utah Prairie Dogs. The proposed SHA and permit would become effective upon signature of the SHA and issuance of the permit and would remain in effect for 40 years. We have made the determination that the proposed activities described in the application and SHA will improve prairie dog habitat and potentially establish a colony of prairie dogs on private land. . . ."*

Allen Henrie signed the Safe Harbor Agreement.

As of January 1, 2007, six other ranchers in the state of Utah had followed Henrie's lead.

February 2, 2008

Prairie Dog Day: A western twist on an eastern tradition with a focus not on weather but climate change. Perhaps we can look toward a forecast not of shadow but of light. May this be a prediction of restoration, not removal.

The 1991 Utah Prairie Dog Recovery Plan belongs to the past century. A new Utah Prairie Dog Recovery Plan will be introduced by the United States Fish and Wildlife Service this fall. If only it would be bold and visionary. If only the prairie dogs had a say.

If only.

If only Utah prairie dogs would speak to us, perhaps they would ask for their status to be elevated from a threatened species to an endangered one, as an offering of greater protection with greater compassion. They would speak of struggle, asking that the future of their families be considered in the path of oil and gas leases, overgrazing, and real estate development. They would tell us that when they are displaced, becoming refugees on unfamiliar land, they cease to speak, and without their voices, they cannot survive. And they would ask to be recognized as the emissaries they are from the Pleistocene Era who have much to teach us about adapting to change. *Can we have a change of heart?* Prairie dogs. Prayer dogs. They are sounding their alarm calls now, recognizing us as the animals we are, unconsciously walking toward the sharp-edge of extinction.

And so it was I entered the broken world.

HART CRANE

A woman stands at the opening of a descending staircase. Her eyes—her red-streaked eyes—see inside me as she puts her arm through mine. We kiss each other on either side of our cheeks, one-two-three—Rwandan style. Her eyes. She directs me down to the basement, where there is a pyramid-shaped glass case of bones rising from a floor of white square tiles. The bones: skulls, femurs, ribs, vertebrae are organized in rows, columns, piles.

You can look through the glass floor of the pyramid case to another floor below where a single coffin rests. We are told that inside the coffin is the body of a mother holding a child. "I saw this woman," a man interrupts. "I knew her. For years, she was exposed for everyone to see." As we listened to what happened to this woman, what was done to her, the repeated rapes and a violence impaled with a gun, I didn't want to hear it. And now that I had, I couldn't get this image out of my mind. How to erase this violence from my mind. Once a witness to brutality, seen or heard, we become accountable.

More bones. I now see them as prairie dog bones, sorted, cleaned, and categorized. It is the only way I can stay in the basement and not collapse under the magnitude of what has been gathered here.

Rwanda. I didn't want to come. I didn't want to be in a place so familiar with Death. I had seen enough in my own family. I was also scared. The only thing I knew of Rwanda was genocide and the weight of that word. 1994, the year we Americans turned our backs. No. I would not go to Rwanda. I said yes. I said yes to Lily Yeh, a Chinese American artist who understood mosaic as taking that which was broken and creating something whole. She helped create The Village of Arts and Humanities in

Philadelphia from the poorest of neighborhoods. She stood in the center of an empty lot littered with glass, picked up a stick, and drew a circle around her. One by one, a curious community came to see who this tiny Chinese woman was and what she was doing. She invited them to pick up shards of glass and together they began making art. Mosaics. A Tree of Life was constructed on the standing wall of a building otherwise destroyed. It was the first of many mosaics to restore beauty to a place of violence and abuse.

"Barefoot Artists," she said as she began to describe the Rwandan project. She had been asked by a member of the Red Cross to help design a genocide memorial in the village of Rugerero, very near the town of Gisenyi, on the border of the Congo. "Will you be part of our team? I need you as our scribe." I said no. And then I said yes. I knew in my heart that my own spiritual evolution depended on it. There are four of us: Lily Yeh; Alan Jacobson, an environmental designer; Meghan Morris, a graduate student whose work focuses on the effects of war on adolescents; and myself.

Rukirande Musana Jean Bosco is our sponsor from the Red Cross, the man who invited Lily to come work with him on this project. He is accompanied by Ndebwohe Damas, a tall, impressive young man with a broad smile. We are driving on a red dirt road outside Kigali, the capital city of Rwanda, on our way to see two churches that are now memorials to the 1994 genocide. Large expanses of wetlands are on either side of us. "This is where many Tutsi hid," Jean Bosco tells us. "It is also where many were hunted and butchered by the Hutu militia known as the Inter-ahamwe." We cross a bridge. "There was a time when this river was choked with bodies," Jean Bosco says.

Nyamata. I look up at the ceiling in the church. Holes from grenades appear as stars. Light is streaming down onto the pews. Empty pews. Rooms full of bones. Bags of bones, bulging, closed. Sacks of skulls. Piles of faded clothing. The altar cloth, once white, is now brown with blood. Ten thousand people were murdered here.

Belyse, a young woman, twenty-one years old, is the witness here at Nyamata who tells the story. She shows us where the door was kicked down. She shows us an identity card. Hutu. Tutsi. "It came down to this," she says. She tells of those murdered, bodies piled over one another on pews. She tells of how the Virgin survived and points to a statue on a shelf, the Blessed Mother perfectly intact.

Beautiful in her ethereal presence, Belyse is barely here. She inhabits the past, hunkered in the grasses, nine years old, listening, waiting. Her parents told her to hide in the fields. She remembers the screams, the silences, looking for her parents, searching for her parents, and then the years of wandering. She has come back. This church is now her home. Her parents' home. Their bones are in the church. Purple fabric covers coffins. Flowers now dried are draped over the wooden boxes.

Belyse is a ghost here on Earth, pulled into the world of the Dead, unable to tear herself away from the skeletal grip the bones have on her. The Dead's grip is so seductive, it is hard to free oneself from its bony hand holding on tight, because in the realm of the Dead, everything is infused with meaning.

Damas is standing in front of an alcove inside the church. The brick wall is stained with blood. Wild with grief, he tells me about babies pulled out of their mother's arms and thrown against the wall by the killers. "In that moment," Damas says to me, "the devil came into the churches and murdered every Tutsi."

My eyes follow the birds flying inside, swallows banking before the stained glass windows—red drops of blood, rendered in glass, below a window of deliverance, blue, yellow.

The woman who led me downstairs and made me look is named Muka-musoni Seraphine. Her husband was killed along with one of her children. Five children survived. "Call me Muka," she says.

Outside, the sun is blinding. I can breathe again. We pass a grave, "Tonja Locatell," an Italian nun. She was killed by Hutu extremists before the genocide. And another grave that reads "P. Manolo Daguerre, 14.9.90, R.I.P." He was a priest. We learn that the pope came to Rwanda in September 1990. He was one of the few international voices that kept calling for intervention during the 1994 war. I look back at the church with its red bricks of sandstone. Swallows circle the white cross.

Purple ribbon is strewn through the white wrought iron fence like crepe paper woven through the spokes of bicycles. Purple petals have fallen on red soil. Jean Bosco sees me pick them up and place them in between the pages of my journal. "Graveria," he says. "Excuse me?" I respond. He picks up some of the petals also, then points to the tree. "That is the name of the tree that produces these flowers." He is a biologist by training.

We descend into what looks like a root cellar. There is just enough light to see that it is filled with coffins covered with purple cloth. Some of the coffins are open. "That is not one person—but many persons," says Belyse. "Each coffin contains many people." She pauses. "Whole families."

This is a hell of our own making—those who killed and those of us who looked away. No surgical strikes, computerized or digitalized by military minds and top gun pilots, the eyes of these killers were on the eyes of those they killed. By hand. One million Tutsis were murdered in one hundred days. Their killers were neighbors with farm tools, machetes, and hoes. Hundreds of skulls, shelves of skulls—thirty thousand bodies—here at Nyamata. This is what we are told. We are walking inside a mass grave, genocidal tourists, underground. I am sick to my stomach. All I can see are the whites of Belyse's eyes in darkness.

I cannot walk any farther down this narrow, damp hallway of bones, shelves and boxes of bones. Damas calls me back. "Here, look, the skin has not separated from the bones." From the corner of my eye, I see a flesh-fallen hand, disembodied. Below, a large amber cockroach scurries across the cement floor. *Inyezi. Cockroach. The Hutu name for Tutsi.*

I emerge out of the cellar, two windows with hand grips are pulled back over the ceiling of white tiles like transparent wings. Muka is outside, one arm wrapped around her waist, her other hand on her forehead wiping away sweat. Can one be soaked in sorrow? I sit next to her in the garden and take a picture of white blossoms against the red sand.

Damas sits down next to us. Lily, Alan, and Meghan are still underground.

"It is impossible to imagine—" I say to Damas.

"It is impossible to accept," he replies. "When I see those skulls, I see me."

I only now realize that he, too, is a survivor.

"You see that purple banner above the door," he asks. "Let me translate it for you: *'If you do violence to me, you do violence to yourself because we are all human beings.'* "

Before leaving, I show Belyse a small glass vial of red sand I brought from home in Castle Valley. She smiles and picks up sand from the ground at Nyamata. Together we kneel in the garden and mix these two sands on the flat surface of an exposed brick. They are indistinguishable from one another. I have a second vial I take out of my pack. We put the combined sands in the two containers, each of us taking one.

We leave and I wave good-bye to Belyse. She runs toward our vehicle. We stop. I get out of the vehicle and we hug again. It was only after we were on the road that Jean Bosco told me that the way I was waving, fingers brought down toward palm quickly, means "come" to Rwandans.

We continue to drive over the red dusty road. People are walking on both sides of the road, coming and going. Meghan, Alan, and I return to the side benches in the vehicle, watching the world through the windows. It is a borage of humanity, a steady stream of people walking, women carrying everything from fruit to wood to charcoal on top of their heads with babies strapped to their waists held close by wrapped fabrics; orphans running on the side of the roads crying, *"Muzungu! Muzungu!"* which translates to "white person." There is a smell of smoke in the air laced with dust.

No one is speaking.

Twenty minutes later, we arrive in Ntarama and are met by a man named Rutaganda Pacifique, another witness. He is wearing the same pin that Belyse was wearing. It reads, "God Loves You."

"This man was in this church," Jean Bosco says after shaking his hand and exchanging greetings in Kinyarwanda. "He will show us how he survived."

Pacifique speaks softly with his hands. I watch him, as Damas translates. His eyes are very far away, as if the voice of the Dead is speaking through him:

"On April 10, 1994, three days after the president's plane was shot down, we came here—Tutsi refugees seeking safety in the church. When we came here inside this church, outside the Hutu militia were burning our houses, eating our cows, goats, destroying everything in the towns and villages. The Tutsis ask the authorities, 'What can we do now?' The authorities say, 'Stay where you are. You are finished; you must be killed. There is nothing you can do.'

"In 1959," Pacifique explains, *"you see there was a semigenocide, a half genocide; the parents and the old people remember. One of the elders, an old man says, 'Let's go to Church. We will be safe there once again,' so the Tutsi's come to church believing him.*

"When the soldiers of government came to the church and asked, 'Why are you here?' we say because in the village, it is very dangerous. The soldiers tell us to bring all our children, the elders, everyone here to the church, and after one week, when everyone is in the church, the Hutu extremists start killing us: five thousand people in all.

"They destroyed the church with grenades. Then they came back into church to check . If you were alive, they killed you again with machetes." He points to skulls on the shelves behind him—many split in half. Pacifique turns to Jean Bosco and speaks. Jean Bosco listens, then says, *"His family— twelve persons—were killed. He was the only one that survived with his wife."* Pacifique points to the skulls, then points to his own.

"I was lying between these pews with dead bodies on top of me. The militia thought I was dead; only the tip of a machete reached me. See here, my scar." (A four-inch scar runs down the side of his head.) He turns around and retrieves a stick with spikes that is leaning against the wall. He then shows us a skull on the shelf with a spike embedded in it.

He tells us that after soldiers and militia left, he tried to lift himself out from under the bodies, and he found that his wife was also alive. Her leg was badly cut. He carried her in a rush of blood to the fields by the river, where many survivors were hiding.

"The RPF [Rwanda Patriotic Front] who were fighting as the resistance army led by Paul Kagame, now the president of Rwanda, finally arrived and found them in the fields." Pacifique clasps his hands in prayer. *"They told us, 'Please don't worry anymore. You have survived this horror. No problem, we are in charge now.'*

"We decided to leave many of the bodies here in the church as a reminder of what happened. Never again. Never again."

Some of the skulls are split in half. Machetes. Some are crushed. Clubs. Some have holes in them. Guns. Some have spikes. Some skulls still have hair on them. Some still wear scarves. There are forty-seven shelves of skulls, some stacked double, with mounds of femurs, ulnas, and shoulder blades also in the church.

There is the same star-blown ceiling. A shattered photograph of the pope. The altar is covered with dried blood, the cross akimbo. A skull leans against the cross. A broken stained-glass window with white and turquoise glass is the only source of light.

Pacifique is standing outside smoking a cigarette. He is a tall, thin man with a narrow face. Mustache. Beard. Short cropped hair. Bloodshot eyes. Red thongs on his feet. He is wearing long green pants with a peach-colored shirt. He is talking with Jean Bosco and Damas. Another man joins them.

Behind the church is an annex. More rooms where tall plastic bags of bones and bags of skulls are stored. There are thousands of fragments of bones on the dirt floor. In another room, pile after pile of faded clothing, shoes, wash basins. A primary school anatomy book is among the debris. Notebooks with careful, beautiful script. The people brought possessions, the things they thought they might need, things that mattered to them, books, photographs—this is what survives—possessions piled against bones.

What possesses us?

The dust has not settled here. There is a distinct smell, a pinched smell of a tincture opened and released that will never dissipate. I do not detect the sweet, sickly smell that precedes and follows a slow death from illness but rather a sharp, cutting stench, like the taste of blood, that metallic taste of taboo.

Next to the church, there is a house. The killers took a mattress, lit it on fire, stuffed it inside, and nailed the door shut. All inside died. The door is now open. Charred remains. I look down at my feet. A child's rib. A baby's shoe.

A baby is crying next door. Chickens are running about. I am dizzy, disoriented. The heat bears down on all of us. Lily has her hand on one of the walls. She is bent over sick.

Eucalyptus trees sway back and forth. A white butterfly undulates in the breeze. Birdsong. Red soil beneath my feet. Everything is sandstone. Broken sandstone.

We leave in silence. Pacifique nods.

Hundreds, maybe thousands of people are walking on the same road we are driving on. Women carrying everything imaginable on their heads, from long bundles of sugarcane to bananas to yellow water jugs to car engines. The soles of babies' bare feet are visible around their mother's waists as they walk facing traffic. The men walk freely talking to one another.

Alan asks me if I have been to Africa before. I tell him I have: Kenya, 1985, the U.N. Decade for Women Conference in Nairobi. He asks me what I brought back from that experience. "A sixty-foot tapeworm," I say. Lily and Meghan perk up. I tell them the story. In 1987, I was growing weaker and weaker, until I couldn't get out of bed. No doctors could determine the source of my debilitating fatigue. Then one day at work at the Utah Museum of Natural History, I suddenly had explosive diarrhea. I ran to the bathroom and I saw it. "Saw what?" Meghan asks. "The tapeworm. I tried to grab it and it snapped back up." They scream.

"I called my doctor, told him what I had witnessed, proglottids and all. He told me to calm down, that it was highly unlikely. I told him I was on my way to his office to have a stool sample tested."

Two weeks later (after a serious fall in the desert as a result of my contin-ued weakness), I was lying on the couch with a hundred-plus stitches holding my forehead together, when I received a call from my doctor.

"Terry, you were right. You have a fish tapeworm. I didn't believe you. We're quite excited by it. We've never seen this in Utah. The tapeworm is site specific."

I am silent.

"You haven't been to Africa lately, have you?"

"Two years ago—" I say. "Kenya."

"Wait just a minute, I want to make some calculations." my doctor says. I waited on the other end of the telephone.

"Let's see, that would make your tapeworm . . . oh my god, Terry, it's approximately sixty feet long."

On a pilgrimage to Lake Nakura to watch the great multitudes of pink flamingos, I remember eating some local fish that most likely had con-tained a tapeworm cyst. After several rounds of heavy-duty drugs, the hearty tapeworm finally made its exit in segments. I deposited it some-where in the Jedediah Smith Wilderness while camping on the backside of the Tetons.

The soil in Kigali is red, erosional red. Every square inch of available land is cultivated in a vertical patchwork of green and yellow squares. Terraced hills surround the city, a city under construction everywhere, a city cov-ering its history with new paint and modern buildings. We are staying in a remodeled hotel, a veneer built over the old one that still has bloodstains in its foundation. It is not hard to read ghosts everywhere.

It is difficult not to see each man as a killer, each woman and child as a survivor, every street, wall, café, and hotel as a backdrop for slaughter. This isn't fair, but I am a foreigner frozen by images of war. Circling the sky, always, I see buzzards and kites.

On the grounds of the Genocide Memorial in Kigali, there is a labyrinth made of roses. You come to it after being immersed in the sorrow of war.

Here, the graves and the gardens are one and the same.

The four of us are escorted into the Secretary General's office of the Red Cross. Dr. Tarsis Kabwesige has been with the Red Cross in Rwanda for eight years. Before that, he was minister of welfare. "I came here after the genocide and was part of the reconstruction. *We are still in reconstruction.*"

Dr. Kabwesige is wearing a perfectly pressed yellow shirt with black pants. The walls of his office are ochre; dark reeds make up the roof, with painted cement floors. Sheer drapes cover the windows. He outlines the fundamental principles of the Red Cross and tells us the Red Cross still means something in Rwanda. "We have over one million orphans that are being absorbed into our communities," he says. Many families have children as heads of their families, as young as twelve years old. Many children who ran away, now they make more children, and many of these children are HIV infected. It is a vicious cycle of violence and neglect. We are trying to reconnect Rwandan children to their families and villages and vice versa. We partner with other governments: Norway, Denmark, and Britain." He pauses. "But the American Red Cross help us very little."

I ask him about America's lack of support. The secretary general's eyes grow angry. "Abstinence is not the answer. We remain invisible to the United States."

Tight Security. We leave our passports and wait beneath photographs of Bush and Cheney. We are visiting the office of United States Agency for International Development (USAID). Ryan Washburn greets us. He is American, young, with dark, curly hair and hazel eyes. He came to Rwanda from Ghana, West Africa, where he was involved with agricultural issues and rural enterprise, coffee-export production and microcredit. He has been in Kigali for a month. Tim Muzira is Ryan's colleague. He is Rwandan and has been with USAID for many years.

We sit down around the table as Lily formally explains our project in the Genocide Survivors Village of Rugerero. She tells the story of her work in Philadelphia. "We transformed abandoned land, trashed land, into beautiful gardens and parks. Drug addicts became not only artists but leaders. We created an 'Alley of Angels' out of mosaics, broken glass, and pottery. The children found safety there. We started school programs and a community theater that addresses the issues of domestic violence, drug abuse, and AIDS. We even built our own kiln so we could create our own tiles for the ongoing mosaic murals and monuments. This became known as the Village of Arts and Humanities." She looks at the gentlemen. "We believe we can do that here. The women in the village are interested. We would like to create these kinds of art projects in the Genocide Survivors Village of Rugerero. We do know the villagers need food, that water is a problem, and that the women want to create their own sense of commerce, so Jean Bosco and I started thinking about chickens, mushrooms, and more intensive farming in small areas." Lily turns to Jean Bosco. "We need your guidance," he says.

"This all sounds interesting," Ryan replies. "But we have a structure to maintain. We have milestones we must adhere to, and then we do the next stage of building."

"What are you building?" Lily asks. The men say nothing. "This is what we want to build." Lily leans across the table, and shows them her drawing of the Genocide Memorial, the colored sketch approved by the governor of Gisenyi in 2004. She explains the undulating white walls that appear as waves and the importance of sacred space inside the memorial grounds. Lily talks about using local labor, local expertise, and local materials such as the lava stones found in Rugerero.

"While we are here," Lily says, "we will build one wall, so the form is set. The project can then continue while we are away. We want to create a sustainable project," Lily continues passionately. "The art project lays the groundwork. We begin with authentic images that arise from the community itself that allows them to express and create their own sense of identity in place. The art itself and the process we will take the children and the community through will create energy and momentum. Sparks for deeper change."

No response across the table.

"Our question for you is how do we find a way to make our project part of the local economy, become an activity that provides economic support? This is not our expertise; we are looking for partnerships." Lily pauses. "We are artists, cultural workers, who dream and believe in the path of the imagination. We are in the process of refining our vision. Storytelling is another way of getting to the root of community problems. For example, we can imagine the children creating story sticks, painting tales of their lives on wood poles, then placing them inside the Village," Lily explains. "We work in interior spaces that move outward into exterior spaces."

Jean Bosco speaks Kinyarwanda to Tim Muzira. "The people in Rugerero have nothing. We want to do something together. I want to bring a sense of possibilities back into these survivor villages. We want to begin here. We need to find a way that the memorial can address the needs of the Survivors Village."

Ryan asks about funding.

"We are self-funded," Lily says. "We are all here on our own expense. We come to you for cooperation and collaboration. We would love to have your blessing."

Ryan explains that the total Rwanda USAID budget is $2.5 million. "The U.S. Embassy does have a small grant project—one hundred thousand to two hundred thousand dollars." He sighs. "Look, we are happy to meet you, to find out where you are working—this is all good. And every April, on the anniversary of the genocide, the U.S. Embassy gives money." Ryan leans forward, his arms folded. "Fact-finding is important—to find out what the needs of the community are. USAID is the funder of the United States government. We are a slow-moving bureaucracy. We don't work with small numbers of people with small amounts of money. But we could approach other people, however, on your behalf that could help. We could say, 'Please assist these nice people with this little project.' "

"So we are too small for you to help?" Lily asks.

Ryan asks if we are a 501-C3.

"Yes we are," Lily says.

"We just had a 50 percent budget cut in terms of the Rwanda USAID/ Agriculture and Rural Enterprise program. Go back home and talk to your congressman," Ryan says. "Rwanda receives virtually zero funding from Congress. Aid to Sudan goes up—aid to Rwanda goes down; aid to Iraq goes up—Rwanda isn't on anybody's radar anymore."

Ryan looks at Lily. "Look, you guys are all over the place—the monument, the chickens, the mushrooms, water, and painting houses with the kids' art. You need to write a detailed proposal as to what you are going to do. I recommend you look for other sources of funding," Ryan says.

We walk out of USAID, Lily turns to me and says, "We have fulfilled our obligation. We have alerted the U.S. government as to what we are doing. Now we will just go ahead and do it. We are more powerful without them."

On the road to Gisenyi, we stop at a Chinese cemetery. Characters are etched in stone marking graves. Lily had a hunch the Chinese built this road we have been traveling on. I asked her how she knew. She said it was just a feeling. "I can't describe it. I just know a Chinese road when I'm on one."

We arrive in Gisenyi at dusk. Smoke. Shadows. Figures caught in headlights. Lake Kivu shimmers on the horizon as a long reflective mirror that creates a liquid border between northwest Rwanda and the Congo. This is known as the Great Lakes region. I am reminded of scenes captured in a ring I once had as a child; inside a plastic orb were the silhouettes of palms against a twilight sky made of iridescent butterfly wings, turquoise blue. We are surrounded by a spectacular crown of peaks, the Virunga Mountains, snow-tipped and jagged, a volcanic spine that creates the continental divide between the Congo and Nile river basins. And then, suddenly, we are all caught off-guard—an eerie red glow is emanating from the Congo. An active volcano.

Jean Bosco refers to the volcano as a woman, *Nyiragongo.* He tells us that three years ago when she erupted, Gisenyi needed no electricity at night, the sky was so bright. Lava flowed for miles. Houses burned.

We are all relaxing on the porch of the house where we will be staying for the month. It is a bed and breakfast, of sorts, owned by Mama Chakula, a distinguished woman I would guess to be in her forties. She owns several businesses in Gisenyi. In candlelight, Lily says, "The results of the violence we witnessed today at Nyamata and Ntarama is not just outside us but within us, capable of erupting at any moment."

As she speaks, I watch the red glare of the volcano throbbing.

We sit down at Mama Chakula's dining table. We are all very hungry and grateful to be eating. Medard, the house manager, brings forward a large platter that he presents to Lily.

"Fish," he says.

Lily, Alan, and Meghan look at me. I grin.

Mama Chakula's house sits on the corner in a neighborhood in Gisenyi. It is a redbrick rambler surrounded by a redbrick wall. The wall is topped with a repeating motif of white barbed arrows to discourage any intruders. From the dirt road, you enter through a painted white metal door to a lovely porch and garden with lime trees and azaleas. The front door opens to a spacious living room with linoleum floors. Two couches are pushed against the white walls with two chairs nearby, creating a comfortable sitting area. On the other side of the room is a long dining room table with a hutch for dishes. The windows looking out to the garden are barred. Each of us has our own bedroom. I make an altar out of the small table against the wall. A green mosquito net is tied in a loose knot above my bed, and we have been instructed to undo it and drape it over us at night. There is a small closet with a lightbulb overhead. My window, also barred with black iron rods, overlooks the outside kitchen that consists of a series of sinks and two fire pits. Meghan and I share a bathroom. Lily has her own. And Alan's room is on the other side of the house off the living room. The house is alive with street sounds, bicycle bells, roosters, children's voices, and birdsong. Twice a day, a parade of prisoners walk by the house, the prison only a few blocks away. At night, you can hear them singing.

I came to Rwanda to step over my fears and find out for myself how a people who carry the history of genocide in their hearts not only begin to heal but move forward in the name of forgiveness and acceptance. This collective crime of cruelty and complicity resides in all of us. I am here in Rwanda floating in the oxbow of my own grief, tired of this ongoing narrative of love and loss. Steve has been dead seven months. And I wonder about the measure and magnitude of one death when weighed against a massacre of millions.

The word "genocide" first appeared in print by the Jewish scholar, Raphael Lemkin in his book *Axis Rule in Occupied Europe*, published in 1944. He took the Greek root *genos* (family, tribe, or race; gene) and combined it with the Latin root *cide* (to massacre or kill). He presented the idea of genocide in 1933 before the Legal Council of the League of Nations conference on international criminal law in Madrid. The concept Lemkin had in mind burned bright through "acts of barbarism" from the calculated killings of Armenians in World War I to the massacre of Assyrians in Iraq in 1933. But the word did not take hold until after the Holocaust. Lemkin finally persuaded the United Nations General Assembly to adopt an internationally accepted definition of genocide crafted during the Convention on the Prevention and Punishment of the Crime of Genocide, on December 9, 1948.

The next day, on December 10, 1948, the General Assembly of the United Nations adopted the Universal Declaration of Human Rights The preamble reads: *Whereas recognition of the inherent dignity and of the equal and inalienable rights of all members of the human family is the foundation of freedom, justice and peace in the world,*

Whereas disregard and contempt for human rights have resulted in barbarous acts which have outraged the conscience of mankind, and the advent of a world in which human beings shall enjoy freedom of speech and belief and freedom from fear and want has been proclaimed as the highest aspiration of the common people,

Whereas it is essential, if man is not to be compelled to have recourse, as a last resort, to rebellion against tyranny and oppression, that human rights should be protected by the rule of law,

Whereas it is essential to promote the development of friendly relations between nations,

Whereas the peoples of the United Nations have in the Charter reaffirmed their faith in fundamental human rights, in the dignity and worth of the human person and in the equal rights of men and women and have determined to promote social progress and better standards of life in larger freedom,

Whereas Member States have pledged themselves to achieve, in co-operation with the United Nations, the promotion of universal respect for and observance of human rights and fundamental freedoms,

Whereas a common understanding of these rights and freedoms is of the greatest importance for the full realization of this pledge.

After witnessing the legacy of bones, these distinguished pieces of paper might has well have been written in smoke. How does a phrase like "Never again" uttered religiously after the Jewish Holocaust, after Cambodia, Rwanda, and now Darfur, translate to "again and again"—the mantra of our collective denial? Code terms like "civil war" and "tribal conflict" give us license not to get involved. The masterminds of all genocides count on our complicity. They plan, calculate, and execute their intent, trusting in our refusal to acknowledge what they are doing. And in the case of America, instead of intervention, our government debated for months whether the mass killings in Rwanda fulfilled the definition of genocide. The manipulation of extinction is done most efficiently through bureaucracies.

We were scheduled to meet with the governor of Gisenyi to go over our proposal for the Genocide Memorial in Rugerero, but the governor had to cancel. We meet with the assistant governor instead. Louis Gakumba is our translator. He is twenty-one years old, elegant and poised. His eyes are almond-shaped and brown with long curled lashes. His skin is the deep hue of chestnuts. And when he smiles, we relax, believing joy can cohabit with hardship. There is a refinement in his speech, and his English is impeccable. His native language is Kinyarwanda, spoken by both Hutu and Tutsi. He also speaks French, Swahili, and two Congolese dialects. This is his first experience as a translator.

Lily shows the assistant governor the design. She explains the white walls around the memorial. How the two towers will also be painted white, then covered in mosaic. She speaks of trees being planted inside, that she hopes it will become a sanctuary of peace and remembrance for all who come to visit.

"Here is the monument with commemorative words," she says, "dedication words. And the purple mosaics behind the words symbolic of the Rwandan color for mourning." Lily talks about painting the village, saying there will be "painted houses, story sticks, all made by the children's designs and drawings."

Louis is trying to stay with her, translating for the assistant governor as she speaks, but he is falling behind, as Lily keeps talking without breaks. Jean Bosco is filling in the gaps seeing what is being lost.

The assistant governor speaks. Louis translates, letting less time go by without interpreting what is being said. "He wants to thank you for coming to Rwanda, and he wishes you a most sincere welcome. And he hopes these things will be done."

"You like right?" Lily asks looking directly into the public official's eyes. "Then we will go together to get permission." She laughs and smiles.

As we walk out of the municipal building, I ask Louis where he learned English. "I taught myself," he says. He sees my puzzled face. "From books. It took me two years." He then smiles. "My brother Michael speaks French very well, better than me. I wanted to speak English better than him." He pauses. "Yeah, that's my brother and me."

The grounds of the orphanage are quiet except for the sound of birds and a teacher's voice. We walk past the open air classroom. The children look up from their notebooks and stare. Some wave. Others look down and giggle. We walk up a flight of stairs on the outside of a building that reminds me of a Best Western Motor Inn. Rosamund Halsey Carr, a formidable presence at age ninety-four, rises from her chair at her desk. She had been in conversation with a woman. She looks anxious. "You couldn't have arrived at a worse time," she says to Jean Bosco. She scolds him for not calling beforehand. "This is Mrs. Merck; her husband was admitted last night to the Gisenyi Hospital because of a terrible kidney stone attack."

We give our condolences. Mrs. Merck looks stressed and frightened. "We had just checked in to the Kivu Sun. The pain came on so suddenly. We didn't know what to do. The hotel sent us to the clinic in Gisenyi. I guess the hospital is all right. The needles they used on my husband were wrapped in plastic." She is pacing. "They have him in a hallway because all the rooms are crowded with patients."

It is an awkward situation filled with silences until Madame Carr says, "But do come in." We shake hands with Madame Carr and Mrs. Merck. We are not invited to sit down. Meghan remarks how beautiful the banner is that hangs behind her desk, the dozens of handprints with the children's names signed inside them to wish Madame Carr a happy birthday.

"Yes, I treasure that. The children made that for my nintieth birthday." She talks about the children, especially the older ones who were orphaned during the genocide, how they were not traumatized until now, when they see these "ghastly images on movies like *Hotel Rwanda*."

When Lily says she had been reading Madame Carr's memoir, *Land of a Thousand Hills,* which Carr wrote with her niece, and how much she was enjoying it, Madame Carr interrupts her. "You are the fourth person who has told me that she wrote the book. She didn't. I did." Another awkward pause and then Lily explains what we are doing here, how she has designed a genocide memorial. She hands Madame Carr the drawing, but she is not interested. "I'm afraid I'm on the opposite side of the fence that you are," Madame Carr said abruptly. "If this country is going to heal, it must focus on the future, not the past." She gets up from her chair and ushers us outside. "I think it's more important for you to visit the children."

Madame Carr, too, is a survivor of the genocide. She belongs to the colonial history of Rwanda, having arrived in the Great Lakes region in 1949 with her British husband, Kenneth Carr, a world-renowned big-game hunter and photographer who was a member of the New York Explorer's Club. They eventually divorced and she ran a pyrethrum plantation in Mugongo, Rwanda. She chose to stay in her home during the conflict until she was finally convinced by the American State Department to leave the country after losing everything, including many beloved Rwandan friends and servants, both Hutu and Tutsi. She lived in California for a year or so but was miserable and returned to her flower farm, only to find her home and gardens in ruins. As a woman in her eighties, she started over from scratch.

On December 17, 1994, she began the Imbabezi Orphanage, fulfilling a need both in Rwanda and in her own heart, having always regretted never having children. Now she has more than one hundred sons and daughters.

We slip into one of the classrooms. The children stand when Madame Carr enters. "Children, we have guests." She disappears and we sit down with the students. One young girl, maybe six or seven years old, comes up to me and says in English, "How many children you have, Mama?" I look at her and say, "None." She looks confused and turns to her teacher, then looks at me again. *"How many children?"* I make a zero sign with my fingers. "Then you choose me," she says, hugging my hips.

Lake Kivu is utterly serene. We are sitting on the beach outside the Kivu Sun Hotel. You would never know that less than a mile away there is a prison packed with genocidaires dressed in pink, that the hospital has no more rooms left for the sick, and that the dusty streets of Gisenyi are filled with orphans begging and wandering among the unemployed men who sit on the curbs and talk among themselves while women farm the fields alone. The stillness and peace of this lake, barely a ripple, belies its history. During the genocide, Lake Kivu was flooded with bloated bodies, an enormous sink of cholera and disease.

Clouds are gathering. Thunder sounds like artillery. Plumes of smoke are rising from the blue haze of the Congo. Night falls in increments. The volcano stands as an open wound.

Jean Bosco arrives at Mama Chakula's house. Alan and Meghan and I are sitting on the patio waiting for Lily. He informs us that someone has died in the village, an accident, hit by a car. "I'm so sorry," I said.

Jean Bosco raises his hands. "It happens." He lights a cigarette and paces in front of the house.

This morning, we tried desperately to get news from the States regarding Katrina. Jean Bosco said he heard on the street that thousands of people were dead because of the hurricane. There is an old television in Mama Chukula's place, run by a generator. We turned it on — no sound. We saw images: New Orleans under water, bloated bodies floating face-down, masses gathered in what looked to be the Superdome, the elderly slumped over in wheelchairs with blankets and sheets draped over them, helicopters rescuing families on rooftops waving white flags. Black faces. The poor. The forgotten. Poverty is exposed for what it is, neglect.

Lily joins us, and we sit down with Jean Bosco on the porch as he explains the Rugerero Genocide Survivors Village to us, providing some background before our first visit. "You see, after the war, the government made a commitment to help the survivors of the 1994 genocide find security and shelter, so they decided to provide housing for those most in need. They set aside small tracts of land and built simple adjoining brick structures covered in gray adobelike material for those who were homeless. One 'house' is built to accommodate two families."

The Village in Rugerero is made up of genocide survivors from Gisenyi, Cyanzarwe, and Kibuye. The individuals and families now living side by side are not related. And for the most part, they did not know each other before being placed together in this makeshift community. (Jean Bosco does not say if the residents were Tutsi or Hutu, only "Rwandans.") In some instances, however, history followed some of the survivors, and all has not been harmonious. Relationships can be strained. But what they all have in common, Jean tells us, is that the killers burned down their houses, murdered family members, and reduced them to refugees in their own country, desperate to find food and shelter. They have moved from place to place, house to house for over a decade. "The people in the Rugerero Genocide Survivors Village have nothing," says Jean Bosco. "Worse than nothing." He goes on to explain, "The survivors would find a house and move in; then the owners would come back and say, 'Move. Get out.' And so the survivors would have to flee again. So you see, the survivors villages throughout Rwanda offer permanent shelter and some manner of security."

"Who decides who is eligible for the genocide survivors villages?" asks Alan.

"Leaders within the larger community decide." says Jean Bosco. "There is a selection process based on need. Once selected, people can live in the houses as if they are theirs, but they cannot sell them. If the parents and children within a particular house pass away, then the government gives the house to another displaced family. If the parents die and the children are left, they can continue to stay in the house."

He tells us that it took five years to complete the Village, which was begun in 1997, because construction was very slow. Very slow. "In this part of Rwanda, we experienced terrible violence after the genocide that remained invisible to the outside world. Ruhengeri, a nearby town, was in a constant state of terror from 1994 through 1998. And here, security was a problem; the burning of cars, the raping of women and killing was still going on even though people around the globe thought the conflict was over. There was great insecurity and instability." He pauses and lights another cigarette. "It's only been recently that we have experienced this kind of peace. During 2000, 2001, and 2002, the Village was still under construction. The government made a contract with the Village to finish the houses, but the construction company stole the money. Finally, in March of 2003, people were able to move in." He pauses. "It's been a very long process."

The Village is stark, with small pueblolike structures built out of cinder blocks. They are covered with gray volcanic stucco containing flecks of mica that reflect light. Painted shutters, some green, some turquoise, some pink, embellish the simple houses. Red azaleas enliven the otherwise drab demeanor of Rugerero. Chickens and goats animate the Village. Dozens of young children follow us, curious and puzzled by these strange visitors.

"How many people live in Rugerero?" asks Lily.

"In the Rugerero Genocide Survivors Village there are close to five hundred people and around one hundred families." Jean Bosco pulls out a piece of paper with a list of statistics. "Out of those families, approximately sixty-seven of them are led by women and eight are led by men. Sadly, there are ten children-led families, the oldest 'child' being twenty-four and the youngest being twelve." Meghan shakes her head, having lost her mother as a child. "Yeah, this is Rwanda," says Jean Bosco. "There are a hundred and ten children in the village. Many of them cannot attend primary or secondary schools because they don't have enough money for school fees."

He explains how in Rwanda, primary school consists of first through sixth grade. This education is free. Even so, most of the young children in the Village cannot afford uniforms and school supplies, and therefore stay home. Each child needs two uniforms that cost five thousand francs, about $10 American. Without uniforms, they cannot attend school. School funds for secondary school costs on the average about $150 per student. There is a government association known as F.A.R.G. that supplies money and materials for those students in need. They select a few students each year inside the Village to support if they have GPA over 60 percent.

My heart breaks. I think of the small hands that are open along every dirt road in Rwanda, hands that could hold a pencil, hungry to learn how to write.

We are greeted by Mukanfwije Emma. Her home is in the heart of the Village. She meets Lily with her hands clasped. Lily places her hands around hers and bows. They had met one year ago. Mama Emma is an elder, seventy-two years old, one of the oldest women in Rugerero. Her face is as a testament to survival, an erosional beauty born through time. Her eyes look down, only down.

Nyiranshuti Dorothée is a community leader. She is a stunning woman with a gracious presence, wrapped in a blue and black batik kaftan, eight and a half months pregnant. She takes us on a tour of the Village. We step to the side of the dirt path between houses as cars and trucks return from the church. A coffin is being carried in the back of a flatbed truck. Walking through the Village, we cross the line of mourners winding their way back through the Village. We stop and shake each hand, kiss the cheeks of the bereaved three times. I recognize these eyes of mourning.

The memorial site is less than a mile from the Village. It is little more than a field of lava stones with a corrugated tin roof perched on four wooden posts to protect where the bones are buried. Banana trees border the field. A primary school is adjacent to the site. Eldefons, one of the community leaders, says, "This is the place we buried our people with the little money we had to keep the bones safe. We will move the bodies while the new memorial is being built. And then we hope to make a big house where people can meet and talk about the genocide." "You mean something like a community center?" Lily asks. "Yes. A place where we can gather." He pauses. "Maybe even with a library where our children could read about our history." Eldefons tells Lily he would like the memorial all on one level so a car could pull up from the road and visit easily. With Louis translating they discuss details.

The children—the children—they gather around us, hundreds of children. Nothing could have prepared me for the joy and the hunger in their large, penetrating eyes. Barefoot. All of them are barefoot, barely clothed, barely fed, many wearing discarded American T-shirts that become dresses for the little girls.

A boy across the road holds his hands together and whistles. We motion him to join us, but he is too wary to come near.

Datura is growing here. Datura is also growing at home in Castle Valley. Moonflower. Gypsum weed. The strongest of hallucinogenic plants. I speak with one of the women tending seedlings adjacent to the memorial. With Louis's help, I ask her what she knows about this plant. *"Very, very powerful medicine."* She says it helps women with abortions. She also says when the seeds are ingested, it creates "a terrible beauty."

Louis explains to the woman that I know this plant in America, that it grows where I live and causes visions, even death. They have a spirited conversation. "This woman knows." He searches for the word. "How do I say this?" "An herbalist?" I say. "Yes, that's it, like my mother. She understands which plants are medicine and can cure people's illnesses. She tends this nursery for its healing herbs." They continue their conversation as I kneel to get a closer look at her seedlings, their roots held together in small black plastic containers.

The vice mayor arrives on a motorcycle driven by a Muslim gentleman, who is dressed in an orange tunic and cap. He gets off the bike and walks over to Lily and Jean Bosco. They shake hands. Jean Bosco and the vice mayor speak. Louis translates: *"The vice mayor met Lily last year and talked to her about this site. Then Lily went home, but she said she would come back. The vice mayor thanks you for coming back. He says after the genocide things were terrible and that it brought terrible things, poverty,* orphans. *The community decided to make a memory, a memorial to take all the parts, the bones, and bring them together as human beings. The genocide was not only one place but every place in Rwanda. Everywhere. The government said we will not just have one memorial, but in each providence, near the road, we will have memorials, so people can remember, can see it from their rearview mirror as they drive on. The way the memorial is built now in the Village is not good enough. To have your help now to make it more comfortable, more beautiful, is appreciated.*

"What happened here can happen anywhere. We are all human beings. We will work together. We will put this memorial back together. Thank you."

The vice mayor then says in English, "I understand you are here for the month. When are you coming back?"

Lily explains that even when we are away, the work will continue under Jean Bosco's leadership.

The vice mayor stands up and claps his hands, then jumps back on the motorcycle and disappears.

We are not tourists. We are not genocide voyeurs. We are here to work, and we are coming back.

We spend the evening with Jean Bosco and his family: his wife, Jacqueline; his eldest and youngest sisters; his sister-in-law. Also present are their seven children: Franceza (an orphan they have adopted); Muhire Jean de Dein, Tuyishime Jean Claude, Twizere Jimy, Kanyange Divine, Mukiza Roger, and Ndayambaje Jules. They sing for us in Kinyarwanda, in French, and in English.

Lily has gifts for all the children—puzzle books, windsocks, pens, paper, Chinese checkers—and a shawl for Jacqueline. On behalf of our team of Barefoot Artists, we present Jean Bosco with a special gift, a white beaded medicine shield from the Ute Nation, a beautiful pendant that a friend, Ruth Cuch, who is Ute, gave our family maybe forty years ago. It is secured on white deerskin. Jean Bosco receives the necklace with great solemnity. He says, "You honor me. You have made me a king." It is as though the mantle of dignity of the Ute People was met with the dignity of the Rwandan People, both peoples of genocide. He says that we are now part of his family and that everyone in the community will help us, whatever we need, that we are one people joined together to heal a great wound.

Lily thanks Jean Bosco for his generosity and leadership. She tells his children about Martin Luther King, Jr. She says that there was a song that strengthened Martin Luther King and other Americans in the United States in their struggle for equality.

"I would like to teach everyone this song." She begins to sing *"We shall overcome . . ."* In Jean Bosco's living room, seven children, a mother and father, aunts and extended family members, and four barefoot artists sing "We Shall Overcome" together.

I think about Pete Seeger in the early 1950s, who adapted the spiritual, "We Will Overcome," an old gospel song from the Deep South during the Civil War, and arranged it for contemporary times. Having been asked to teach at the Highlander Folk School in Tennessee, a school for activists interested in labor organizing and social change, he included music as an essential part of the curriculum. Seeger introduced the song to the participants at the conference, Martin Luther King, Jr., and Rosa Parks among them. They heard this song for the first time here, a song that would be burned into their hearts and would sing the civil rights movement forward.

Whatever boundaries and borders had been drawn inside of me are trembling, breaking down and shattering. We stand in a circle holding hands and sing with an understanding that our lives depend on the solidarity of our voices rising in the humble household of a family in Gisenyi.

One heart opens to another, as we dare to engage, to feel, to speak, to sing. Why do we hesitate?

In matters of justice where is our outrage? Where is our love?

I hear William Coffin's voice, *"The world is too dangerous for anything but truth and too small for anything but love."*

Social change depends on love.

For this one night in Gisenyi, we are taken into the arms of a family in Rwanda. Inside the warmth of Jean Bosco's house, I can still imagine the terror of those years of war when a knock at the door meant death.

I just spoke with Brooke on Alan's satellite phone. What to say in one minute?

Is everything okay at home?

Katrina. One thousand dead.
Bush absent, incompetent.
America is outraged.
And you?

I am well. It's good. It's hard.
The full range of emotion:
A bag of skulls, a bag of potatoes,
both tilled from the same fields:

I love you. I miss you.
Give everyone my love at home.

I love you, too.
Please take special care—

Good night.

This morning, I take a brisk walk through Gisenyi to orient myself. I want to get a sense of the town where we are living, roughly nine miles from the Village in Rugerero. As I head toward the market, groups of men, young and old, begin to heckle me, jeering and laughing. I look straight ahead only to be approached by a man with a crutch who is missing his left leg from the knee down. He speaks to me. I don't understand. He holds out his hand. Now I do, and I give him the Rwandan francs that I have in my pocket. It isn't enough. He grows impatient, shakes his head, and moves on. Women pass with baskets of bananas on their head and smile. I smile back. Four small boys follow me, practicing their English, tugging at my shirt. "Hello, madame, how are you?" *"Muzungu! Muzungu!"* Bicycles flash by, their drivers ringing bells to tell me that I am in their way; trucks and motorbikes speed by too close for comfort. Dust envelops me, and I cover my mouth with my scarf. The chaos grows as the crowds grow. All roads lead to the market, as the pulse of Gisenyi intensifies. Western Union is on my left. An internet café with wooden benches outside is on my right. There is a bank with people openly making deals for the best exchange rate. A barber shop. A bike repair shop. A hardware store with men next door shining shoes. Six women are crouched down around a blue plastic tub in front of what appears to be clinic. Looking sideways, I see a baby with its eyes closed and legs folded. I think the baby is dead. On either side of the dirt road are trenches half filled with water and trash, the acrid stench of urine and rotting food swirls around toilet paper, discarded diapers, and single shoes floating sole side up.

Inside the market, the labor of women is in full display: tall triangular mounds of potatoes, purple, red, and white; beans, string beans, yellow beans, black beans, kidney beans, more varieties than I could ever imagine, which women dip from full burlap sacks with tin cups, selling them to other women; carrots; cabbage; corn; cassava; spinach; sorghum and all manner of grains from oats to barley to wheat create a colorwheel of produce next to piles of polished avocados. The smell of coffee alone induces a euphoria in me, and I purchase a pound. Young women stand with stalks of sugar cane taller than they are. Older women sit on stools with rainbow umbrellas shieding them from the sun as their daughters sell their harvest. On the periphery of the market are lines of black sewing machines with gold trim, the kind my grandmother had, with men sitting behind them rapidly stitching together school uniforms out of royal blue cotton and khaki as mothers wait with their children. Deeper into the market, there are clothes of every kind, shirts, blouses, skirts, and pants, new and used, and I duck to avoid brushing my head against all that is hanging. An acre of shoes stretches toward socks and bras and panties and briefs. Bolts of colored cloth, Indonesian batiks, some already cut to wrap around waists, are clothes-pinned on rope lines that flap in the wind; soccer balls; brushes and combs; creams and cosmetics; radios; records; a tower of cassettes from rap to jazz to African music; videos; magazines; dishes, pots and pans, appliances; and then at the far end of the market, I can first smell, then see live chickens, eggs, baskets of fish, fresh and dried minnows from Lake Kivu, and then hanging from hooks is the red marbled meat of goats and cows, with the large pieces being cut into smaller ones on a table. Anything you could want or need is here.

I am sitting against a tree wishing I could disappear. The physical and psychic assault of Africa has deflated me. I close my eyes. Three girls suddenly grab my hands and pull me up, pushing me toward the school where dozens and dozens of children follow, running, laughing, and tugging at my skirt. Meghan is behind me with her own group of children. Desperate to stem the chaos, I sit down on the ground, making a circle with my hands. Miraculously, the children sit down with me, and then with Louis's help, they move back to enlarge the circle so more kids can join us.

"My name is Terry," I say, then clap, looking at the child sitting next to me. "My name is Olive," she says and claps! "My name is Jean Claude." Clap! "My name is Vincent." Clap! The tempo picks up. "My name is Yvonne." Clap! And so the children's names become a game if cadence and rhythm moving energetically through the circle like an electrical current. And then spontaneously the children begin to sing. Olive sings with a deep, haunting voice. More songs emerge, many of them Christian songs the children learned in church.

Suddenly, the children start clapping their hands and calling my name. I don't know what they want. Louis turns to me and says, "They want you to sing them a song—teach them a song." My mind, in a panic, goes blank. A song? I can't remember any song. Finally (with Louis translating), I say, "Okay, this is a very silly song. It's about a food called 'Jell-O.' " I jiggle my body, and they jiggle theirs, all of us laughing.

I began to sing:

> *Oh, the big red letters stand for the Jell-O family—*
> *Oh, the big red letters stand for the Jell-O family—*
> *It's Jell-O—yum, yum, yum*
> *Jell-O Pudding—yum, yum, yum*
> *Jell-O Tapioca pudding—try all three!*

The children are laughing hysterically, at me, at my singing, and I cannot believe that the only song that came to me was a Mormon camp ditty, that I learned when I was eight years old.

Louis tries to explain to the children what Jell-O is. He looks at me completely puzzled, "What should I say?" "Tell them it looks like a fat man's belly that jiggles when he's laughing. Tell them its green and comes in cold square cubes." Louis raises his eyebrows. "Tell them it's like squishy candy and you can eat it with a spoon."

Whatever Louis tells them, the children are rolling with laughter.

Meghan moves us foward with a chant of her own. We enter a musical trance. In the dreamscape of afternoon heat, the African sun beats like a drum, moving one tiny girl. She jumps into the center of the circle and dances. With her eyes closed, she twirls and twirls. The children clap as she rises and falls like a scarf being blown up and down by the wind. Other girls join her, one with her hands in a prayer shape above her head. More begin to dance and sing on the edges of bones, impatient bones that are crying to be buried.

Louis whispers in my ear, "No one can rob these children of their joy."

At the genocide site, where there are more children still, Lily calls them together. All eyes are on her. She picks up two rocks and raises the lava stones high above her head. She then ritualistically places them down by her feet beneath a line of twine that Alan and Damas used to mark the boundaries of the site. Lily makes a rectangle with her hands in the air and then points to the children and claps her hands. The children understand and begin gathering rocks and placing them below the twine. Within minutes, the children have enclosed the sacred space with lava stones. The boundaries of the memorial are set.

When I asked Lily how she had thought of this, she said smiling, "I'm Chinese; I know a workforce when I see one."

"Right now, I think God is with us," she says to Alan, Meghan, and me, as we sit outside on the patio. "The Chinese contractor is here in Gisenyi once every two months. Mr. Yu works for a company based in Beijing with ties in Rwanda for the past eight years. I spoke with him on the telephone today. He will meet with me tomorrow. Cement is very expensive, eight times what it costs in China. I will show him the design. He said they will do whatever we need

"The first stage will be to level the site. We will need surveyors. Mr. Yu promises to give me the best price because I speak Mandarin. But, I have no idea how much it is going to cost . . . thousands, tens of thousands?" "Lava stones or bricks?" she asks Alan. "We'll just have to price it out," says Alan, "and see what is available." Lily tells Alan she will price out the room for bones with Mr. Yu as well. "There has to be an underground room for the bones with ventilation." Lily is thinking outloud. "Cement is too expensive. Lava with cement binder will be better. Mr. Yu will supervise." Lily looks at Jean Bosco. "So we start on Monday."

Damas stands up and begins chanting, *"Oh—oh—oh—oh,"* clapping his hands. Jean Bosco lets out a deep belly laugh and raises his hands up to the sky. "God places his benediction on this," he says. It begins to rain.

This morning at breakfast, I ask Lily when compromise is appropriate. After a moment of silence, she says, "Compromise is fine on anything that is not essential, but you cannot compromise your principles. You cannot compromise the dream or the dream dies, and you suffer spiritually."

She spoke about not liking to talk about politics, per se, that her reasons are rooted in her strict Chinese upbringing. Her father, Pei Kao Yeh, was a general in Chiang Kai-shek's army, the only victory China sustained in World War II, what the Chinese call their Normandy. "By living your principles, you are political," she says. "Living your values is political."

In the Municipal Center in Cyanzarwe, you feel the cold, sharp-edged reality of poverty. Women line the benches outside, most with babies wrapped around their waists. Their eyes are distant and tired, even though their clothing is bright. Soldiers dressed in maroon uniforms stand around a tree in the courtyard waving their AK-47s as they talk. We enter the community building. The smells, how to describe them? Walking down the long hall painted turquoise, light paints the side walls green, walls covered with handprints and stained with mold. The closed air in this narrow space smells of tin, sweat laced with dust. It has a bite to it.

Mr. Safari Kazindu Patrick, mayor of Rugerero, welcomes us into his office and invites us to sit down. He is wearing a green sport coat, pink checked shirt with a peach tie and khaki pants. A portrait of President Paul Kagame hangs on the wall behind him. The new Rwandan flag sits on his desk. He explains the colors and their significance within the three bands: a green base which is emblematic of the land, a yellow line that is the horizon, and a large light blue space with a sun in the corner that appears as the Rwandan sky. The mayor stands and shows us the new Rwandan coat of arms that is displayed as a wall hanging with its various images: a basket, a wheel, and a shield for protection and security. "These symbols represent patriotism, unity, and work. All of us in Rwanda are working for the reconstruction of our country."

He introduces us to members from the Survivors Village in Rugerero. Once again, Louis translates. Liberata is the president of the Council of Women in the Survivors Village. She is a well-dressed woman in Western clothes who has the same eyes as Belyse from Nyamata, heavy with sorrow. Eldefons sits next to Liberata. We had met him before at the memorial site. He is the president of the Survivors Village. And next to him sits Roselyn, a student at the university in Gisenyi, who is the Village's secretary. She must be in her midtwenties, beautiful, vibrant, and poised.

Jean Bosco introduces us as "Barefoot Artists" and then tells the mayor about Lily coming to Rwanda, how she saw the memorial site, visited the Village at Rugerero, and then created a sketch of the Genocide Memorial. He tells the story of taking us to Nyamata and Ntarara and how moved we were, how we were strengthened by all we saw, felt, and heard. "Lily has a heart to do something and there is a whole community with great hearts who want to do something together," says Jean Bosco as he points to Liberata and Eldefons and Roselyn.

Lily stands. "Thank you for this opportunity to show you our design for the memorial." She places the drawing on his desk. Everyone gathers round to see the white stucco Gaudi-like pavilion surrounded by an undulating wall. Lily references the colors of Rwanda—green, yellow, blue—on the Rwandan flag and the use of purple to commemorate mourning, colors that could be incorporated in the art of mosaic. "We can find broken tiles, very inexpensive. Very colorful. We can train people within the community and teach them how to make this kind of art. We can make the memorial beautiful with mosaic."

Lily shows the community leaders photographs from the Village of Arts and Humanities to give them an idea of her work. "This is a very poor community in America." She flashes the images before them. "Before—after; before—after. Empty lots become gardens. Abandoned land becomes a meditation park. Employed adults."

The community leaders look at the photographs of the people working together in Philadelphia, the details of the murals, the mosaic sculptures, and the walls embellished with flowers, trees, and angels.

"This is our angel." Lily kisses her fingers and touches the angel's mosaic face. "This is good, no?" She shows them a photograph of a community garden. "You see here how we are planting vegetables, training young people to be farmers."

Liberata smiles and nods to Safari.

"See here the celebration, the ceremony. The art, the colors, the transformation of the neighborhood brings people together."

Lily's words have the sound of incantation.

Jean Bosco tells the mayor that the land at the memorial site has been measured, the boundaries set with stones, placed by the hands of children, and that a Chinese contractor has been found, and that Lily has met with him and negotiated a contract. Mayor Safari asks, *What about the memorial that is already there and the bones that are already buried at the site?* Jean Bosco explains that the community knows it is temporary, that the land must be leveled and the bones will be transferred to a safe place until the final bone chamber is constructed beneath the memorial.

The mayor listens intently and then he speaks: *In this district, we have big problems and many big challenges. The government has a Development Millennia Goal known as Vision 20/20. After twenty years, we believe we can eradicate poverty, alleviate welfare in Rwanda by focusing on the genocide survivors. This is the target and priority of the government to raise their welfare. These are our priorities in Rwanda and in Rugerero:*

1. *Security*
2. *Shelter—shelter for both the bones of our dead and the living.*
3. *Welfare—food and medical care, with an emphasis on widows and children-headed households created by the genocide.*

The pillars of our developmental goals are as follows:

1. *to raise our economy*
2. *to struggle for the educational and medical welfare of the population*

There are a large number of women-headed households and children-headed households, many in the Rugerero Survivors Village. Victims of genocide are more vulnerable than others in terms of access to medical care, clean water, and welfare.

He outlines a plan set forward by President Paul Kagame:

1. *A national insurance program is under way. They pay three thousand francs a year for those who can pay. Genocide survivors are free.*
2. *The government is trying to solve the problem of shelter because of the small amount of land. This is a big problem. People are living in plastic sheeting and small huts made of banana leaves.*
3. *The problem of water is very large in villages within my district. Because it is a volcanic area, there is an absence of water. This is a critical concern. We get water from the river, take water from the river. It is not sufficient. UNICEF is assisting us by supplying pipelines. Another program is to train people to collect water from roots with rain water. Water is captured in storage tanks. The population is aware, but it requires technical assistance.*

"This can be done," says Lily. "We can help with this technology."

Mayor Safari talks about the Kigali Institute of Solar Technology and how they are implementing new energy technologies in Rwanda. He explains the shortage of firewood and the importance of solar cookers over charcoal in how women cook food.

"To save our forests is imperative so Rwanda doesn't become a desert. Without forests we cannot hold the rain, therefore we have a degraded environment."

"All these issues relate to each other," says Mayor Safari *"to the structures of poverty compounded by the genocide."* From Mayor Safari's perspective, the Genocide Memorial Project falls under the category of "shelter." A sheltering of bones. A shelter for surviving hearts. A refuge, a sanctuary where loved ones can unite, body and spirit, in peace and in place. And the Rwandan people wish it to be beautiful and near by the road for all to see. He looks at Lily. *"How long will it take to complete the Genocide Monument?"*

"I imagine two years, and we will need the names of those who will be buried there, so they can be honored."

"We would appreciate it if the memorial could be completed and dedicated by April 7, 2006," the mayor says abruptly.

Lily whispers, "Oh my god," and leans into Louis with her hand over her forehead. "With my friends," Jean Bosco says, *"Take bazo"* "No problem." "We will try," Lily says.

"I will need a well-established document of your plan of action: the timeline for this project, your schedule, and the budget." The mayor smiles, *"I learned about you from President Kagame, who was here last year at a special town meeting when you visited Gisenyi."* The mayor folds his arms. *"We appreciate your initiative. You have a humanitarian heart. You have created a plan that reflects our feelings."* There is a long silence. *"The angels are ready to receive these restless souls to heaven."*

We stand. Jean Bosco thanks Mayor Safari for his time. We shake hands.

We return to the memorial site. Mr. Yu is engaged. By the time we leave, he promises Lily that the ground will be cleared, leveled, the room below the memorial will be dug and the platform foundation poured. Lily also wants the stone path leading up to the monument finished. She also imagines the curving design around the memorial to be drawn in flour so they can follow the undulations. "The last stage will be to cover the memorial with mosaics." she says. "We can find broken pieces of tile that can be used to decorate the surface of the outside walls." She smiles. "I will teach the men and the women in the Village how to create beautiful mosaics with what has been thrown away." She bends down and picks up terra-cotta shards. "These are everywhere." Lily turns to me. "We are all broken somewhere. Putting the pieces together while using vibrant color creates joy in the bleakest of places."

Lily and I are sitting on the porch of Kivu Sun with Damas and his friend, Brown. Both are from Kigali. Damas is the only survivor in his immediate family. He is supporting fifteen orphans. Brown is assisting ten orphans. Damas asks us to help him pay for the education fees for his fifteen orphans—twenty-five dollars per child, per year. His phone keeps ringing; it is his cousin from Ruhengeri, who he has asked to come see us. "She is poor," he says. "She needs help." Throughout the evening, Damas asks for more and more. "Terry," he says his head turned sideways, "a car—I need a car—only eight thousand American dollars." He talks about not being able to go to the university because he has to provide for his family.

"What would you like to study?" I ask.

"What would I want to study?"

"Yes," I say.

"What do you want me to study?"

"That doesn't matter, Damas. What matters is what you want."

"Law," he says. "I want to study law. I want to study law so I can help the orphans."

His cousin-sister arrives, dripping wet, from Ruhengeri, having ridden on the back of a motor bike in the rain. She walks in, soaked, in her black leather jacket, her eyes focused down. Damas introduces us. Yvette Uwizeyimana wants to be a journalist. She is nineteen years old. She was nine at the time of the war. She looks frightened. She understands English but is shy. Yvette tells me in an almost hushed voice that she wants "to tell the story of Rwanda—it's beauty, the mountains, the story of the genocide."

Lily, Damas, and Brown walk outside to get into the vehicle. Yvette and I follow them. Suddenly, she speaks. "Please help me. I want to go to school." She looks directly into my eyes.

Anywhere we walk, hands are open from beggars on the street to those we are working with. How can we turn away? What is fair? Are we supporting and encouraging a culture of dependence?

The only thing I know how to do is listen. Overwhelmed and confused, I understand Damas's desperate plea but don't know how to handle his requests.

In bed, beneath a green mosquito net, I listen to the rain fall on our tin roof. I cannot sleep.

We speak and act out of our own understanding. Rwanda is changing me. To see steep green hillsides plowed by women, eroding, as they feed their families, to feel the fragments of war lodged in every story told, to smell death trapped in walls, and taste dust, even in rain, is to hear a very different rhythm in the way people live. The backdrop and context of genocide is flooding my imagination.

A spectacular lizard is climbing a tree: turquoise head, black shoulders gradually changing into dark green to green-yellow to a bright yellow tail. The stunning reptile is three feet long. It feels good to walk, to rest my wild eyes on lizards, trogans, and colorful unknown birds, all of them new species for me. Beauty is not a luxury but a strategy for survival.

I visit an arts and crafts store. As my eyes adjust to the dark interior after coming in from direct sunlight, I notice a spiral carved on a flat piece of wood, painted in black and white. I am walking a spiral. The shop is crowded with masks from the Congo. Each one is an animated emotion. Anger. Fear. Awe. War gods and fertility goddesses. Objects that once belonged to the reliquaries of the dead. Who knows whose eyes have peered through them. I worked in a museum for too many years not to understand that no artifact is neutral. Out of context, they frighten me. They are imbued with the powers and intentions of their creators.

I meet Vincent Juarez, a U.S. Marine just sent to Rwanda on September 1, 2005. He can't tell me why he is here in Rwanda. But he does say, "The government doesn't like the vibes in Kigali. We're here to protect the U.S. Embassy."

He is the first marine to be sent to Rwanda, and five more troops are being sent in October. He is staying at the Kivu Sun with his new girlfriend, who works with USAID. He has been in the country all of five days. He is from New Mexico and recently served in Iraq but was sent home because of injuries. A long, jagged scar runs across his shoulder and down his right arm. "I'm fine, now." he says. "Listen, can you help me out with something?"

"Of course, if I can."

"There was a war here, right?" He looks side to side. He is serious. "I mean, could you sort of fill me in on what happened?"

In the midst of the genocide, Ingabire Fedele was nine years old. Right before she was murdered, she turned to her mother and said, *"Gusenga"* which means "pray."

Mr. Yu has delivered. The ground is being leveled. Hundreds of children stand on stone walls watching. This rich black soil is being moved. There are twelve Rwandan men with shovels. One caterpillar with a central blade is clearing the lava field. What is the name of this tractor? My brothers would know. I watch these men with shovels in hand. I am mindful of the intersection made with my own family. My father. My grandfather. My great-grandfather. Of my brother who mobilized his men from his deathbed to help the town of St. George, Utah, as the Santa Clara River was flooding. "I want our trucks to be in front of the mayor's office before sunrise," he said to his cousin Bob passionately over the telephone. "And when the mayor arrives at work, I want our men to ask one question, 'How can we help?' "

Mr. Yu is helping. The men with the shovels are helping. The Bone Room is being dug.

Dirt—the prairie dog mounds, the graves of genocide, the grave of my brother—who can fathom the meaning of holding a fistful of dirt?

We are all laborers.

The site for the Genocide Memorial is cleared. One sacred datura still stands. Its white luminous blossom survives.

We are about an hour away, maybe less from Ruhengeri, the town where one begins the trek to the Volcanoes National Park where Dian Fossey and Amy Vedder did their historic work on gorillas. There are approximately 300 mountain gorillas living in 420 square kilometers that cuts across the Congo, Rwanda, and Uganda. Researchers say there are between 140 and 150 gorillas in Rwanda. In 1983, Dian Fossey talked about the fate of gorillas being directly tied to the well-being of local Rwandans. She believed that the Volcanoes National Park could not be protected for the gorillas' sake; it had to be for the Rwandans' sake because the mountains are where the water is stored, which is essential to the farmers' survival.

She writes:

> American and European concepts of conservation, especially preservation of wildlife, are not relevant to African farmers already living above the carrying capacity of their land. Instead, local people need to be educated about the absolute necessity of maintaining the mountains as a water catchment area. The farmers need to know, not too much about what foreigners think about gorillas, but rather that, 10 percent of all rain that falls on Rwanda is caught by the Virungas and is slowly released to irrigate the crops below. Each farming family's personal survival depends upon the survival of the Parc de Volcans. Cultivation of this vital catchment area would mean virtually the end of both present and future crops. If the importance of the ecosystem to the lives of the populace becomes a prime local priority, which is not the case, the rain forest might stand a chance to survive, and with it the animals it contains and the people who rely upon it.

This is the argument for the surviving wilderness on the planet. It has to be inextricably linked to cultural values as well as ecological ones. Amy Vedder, who has served on the Governing Council of The Wilderness Society (and now works for them), came back to Rwanda shortly after the war in 1995, to find most of her friends, many of them Hutu, dead. The gorillas were also victims of the genocide. Much of their habitat was burned for charcoal. Poaching escalated. Who was enforcing laws to protect gorillas when no one was adhering to laws of any kind, except the prescribed law of killing innocent people?

I have met only one person in the Village who has ever seen a gorilla. It was a woman who was running from the *genocidaires*. As she was fleeing up the flanks of the volcano, she saw a silverback from the corner of her eye.

I dream of one day being able to enter the bamboo forest, slippery and steep in the upper reaches of the volcano. It is an arduous trek, and one must have a permit. The Rwandan government gives out between sixteen and thirty-two permits a day. You must have a Rwandan guide. I would love to visit the gorillas, to witness them in the wild, to experience our kinship as primates. But the expense is high, around six hundred dollars per person. It is difficult to justify the cost when we are working in the Village where the needs are so great. For roughly six hundred dollars, six orphans could attend secondary school.

From the Village, I look to the flanks of the volcanoes, knowing bands of gorillas are surviving, slowly, deliberately, going about their business of foraging and socializing as they quietly move through the forests, families, watching change come to them from all directions. There is less and less room to move. The gorillas gaze is looking down on us. They are a hidden but felt presence.

The clouds—the clouds have become my refuge—the clouds and Lake Kivu. Looking up and looking out to the horizon—the only release from the high population density of Rwanda. No silence. Buddhism originated in densely populated countries, where there was little open space. You turn inward from the outward chaos searching for peace. For the first time in my life, I am sitting. Call it meditation. Call it survival.

Sanity is a stillness of soul.

I wasn't the only one who noticed the sacred datura that survived the bulldozer. Today, as I left the site to return to our vehicle, I felt a tug on my shirt. I turned around and there was my young friend, who does not speak, holding the plant, which was as tall as he was, roots and all. He had noticed my affection for the flower. Startled, what could I do but bend down and smile, eye to eye with this orphaned child, and accept his gift. "*Murakoze*," I said.

Gisenyi at night is dirt roads pocked with ruts and holes and wandering shadows. Goma, adjacent to Gisenyi, is where millions of Hutu refugees gathered after the genocide, many of them killers, who suffered from hunger and disease, especially cholera. Mistaking the perpetrators for the surviving victims of genocide, the United States offered them humanitarian aid.

Gisenyi at night is also filled with surprises. I walked into the house alone, lit a candle, and found four men in the living room staring. The prison is not far down the road. Groups of prisoners walk freely through the streets of Gisenyi, twice a day, with only one armed guard watching them. They pass by our residence frequently. Mama Chakula's well-meaning guard sees himself more as a greeter, bringing into the house a stream of visitors from the street. On another night, a frantic woman entered the house and searched madly through our rooms after dinner. There was no one in the house to translate; we had no idea what she was saying or wanting. We felt helpless. A man began knocking on the door, vehemently, adding further confusion to the situation. We later learned he was her husband, and they were anxious to find a place to stay.

Afterward, with no electricity, the house dark with candles burning, we fell into fear. Imagination seized our throats. We realized we were prisoners in our own habitation. The windows were barred with metal grates. The back doors were locked. None of us had keys. If a fire started in the back bedrooms, we had no way of getting out. In truth, the real prison that held us captive was our own minds.

It is so easy to spiral into fear toward paranoia. We become the terror that possesses us.

Over and over again, I am reminded to live and work out of my strength, not my weaknesses, to stand in the center of my most generous self and trust what is good in humanity. More often than not, we will draw the generosity of others toward us. But here in Rwanda, all these platitudes of what one believes and how one behaves evaporate on the dusty red roads. Neighbors murdered neighbors. Priests called the machete bearers into their churches and allowed them to slaughter their congregations. Nothing makes sense. Everything and everyone becomes suspect. My heart trembles. I become my own darkness. At night in Gisenyi, the only buffer between me and the haunted streets of Rwanda is a torn mosquito net.

Lily Yeh: I have seen her worry as she carries the weight of this project. None of us can ease her burden. I have seen her grace, her enthusiasm, her deep sorrow and tears at Nyamata, with her hand on the brick memorial, bent over, wretching in grief. I have seen her as tyrant. "Do you want to build this monument or not?" And the impatience that is hers when nothing is happening. I have also seen her as pied piper, facing the children with a full-bodied joy, her eyes locked on theirs, as she teaches them Chinese folk songs, gestures and all, her head rising only a few inches from where they stand—and her delight as the children follow her, chanting these new foreign words at the top of their little lungs. I have felt her great humor as we have laughed louder than I thought possible and processed together the complications of being here. We have to laugh or we will not survive the sadness that can be felt like humidity as it seeps into our skin. It doesn't mean we are not scared. I am scared most of the time, but it can't get in the way of our work. I am just trying to stay present, to be of use.

Nothing is set; all is fluid. Every day we make adjustments as we work together as a team. Alan knows how to take Lily's vision and make it concrete. While she takes the children's images and transposes them onto the walls of houses in the Village, he organizes the Village to help paint them; then he chalks in the border designs that will run below Lily's artistry.

"Do I know a lot?" Lily asks. "No. I only know how to paint. My work is about reconnecting what is broken, healing what is wounded, and making visible the invisible." Lily told me yesterday as we were walking in the Village. "In this way, the work cuts through racial, class, geographic, and ethnic separations directly connecting people to their hearts, minds, and emotions. When this happens, transformation occurs." She stops and looks at me. "So often people ask me what they can we do; I just say, 'Do something.' "

The governor of Gisenyi, Barengayabo Ramadhan, invites us to his office for a conversation. His countenance is stern. His eyes unwavering. He asks us to explain the project since we are working in the region of Cyanzarwe in the village of Rugerero, all part of the Gisenyi Province.

Because Jean Bosco is attending a Red Cross meeting, his associate, Habumugisha Michel, recounts our history:

"Everyone is an ambassador of Rwanda, to build pride in our country, to forgive, to forget. This is the message Paul Kagame presented last year to the people of Rwanda. So, when Jean Bosco attended an international meeting in Barcelona, he was our ambassador, telling the people present about our past, our pain, our beauty. Lily Yeh, who was sitting in the audience, was very moved by Jean Bosco's story. Lily asked, 'How can I help?' Jean Bosco said, 'Come to Rwanda.' And she did. She heard President Kagame speak. Jean Bosco took Lily to the Genocide Memorial Site in Rugerero. She was very touched and asked if something beautiful could be created."

With each public official we meet, the story of Lily and her Barefoot Artists becomes longer and more involved. The longer we are here, the longer the story.

Michel tells the story of how the children created the boundaries with stones and how the Chinese showed up with their backhoes and trucks, how the memorial site is now cleared.

The governor looks puzzled; he is concerned about the bones, how they will be moved from one memorial to another.

Michel steps in to explain. The governor wants to have metal shelves for bones, not cement. Mildew would enter the bones and begin to deteriorate them. The governor says if you place coffins on cement, they deteriorate in this humid climate. He wants a detailed plan of action just like Mayor Safari.

Meghan speaks about how she is so impressed by the way in which everyone is working together, how engaged the village of Rugerero is in the project. She explains how excited the children are about their artwork and how their original designs are appearing as paintings on their houses in the Village.

Now the governor speaks. Louis translates:

He is happy to receive you and thanks you for addressing our wound. This is not a Rwandan problem. This is a human problem, and it should make all of us rise together in unity and reconciliation and say, 'NEVER AGAIN.' Genocide was first committed in the heart. The people who committed the genocide, those who fled to other countries, those individuals, those countries who turned their backs, must bear the pressure and the pain of what happened also. The sin will remain in their hearts. They cannot hide. What you saw is enough in Nyamata, Ntarama, but there are hundreds more. Even though we need reconciliation, those genocidaires must be punished. We have to look at what will build a good society. We must punish the ones who did this, who committed these horrific crimes against neighbors and fellow countrymen and women and children. Here in Rwanda, 'Gacaca' is where people get together and talk among themselves, 'I saw this; I saw this'; 'the scene was so heavy.' We need to have 'a forgiving heart.' But it is very difficult to forgive and forget.

I begin to understand how he wears his responsibility of governance like a heavy cloak.

He continues to talk; now he is speaking English.

In Rwanda, we lost more than one million people. To put things back together is very difficult with little resources. This requires people to give of themselves.

The first donation given is in the mind—actions follow, the governor says.

This is the way we work together. As you have seen the problem and felt it, we ask you to be ambassadors. He smiles. *I would like to ask each of you to become ambassadors of Rwanda.*

He stands up behind his desk and walks around the room shaking hands with each of us.

The mood in his office lightens. We take photographs with the governor. He takes off his suit coat and puts on his leather jacket and is completely animated. We are laughing and joking together.

What changed and how?

Sitting on the porch, with a cup of ginger tea, my journal and bird book, I am watching through my binoculars what I believe to be sunbirds in the garden—elegant, iridescent-purple birds with a decurved bill. I put down my glasses and flip through the pages of *The Field Guide to the Birds of East Africa*. Yes, here: the tacazze sunbird; long, central tail feathers, brilliant, metallic violet. I think this is the one. So exotic looking to a desert dweller used to seeing Say's phoebes and meadowlarks.

It is cloudy with intermittent rain, muddy roads with puddles. Smoky. Eyes burn. Again, the sound of children playing, chickens and roosters, birds, quiet conversations on the streets, the clicking of bicycle bells.

A wagtail, black and white, has just landed between the upright metal arrows that serve as a deterrent along the top of the cinder block wall. Its lyrical song softens the edges between this porch and the street.

I am touching only surfaces.

Dorothée welcomes us into her home. Her baby is due any day, and she continues to extend her grace our direction. We gather in her living room and sit around a small coffee table with six volunteers from the community interested in teaching the children how to paint. Their names are Rosette, Liberata, Hussein, Eric, and Clementine. Dorothée joins the teachers. Filtered light is dancing through the doorway. As my eyes adjust indoors from the intense sunlight, I notice a couch and four chairs, each one with an embroidered cloth in the shape of a triangle covering it. Embroidered on the cloth is *"Arakiza,"* which means "He heals." The earthen walls are whitewashed, and the door is painted turquoise. Tree beams called timbers—literal, rough branches—hold up ceiling and the home has a dirt floor. On the shelves of a large wooden cupboard are many traditional Rwandan baskets with their characteristic pointed lids. Dorothée had told me earlier that these were historically used to carry messages from one village to another.

Lily begins to explain the idea behind painting houses with original designs. "Let me show you a book of photographs and show you what is possible." The images are from Kenya, Ghana, and the Village of Arts and Humanities in Philadelphia. They are all brightly colored murals designed by children.

After the teachers look at the various designs in the photographs, Lily spreads out paper and various colored markers, pencils, and crayons on the table. "See what you might create on your own."

Each teacher pauses and then gravitates toward particular colors. They begin to create their own strips and squares of designs, lost in their own concentration. They enter a trance. As they draw, Lily talks about the importance of pattern, abstract patterns that repeats themselves. These designs and patterns from both the teachers and the children will become the motifs for the paintings on the houses.

The children outside are watching their teachers inside. They are packed in the doorway and peeking in through the window. Dorothée's children are also watching, hiding behind a gauze curtain in a doorway. When it is the children's turn, they are eager. They have watched and anticipated and are ready. Lily encourages strong colors and contrast. "Three colors," she says. "Contrast creates tension."

The teachers become bolder in their second designs.

I am distracted. Flying ants burrow into Dorothée's hair and fly back out. Many of these children have ringworm that appears as white circles on their scalps seen through short-cropped hair. Mama Emma sits on a stool in front of her gray house across from Dorothée's with her hands clasped, her hands perpetually clasped in prayer. Her face bears the history of her people. I watch her through the open door.

After class, as I walk through the Village, an old man approaches me and begins speaking with great desperation. I try to tell him that I do not understand Kinyarwanda. He keeps on talking, crying, pleading, waving his cane in the air. I put my hand on his arm and gesture "stop" and "one moment" with my other hand, and run to find Louis to help me understand what he is saying.

Louis is standing with Lily in front of Mama Emma's house discussing which houses the Village wants painted. I interrupt and ask them to come with me. We run back to where the old man is standing, waiting. Louis introduces himself and then asks the old man his name. His name is Sharamanzi.

My name is Sharamanzi. I have no work. I have no dignity. I used to be an electrician. I used to be able to provide for my family. Now I do nothing. I am worthless. Can you help me? Can you give me a job?

With Louis translating, I tell Sharamanzi that perhaps he can help paint houses tomorrow in the Village. Sharamanzi says that is no good. He is too old and too frail. His legs are too weak from what happened to him in the war. He lifts up one of his pant legs to show how they are badly scarred. "I cannot stand and paint," he says. I ask Sharamanzi what he would like to do. He says he would like to teach the children. Could we pay him to teach the children?

Lily agrees we can pay him a daily stipend to teach the children. The Village needs teachers. The old man's sorrowful face brightens. There is a spark in his eyes. He says he will begin tomorrow. He says he would like the children to come to his house at three in the afternoon. He says this will be "Sharamanzi's School of Knowledge." We shake hands. *"Merci,"* he says.

Twilight. Insects chirping. A very long day. We just returned from the Village. Four hours of teaching the teachers and always engaging the children or, more accurately, being engaged by them. I cannot stop thinking about Sharamanzi, his plea for work. The call for prayer wafts through Gisenyi from the mosque. I have come to love their haunting regularity at five in the morning and seven at night. I think of Michel in his pink bobo, his wisdom, his commitment and generosity. How he teaches me something every day, be it language, a new word, or something inside his Muslim culture.

During dinner, by candlelight, Lily shares her thoughts. "Every time I build a park, it is like a zen experience finding peace through the chaos. What I do is create 'pristine space' that is luminous, clear, quiet, potent in its action. It's like sunlight, transparent with seven colors. That dis-stilledness comes through the depth of humanity; then you find the equilibrium—the balance—a circle of emptiness. Emptiness becomes fullness."

She tells us what it was like coming to America in the 1960s and '70s when the women's movement was in full bloom. She told of how it did not affect her, at least consciously. She was focusing on how to retain her identity as a Chinese.

"It took me twenty years of teaching art history, getting married, raising a child to find out who I was and who I was not. I was an artist but not a particularly good one. With the Village of Arts and Humanities, I felt my work had weight and then my life unfolded. I began to root in my essence. Man, that was huge. I became connected to the source of life, and then you become strong. It's not something out there; it's in here—in you. Once you are rooted, you are confident; nothing threatens *you*. You are 'connected' to 'God.' You cannot build peace out of the peace in the Village. It isn't there. You must create it together through our shared brokenness."

Lily looks down and folds her small, strong hands. She continues, "It is really through the depth of living, the chaos, the brokenness that I find peace. Joy is rooted in the depth of our suffering. It is out of my own brokenness, and the brokenness of others in the darkest of places, that I find that sense of joy. This is my special gift—to build sacred space out of the chaos in forgotten places. I feel it. The need to create beauty. We all have it, and we've lost it. The vehicle for joy is Beauty. Beauty is a right—an angelic quality that heals."

"We want to create. We long to create. We can transform a very bleak situation into a place of joy and color. I am a painter who builds things. That's all. When your environment is beautiful, it gives you dignity. You feel more dignified and your sense of self-esteem grows. All this is nurtured from working together. Seeds. Planting seeds of beauty helps the tree of community with all its branches to grow."

Lily becomes quiet. We eat in silence.

When we are in the heart of our work, we are in the heart of our power. One informs and inspires the other.

We cannot work in the Village today because they are holding *Gacaca* this afternoon. This is a mandatory meeting that all villagers must attend. *Gacaca* translates as "grass courts" and is based on an old tribal model of justice.

Sitting on the shore at Lake Kivu. Three kingfishers fly by. This morning, I watched two ibis and a heron. Two men in a kayak paddle toward Goma. I keep wondering how such a peaceful paradise could harbor such violence. Hutu extremists still inhabit the North and South Kivu regions of the Congo, committed to seeing the genocide of all Tutsis complete. There is a stratigraphy of color that defines the lake, brown closest to shore, then aqua, bleeding into turquoise, followed by a slate blue horizon. Facing Lake Kivu, flocks of pied crows inhabit the palm trees, their voices create an avian rhythm akin to jazz. Goma is to my right, with smoke rising; terraced hills create a quilted terrain to the left. There is no one here on the beach. This is one of the few times I have been alone. The sun massages my neck and shoulders like a lover. It is such a relief to be away from the Village and the heartbreak of the children, so many hungry and sick children. Children who are fourteen look half their age.

After learning "hello" (*muraho*) and "thank you" (*murakoze*) in Kinyarwanda, the first phrase I sought was *"Please move back"* (*Egerayo*). Afraid of getting sick, I was afraid of touching the children as they were touching me. Now, I do not have enough arms to hold them all.

Walking in between some of the houses in Rugerero toward the back of the Village, I saw a baby left alone sitting in his own excrement, crying. A little girl picked him up, gave him her little finger to suck on, and carried him on her hip as she walked to the one water spigot to wash him off.

I kept on walking.

The volcanic soil shimmering with mica beneath calloused feet, the golden sand on the shores of Lake Kivu, the sterile ground between the banana trees shaded from light, every square inch of this forgotten country has been bled on, cried over, and mourned.

Can that much bloodshed ever be absorbed?

Today, the first thing Louis says as he jumps into the back of the Red Cross vehicle that takes us from Gisenyi to Rugerero is "I have my answer." It took me by surprise. Yesterday, I had asked him what he has learned through the work of translation, and he told me, "I will tell you tomorrow." I had forgotten.

"There is something beyond language." he says. "There is something else."

"What?" I ask.

"Hunger. You are hungry to understand. You are hungry to be understood. But without translation we just talk to ourselves, and no one eats." He pauses. "How can I say this . . . As a translator, I see hunger on both sides. I can create a place where these two hungers can meet."

He stares out the window as the landscape flashes by. "Birds have their own language. Cows have their own language. If there was a bird who could hear a cow, I mean really understand what that cow was saying, then that bird could stand between cows and birds and be the mediator between these two different groups, and perhaps they could help each other. That's how I see it."

Without Louis's capacity to listen to, understand, and translate what is being said, I have no access to the hearts of the Rwandans with whom we are working.

Words are our tools for understanding and misunderstanding. Words can ignite and incite, kill and cull, and at the same time, words can create bridges between cruelty and compassion. A chain of words becomes a history: Neighbors. Hutu. Tutsi. Colonialism. Identity. Power. Resentment. Propaganda. A Plan. A Purpose. A Genocide.

Louis is the channel by which I can enter into this foreign landscape. He is right to use the word "hunger." I am hungry to understand where I am and with whom. I am hungry for story. My insatiable appetite begins with a question. I hate to think what violations of privacy, taboo, and manners I have committed to feed this hunger.

"You asked me what I am learning."

"I did."

"What I am learning is that if I love what I am doing, then that translates to a love for the one who is speaking and those that are listening. This is what I mean when I say there is something else, something else at play and at work." He looks at me intently. "I think you know what I am saying."

I look at him. This unexpected companion who has become my eyes, my ears, and my voice is entering my bloodstream in ways unknown to me.

"It is deeper than just trading words," he says.

We arrive at the memorial site. Louis jumps out, turns around, and takes my hand to help me down. "I can read your mind through your language. Even though I can't go word for word, I can give your core message." And then suddenly, he laughs.

"What?"

"I just remembered the one time I could not translate for you. Do you remember?"

We both laugh.

"Why couldn't I have taught the children to sing, 'Amazing Grace.' I just didn't think of it."

"No, it was good to make the children laugh."

Louis is wearing a black and red cap turned backward, a black T-shirt, and jeans. He dresses with style and attention to detail. He wears a nasty scar on his left hand. A visual story, untold.

Six Rwandan men are digging a trench where the cement footings with rebar for the wall will stand. Shovel to dirt, shovel to dirt. Body as lever.

Louis and I walk the ground where many bones from the Village are buried. "Wherever Life is, Death is there." Louis says. "I am here, yeah, and Death is standing behind me." He pauses. "Death has been chasing me most of my life."

We follow the trench toward the school. "I am old, even though I am young," he says. "I took responsibility for my family at eleven."

"How many brothers and sisters do you have?"

"Four brothers and two sisters. I am the third oldest. I am responsible financially for all of them." He smiles. "Can you guess how old I am?"

"Tell me."

"Twenty-one. We live with our mother in Gisenyi. She is a farmer." He pauses. "And she can heal people with herbs."

Louis tells me that he works for a South African mining company called MPA (Metal Processing Association). He has worked there for three years and is a laboratory shift leader. His expertise is working with a spectrometer that measures and analyzes the grade and quality of ores like copper, tin, tantalum, aluminum, and lead, the majority coming out of the Congo.

"Can I tell you my dream?"

I nod.

"My dream is to see my family in good health, stable, with my brothers and sisters in school. I feel the same satisfaction toward my younger brothers and sisters that a parent feels."

At the end of the day, Meghan, Alan, and I pass out pens and notebooks to the children at the memorial site. They form two long lines: one for girls, one for boys. Hundreds of children walk through the line.

"Thank you, my friend. Thank you, my friend." This was the mantra uttered by each child. It is only a notebook and pen. We did not have

enough. There is never enough; hundreds more children came running toward us from the school, older children.

The teachers would not allow the orphans from the street to have a pen and notebook, although they are the ones who need them the most because they don't attend school. Even among the poorest of the poor, there is still a hierarchy. We gave them pens and paper anyway. Are we contributing to dependency? Are we hurting more than helping? Why do I feel guilt for giving when we have so much?

On our way home, I look out the window of the vehicle. The evidence of the war is everywhere: burned cars, razed houses, bullet holes in the walls of schools, collapsed churches. There are, as well, the visable scars on the people, the amputated arms and legs, the hollow stares from the burdened women as we pass by. I sit with my own demons as I wonder what violence I am capable of. None of us is immune from inhabiting the dark corners of human nature.

"The future of Rwanda is education," Damas tells us back at Mama Chukala's house. "The governor of Gisenyi, as smart as he is, did not finish secondary school, and because of new standards set for public officials, he will have to step down. To be a governor in Rwanda now, you must have a university degree."

He tells us that the weight of educating the children under his care does not allow him to sleep at night. Bloodshot eyes. Fatigue. I wonder what the future of Damas and Louis will be?

Lily promised our well-meaning guard that we would find him some new clothes today. So tonight when he came to the house, Lily brought out a sack of brightly colored clothes—yellow, to be exact—that she purchased this afternoon in the kiosk by the road.

The guard pulled out the shirt and pants. It was an L.A. Lakers basketball uniform. A tank top with long yellow net shorts to match. Alan, Meghan, and I burst out laughing. "What's wrong?" Lily asked. When he could finally speak, Alan pointed out that this was an outfit for a point guard, not a security guard.

The guard was delighted, completely delighted, as he held the top with the number 12 up to himself. Lily, once again, had kept her word. It didn't matter that she didn't know a basketball uniform from a pair of shorts and T-shirt.

For the first time, I slept with a light heart.

Lily asks Mama Emma, the matriarch of the Village, for permission to paint her home. "With respect," Lily says, "if it would please you, the community would be honored to paint your house first." Mama Emma bows her head and quietly says yes. Wilson, an artist from Gisenyi, and Alan begin to chalk out a geometric design that will grace the front of her house like a running border.

An art teacher from the nearby school shows up this morning saying, "I would like to be involved. I can help teach the children to draw." He smiles. "My name is Fabrice." He immediately gathers the children together, passing out paper and pencils. Sitting in a circle on the ground, he asks the children to look around them. *What do you see around you? What do you hear? What goes on in the Village?* As if by magic, Fabrice is able to coax and inspire the children's powers of perception and imagination. Cows, goats, cats, roosters, trucks, motorcycles, banana trees, self-portraits, and portraits of their families all find their way onto the page.

Delighted, Lily pulls various images from their drawings for the houses; a red-faced angel and two flowers are the first designs chalked onto the side of Mama Emma's house. Lily climbs a ladder and begins to transfer the children's images onto the gray stucco. The young artists gather and watch with great excitement. The canvas is the earthen wall; the medium is chalk, then paint. Bowed heads are beginning to be raised.

Sharamanzi is an electrician. He was born in the town of Gisenyi in 1936. He married his wife, Spacious, in 1959. She is from Kigali, where they met when he was working for an electrical company. They moved to Gisenyi. In 1959, the Hutus were burning houses and killing people throughout Rwanda. Sharamanzi and Spacious fled to the Congo with his Belgian employee. From 1959 to 1966, Sharamanzi and his family lived in Goma, just across the border from Gisenyi in the Congo. "The white man left and returned to Belgium," Sharamanzi told me in the Village. "He was a very good man."

"We stayed in the Congo after the first genocide," he said. "We had five children." All five of their children were murdered in "the second genocide" in 1994. I ask Sharamanzi if he can follow President Kagame's plea to forgive. He brings his fingers to his mouth and blows them apart, "Poof!" he says. He shakes his head side to side. "No." Spacious says nothing can be done. "Paul Kagame is releasing prisoners. If the prisoners come and ask for forgiveness, yes. If they don't come we just keep quiet."

There is a long silence between us.

I am afraid to ask if they know who killed their children.

"Our children were murdered in the church. All of them went to the church." Sharamanzi pauses, then says, "The priests were the promoters of death."

"How did you survive?" I ask.

He puts his hands over his head and drops it between his knees. Spacious talks to Louis for a long time. "This is not easy to explain," Louis says. "They hid. Only God knows how they survived. They spent weeks in the bush—a young friend of theirs helped them, brought them water. It's a long story."

Sharamanzi and Spacious begin to argue. She puts her hand on her forehead.

"Our son had already completed his university studies. They killed him, and then they came for us."

Louis puts his hand on Sharamanzi's knee. Sharamanzi talks directly to him.

"After two weeks in the bush, Sharamanzi and Spacious learned their four other children were killed in the church," Louis says.

"A young man like me," says Louis, "came to them at three A.M. in the bush and led them over the border once again to Goma. They knew him. He was a neighbor. When the war was over, they came back and found their house was destroyed, so they stayed with their neighbors until the Survivors Village was constructed. It took about a year." Sharamanzi breaks into Louis's words to tell him something. Louis translates: "It took too long."

"When you were in the bush, what did you eat?" Alan asks.

"Nothing—because during those two weeks, we were in such danger, we just hid in the bush. We didn't move. We ate nothing; we didn't dare."

Spacious points to her stomach and tells of a subsequent operation because of the effects of long-term hunger.

Sharamanzi then tells of the tools of torture. "The Interahamwe took nails and dug them between two sticks and hit his ankle; the nails went through his ankle," Louis says.

They were tortured. Something passed through Sharamanzi's thigh. He shows us scars on his thigh and ankle.

Spacious and I hold hands, and I feel guilty for even engaging them in this story of horrors.

"Now they do nothing," Louis says. "He is doing nothing. He has no work. They only survive like this. No job. They just sit home. When they get money, they buy soap."

Louis takes Sharamanzi's hand. "He has no strength to work." Sharamanzi looks down at his lap with his hands over his face.

"Enough," Spacious says.

Louis turns to us and says, "It is a shock in their hearts when they remember."

Alan and I are quiet.

Sharamanzi says to Alan, "When I look into your eyes, I see my son. I love you. You are my son." And then Sharamanzi turns to me: "When I look into your eyes, I see my daughter. I love you; you are my daughter."

"What was your daughter's name?" I ask. "Our daughter's name was Terry," says Spacious.

After we left Sharamanzi and Spacious, I whispered to Louis, "I cannot believe the history that is yours." He stopped. "It's not just my history. It is your history, too."

The sun is setting over Lake Kivu. I retreat to reflect. The healing grace of sharing one's story is another form of witness. In tragedy and loss, it is the story that remains and reminds us of our shared humanity.

An orange disk is dissolving into the liquid horizon. Alan is playing his drums. Meghan has her eyes closed as she sits on the sand with a cotton shawl wrapped around her.

I am fifty years old. I can still hear the voices of the children in the Village singing "Happy Birthday."

Twelve white egrets skim the lake, their wings barely, just barely, above the surface.

I return to the Gisenyi market with Lily. She, too, delights in the mosaic of baskets of beans, black, red, and white; maize, white, yellow, and blue; flours, powders, and potions; cabbages and potatoes, yams and mounds of avocados. There is a wealth of fragrances wafting over us that strangely reminds me of my mother. "This is a testament to Rwandan women's prowess as farmers," says Lily.

We gravitate to the drapes of batiks hanging from the metal rods beneath the large canvas tents. The prints are celebratory, with birds, flowers, and leaves, many with bright geometrics. A collage of colors arches over us. We buy some fabric for gifts. I imagine making quilts and pillows for friends and family.

Lily and I wonder why we wear black as we pass Rwandan women shielding themselves from the sun beneath their enormous red, yellow, and blue umbrellas.

I met two boys this afternoon in the Village. They live on the periphery. They are orphans. Their names are Vicmanotor and Firkovitch. They are shy and intense. They speak a little English and want to learn more. They told me they are in sixth grade and are thirteen years old.

"We are hungry."

I had two granola bars in my pocket, which I gave to them. I watched them devour the bars as they ran through the fields.

Sharamanzi is waiting for us in the Village. He will teach the children in his own house. "It will be called 'Sharmanzi's School of Knowledge,'" he repeats to Louis.

The image I have is this: dozens of children walking up to his gray stucco house, so excited, some running. Thirty, maybe forty children packed inside, sitting, standing, perched on the windowsill. The flower that Lily chalked on the gray wall the day before towered above the children. I watched from outside through the window as he tells them stories. Louis is assisting him. The children are rapt.

The first thing Sharamanzi does is show them his hair. He explains that if they are lucky enough to one day have white hair, a gift from God, then they, too, can have respect. He tells them that they can begin to respect themselves now. There is no time to waste; they should work together and take care of each other. He shows them the lines on his face, his scars. He tells them never to kill or steal from one another. He tells them that if they will respect themselves and each other, one day, they may have a chance at old age like him.

What is important for the children to know? Sharamanzi tells me after his first class that this is the question he is asking himself as he prepares to teach the children of the Village.

He will think about all the lessons in this way.

After the class, three girls and one boy did not want to leave. With Louis's help, I ask them what they learned from Sharamanzi. The children told me that Sharamanzi Tate (a Kinyarwanda word that means "grandfather") taught them that:

1. They should respect themselves and each other.
2. They should love themselves.
3. They should avoid fighting and insulting each other.
4. Boys should help in the house, too.
5. Boys should not take girls by force.
6. They should respect their parents and help them.
7. They should not throw stones at children who are orphans.

When Sharamanzi walked out of his house with his cane, these children followed him saying, "Tate, Tate . . ."

When we return from the Village, Medard, who manages Mama Chukala's house, hears me cough again, an aggravation that is growing worse. He disappears and then offers me "medicine" on a silver tray—a raw egg, a lime, and some honey. I watch him elegantly break the egg with the edge of his knife and let it fall into the cup. He then carves a little V into the lip of the lime, creating a spout, and squeezes the juice delicately into the cup. He then drips honey with a circular motion into the concoction and vigorously stirs it together. He hands me the cup gently, saying, "This will help your cough."

I thank him and drink the potion, figuring I am good for one gulp. Meghan looks on with eyes as wide as saucers.

Louis arrives after working his shift at MPA. He has written a poem called "Let's Talk About It." We sit down on the couch in Mama Chukula's living room. He reads it to me:

LET'S TALK ABOUT IT

For Africa, for My Father and Mother

Rwanda, my country—
Wake up and talk.
Let everyone hear your voice.

Do not keep silent.
Speak to save our lovely nation.
Important people are dying of AIDS.
The streets are full of orphans of AIDS,
    begging in the streets, crying for help.
They have no one to take care of them.
They cannot dream of a good life.
What a horrible life!
The children are innocent.
We need to assist them.
Let us be close to them.
We cannot leave them alone
    in such a condition.

Listen, my brothers and sisters,
It is our time to break the silence.
We cannot allow this epidemic
    to eliminate our people.
Important people are dying of AIDS.
The streets are full of orphans of AIDS.
Let us set an example among friends.
Let us become a lit candle for those
    in darkness—
Let us learn from them.
Let them learn from us.
All my best friends are dead from AIDS.
Their families wasted money
    as they wasted away.
Believe me, they wasted a lot of money
    treating them in vain.
They are poor until death.

Whoever you are, buy the time
to think about his problem.
It is all of our problem. Let's talk about it.
Respect yourself.
Keep yourself safe.
Avoid illicit sex.
Our future is bright if we don't stand still.

To the young, do not stand still
Move around and around, side to side
to save the lives of many.
Let our voices be written on small scraps
all over this country
across Africa, America, Asia
and the world—
We have lost too many of us.
Enough is enough.
It is our time to make sure
we all understand
Important people are dying of AIDS.
The streets are full of orphans of AIDS.

This is the first time anyone has brought up the subject of AIDS. There has been no mention of it in the Village, yet you know it is the ghost that haunts and inhabits millions of residents in Sub-Saharan Africa.

From 2003 to 2007, reports from the United Nations to the President's Emergency Plan for AIDS Relief (PEPFAR) indicate that 4 to 8.9 percent of the population in Rwanda is living with HIV/AIDS. For the most densely populated country in Africa, with 8.1 million people, this translates to close to half a million people living with HIV; 50 percent of those individuals are women and 13 percent are children under fifteen. Seven out of ten female genocide survivors are living with AIDS because of the brutal use of rape during the 1994 war. And an estimated 270,000 Rwandan children have lost one or both parents to AIDS-related illnesses, leaving the country with the highest number of child-headed households in Africa.

But the Rwandan government's distribution of antiretroviral drugs to individuals living with AIDS is beginning to have an impact. Statistics indicate a significant decline in AIDS deaths and a rise in quality of life.

The work of organizations like Partners In Health in collaboration with the Clinton Foundation at sites like the Rwinkwavu Hospital outside Kigali, as well as that of individuals like Dr. James Plumb and the medical students from Thomas Jefferson University, who are now working in Rugerero, are emblematic of the efforts of thousands of individuals and organizations who are teaming with Rwandans to create a system of wholeness, not fragmentation, within a national health care plan.

Rwanda is the first of the so-called focus countries identified by PEPFAR as reaching its five-year treatment goal a year ahead of schedule. An estimate of fifty thousand people will have been treated with antiretroviral drugs. As Dr. Paul Farmer has said repeatedly, "The hope is that those infected with the HIV virus who are given these drugs will continue to have access to them and keep taking them."

Dr. Innocent Nyaruhirira, the state minister in charge of fighting HIV/AIDS and other epidemics points out, "We have adherence which is beyond ninety percent."

There is a woman who lives across the street from Mama Chakula's house. Her name is Elena. She is so thin and struggles each day to sweep her porch with her young children playing around her. She sits on the cement steps with her elbows on her knees and her hands holding up her head. Each morning, we wave. And each day, I wonder about her well-being. She reminds me of my mother a few weeks before her death from cancer, that unmistakable gaunt beauty very close to the bone.

I recall listening to Dr. Paul Farmer speak at the University of Utah a few months before coming to Rwanda. He spoke of structural violence, how most people in power say "data is the cure for antidote." Farmer says no. That the importance of listening to life stories is crucial to our understanding of how a community exercises their right to be healed.

> *If I look at the mass, I will never act. If I look at the one, I will.*
>
> MOTHER TERESA

Genocide. The Holocaust. The displacement of indigenous people in North America. Habitat destruction and climate change. It is not in our psychology as human beings to respond to the grand abstractions of catastrophe. Paul Slovic, a psychologist at the University of Oregon, calls it "psychic numbing." We turn away. But we can respond to the suffering of another human being. To hear and share one another's stories becomes the open channel to compassion.

What I see in Rwanda is what I know in Utah: Illness is not part of our fate. The occurrence of AIDS among women in Rwanda is about rape and the brutality of a war predicated on the seeds of colonialism. And it is carried on, transmitted, through the generations. In the same way, cancer in Utah is not our spiritual fate but the raining down of radiation from the nuclear bomb testing done during the Cold War in America. Another kind of colonialism that said those living in the deserts of the American West were "a low-use segment of the population."

The colonial world is a compartmentalized world.

FRANTZ FANON

We cannot understand social problems without looking at historical roots. It is impossible to change society without changing the societal stories. We must listen to the stories being told on the ground by those who have survived the abuses of power, those who bear witness and embody the resiliency of the human spirit. And resiliency is what I see in Rwanda.

Social, political, and religious hierarchies are responsible for creating poverty and structural violence that is not just reserved for Africa. Bureacracies breed contempt, and no one is accountable. An institutional mind tries to crush a creative one. The individual becomes powerless against the collective unless the community rises to a man's or a woman's defense. The question that keeps haunting me on issues of power, corruption, and cruelty is "Who benefits?"

Madame Head Wide Apart is no exception. Who benefits when her home ground is taken? Or when her clan and coterie are shot and killed for sport? She is among the planetary witnesses standing her ground in this Global Community of Life.

When you walk into the Village, a painted angel greets you dressed in a light blue and black sarong. She floats between two blooming flowers in a palette of blues, blacks, whites, and reds. Her eyes are wide and knowing, and the smile on her face is the smile of the child who imagined her. This angel resides on the side of Mama Emma's house. Her hands are hidden behind her back as though she holds a surprise.

Across from Mama Emma's house and the painted angel is Dorothée's place. Above her turquoise door lives a red and white striped painted Cheshire cat with extended claws, another design created through the eyes and hands of the children. A border of large diamonds alternating from turquoise to yellow to white creates a bright geometric band around the house. For days, the children, some barely three feet tall, stood with a cup of paint in one hand and a brush in other, creating strokes of color on a gray canvas. These are the "barefoot artists," not to be distracted by anything but the task at hand, trading places with those lined up behind them.

Two houses have been painted in the Village. Our goal this month is five. The other designs have already been chalked on and partially painted on the cracked stucco walls: a turquoise tree of life; a yellow cow with a generous udder; a black-and-white rooster with a red comb; a yellow and black giraffe outlined in red; a Rwandan pointed basket; two boys on a motorcycle; and a fountain of red, yellow, and green flowers.

Dorothée went into labor this morning. Early. Yesterday, she said her baby was due in October.

In Rwanda, a child is often named according to the circumstance he or she is born into or is named as a wish for the future. A beautiful child in the Village holds in her tiny hands a bouquet of flowers which she has spent the morning gathering. I bend down to greet her. When I ask her name, *"Witwande?"* She whispers in my ears, "Tuyishime." Louis later tells me it means, "To thank God."

Sharamanzi continues to teach the children. "Sharamanzi's School of Knowledge" is open daily at 3:00 P.M. He has enlisted his friend Foster to help him. There are so few elders within the Village. Most did not survive. The children are eager to sit at their feet and simply listen to their stories.

Every day, new people appear and want to become involved.

Joy has entered in. Word is getting out.

Lily and many of the women in the Village, Spacious and Clementine, Liberata and Rosette, among them, are sitting on Mama Emma's lawn mixing paints. Lily says, "The Genocide Memorial looks to the past and honors it, both the violence and the death, that it might never happen again." She pauses. "It holds the collective memory, and each of you feel it through your own memories and loved ones." The women are listening. Louis and Damas are translating. "Painting the Village honors where we are now, inspiring us to see what else is possible."

Spacious's tears followed the lines down her face as she showed me photographs of her daughter Terry and two of their other children. The tattered and crumpled pictures had traveled with her throughout the war and all their wanderings.

We spread all of her pictures on a wooden table in their home. She showed me photographs of when she was in the hospital for a stomach operation, shortly after she and Sharmanzi had been surviving in the bush without food or water.

A handful of photographs—all she has, all they have together, of their life and children. I kept wondering how she carried them, how these images survived.

Didien Yutti is the brother of Mr. Safari, the mayor of Cyanzarwe. He told me that his older brother had been away at school, attending the university in Butare, when their family was murdered by the Hutu militia. To hide from the Hutus, Didien, his mother, and two sisters lowered themselves into the pit toilet outside their home. Didien descended first to protect the women in his family from the filth. The Hutus found them anyway and murdered his mother and sisters, who were on top of him. He stayed in the pit toilet with his loved ones' bodies rotting above him for days. Finally, close to suffocation from the weight pressing down, he had to get out. From there, he ran, leaving his mother's and sisters's bodies behind. He hid for days, weeks, months, years. Alone. Two years later, dazed and despondent, he found himself wandering the streets of Butare. He saw his brother walking down the road, the brother he assumed was dead. Didien said they both looked at each other in disbelief and then ran toward each other, hugging and sobbing uncontrollably. "We cried for three months together," he said.

Sharamanzi's lesson today included the history of Rwanda, beginning with the first king whose name was Musinga. And when he was old, his son Rudahigwa, replaced him. He told the children that the old Rwanda was very different from the Rwanda they are living in today. For example, the way Rwandans dress. Before, women took the bark off trees, smoothed it, and wore it as cloth. Men used to kill animals such as a goat and then take the hide and make it into clothing. Before, there was no difference between Hutus and Tutsis. "We were all Rwandans," he said. "I advise you not to create differences between each other but to realize we are all one nation. After the war, when Paul Kagame became president, he did away with identity cards.

"Please avoid this distinction," Sharamanzi told the children. "It is good. Once you do this, God will help you as you play together with your friends."

He advised them to obey their parents, especially after school. "It will help you to develop a good heart," he said.

The children had many questions.

"When did mzungus */white people come to Rwanda?"*
"When did Rwanda gain its independence?"
"When did the white men leave and Rwandans take back their country?"

Sharamanzi said these were all very good questions and he would answer them in the next class.

None of the children wanted to leave.

Jean Bosco said it reminded him of when he was a child listening to stories around the fire.

We were walking along the shore of Lake Kivu. Our walk was stopped short as we were too close to the Congo for comfort. Men approached us asking for money; others walked next to us, mocking us, intimidating us. It worked. Young men sitting on the beach drinking banana beer made loud comments that we couldn't understand. We just kept walking.

But what made me the most nervous were the stares.

This was supposed to be a "nature walk," at my request. Lily smiled and quietly said it is because of my binoculars and fanny pack full of field guides that we are being harassed.

"We deserve whatever they are saying." she said laughing. "Look at us—not to mention the fact that we are stopping every few feet with some magnifying glass to look at sand."

Alan and Meghan joined in the teasing. At least they were feigning an interest in birds.

We saw a tawny eagle, an African black kite, pied crows, a sunbird, turacos, and a white-necked cormorant. And of course, many kingfishers.

Our days here are taking their toll. I see it in our eyes. It is not the physical fatigue of working in the Village but the mental stress of moving in a world we don't understand; the land mines we are trying to dodge with almost every move we make.

Who are we to be painting somebody else's house? What do we know about sustainable development? How can I even begin to think about asking a woman about the genocide when it inevitably leads to memories of physical violence and watching the death of her children? And what are we doing disturbing the dirt where bones are buried?

Echoes of the war reverberate in each conversation. Nothing is neutral but perhaps the sky. Even the thought of God feels suspect. It is hard for me to reconcile myself to a god that allows this kind of suffering and one that is indifferent to it. Both action and inaction cut into my conscience as a sharp-edged conundrum. Those who were perpetrators and those who survived now all bleed into victims, with the exception of *genocidaires* who helped plan the killings. We cannot tell a Hutu from a Tutsi. The people we are working with all know, but it is never spoken. Real tensions live here; I watch eyes, and they know one another's histories. It's as if we Americans are walking inside a hologram Rwandans can see but we cannot.

At dusk, enormous bats emerge from the canopy of palms and flap heavily through twilight. They appear as large flying cats. Damas told us people in the Congo eat these bats but nobody in Gisenyi does. You can buy them in the market in Goma, along with a variety of bushmeats, monkeys, even gorillas, among them.

Black-bodied rowers in lime green kayaks on light blue water traverse Lake Kivu in twilight.

I close my eyes and still see the dust rising from the chaos of Rugerero. I wonder what we are not seeing, what the women are not saying, and what we are not understanding. I suspect almost everything.

Aboveground. Bodies in motion. Belowground. Bodies animated by beetles, leaving behind bones. And the women's hands on hoes that cultivate the soil of their grief while they sow the seeds and harvest food for their families. Poverty is fed by wars. It is the great continuum. What lies below the surface is this silence of women who bear the burden of both witness and survivor.

Dorothée gave birth to a baby boy. All went well. She is back home in the Village.

It has been difficult to locate local writers or poets. When I ask who they are, no one can tell me. They have to be here. I know they are here. Perhaps they are holding their stories inside like Mama Emma, like Louis, believing one day there will be a safe time for them to speak. The other answer is a pragmatic one: *"We have no time for that."* Damas and Brown may not be writing down their stories, but they want to share them. "It helps us," says Brown. He has a long scar on his neck. Damas has scars on his right wrist and his arm, then lifts his shirt to show more. In most stories I hear, people survived because the dead and, in most cases, their loved ones, were piled on top of them, and they were mistaken for dead by the killers. Then, with the passing of time, usually days, they crawled out from the bloating bodies and fled. Some were helped by friends and strangers; others surely suffered and died alone on the sides of roads or hiding in the bush.

Damas says to me on the banks of Lake Kivu as clouds gather, "It was so horrible—*horrible*. My whole family—we were wealthy; we had a beautiful home in Kigali. The militia destroyed everything." He was away from home at a boarding school in Butare. When he was finally able to return home, in July 1994, several months after the beginning of the genocide, he found his entire family dead, their bodies decomposing in an open-pit grave outside the burnt cinders of his house. "I had to bury my family alone. Nyamata was very hard for me. Very difficult. When I was there, I saw me. Each skull was my mother, my father, my brothers and sisters." He looks toward the lake. "It never leaves you—*never*."

Brown lost five out of his seven family members. It took him three years to locate his father's bones. He said that when he found people whom he thought had died but were alive—neighbors—they said, "Brown, we saw where your father was killed. We know who did it." "And then they told me the name, and I know him. He was a friend of our family. You just can't believe that they could do such a thing." Later, says Brown, "the killer came to me and confessed, bore witness to the killings, and told me where my family was buried." Brown's family was thrown into a huge mass grave. He had to dig through the bodies until he found his mother, his brothers and sisters; then he brought them home for a proper burial. I did not dare ask how he recognized the bones or if their bodies were still clothed. I'm not even sure I heard him correctly. At some point, I stopped listening. Brown said that in some places like churches, lines of clothing were created so you could walk up and down the aisles to see if you recognized a sarong of fabric worn by your mother or if you saw your brother's or father's shirt or jacket or hat. In this way, you would know if members of your family had been buried in a particular mass grave. Brown went on to say, "Even if the killer tells you that your father's bones are in a toilet, you go to those pits and you pull them out."

Again, I am mindful of the women in the Village. They are not as forthcoming with their personal histories. Perhaps it is because our translator is male. Perhaps it is because their humiliation is of a different nature. The word not spoken. The women we work with—Liberata, Roselyn, Dorothée, Clementine, Rosette, and Mama Emma—do not speak about themselves. Half of them are widows.

What is the word not spoken?

Hot springs boil on the western shores of Lake Kivu. Orange and chartreuse algae grow along the edges like lace. There are no birds here. An old man with white hair sits in the deepest pool with his eyes closed. And beyond the hot springs, three children laugh and splash in the lake, as one child rides an inflatable whale.

We have traveled along a narrow dirt road that cuts through such deep poverty and deadly erosion that whatever solace may be found here evaporates with the steam. Children, barely clothed, sit on red hillsides, lethargic. Their bones push through transparent flesh like unstable scaffolding. Hunger follows our vehicle, and I shamefully look away. Deforested hillsides hang precariously on the mountains, and I fear whole slopes may slide, burying these vertical villages alive.

My hope is eroding the longer I am here, even as my faith is deepening. I am too tired and overwhelmed to reflect on why.

Who has time for reflection?

Time, here, does not seem like a horizontal line but rather a circle drawn tight around Rwanda that contracts and expands like traumatized lungs.

Lily chalks in more motifs on more houses, the designs inspired by the children: a cow with many teats and a banana tree. Alan is finishing chalking geometric designs, the joyful borders that wrap themselves around the bottom of the linked houses. Meghan mixes paints, pouring various colors in paper cups for the children and teachers. Rosette, Clementine, and Roselyn hand each interested child his or her own cup of paint and paintbrush.

Every night, our guard greets us in his Lakers' suit and invites everyone in. No doubt, he is a victim of the genocide. No doubt, Mama Chakula has taken pity on him and given him a job. He rarely speaks. We try to explain to him that he must keep the door locked for security. I raise both my arms in a gesture of strength and flex my muscles. "We need you to be strong," Alan says. "Protection" gestures Lily with her hands in the form of a boxer. Meghan is doubled over in laughter, "You look like fools." There is no one to translate for us, so we are reduced to charades. The guard thinks we want to play soccer and kicks a ball in the living room that Alan returns. Lily gets some mosquito repellent and offers to spray his legs for "protection against mosquitoes." Laughter turning into tears. There is a term for uncontrollable laughter during inappropriate times: *corpsing*. We are corpsing and we cannot stop.

Exhausted. In bed. It is raining. A cat screams. My heart is pounding. Mama Chakula has asked that even our bedroom doors be locked. At night, a physical darkness envelops the emotional one. These nights trying to fall asleep with a racing mind seem endless. Demons, spirits, all shapes and sizes, primarily of the dead, from my own life and the lives I am entering, become smokelike cohorts with the lives that still stir within this house. *Who knows what happened in this house;* they are alive in this bedroom and I cannot sleep.

Rosette, one of the most gifted of the teachers, tells me on our way to the school a story about the only gorilla she has ever seen. Her school had organized a trip to Lake Ihema. Before reaching the lake, they saw a zoo on the side of the road. They stopped and visited some of the animals. "There was a gorilla in a cage. It looked so unhappy. Lonely. We fed it bananas. The gorilla ate it, peeled it just like a man. After it finished the first banana, it held out its hand for another one."

Rosette was born in Gisenyi. She is twenty-nine years old. She has lived her life here in Cyanzarwe. She now lives in Gisenyi and works nights as a waitress at an outdoor cabaret called Gloria that Liberata manages.

She tells me she has four sisters and one brother. Her dream is for them to have good jobs and good health.

"And for you?"

"Just to live each day." She pauses, then smiles. "I would like to be a teacher."

"You already are," I say. She is patient with the children. They absorb her calm. She wants a formal education and a teaching certificate.

Rosette is a mother with three daughters. Her husband is away working. She is hesitant to talk or say too much.

When we arrive at the school, she stops and asks me directly, *"What is your purpose in asking me these questions? How is it going to benefit me personally?"*

We talk to Sharamanzi and Spacious this morning. He has close to forty students today. He wants to build a classroom behind his house with shelves for books, a library. Yesterday, Lily gave Spacious some blue batik cloth that she bought in the market. Today Spacious came into her living room modeling her new clothes. She had cut and sewn a beautiful outfit, complete with tunic top, skirt, and head scarf. The enormous flower that Spacious desired for the inside of her house instead of the outside is finished. Lily steps down from the stool in their living room with a drop of green paint on her cheek.

Clementine is an athlete who participated in the 1984 Olympics in Los Angeles. Her passion is ten-kilometer and twenty-two-kilometer races. She has competed in the United States, Morocco, China, Korea, Tunisia, Kenya, and Burundi. "Running saved me," she says. "It's why I've become a coach, committed to teaching the girls how to run and play soccer. You learn how to own your body."

Clementine came to the memorial site on the first day we arrived and immediately stepped in to help with the children, recognizing instantly my inability to find control or discipline. In thirty seconds, she snapped her fingers, spoke a few strong words, and the children's minds were focused. Clementine brought birds into the children's imaginations as we laid on our backs behind the memorial watching red-tailed hawks. She created a language game alternating *ikwibi* with "hawk" as a way to teach the children both natural history and English. Her buoyancy of spirit creates rain. The children both fear her and delight in her good nature.

Clementine has three children of her own: Jean de la Paix, who is sixteen; Delphine, who is ten; and Richard, who is seven. Her husband died in a car accident in 1998. And her father died in the war in 1994. From 1995 through 2002, Clementine was a volunteer for the Red Cross helping to unite families that had been separated during the genocide. They took notebooks with photographs of orphans from village to village trying to locate their parents or family members, seeing if anyone could identify them.

"No one was taking care of them. It was very sad, very difficult."

"There was one child that was three years old. I remember her in particular. All she could say was 'Kigali.' I could not leave her and kept her with me for two weeks. I had this photo album, part of the Red Cross system of relocation, trying to match parents with their children. We finally found her family. The parents of this child saw a picture of their little girl. They were overcome with joy. They had fled to Tanzania and later returned to Gisenyi. They had to leave their child with friends. They feared their daughter was dead, but here she was in this camp in Gisenyi."

"How did you keep your strength?" Meghan asks.

"By helping the children, by comforting them, holding them." She looks down at her lap. "I held so many, many children."

Clementine abruptly changes the subject. "I have three questions for you, Terry."

"I'd love to hear them."

"Where do you live?"
"What do you cultivate?"
"And how many children do you have?"

I tell her I live in Castle Valley, Utah, located in the American Southwest. I describe the red-rock cliffs and mesas, telling her that it is a desert, a place of little water and much wind. I draw her a map of the Four Corners region in relationship to Los Angeles, California, where she has been.

"Compared to the lush green, terraced hills of Rwanda, Utah looks like Mars," I say. Clementine laughs.

"What do I cultivate? And what are the names of my children?"

"Yes."

"I cultivate nothing. And we have no children."

She looks puzzled. "What do you mean you don't cultivate anything? What do you eat? How do you eat?"

I explain that we live in a desert and buy our food at a local cooperative that is part of a larger community garden, that one day I would like to make time to create a garden of my own.

And then I tell her that Brooke and I made a decision not to have children.

"We chose not to have children for a variety of reasons—because of health considerations, because of my commitment to my work, because I believe we can create an extended sense of family that is not just of our body but born out of community." I pause thinking this all must sound so absurd in regard to something so instinctual.

Clementine remains silent and thoughtful. Her eyes never stray from mine. "That is really interesting."

She expresses her concerns about many Rwandan women choosing to have as many children as they can to make up for those lost in the genocide. "And then they can't feed them and they suffer." Clementine does not feel she can have any more children. She says that, now, if she got pregnant, she would not continue with the pregnancy because she would not be able to take care of another child.

Clementine talks about how difficult this is to give up. "Children are our pleasure. But it is more difficult not to be able to feed them and to watch them die," she says. "When people outside Rwanda hear about women who kill their own babies, drop them in pit toilets so they won't have a lifetime of suffering, they judge the young mothers. They don't understand what it's like to watch your baby starve. There are so many sick and hungry children in Rwanda."

There is a long silence.

Clementine turns to me, "Do you, Lily, Alan, and Meghan, take care of each other when you go back to America? That is important to me because if I talked to you and asked you how Meghan is and you say, 'I don't know; we haven't been in touch,' well, it would be very disappointing because we feel your love for each other and that is important for us to witness."

The children are calling for Clementine to paint. She smiles, "My children—I must go to them."

There is a knock on the door at Mama Chakula's house. It is our guard. He is very upset and agitated. We invite him in. Louis translates. The guard informs us that his child has been lost for a month. He thinks his son is somewhere on the streets. The boy's mother died in the genocide. This is the first we have heard him speak of anything personal. We learn his name is Kabanda.

We all feel so helpless.

Meghan's research for her master's degree focuses on how young people find dignity after war. With Louis's help, she interviews Firkovitch and Vicmanotor, two boys who became orphans during the war, close friends, both thirteen years old. I had met them earlier and explained that they are in sixth grade, their last year of primary school. Neither boy has the money to continue his education.

Both boys were born in Rugerero. They lived in the Congo during the war. They lived inside refugee camps for many years, moving from place to place. They did not know each other. They met in the second grade when they were seven years old.

Who do you live with?

"We have no parents. We live with an old woman. No family. No brothers or sisters, only each other."

When you think of healing, what do you think of?

"Healing in what sense?"

Firkovitch: "No one can heal you, only God. We can strengthen one another by taking care of one another."

What helps you to feel stronger?

Firkovitch: "The word of God through the Bible."

What makes healing hard for you?

Firkovitch talks to Louis. Louis says, "When he has problems, what makes him strong is that he finds other people who know the Bible better than he does, and they show him passages that help him find strength and understanding.

"What makes him sad is when he doesn't have a pen or notebook or school fees."

Vicmanotor talks to Louis. Louis explains, "They have no one to cry with or to comfort them."

Meghan asks, *What is dignity?*

The boys are puzzled. Louis explains the question to the boys. They engage in a lengthy conversation.

"They say when you feel a dignity in your own life, you can then proceed with confidence and self-respect. Before you respect someone else, you first have to respect yourself. Before you honor someone else, you first have to honor yourself, then you can get whatever you want. This is the key to life."

What takes dignity away from people?

More conversation ensues.

Firkovitch: "What I see is that even when there are so many problems, no one can take away your dignity.

"To drink is not bad, but if you drink too much, you will break things in your house. When you are drunk, people view you as strange and dangerous. Here it is easy to lose your dignity. But no one takes your dignity from you. It is something you must hold on to and maintain for yourself."

How do you see this project in the Village—the building of the Genocide Memorial and the designs being painted on the houses?

Firkovitch: "This project has brought a new mind to the people here. Usually when people come and help, they help 'Rwanda.' But this project is being done specifically for us—here in this Village. It elevates our dignity, our self-respect.

"I believe this project is doing something great to this community. People here have so many problems from the war, the deaths of many loved ones. When they see such beauty created for them, they feel that they are not alone, that we are together. It helps us."

Louis translates Vicmanotor's words:

"In this Village, a lot of people found themselves in unbelievable events. Horrible events. The genocide. When they see this [he points to the painted houses], they start thinking about their friends, their children, their families. This is a sign that we will be here for a long time, and we feel encouraged. It helps us."

Damas is at the wheel. We are on our way to the village of Gatumba. Jean Bosco and Lily are talking in the front seat. I am in the back. We are being thrown left and right over this hellish, steep, winding, dirt—no—rock-strewn road. Much of the road has washed away. We disappear for minutes at a time in gullies with a thousand-foot drop-offs on the passenger's side, steep and treacherous with rocky, eroding shoulders that make driving the slickrock roads of Utah's Canyonlands child's play. Mudslides around every corner. Rivers below running red. The road not only jars your back but also your head as you enter into some sort of stupor.

At one point, we pass hundreds upon hundreds of people with pickaxes, sledgehammers, and shovels who are helping to build and rebuild this deteriorating road—men, women, and children. Lily says it looks like the massive work projects in China. Rwandans are wearing America's discarded T-shirts. The people become walking billboards for American consumption, from Old Navy to Abercrombie & Fitch to Eminem to "Harry and Elaine's 50th Wedding Anniversary." One young man pounding a pickax into stone is wearing a T-shirt that reads, "Having a frickin' good time."

We left at 6:30 A.M. We arrive in the village of Gatumba at 9:45 A.M. and enter the assistant mayor's office. Jean Bosco tells the story of meeting Lily in Barcelona and how the Barefoot Artists project began. The mayor, a large, impressive man, has just walked in. His office is small, painted turquoise on the bottom half and orange on the top half with drapes made of navy blue fabric in a '60s floral print. The drapes are drawn.

The Rwandan flag and the Rwandan coat of arms are standing on either side of the mayor, with Paul Kagame's photograph hanging above. I have seen his picture on the wall of every bureacrat's office. His face is everywhere—moving across the country on buses, advertising peace on billboards, and being worn on T-shirts. He is hanging in the front room of every home we have visited, seeming to confirm his 96 percent approval rating. His eyes are watching the most minute of details of this country in reconstruction.

As Lily is explaining our work to the mayor, my mind is wandering, still bouncing around somewhere back on the winding road. I can't concentrate. I feel myself shutting down. It has become too much—the residue of violence, the brokenness, the instability of the land and the people. Rwanda is an open wound.

But not without beauty. Driving into this mountainous region, the most culturally remote place I have ever been, the most exciting moment for me, was to see the yellow bamboo, so elegant in the landscape. It became a pause of wildness in the midst of overwhelming deforestation. I wept.

The mayor speaks:

Thank you. I tell you a brief story. This is the district of Nyagisagara. In the past, it was called la Commune Kibilira, during the genocide. We now have a population of eighty-four thousand people. Kibilira has fifteen sectares. Gatumba is one of the sectares. Kibilira's history is very sad. Kibilira was the first commune where the killing of Tutsis began. The date was October 6, 1990.

Jean Bosco interjects the fact that of the seventeen massacres that occurred during the years between 1990 and 1993, fourteen took place in the northwest quadrant of Rwanda, which is where we are working, in the region of Gisenyi. The reason, he explains, is that this was where President Habyarimana and the Hutu extremists had their supporters. The mayor continues:

As a result of this growing Hutu Power, three hundred people were killed on October 6, 1990, all Tutsis. Two thousand more were killed that year. The killings continued. March 1992, December 1992, and into January 1993. These were dress rehearsals for what was to come. The slaughters were denied because of the inaccessible location.

During the genocide, more than twenty-three thousand individuals were killed here, murdered, in Kibilira. Twenty-three thousand. We will go see the site where their bodies are now. At the site, there are a total of around twenty-five thousand people buried in a mass grave adjacent to the church.

(In the background, a baby cries. The number twenty-five thousand is screaming in my head like a verbal migraine, pounding, throbbing. I look up from my notebook, everything is blurry.)

We have one hundred and two orphans.

We have three hundred and seven women-led families with no houses because they were destroyed during the war.

We have two hundred families who do have houses now in the Survivors Village.

One hundred families have nothing. Very, very poor. You will see the bodies are not covered; the families are very, very sad.

We have tried to observe other genocide sites like Nyamata and Gizozi, but we have no money. We have even made a plan.

The mayor pulls out the plan and places it on the table in front of us.

Muhororo is the name of the genocide memorial site. Muhororo Genocide Memorial Site.

The mayor shows Lily the design in detail. Lily explains that if she raises money for this, she must be able to design it and have total artistic freedom.

The mayor tells her they need to raise seventy-five thousand dollars for the memorial site.

Lily says she will consider this challenge and shakes the mayor's hand. I see the reflection of Paul Kagame's face in a mirror with a carved raven as its frame.

The mayor presents Lily with a basket that looks like a woven challis. Our photographs are taken, and we walk down the hall where there are endless lines of people waiting—for what? Documents? Money? Help? I look into their sunken eyes. Many appear already dead.

"This is the mass grave," the mayor says. We are standing in front of a huge hole. We are told the graves are three meters deep, almost ten feet— "Twenty-five thousand people, their bones are piled on top of one another." Jean Bosco explains to Lily and me, in case we didn't fully understand.

"There are actually four mass graves here," the mayor says, "all in a row, covered only by the tin roofs—open air—it's not good."

I look down at my feet and see the bones of children, even as I hear children's voices playing the schoolyard across the road.

A tall, thin man approaches us slowly. He hangs his head and puts his hands behind his back as he looks at the graves. The mayor introduces us to Paul Musabyimana. He is a survivor. He shakes our hands but does not speak. I am distracted by the children's voices. They are lining up for class. The school is directly across from this mass grave, which is bordered by purple and white flags. To our right is a large, impressive sanctuary. This is all part of the church grounds.

The graves look more like lean-to structures. This burial site feels so tentative—"temporary" is the word that comes to mind. Porous. A place where ghosts can come and go freely.

Cement slabs with rebar handles create coffinlike rectangles. There are four down and eight across. These twenty-four vaults, for lack of a better term, are lined with wooden crosses. Above them, the purple and white triangle flags snap in the wind.

We leave the graves and walk to the church. "I'm so sorry," I say to Paul. He shrugs his shoulders. "And so we go on," he says.

The church at Muhororo. We stand before it under a cloudy sky with the wind picking up dust. I cover my mouth with my scarf. Deep soulful voices escape the confines of the church and reach us like heat waves.

"A prayer song" says Jean Bosco. "I Sing for You, God." It is a song well known here in Rwanda.

We look through broken windowpanes into a dark room of the brick annex to the church. Women are singing, their hands undulating like butterflies. A choir of older women. They sing with their eyes closed. It is the same chorus being sung over and over again, like a musical rosary being moved not through their fingers but through the vibrations of their voices. Children from the school surround us as we listen together.

Inside the church, we sit forward facing the altar. The children sit on benches to the side and face us, staring. It is unsettling. Jean Bosco tells us most of the people were killed here—inside this church.

"It has been restored," he says. "And I believe they have restored the peace."

It is a beautifully sublime space with a history that screams from the mass graves outside.

The walls are red brick. The altar face is white. It is true; this internal space is serene.

We sit in silence, aware of thunder rolling outside.

This is the recurring story throughout Rwanda. The majority of the killings happened inside churches. In a 1991 government census, 89.8 percent of the population claimed membership in a Christian church; 62.6 percent said they were Catholic, 18.8 percent Protestant, and 8.4 percent Seventh-Day Adventist.

The complicity of the churches in the Rwandan genocide emerged from the complex web of colonialism, religion, politics, and power that ultimately made the slaughter of hundreds of thousands of Tutsis possible.

Nineteenth-century colonialism helped to prepare the soil for ethnic divisions fostered and promoted by the German and Belgian authorities. Tutsis were favored by the Belgians for decades. White missionaries regarded the Tutsis as more closely related to Europeans, with finer physical features and more "aristocratic" behavior as herders of cattle, than the Hutu peasants, who resembled the Bantu-speaking tribes of West Africa.

Hutus, 85 percent of the Rwandan population, became resentful. Omer Bartov writes in *In God's Name: Genocide and Religion in the Twentieth Century,* "The new 'progressive' missionaries who championed the cause of the Hutu in the 1950s promoted an ideology of exploitation that identified the Tutsi as the culprits in Rwandan history while ignoring exploitation by the German and Belgian colonial rulers. Hence, when a Hutu uprising occurred in 1959, attacks were directed against the Tutsi rather than the Belgian administrators. The inaccurate ideal promulgated by the missionaries that Tutsi had grossly exploited the Hutu for centuries continues to shape Hutu understandings of Rwandan history and eventually became a primary ideological justification for genocide."

Tom Ndahiro, a commissioner of the Rwandan National Human Rights Commission, states, "Stereotypes used by the Hutu-dominated Rwandan government to dehumanize Tutsis were also spread by some influential clergymen, bishops, and priests, before and after the genocide. The Catholic Church and colonial powers worked together in organizing racist political groups like the Party for the Emancipation of the Hutu."

Prior to the 1994 genocide, power in Rwanda was found in both the state and the churches. Soliciting support from the government helped secure support for the religious leaders. Obedience to public officials was part of the missionary message. As the dominant religion in Rwanda, the Catholic Church supported the status quo, even though Pope John

Paul II was one of the few world leaders religious or political to speak out against the genocide.

On April 27, 1994, at his general audience, the pope said, *"I invite all in positions of authority to work generously and effectively to end this genocide."* And on May 15, he made a public statement to pilgrims in St. Peter's Square. *"Again, today, I feel it is my duty to recall the violence to which the peoples of Rwanda are subjected. This is an out-and-out genocide, for which unfortunately even Catholics are responsible."*

What people do is much more important than what people say. It can be argued that sins of omission committed by priests during the genocide inspired more deaths than those by individuals who grabbed a machete and chopped their neighbors to death. The current government has accused at least twenty Catholic priests of war crimes.

On April 22, 1994, two Benedictine nuns, Sister Gertrude, the mother superior of Sovu, and Sister Maria Kisito willingly turned over refugees seeking shelter in their convent to the Hutu militia, which resulted in the slaughter of seven thousand people who were burned and butchered to death. Both sisters were Hutu. Ethnic loyalties transcended religious convictions—they believed that if they apologized to God, no matter what they did, they would be forgiven. They were convicted in Belgium in June 2001 on charges of homicide.

Witnesses tell of seeing the sisters carrying jerry cans of gasoline into a garage and dousing more than five hundred women and children trapped inside, setting them on fire, and then bringing in dried leaves to fan the flames and let the Tutsis burn inside with the door locked and bolted.

One of the most gruesome massacres took place at the Sainte Famille Church in Kigali. Hundreds of refugees were murdered at the hands of the Reverend Wenceslas Munyeshyaka, who let Hutu militiamen into the church to rape and kill Tutsis hiding there. But there are also stories of courage and compassion within churches. A Hutu priest, Father Célestin Hakizimana, who presided at the St. Paul Pastoral Center in Kigali, bribed the Interahamwe with beer and wine while cajoling them with his wit. On other days, he chose to intimidate them with the authority of his robes when they tried to break into his church. He was constantly on the streets, walking through the carnage, relentlessly trying to secure food and water for the refugees under his care. Eventually, he was shot and killed, but today he is still revered, remembered, and honored as a hero of the genocide, credited with saving more than fifteen hundred refugees who sought shelter in his church.

"Genocide depends on raising voices," writes John K. Roth. "It cannot exist unless divisions between people are constructed by speech, fears are expressed in ideology and propaganda, and killing is unleashed by voices that proclaim it to be necessary."

There is an uncomfortable corollary between the "hate radio" in Rwanda, the RTLM (Radio Télévision Libre des Mille Collines), used as an instrument of Hutu extremists to further their agenda of fueling and igniting the genocide, and the "shock jocks" that flood the airwaves in the United States with their simplistic and charged rhetoric to ignite the masses against "environmental wackos" and "feminazis." It is a hair's width between intolerance and hatred, between verbal abuse and physical violence. A cockroach in Rwanda is a Tutsi. A "varmint" in America, according to Michael Savage, is a liberal.

Each day, I hear stories of those who survived the killings inside churches. They wonder why they are alive and not dead. It's as if by telling their stories, they come closer to making peace with their own survivor's guilt. That if they can make me not only believe in the horror but see it with them, some act of redemption can occur between the dead and the living.

What I do believe is that if human beings are capable of mass murder within mass hysteria than I, too, as a human being am also capable of such things. My only protection is my independent mind. Fear is the mechanism used to get both the masses and the bureaucrats, clergy, or clerks, to carry out the anonymous orders of those in power.

At each memorial, I read "Never Again" in Kinyarwanda. But each time I see these coupled words and realize what is occurring in the Congo and Darfur, I want to add a comma between them: Never, Again.

And still, we look away.

Through the countryside the women walk, walk, walk, carrying everything imaginable on top of their heads: firewood, charcoal, potatoes,
yams, all manner of fruits and vegetables; baskets; water jugs; large bundles of herbs; long shoots of sugarcane; plastic basins of supplies; tiles;
car motors, the list goes on and on. The women work hard and long,
plowing in the fields, planting, hoeing, harvesting—and the men? The
men sit around, talk in town, any town, all towns. Out of work. Nothing
to do. Especially young men. No wonder that during the war, this population of Rwandans were eager to "go to work," an opportunity to use
their "tools" (i.e., machetes). Those in charge made sure the young men
had plenty of banana beer to drink as they became "a marching choir"
flashing the bloodstained machetes above their heads on their way to the
next house or village or field, singing.

Jean Hatzfeld, a French reporter, asked young members of the Hutu militia who were in jail after the genocide why they participated in the killing.
One prisoner replied, "It was easier than farming."

All I can see are rivers running red, this time not with the blood of the
people but the blood of the land. Steep mountainsides are cultivated clear
to the summits. The green and yellow squares looked like a stretched
quilt pulled apart by rain and gravity.

Genocide is not just about the killing of people but the taking of land, killing
those who have it, claiming it for yourself. Land ownership was one of the
incentives those in power gave to those who did their dirty work for them.

Erosion—the other genocide in Rwanda, the one rarely mentioned.
Rwanda is a country that is literally slipping away.

Land—the taking of prairie dogs for the taking of land, the toxicity in the
land from pesticides, from radiation that enters our bodies, Steve's death,
Mother's death, the millions of deaths around the world from environ-
mentally caused cancers. We are suffering from habitat fragmentation
resulting in a breakdown of overall health.

Erosion of hillsides, the inability to hold on, to come to terms with the
immense cruelty of the past—no wonder there is a catastrophic erosion
of belief around the planet.

But every day, I watch women walking the steep, winding roads of Rwanda carrying their burdens on their heads so they can continue to feed their children. Even under the most severe circumstances, we adjust and find our way. It is more than survival; it is how we ground our dignity and purpose in the mundane occurrences of a day.

Medard just brought me a mirror with a napkin, gesturing that I had toothpaste on my face. What a mess we Americans are. Rwandans are proud. Those with jobs are meticulous in their appearance—pressed shirts, pants, crisp blouses and skirts. Polished shoes. I look down at my work boots, which Jean Bosco insisted be shined. I brought the worst clothes I have, clothes to work in, paint in, and give away.

Next time, out of respect, I will dress well for those in the Village.

Today, Meghan and I picked some white lime blossoms, deeply fragrant, and placed them in a beautiful black ceramic vase with mica flecks made by the Batwa. These forest dwellers (formerly known as Pygmies) comprise 1 percent of the population in Rwanda. We bought the vase from a man who was selling red and black pottery on the edge of the Village. A few miles behind the memorial site, there is a Twa community. The Twa children who come down to the school are shunned.

We gather outside on Mama Chakula's porch, light several candles, and listen to Rwandan music. Louis joins us after work. "This is a very sad song," he says standing. "Do you know what Jean Paul Samputu is singing?" He sits down on the couch and translates the Rwandan musician's lyrics:

> *God, where were you during the killings? God, you leave Rwanda during the day, but you come back here to sleep. Where were you during the genocide? God, where did you go during the genocide?*

Listening to Louis's voice as Alan quietly plays the drum in the background sends me into an altered state, with the red glow of the volcano emanating from the Congo. Meghan and I are not Americans, Louis is not Rwandan, Alan is not Jewish, and Lily is no longer Chinese; we are simply human beings inhabiting the Earth, together.

Louis shared how he got the nasty scar on his left hand. "Some boys I went to school with were following me home. They were Hutu and calling me and my mother *inyenzi*, 'cockroaches.' It was raining hard. One boy started chasing me down a muddy hillside with a raised machete. He slipped just as the machete fell on my hand, but I escaped."

A long silence.

"I was lucky," he said.

Candles are burning. It is close to midnight. Medard has prepared a late dinner of rice and chicken with spinach and peas. Avocados and pineapple are served for dessert. All fresh. All food cooked outside over a wood fire. We are tired. No one is talking. Lily has her hands folded on the table with her eyes closed. She opens them. "I'm not happy with the project."

We look up from our plates.

"I need to retreat," she says. "I'm tired. It is time for me to create my own sacred space internally."

No one responds.

"I understand that I must let go, that the aesthetic in the Village has its own momentum, and the people are now painting their own designs in the Village . . ." She pauses. "It's good. It's as it should be. I'm just not that interested."

Lily is as surprised as we are. She came to Rwanda and made an enormous commitment, both physically and creatively. How can she continue to carry the responsibility that is on her shoulders and yet still be responsible to herself?

Rwanda is more than any of us imagined.

"Does any of this matter? What are we really doing here? It's not going the way I thought it would. The designs are . . ." her voice fades away as she lowers her head. "What I need to do is go home and find my own art in my own solitude."

As we listen to Lily confront her own soul's doubts with honesty and anguish, I wonder how much of her anxiety is fatigue and how much is the daily accumulation of sorrow that one cannot help but absorb as a porous being engaged with others. Her doubts begin to compound our own.

And I followed her . . . I thought to myself.

In Louis's words, I begin to "hunt myself" as my own mantra of anxiety begins to speak.

Why did I come to Rwanda? Because Lily asked me. Because I believed in her. Because I trusted her vision and now she does not trust her own. I said no—I said yes, realizing that if I refused her invitation I would be saying no to my own spiritual growth. Perhaps I am just selfish. Perhaps I came to Rwanda to better understand the nature of my own grief after Steve's death, to have my own sorrow absorbed into a larger one; perhaps I came to learn something because on some fundamental level, I trust the opportunities that come to us even when we are afraid. Bullshit. I don't know why the fuck I am here.

As we hold Lily with our silence, I realize we are the broken ones.

I am scared to death that if Lily chooses to disengage, everything will fall apart. Alan and Meghan go to bed. Lily and I stay up for the better part of the night and talk about our mothers. Mine is dead and hers is in her late eighties. Who can say how our mothers appear to us in times of discontent, to provoke and to console at once.

"I need to spend more time with her before she goes," Lily says.

The Sacred Ibis.
The Sacred Abyss.

This morning on the porch, I experienced both—the ibis flying outside; the abyss, present inside. Lily's shattering realization last night has left us uncertain and insecure, qualities I cannot afford right now. We have held on to the illusion that we were standing on solid ground. We now know we were standing on top of a trap door. Last night, it opened and we found ourselves in a free fall.

Almost a month has passed. We gather in the Village at the request of the women. Mama Emma, Spacious, and other women from the Village gather. They are dressed up in their head scarves, bright blouses, colored shawls, and batik sarongs. Dozens more women with their children are seated on benches in front of Mama Emma's newly painted house.

Liberata stands and begins the meeting. "Every day we see you here, having come here from America working on the construction of the monument and painting this Village. When the children greet us each day singing, *Turabishimeye* (We are happy to be together), we feel the same. *Kujenga pamoja*. Together we build."

Lily stands before the community and speaks: "We recognize there are many problems in the Village, emotional trauma and poverty among them, but we feel beauty and joy are the first steps to solving them together.

"We recognize jobs and education are paramount. We are not a government organization, but we will go back and tell your story, and hopefully, other people will be moved to help and participate in this struggle."

"We hope the 'School of Sharamanzi' continues to teach the children about both the old and new Rwanda and how to behave with respect. And we hope that Fabrice will continue to help the children draw and understand their world around them. We hope you will continue to paint the houses because when I come back in the spring, the big project will be to complete the monument."

Lily asks for requests, what they need to make their village sustainable, saying "We cannot do it, but we can find the right people to work with you who can."

Many of the women present speak words of eloquence, others, words of heartfelt simplicity. Spacious speaks as one of the senior women: "Thank you. God bless you."

Damas: "You have become like family. You can go back to the States and talk about us, share our problems with your friends and bring back many visitors. And it is my wish that this project can continue, not just here but throughout Rwanda. Psychologically, people in Rwanda have to change the minds and perceptions of the world."

Husein: "Some may say painting these houses is a simple project, but for us, it is very important for us to see what is possible."

Wilson, an artist from Gisenyi, speaks (Jean Bosco translates): "When we arrived in the Village, we saw a change in color, in the children, in the whole village. In Gisenyi, there is a forum of artists, that want to share in this project. And this program could go all over Rwanda with Jean Bosco's help."

Jean Bosco explains to the mothers what we have been doing together in the Village. Again, he uses the phrase *Kujenga pamoja*. The children do not take their eyes off of him, enthralled by his booming voice and oration. I am sitting next to Liberta and cannot help but notice that she is copying the names of the dead from a master list for Lily. In the smallest of writing, the names fill both sides of the paper, along with their ages:

89 years
84 years
32 years
49 years
38 years
13 years
12 years
7 years
60 years
14 years
11 years
36 years
9 years
6 years
4 years
2 years
23 years
40 years . . . and so on

Jean Bosco finishes his speech, pauses, and looks around. "You see what has happened in one month? It is just the beginning. I ask you to become involved."

Lily speaks once again. This time with great emotion; for the first time, she weeps. The women weep with her, wiping their eyes with the edges of their sarongs.

Jean Bosco leans over to me, "Terry, we have a problem; all the women are crying. In Rwanda, when one woman cries, all the women cry with her." I whisper back to him, "Jean Bosco, this is not a problem." We hold hands.

Lily talks about her Chinese background, how as an artist she is drawn to broken places, that out of brokenness beauty emerges. Rwanda has taught her about humility, to let go, to trust in the wisdom of the people. She says that she believes leadership emerges from community needs. She thanks the women for their wisdom and strength.

She looks down and then directly into their eyes. "I feel this is not just Rwanda's story but all of our story."

As I listen, I realize Lily's need to voice her disengagement last night has allowed her to fully engage today. Nothing is as it appears.

The meeting ends with Liberata giving us statistics about the children:

THE CHILDREN IN THE VILLAGE

1 year to 10 years—112 children
11 years to 20 years—75 children

Liberata then reads off another list to the women in Kinyarwanda, and they begin to organize the distribution of clothing.

A woman in the Village speaks as she balances her young daughter on her hip, with another tugging at her skirt. "To see you is very interesting for us. We see you through our children. They are happy. Thank you for coming."

Sharamanzi slowly stands; he has painted his wooden cane yellow and raises it up to the sky, smiling.

The meeting is over.

There was a day when I walked away from the Village. I didn't want anyone to see my tears. Suddenly, I felt a pull on the back of my shirt. I turned around. It was Jean Claude, one of the children who, at age twelve, is head of his family. He looked at me, smiled his big broad smile, and shook his head as he waved his index finger side to side. He grabbed my hand and walked me back to the Village. When he snapped his fingers, thirty, maybe forty children came running and created a circle. Jean Claude started singing, and all the children joined him. He pulled me into the circle, then started "Congo dancing." Ferdinand jumped in and also started dancing around me; he put his arms inside his shirt with one hand down his pants in the gesture of an erection. The children were wild with laughter as we danced in the center of the painted houses. And then I noticed Jean Claude standing outside the circle, perfectly still, his arms folded, staring at me, pleased with what he had set in motion.

Sitting on the shores of Lake Kivu again, I watch lightning over Goma. Four million people have died in the Congo since 1998, and most of those deaths have been children five years old or younger. Many of the Hutu *genocidaires* fled Rwanda to the Congo. And Tutsi rebels have not forgotten their sins on their own people. Like Rwanda in 1994, the violence in the Congo is both ongoing and invisible to the outside world.

On the shores of a lake that joins both countries, Louis tells me, "Since the war, the Hutu extremists have infiltrated Congolese culture without any retribution for their actions. They have a strong presence in North and South Kivu." He throws a stone in that direction. "Being a Tutsi on Congo land today is a big problem. The Interahamwe have never lost their dream of the extermination of all Tutsi. Their commitment to violence has never stopped—be it rape or maimings or murder." He looks across Lake Kivu. "It's happening now and the world has gone to sleep once again.

"But this quiet massacre cannot be heard because even most Congolese believe that sweeping the Tutsi away is the only solution to the Congo's problems of war. They are refusing to focus on the real threat that lies in the heart of the country: poverty. The unsaid in the Congo is the physical and emotional poverty caused by the Hutu militia, alongside government soldiers. They loot and beat and terrorize the local people. They rape without exception. A five-year-old girl is not too young for these beasts.

They will enter her, digging and widening something so small just to feed the desire of wild men—and then they leave her little body limp on the ground. I have seen it, her mother in agony as she is forced to watch. Old women are not seen as mothers or grandmothers, just discarded flesh to rape. Women are not free after rape but become outcasts who take to the forest and live out their lives in shame, victims of further abuse."

Louis gets up from the sand. "The sad thing is," he says, "since the Congolese government cannot disarm the Interahamwe and send them back to Rwanda for justice, there will never be full disclosure of what is behind the politics. Add to this fact, the immense riches of the Congo's natural resources from gold to oil to uncut forests the size of other countries, there becomes little doubt as to why power chooses to support power. Rwanda becomes invisible once again. We have nothing America wants.

"Here's what all Tutsis know: The Hutu extremists were not satisfied with the bodies they chopped and ate and the blood they drank in 1994 in Rwanda. They are still hunting us. Their job is not complete. It is the people in the villages who are suffering."

Staring out at Lake Kivu with Louis's words on the wind, the lake's surface appears worn and wrinkled. Can a lake grow weary of war?

The children's clothes have been organized in piles in Mama Chakula's living room. It feels like a rainbow of comfort—the cotton T-shirts, the flannel dresses, the pile coats. Today we will sort through the clothes bought at the market for the children at the village. We will need close to two hundred outfits.

The story I don't know if I can tell, the one that words will never be able to convey, belongs to the haunting, charismatic waif who has followed me at the memorial site ever since we arrived. He is constantly by my side, the one who wants to be in every picture, the one who wants to see himself in the digital lens stopped in time as an assurance that he exists in the world, that he has been seen. He is my shadow. Whenever I turn around, he is behind me, staring.

He is the child who watched me take a photograph of the sacred datura that survived the bulldozing and leveling of the land at the memorial site. He is the one who picked the flower and handed it to me.

He is the child whose name I do not know. Nobody seems to know.

This morning in town, as Lily and I were heading into the market, there he was—a beggar boy—one of the street kids. He had a small gunnysack on his head with his possessions, a few potatoes, some beans. He was with another boy, older and taller. Of all the children we have met, he seems the most in need, and I have been tormented by the fact that these clothes for the Village will not reach him. We are told by the other children he lives outside the Village, in the forests where the Batwa live.

Lily and I looked at each other and had the same thought.

We went to a clothing stall for children. The boys followed us. He picked a long-sleeved T-shirt that was gray with bright yellow stripes. His friend also picked out a shirt with stripes. Then we quickly moved to pants. People were watching, gathering around us in the market. It was uncomfortable. He packed the new shirt deep in his bag of potatoes as if to save it, secure it, so it wouldn't be stolen.

He found some navy blue bermudas, quickly took off his one-shouldered long sleeved T-shirt that looked like a dress, put on the new shirt, and tried on the blue pants, which he liked because they fit around his distended belly. Mothers in the market clapped. It was all happening so fast. His friend put some light blue pants on over the faded ones he was wearing. Cash was exchanged between the buyers and the vendors.

The two boys looked over their shoulders and, in an instant, disappeared among the throngs of people.

Big rains last night. And at dawn, pied crows were jumping on the tin roof. My Rwandan morning alarm.

Dignity creates a pause in others and attracts respect. We want to know what a dignified person knows and how. I think of Mama Emma in the

Village. She is a woman of dignity. What she doesn't say, you feel. Her restraint is her power.

Dignity is a presence, a suffering withheld, a reserve and a patience learned through difficulty, a broken heart held together through acceptance, not bitterness.

So many of the children we have met in Rwanda have dignity. Dignity has nothing to do with age. It does have something to do with survival.

My father has dignity. He is a man of principle and a straightforward awkward empathy. He is direct and unapologetic in the losses he has suffered. He sees the sacrifices of the men who work for him and carries the weight of their lives on top of his.

Ann Tempest, my brother's wife, has dignity. I see her supporting her daughters. I see her kneeling in her garden with a bulb in one hand and a trowel in the other, planting tulips in rich black soil.

There is dignity in Beauty.

Lily has dignity. She watches. She listens before she speaks. And she not only sees but feels what needs to be done. And then she does it.

Lily is at the memorial site, trying to figure out how to build the Bone Room so that it will not fill up with water. Dignity recognizes a force beyond oneself and serves the community in underground ways.

Prairie dogs have dignity each time they stand and greet the sun. And in Rwanda, a cow carries the dignity of the family who cares for it.

Every day, I pass cows, some of them very gaunt, their ribs a ripple beneath their hides, and I think of Louis's love for them. Milk is his sacrament. His name, Gakumba, means "many cows." For him, they were the measure of his family's status and well-being. As a nine-year-old, from the vantage point of a tree branch, he watched forty of his family's cows being butchered by the Interahamwe in Masisi in the Congo. "It was at that moment, I understood genocide," he said.

We have been invited to be guests at the local Gacaca in Gisenyi, just down the road from where we are staying.

"Gacaca," says Jean Bosco, "is pronounced *ga-cha-cha*. It refers to the traditional form of justice practiced in villages throughout Rwanda before colonial times. It was a way the community handled disputes over property rights, goats, cows, all manner of discord from marriage to theft. The community would sit on the lawn or hillside, listen to the quarrel at hand, and decide the outcome through consensus."

On November 8, 1994, the International Criminal Tribunal for Rwanda (ICTR) was created by the United Nations Security Council. Its purpose was to hold perpetrators accountable for acts of genocide and other violations of international law that took place in Rwanda or were committed by Rwandan citizens in neighboring countries, between January 1 and December 31, 1994.

On February 22, 1995, the Security Council by Resolution 977 determined that the seat of the tribunal would be located in Arusha, Tanzania. The tribunal precides over genocide, crimes against humanity, and war crimes, defined as violations of Common Article 3 and Additional Protocol II of the Geneva Conventions.

"Arusha is moving too slowly and shows signs of corruption," says Jean Bosco. "So far, the tribunal has completed less than two dozen trials and only convicted twenty-eight people for acts of genocide. Because of the hundreds of thousands of trials pending as a result of the genocide, and the overload of the courts and prisons, President Paul Kagame has reintroduced the concept of Gacaca. This process, inspired by South Africa's 'Truth and Reconciliation Commission,' has been ongoing for several years with a goal for completion by 2008."

Aside from trying and convicting the lead *genocidaires*, two cases brought before the International Tribunal in Tanzania were especially significant. The trial of Jean-Paul Akayesu established the precedent that rape is a crime of genocide. The Trial Chamber held that "sexual assault formed an integral part of the process of destroying the Tutsi ethnic group and that the rape was systematic and had been perpetrated against Tutsi women only, manifesting the specific intent required for those acts to constitute genocide." The presiding judge, Navanethem Pillay, said in a statement after the verdict: "From time immemorial, rape has been regarded as spoils of war. Now it will be considered a war crime. We want to send out a strong message that rape is no longer a trophy of war."

The other noteworthy trial in Arusha acknowledged the role of propaganda in inciting the Rwandan genocide. The trial began on October 23, 2000, and investigated the role of "hate media" in encouraging the genocide of 1994.

On August 19, 2003, life sentences were recommended for Ferdinand Nahimana and Jean-Bosco Barayagwiza, cofounders of Radio Télévision Libre des Mille Collines, along with Hassan Ngeze, editor of the *Kangur* newspaper. They were charged with genocide, incitement to genocide, and crimes against humanity, before and during the period of the genocides of 1994. On December 3, 2003, the court found all three defendants guilty and sentenced Nahimana and Ngeze to life imprisonment and Barayagwiza to imprisonment for thirty-five years, but due to time spent in detention deducted from his sentence, he will spend twenty-seven years in jail. The case is currently on appeal.

Jean Bosco tells us that ten thousand Gacaca courts throughout Rwanda are now trying genocide suspects in the communities where their crimes were committed. Perpetrators currently in prisons and jails will be tried by their friends and neighbors. If the suspected criminal shows proper remorse and tells who he killed, how he killed them, and where their bones are, the community will grant him forgiveness and fold him back into the community. But if the suspect lies or shows no remorse, or if the crimes waged against him are particularly severe, the judges in the name of community can exact a sentence, including execution, and send the perpetrator back to prison.

He tells us there are three categories of suspects: Category One belongs to those who were the planners and organizers of the genocide, known murderers who led the killings, perpetrators who were in a position of religious or political authority; Category Two belongs to those who were both perpetrators and accomplices with an intent to kill; Category Three includes those who destroyed property.

He quotes statistics that are difficult to comprehend: There are 1.7 million displaced Hutus who are afraid to return to Rwanda for fear of reprisals. Many of them have taken up residency in the Congo. There are 400,000 widows and 500,000 orphans created from the 1994 war. And 130,000 individuals in prison on suspicion of committing acts of genocide.

"Gacaca's goal is to bring restorative justice back into the country so we can live in harmony with one another," says Jean Bosco. "Gacaca is held once a week in every village. Attendance is mandatory. There are nine judges who oversee the proceedings. They are voted on by the community for a three-year term and have the task of collecting information and creating profiles documenting the truth of what happened during the genocide."

Louis meets us at Mama Chakula's House. He quietly says to me, "I don't like to go to Gacaca."

"Why?"

"It brings me nightmares." Even so, he accompanies us.

Lily, Meghan, Carol (a minister who joined us), Louis, and I walk to the community center. A crowd is standing outside. We enter the concrete room through its only door, and as our eyes adjust, we see it is packed with several hundred people. We stand in the back. Immediately, the proceedings stop.

The senior judge addresses Louis in Kinyarwanda. Louis walks up to the judges' table. They engage in a lengthy conversation. We are self-conscious and unsure of what is happening. Women are fanning themselves with folded pieces of paper. Men are sweating.

Louis returns to us and says that the judges welcome us. They say that the community is aware and appreciative of the work we are doing in Rugerero. They are pleased that we wish to bear witness to Gacaca. They say there are over 20,000 prisoners in the jail here in Gisenyi. It is too crowded, and the tribunals are too slow. This is the only way Rwanda can move forward. Each community is in charge of its own justice. The judges ask that we sit up front, in the side pews to witness the trails. They need us to turn over our passports.

"Please come forward," says the judge in English.

We walk up to the front, each one of us placing our passports on the table. Louis publicly thanks the judges and those in attendance for letting us be here, and we find our seats on the side benches. I am seated next to Louis and a man named Mugensa Joshua from the Anglican Church.

The prisoner standing before the judges is a man that I guess to be in his early forties. He is dressed in the customary pink prison shirt and cropped pants and is wearing a black crocheted cap and black leather hiking boots. He is agitated. The community is uncomfortable. There is a great deal of shuffling in the room, coughing, and chattering among people. When the prisoner speaks, there is heckling from the crowd.

Seated on the pew is another prisoner, an older man in his sixties, whose head is bowed.

Joshua whispers in my ear, telling me that the government is feeding all the prisoners, providing them with medical care, clean clothing, and good shoes. They work at odd jobs and get exercise. "In so many ways," he tells me, "they have a better life than most Rwandans." By appearances, these prisoners certainly look better off than those individuals living in the Rugerero Survivors Village.

Joshua helps me understand what I am witnessing:

The prisoner before the judges with a black crocheted cap says he was cooking with a Mr. Hasim Kasimu. He was guarding him from twenty-eight Tutsis.

The judges say this does not make sense.

A witness from the community says to the prisoner, "When you killed Kasimu, I saw you with twenty-eight other killers."

The prisoner says, "No, I was not there. I was at Mama Solange. You saw someone else."

Black-Cap Prisoner and Old Man Prisoner (who is the other prisoner being tried today), evidently had bad blood between them; Black Cap Prisoner accuses Old Man Prisoner of killing Kasimu.

Both prisoners give conflicting details of who saw Hasim driving.

When Black Cap gave his account, the crowd started chanting, "No, tell the truth. This doesn't make sense."

Black-Cap Prisoner continues to contradict himself.

The judges point out to Black-Cap Prisoner that he said he killed Kasimu and threw him in the toilet. A man from the audience says, "You say this in the file; then you say something else to us here at Gacaca."

Black-Cap Prisoner tried to eliminate whole family of Kasimu so there would be no witnesses.

The man in the audience bears witness to this.

François, the secretary of the judges, rereads file of proof of this prisoner killing Kasimu.

People in community say, "Don't waste our time. You came to kill Hasim with Interahamwe and militia troops."

A Muslim man in a white bobo and white cap says, "When we hear you say you are innocent, that you were at Mama Solange, we do not believe you, when in your own file you admit to the killing. We have proof of your killing. We grow impatient."

Black-Cap Prisoner begins to explain himself as he takes out a yellow cloth and wipes his eyes, his brows, and under his arms and neck.

"Sit down—you are talking too much," the Muslim says. "You are wasting our time. Tell the truth or sit down!" The Muslim man is very angry at prisoner.

One of the judges says, "My wish is for the community to hear your case once again. Yes, we invite witnesses to come forward." The judge continues, "Look, the Americans have come to witness our Gacaca; they are moved by this process. Tell the truth; do not contradict yourself.

"We are all brothers, black skin, white skin."

The Muslim stands up again. "This man is not my brother. If you go into my village, they will not know his name. I know my brother's name. You are not my brother."

The judge says, "I meant spiritually."

The tall, impressive man who is Muslim gets up and walks out with many others.

Old Man Prisoner, whose name is Enias, stands humbly before the judges. The judges call for witnesses to speak on his behalf. Old Man Enias was accused of killing Kasimu. It has been said that he had three cars used to transport the Interahamwe.

"This is not true," Enias says. "I only had a Renault truck; that is all."

Old Man Enias tells his story quietly, with his hands formally clasped at his waist. His pink prison attire, perfectly pressed with long pants that break at the top of his polished black shoes with silver buckles, adds a strange air of dignity.

Enias was married to a Tutsi. On April 10, 1994, he took his wife to the Congo so she wouldn't be killed. He is Hutu.

When he took his wife to the Congo, a group of Hutu extremists there turned against him and accused him of giving away information and telling secrets.

Black-Cap Prisoner, the one the Muslim says is not his brother, contradicts Enias.

The judge asks Enias, "If we get proof today that you were driving a car of Interahamwe with an intent to kill Hasim . . ."

Enias replies: "If anything proves that I was transporting Interahamwe, KILL ME. I will support your decision."

The judge says, "When you said . . ."

Old Man Enias interrupts, "Try me; I am ready for any punishment. If you have proof that I transported Interahamwe to kill people," Enias replies, "then give me what I deserve, but I am an innocent man."

There is much talk among the audience. The crowd supports Enias's claims.

The judge explains to Enias the process of Gacaca, that it is for the public, not for police. The public decides according to the witnesses and testimony given. Gacaca has a committee of nine people that has the power to release prisoners with a piece of paper, but we will keep an eye on you.

Someone in the room asks Enias a question, "Do you know where Kasimu was living?"

"No, I don't," says Enias.

"Do you know where Mama Solange was living?"

"Yes."

The prisoner in the black cap says, "I know Enias had a car in 1994 and took Interahamwe into the Congo."

Black-Cap Prisoner says to Enias, "Look, we can figure out a way to free ourselves with fake documents if you would only give enough money . . ."

Black-Cap Prisoner goes on with incoherent details. He keeps looking over at Meghan. His eyes keep darting back and forth.

Enias turns to him and shouts, "Why are you saying this? I am innocent."

In walks another prisoner, confident and brisk, with a long scar running down the side of his face. The energy in the room shifts. Some women begin crying. An elderly man drops his head into his lap and begins moaning.

The head judge turns to Louis and says in English, "Tell our guests who this man is."

Louis leans over and explains that this man's name is Kawawa. He fears nothing. He tells the truth. He is not afraid to say how many people he killed *or to say who the other killers are. He was one of the worst leaders of the genocide and responsible for most of the killings in the Gisenyi region.*

I note the sidelong scar on the left side of his head that divides his face, his long fingers on small hands, his shapeless legs visible from the cropped and creased pink prison pants, the black leather high-top running shoes.

Joshua says to me, "He is the killer of all killers, one of the masterminds responsible for the deaths of thousands. They say he ate the hearts of all those he killed."

Kawawa sits on the bench behind the two standing prisoners, his elbows on his thighs, his fingers tip to tip pulsing up and down, staring at us. His gold watch catches late-afternoon light. A man from Rugerero sitting behind Kawawa looks at us and draws the gesture of a machete with his hand and slashes it through his own heart and points to Kawawa's back.

The judge asks Kawawa to stand. "We know you know everyone who killed Tutsis in Gisenyi. Did you see Enias drive Interahamwe around, and did he kill Kasimu?"

Kawawa looks directly at the judge: "No."

Appearing weary, Enias reiterates again in a soft voice, "I am innocent. If you find proof that I killed Kasimu, I will accept punishment." Enias tells how he got his wife a refugee card in the Congo.

Black Cap Prisoner says Enias left the car in the Congo and makes more accusations.

The judge says to Enias, "If this is true, what are you ready to accept?"

Same response from Enias: "I will accept my fate, but I tell you in the burning truth of my heart, I am an innocent man who has been held in prison for seven lost years."

The judge turns to Kawawa again. "Is this man lying?" He points to Black-Cap Prisoner.

Kawawa stands. "Yes. He's lying. He killed Kasimu, and he killed with me."

The judges leave the room to make a judgment. People walk outside during the break, talking to one another, some arguing, others listening.

The judges return. A gavel is pounded on the table. Silence follows. And then the verdict:

"Based on witness accounts and contradictions within your own testimony, we find you, Manquent, guilty. You will return to prison. And based on witness accounts and testimony, we find you, Enias, innocent. We release you from prison."

The community erupts with joy. People clap and cry and make birdlike calls. Documents are signed. Kawawa walks freely up to the table of judges and signs the declaration of innocence as a witness.

What I remember is this: After the judgments had been delivered and the Gacaca was over, I walked up to the judges still seated behind the table and asked if I could get their full names and the names of the prisoners. I told them I was a writer and the scribe of our group. I explained I wanted to make certain my notes were accurate.

"No problem," the head judge said to me. He proceeded to write all of the names down in block letters on the piece of paper that I handed him.

NAMES OF THOSE PRISONERS HEARD IN GACACA ON SEPTEMBER 18, 2005:
BAHINZI   ENIAS
NTIRENGANYA   MANQUENT

I noticed when he was finished that Kawawa's name was not on the list.

"How do you spell 'Kawawa'?" I asked.

"K—A—W—A—W—A."

I looked up—Kawawa was leaning forward on the edge of the table, spelling his own name.

Our eyes locked. I became frozen with fear.

Louis, who witnessed what was happening, rushed up behind me, "What's going on? Are you okay?"

I turned to Louis. "Kawawa just spelled my na—I mean, *his* name." quickly correcting myself.

Suddenly, chaos erupted. Kawawa grabbed the guard's AK-47 and started waving it around the room, his hand on the trigger. They struggled. People were screaming. All I saw was the barrel flashing above the crowd. I heard the safety click. *My God, Kawawa is going to kill us all.*

And then it was over.

Two men tackled Kawawa and fell to the floor. The gun didn't fire. The guard recovered his weapon. Kawawa stood up and looked at us: four Americans, seven judges, Louis, and half a dozen street kids hiding behind us. We were the only ones left in the room.

The guard pointed his gun at Kawawa's back and herded the remaining prisoners outside. No handcuffs. No shackles. Nothing. They walked out of the building like free men and headed back to the prison on the dusty roads of Gisenyi at dusk.

From a distance, Lily followed Kawawa and the three other prisoners down the dirt road. I have a photograph of her walking behind the men dressed in pink. When she returned home, I walked into her bedroom. We held each other for a long time.

"I told you, I don't like Gacaca," Louis said as we sat on the couch at Mama Chakula's house holding hands. "This is only the second time in two years that I have been. That time, I heard the testimony of a man who killed fifty people, twenty women and thirty children."

"You are feeling the terror that we all know."

Louis talked about the years after 1994—1995, 1996, 1997, and 1998. "Those years after the war were another kind of terror," when the outside world thought the killing in Rwanda was over.

He was living in Ruhengeri with his grandmother. Every night, there were killings. You could hear the cries. You could hear the Interahamwe coming, marching, singing. There was a shooting in his school. He ran, he ran out of the school, across the road, into the fields, when a shoulder launched grenade exploded above him. He fell down; he thought he was dead. He was alive.

"I survived."

"Jenda—that village where Interahamwe came; they killed and killed and killed until morning," Louis said.

He must have seen the looks on our faces in candlelight as we sat around the dinner table in near darkness.

He stood up, rail thin, and looked out the barred window. "Rwanda is not just a country anymore. It's a people on the move with no place to go."

At night, my mind is racing, forward and back, unraveling and rewinding, playing the terror over and over: Kawawa grabbing the gun from the one guard, the only guard's gun? The scattering. The chaos. Everyone running out as we remained. It happened so quickly. Yet in my mind it unfolds in slow motion, evil in motion. I remember afterward, Louis and I holding each other, shaking in terror.

How Kawawa walked out with four other prisoners, freely, down the street, past our house, as though nothing had happened. No handcuffs, no shackles, just walking back to the prison in twilight. How?

Kawawa—those hooded eyes, his stained hands *(can blood stain hands?)*, black fingernails gripping the edge of the table. K-A-W-A-W-A. No whites in his eyes, only red, blood-filled eyes. There is a charisma to evil, and I saw it.

Kawawa just spelled my name. His name. My name.

Rewind racing mind. Kawawa is staring. Racing mind. The face of evil. The charisma of evil. Turn around. The gun. The screams. Down on the ground. Rewind racing mind.

And if the gun had fired?

Jean Bosco arrives at Mama Chakula's very early this morning. He is not his congenial self, the man with the mantra, *"Ntakibazo"* (translation: no problem). He is tense, disturbed, pacing back and forth on the porch smoking cigarettes, one after the other.

"People are saying," Jean Bosco tells us, "that Kawawa tried to kill the Americans at Gacaca. He wanted to create an international sensation to let the world know that the Interahamwe are still alive, that their work is not finished. Kawawa made a calculation and took his chance."

Michel has just arrived. *"Kawawa?"*

"Kawawa," says Jean Bosco and speaks to him in Kinyarwanda for a long time. They argue, go back and forth.

Michel turns to me, "I know Kawawa—*Kawawa Bizimana Djumaapili*— I was one of his judges at Gacaca in 1995." He pauses and turns away from us. "Horrible," he says. "The trial was two weeks. Kawawa spared no details. The most gruesome of storytellers. It was horrible." He turns toward us. "We sentenced him to death. But he still lives."

Michel, Damas, and Jean Bosco talk feverishly among themselves. I ask what they are saying.

Michel grows angry and says, "This is a problem here in Rwanda. The government says the killers can be released and that they have the capacity to change, but with a killer like Kawawa, I do not believe it." They reiterate how dangerous it is to have Kawawa on the street, walking free, with only one guard, a guard whose gun does not even work. Michel shakes his head. "Kawawa travels all over Rwanda as a witness to who killed whom during the war."

"Kawawa," Jean Bosco explains "was the chief of all the killers in this region. Before the genocide, he was a thief; he was nothing. I knew him. During the genocide, he became a big man."

"And now," says Michel, "they say he has impeccable integrity because of his ruthless truth telling."

On our way to the Village, I was sitting next to Michel in the back of the Red Cross vehicle. We passed a truckload of prisoners. Michel grabbed me. "Terry—look, there! Kawawa! He's looking for you!"

We all laughed very, very hard. Especially Louis.

We arrive at the Village. I walk down to see how Dorothée is doing and see her baby. She is standing in her doorway looking elegant as always but very tired. She is talking to Damas.

We greet one another—kiss three times on either cheek. I ask her how she is feeling. She tells me she is not well, malaria. She's had it for three days and cannot take the strong medicine she needs because she is breast-feeding.

She is weary, spent. She looks as though she has just stepped out of a steaming hot shower, wet with fever.

Even so, she is pleased with her painted house. Above her door, a striped Cheshire cat stares, and turquoise, white, and yellow diamonds create a border around her block of houses.

I tell her that we went to the Gacaca in Gisenyi on Sunday, but before I can give her any details, she interrupts me and says, "I heard. . . ."

Damas looks ahead, away from me.

"I know Kawawa." She pauses and gets control over her emotions. "He is the murderer who killed my parents in the stadium in Kibuye. He brought a busload of killers—Interahamwe—and murdered thousands of Tutsis who had gathered in the stadium; seventy of my relatives were cut to pieces."

She folds her arms and continues in Kinyarwanda. Damas translates and tells me that she escaped with her brother and cousins. They fled to Lake Kivu, swam for three days, fighting their way through the floating bodies, hiding beneath them, underwater, taking in little breaths of air so as not to be seen. They swam all the way to Goma. They lived in Goma for months in the refugee camp. She and her brothers and sisters survived.

"Kawawa—evil," she says, spitting on the ground, shaking her head. "You saw the face of evil just like the rest of us." She clicks her tongue.

Jean Bosco wants us to visit his village of Belinda. This is where he calls home. It is a long drive from Gisenyi through the corridors of banana trees and severely eroding dirt roads.

He tells us the community is made up of 820 families, 140 led by women, and there are seventy-four orphans.

Water is the main problem: It is over seven miles to the reservoir. Women have to walk for water all the way back to the main road, which is nearly two miles to the closest pump. What is needed is a water pipeline to the village.

We meet the mayor at the community center. The mayor gives us these facts: Malaria is very severe here. Diarrhea is a big problem with the children. They become dehydrated and die. AIDS is also a serious problem here in this village. If a person has AIDS, they say that person has been "poisoned."

Jean Bosco explains the needs of this poor community. Not only do they need clean water. They need medicines and a health clinic. They need cows. They need microloans.

The mayor says that not all is bleak in Belinda. They have bananas, beans, potatoes, and vegetables that the women cultivate. And Belinda has a professional troupe of dancers. Perhaps we would like to help bring them to America?

Wherever we go, wherever we look, the poverty, the needs, the expectations and requests are like quivering leaves on a tree dying of drought. We are nobody visiting a village in Rwanda, but we are privileged and seen as somebody who can help. It is about the underclass and how they are desperate to be seen, counted, then served, whether it's in the remote community of Belinda or in the Ninth Ward in New Orleans. Hands out and hands in our pockets. Will there ever come a time when it is simply hand in hand, when we can literally pull each other out of our collective despair and dance?

I have clawed at my own conscience until my mind is ragged.

We sit in this tiny room of exposed red brick, the hand-made bricks we see drying on the side of the roads. I look upward through tiny holes in the corrugated tin roof. I have seen these constellations of light before. I cannot breathe and begin coughing uncontrollably. I apologize, excuse myself, and walk outside.

There is a young woman, very young, breast-feeding twins; one does not look well. The minister traveling with us, pays her five dollars to take her picture. The young woman becomes ecstatic, runs over to a circle of women, and shows them the five-dollar bill.

I am ashamed. I sit under a tree with Damas.

We meet Jean Bosco's friend Michael. He invites us into his house. It quickly fills with family members. Jean Bosco tells us that for many of these people, especially the younger ones, we are the first *muzungus* they have seen, certainly the first ones who have ever visited this house.

Michael and his wife offer us Coke and Fanta.

I wonder if this visit was predicated on promises made by Jean Bosco that he would bring a group of *muzungus*, which meant money, to help. There is so much we do not understand. There is so much we are missing through translation. I feel the weight of expectations that we are unable to deliver. We know little about development issues; there is little we can do.

Claustrophobic—little light, so many people staring at us in this tiny space. One room, one window, one door. Twenty or thirty people standing. Everywhere children. Everywhere babies. All around us, eyes staring from gaunt faces, so many people with distended bellies. An exploding population in an eroding landscape.

I think of the discussion at the Red Cross in Kigali weeks ago, how malnutrition is epidemic in Rwanda, all over Sub-Saharan Africa. Deprived of necessary nutrients, the children become stunted and sickly. We have seen this in the Village in Rugerero. Children who look five or six turn out to be ten and eleven. The statistics that won't leave me are these: Five million African children under age 5 died [in 2006] (40 percent of deaths worldwide) and malnutrition was a major contributor to half of those deaths. Sub-Saharan children under 5 died not only at 22 times the rate of children in wealthy nations, but also at twice the rate for the entire developing world.

The woman sitting next to me, whose name is Immaculate, turns and says, "Please tell people about us."

On our drive home, dozens of children run behind the vehicle crying out, *"Agacupa."* Jean Bosco throws plastic water bottles out the window. One boy runs and runs more than a mile, until we get to the road. He stops and waves. The smile on his face does not fade.

What to do—*Do something.* *"Agacupa,"* they cry. They cry for water bottles. All the children ask for is the pleasure of a water bottle, a container of water saved and shared, their thirst momentarily quelled.

This morning at the Village, Dorothée said she would like me to name her baby. It is customary in Rwanda that parents wait seven days before bestowing a name on their child.

I wasn't sure I was understanding what she was saying. Damas reiterated that Dorothée would like me to give her son a name.

Dorothée said, "Please pick a name for my son."

I told her that this was a great honor. I thought for a moment and then said, "Dorothée, I would like to name your son after my brother. My brother's name was Stephen. He worked hard and helped many people."

"Stephen," she said, smiling.

"Etienne in French," said Damas.

"Etienne." She handed me her son, and I rocked him in the morning light.

We watch a full moon in Rwanda, the color of butter, slowly dripping behind the mountain.

God leaves Rwanda during the day and comes back to sleep at night.

Tomorrow is our last day in Gisenyi.

Outside Mama Chakula's House, Alan is playing soccer on the dusty streets with the kids. Dozens of children are screaming, "Alain! Alain!" and then you hear the ball being kicked and children laughing.

Alan leaves tomorrow. I will miss him. We all will.

Earlier today in the Village, Vicmanotor and Firkovitch asked if I had a photograph of my husband. I put down my pack and pulled out a picture of Brooke and our basenji, Rio. They held the image between them, looking very puzzled. They handed it back to me. "Why this dog?" Firkovitch asked.

I later learned from Louis that during the genocide, dogs ate the bodies of the dead. When he was a child, he feared dogs as much as the men with machetes. "They were big and traveled together in large packs." He said, "Really terrifying. When we see a dog, we see the pain of war." I have not seen any dogs in Rwanda, not one. In America, we sleep with our dogs. In Rwanda, they shoot them.

What is understanding but a shifting set of perceptions, each of us with our own associative memories?

Rwanda is a compelling paradox, and why it is so seductive, the heartbreaking allure of its paradise. One can see both the hope of a nation trying to right itself in the aftermath of genocide and the bold despair held in the eyes of the people as they struggle to address the enormity of their problems—poverty, hunger, disease, population density, erosion, lack of land, and the underlying quicksand of violence that can erupt at any moment, pulling Rwanda on the edge of the Congo into another conflict.

The example of Paul Kagame's leadership is seeping into the collective mind of Rwanda. There is a brave generation of leaders throughout this nation that is planting seeds of restoration through education and the pragmatic dreams of a renewed economy, the leadership of women, and forgiveness, reconciliation, and peace. It is not only rebuilding a country but the self-esteem of its citizens.

And then the face of Kawawa flashes before me—and his tribe of extremists—those in jail and those still breathing in the bush, others living in the Congo, carrying their dreams of Tutsi extermination to their graves. Scratch the soil and blood still pools.

I think of Enias and the restorative justice that is his and how a community through Gacaca brought him back into their embrace after being wrongly accused, a Hutu who was not a killer but another victim.

I look at my two hands. On this hand, good. On this hand, evil. I am capable of both altruism and atrocities, blessings and brutalities. With both hands open, how can I judge another?

This I have witnessed: There is a village in Rwanda that is in the process of painting itself alive, breathing life back into its community through color and the joyful emancipatory gesture of creating beauty. The children are leading their elders toward restoration through their insistence on hope and will continue to do so, given half a chance. It is the stories that move us to a place of change. One man, Jean Bosco, inspired one woman, Lily Yeh, with his story of war and the need for healing. She responded to his call for help and visited Rwanda. She returned home with a vision and inspired three more colleagues to accompany her. They came as Barefoot Artists, in spite of their fears, and there will be others who follow.

I take my last walk on the shores of Lake Kivu, flecks of mica become tiny mirrors in the glistening sand. The lake's reflective nature held my own in all manner of moods. A Pale Chanting Goshawk flew over me—the gift of a feather in front of my feet.

Bones and Dirt. I dream this morning that Brooke and I are presented with bones—leg bones—femur, tibia, fibula—the bones by which we stand on the Earth, the bones that give us stature, upright and tall.

We cannot see who is giving us these bones.

Bones as weapons, we now hold them in hand. We rattle them. We play them as flutes. We use them as drumsticks on hollow logs. The bones of our ancestors are speaking. We listen. Advised by bones. There will be nothing left if we do not listen. The scaffolding of our communities is collapsing.

We are striking two bones together on a mound of dirt.

In the continuing dream, we are shown other mounds of dirt in various colors—where life begins, where seeds are planted, where food is grown. We place our hands in the soil, our fingers turn to roots and wrap themselves around bones until they become trees.

The foundation for the Bone Room is dug and finished.

The children who live next to Mama Chakula's House and I were looking into the leaves of the lime tree with the last of my insect-eye kaleidoscopes. They were were amazed to be looking at the world like bugs.

Jean Bosco walked onto the porch and reprimanded me, saying, "No, not these children, please save for my children—my own children!" And he took a lens from tiny hands and looked up toward the sun for himself.

If there is an untold story, it is the story of Jean Bosco. We know little of his past, where he was, what he saw, how he and his family survived the war.

We know from Clementine that he worked for the Red Cross, that he took photographs of orphans from village to village to help identify them and bring families back together.

We know that he knows everyone, Hutu and Tutsi, that he is smart and clever and opportunistic.

We know he is an eloquent spokesperson for justice and restoration. And we witness every day how hard he is working for the genocide suvivors of Rugerero and communities in need.

In this unfolding story, he is my protagonist, the one who stood between perpetrator and victim, caught and captured, carrying both the wisdom and wounds of the genocide.

We arrive at the Village. The painted houses look bright and joyful. Medard and Mama Chakula have joined us to see for themselves what has been happening. They are surprised to see the transformation, a once gray village is now ablaze with color.

Jean Bosco gathers the children together and asks them to share with us what they have learned in this month. Fernando, ever the trickster, raises his hand, "We would like uniforms to play soccer."

Jean Bosco scolds him and says, "I did not ask you what you wanted, I asked you what you have learned."

Fernando gets a big smile, "I learned that our houses can be beautiful!"

Little Eric says, "I learned we can be happy together." Suddenly, all the children are speaking at once. Jean Bosco points to a group of girls, Olive among them. As they shout out, Jean Bosco translates:

"They now know the story of Old Rwanda from Sharamanzi.
"They know how to draw.
"They know how to paint.
"They like playing football [soccer].
"They learned to be polite and respectful from Sharamanzi.
"They know how to be happy with you."

Jean Bosco turns to us. "They ask you to please bring pens and notebooks with you when you return."

Clothes. Two areas are roped off in the center of the Village, each with three chairs in the center. The children are standing in line behind a rope in front of Mama Emma's house. Liberata points to one family at a time. When it is their turn, each family, primarily a mother with her children, walk up to the designated area and receive one item of clothing for each child—a dress, a shirt, a pair of pants. The teachers hand out the clothes. Orphans like Firkovitch and Vicmanoter receive nothing—they have no advocate. The Twa boy whose name we do not know is hiding behind a cluster of banana trees on the periphery, watching. Jean Claude, twelve, head of his household, is last. He receives what is left, a pair of pink tights for a baby. He takes them and looks at Meghan and me.

I retreat behind the Village to one of the back roads that intersects with a field of sugarcane. Half a dozen women carrying their burdens pass me as I am squatting with diarrhea. They permit me their dignity, even as I place both hands over my face.

I walk over to Dorothée's house to say good-bye and knock on her door. Her sister answers. She invites me inside. The green shutters are closed. It is dusk. We walk into her bedroom, where she is in bed. Dorothée is wet with malaria. I put my hand on her forehead. She is burning with fever. She insists on getting up and walks slowly over to the corner and hands me a beautiful, large mat, rolled up to take home.

"For Barefoot Artists," she says. "Take."

A man is waiting for us. He leads us through a tunnel of banana trees, shooing away the chickens until we come to a small clearing and two huts. Smoke. Flames. The kiln is an open fire. The man's wife is tending it. On the ground are samples of his red and black wares. Some are vases and pots, some are clay birds, and some are candlesticks and incense burners. Suddenly, the little boy who follows me, who appears each day at the memorial site, the one who handed me the sacred datura after the ground had been leveled, the one who appeared in the market, the one who smiles and disappears, the one who was just hiding among the banana trees, walks out of the hut. He grins and hides behind the man. The man sees we know each other. He explains to Jean Bosco that this boy is an orphan. Nobody knows how old he is. He lives with them.

I ask Jean Bosco to ask the man the name of this little boy.

His name is Dusengimana Kigemza. He has a name. He has a family. I see him in place. Kigemza picks up the clay bird and holds it in his small hands. I kneel down to his height and stroke the back of the red bird. "It is beautiful."

We buy everything they have.

Lily explains to the Twa potter that she would like to work with him in creating cisterns for the Village that can catch rainwater from the roofs. She explains through Jean Bosco that this is a common practice in Egypt. They shake hands.

The Twa. Their land has been taken. They are displaced and disdained. They are not allowed to be educated. In the eyes of many, a cow is worth more. They have nothing, only their red and black pottery smoldering beneath ashes in the remembered forests.

It rains. It rains in sheets. I run outside and delight in the shower. I cannot enjoy it alone, and I run back into the house and grab Lily's hand. We stand in the rain and allow ourselves to be drenched. *We did the best we could.* We run back into the house and open all the windows and listen to the deluge dancing on the tin roof.

Late in the afternoon, there is a knock on the door. It is Gapasi Desmites, the president of the Gacaca judges in Gisenyi. He asks if he can come in. We all sit down in the living room. He gets straight to the point. He has come to tell us that Kawawa was sent to Gitarama after Sunday's events.

"We realized that Kawawa is too dangerous to be allowed freedom within the Gacaca. In our desire to move the trials forward, we became complacent. He is still a killer. He will be executed."

The sun has set. I sit on the dusty road of Gisenyi with my back against the redbrick wall that surrounds Mama Chakula's house and watch the light become absorbed by night almost instantly at the equator.

Three ibis fly by—

"The Genocide Memorial at Rugerero holds the bones of 193 people in its keeping as of September 21, 2005," says Liberata. "Here are their names."

Lily and Louis are sitting with Liberata around the table and read through them. There is no electricity. We light candles. "And here is the translation of the words the Village would like to see on the Genocide Memorial," Louis says.

"Will you read it out loud?" Lily asks.

In candlelight, he reads these words with solemnity:

NTITUZABIBAGIRWA
(WE WILL NEVER FORGET YOU.)
MWISHE URWAGASHINYAGURO
(YOU WERE TORTURED TO DEATH.)
MWAGIYE TUKIBAKUNZE
(YOU ARE GONE. STILL WE LOVE YOU.)
MWAZIZE AKARENGANE
(YOU WERE VICTIMS.)
IMANA IBAKIRE MWARI INTWARI
(MAY GOD RECEIVE YOU AS VICTORS.)
TWE ABO MWASIZE TURABIBUKA
(WE STILL REMEMBER YOU.)
TURABASABIRA
(WE PRAY FOR YOU.)
NTITUZABIBAGIRWA
(WE WILL NEVER FORGET YOU.)
MURUHUKIRE MU MAHORO
(REST IN PEACE.)

Louis and I are standing in the living room. Candles are burning. Our shadows are dancing on the wall in flickering light. How to say good-bye? He hands me a brown paper sack. I look inside. There is a pair of shoes, turquoise beaded sandals embellished with cowrie shells. I take them out, place them on the floor, and slip my bare feet into them.

"When you walk in these shoes, I walk with you," he says.

Beneath the open sky, there is no fixed horizon on humanity, only lives lived and stories shared from one broken heart to another.

We have not lost faith in God.

We have lost faith in Life.

Feeling the lift of the plane in my lower back, I close my eyes. I see a procession of Rwandan women walking, each woman is holding a pointed top basket with a tightly closed lid. The women are walking from one village to the next carrying their secrets inside.

Turning shadow into transient beauty.

T. S. ELIOT, Four Quartets

When we arrived in Kigali on March 28, 2007, the first call I made was to Emily Shaffer at the U.S. Embassy. I had one question.

"Where are we on Louis Gakumba's visa?"

Her response was simple and direct. "He picked it up yesterday."

I hung up the phone and sat on the bed of the hotel room. *Louis is coming to America.*

Brooke and I called my father in Utah. "That's great," he said. "When will he be here?"

"He'll be coming home with us," I said. "Three weeks."

"I'll let the college know right away." Dad said. He had agreed to sponsor Louis at Salt Lake Community College for two years.

I hung up the phone.

My body was trembling—*How will we pay for his airplane ticket from Rwanda to Utah? When does school start? Where will he live? How will he support himself?* It didn't matter. What mattered was this: After two years, and having his visa denied three times because, according to the United States Immigration Office, *"Unfortunately your expressions of commitment to Rwanda are not sufficient,"* against all odds, he finally has his visa in hand. I think back to various memos, letters, and e-mails Louis and I have exchanged over these two years, when I would never allow myself to imagine where all this would lead. I have a folder of letters that I am carrying with me.

Dear Terry,

I am strong and believe in God. I know that what a man cannot do, God can. It is better to trust in God and believe that He can do all for those who believe in him.

Let me tell you a short story of my studies:

I went to primary school, but I did not even finish it because of the war. During this period, the security in the Congo where we were living was not good at all. Killings started when I began primary level 4 and I had to stop because of this. Two years later, without studying I went for the national exam to see if I could enter secondary school. I succeeded. It was a big surprise to all my family.

In 1994, [after] the genocide in Rwanda, which spread all over the neighboring countries like Burundi and Congo, we fled the Congo for the safety of Rwanda. In 1995, I started secondary school. I was brilliant and things appeared difficult on one side, but I understood all the subjects as if I had finished grades 5 and 6.

But in 1997, the year went blank. It was nothing but violence and so once again, I had to leave school because of security. The Interahamwe used to come and kill students in the schools. On one occasion, I barely escaped for my life, a shoulder rocket scraped my head as I fell to the ground. The insecurity was unimaginable.

In 1998, we moved to Gisenyi, where I went to Goma in the Congo to study. It was not easy. My mother had no job, not even simply a business to run to help us go to school. My eldest brother (there are seven of us) was already in the 4th year of secondary school. I suggested to my mother that I study mechanics so that I might be able to get some work after school in garages, simply to see if I could help my young brothers to keep on with their studies. It was so hard for us. Life was not easy, but we lived on. We were lucky enough to live with our grandmother. We did not have to pay house rent.

I did my mechanic job up to the 4th form whereby I got a certificate in 2001. I was first in the whole region. Later in 2002, I started reading English books, getting more and more interested in English, listening to English radio, watching English television. And in time, I was able to speak and write English up to the level that I was able to teach myself.

I never attended any English club or did any training in English. It is hard to believe, but true.

In 2005, I decided to go for the national exam in Rwanda. The least acceptable grade is 1.5. I realized I had not been in school since third grade. Luckily, I received 1.8 and passed with great appreciation and received my diploma.

I helped and supported my family since 1995 up until now. So many years. But there is a great hope that my brother Michael is going to help as much as he can. He is good. If I come to America, I won't worry about my family.

I studied in many difficult situations, finishing the four years of secondary school with only two pairs of pants. I think I told you once that I was never happy in my life. Sometimes, I think of all my past and see that there has been nothing to make me happy apart from my believing in God, who does operate miracles in my life.

I am so happy to have met you, Terry. When I read all your e-mails you have written me, I imagine that you also had problems in your life. I want you to know that if you cannot get everything done for me or make this visa happen, I will understand. I won't blame you. You have tried.

This is a long letter I know. You are among the few who now know my history, this little portion of my story that I tell you.

I praise God to not let me be living on the level I have been living on in these past ten years and that I will not even be on the level I was on just five months ago. My hope still lives with the dream of improvement.

I hope Salt Lake Community College will still be my chance to come to America and study in school. No matter what happens, we will still care about each other and stay together as friends.

I wish you luck in all you do,
Louis

2 March 2007

Louis—

Unfortunately because:

My predecessor interviewed you and did not find you eligible.

You chose not to consider his suggestion about using your sponsorship to study here in Rwanda to establish yourself and demonstrate a record of academic achievement related to your proposed area of study.

And you still have not shown me ties to Rwanda which are necessary under law.

It will be impossible for me to grant you a student visa at this time.

I have spent a lot of time researching and I regret this, but I must consistently apply the law.

Emily Shaffer
Consular officer

21 *March 2007*

Dear Emily Shaffer,

Thank you enormously for your concern and time.

Emily, if I dare say that you are my last chance. Perseverance, persistence and tenacity are words we should always have at our fingertips because all great achievements require the use of one or all these virtues.

Unfortunately, my patience has become thin and I wonder why God is doing all this to me. . . . Of course he has a plan that I don't know, and at the other hand I say why did he start this rough road? But I still believe that God is able.

I haven't yet brought any tangible evidence to your request and this is why I am worried to be interviewed by the third other officer authorized to do consular work as you said to get a fresh perspective. . . .

What if he asks me to own a residence moreover not everyone has a house in Rwanda? What if he asks me to show financial assets and other things that would tie me to Rwanda when I expect all these through my own education? But you have learned a lot about me and this is the reason why I say that you are the last person to decide on this case.

There are people who give up so early. Many people fail in life because they believe in the notion that "if you do not succeed in what you are doing, try something else." This is not right because if the dreams become true it is because people who held the dreams stuck to their ambitions. They refused to be discouraged and never let disappointment get the upper hand. I would look more at the future than the past. Going to the US will certainly give me knowledge that will form the bedrock of my life . . . now if this does not happen, well, it will result in high cost.

When you get into a tight situation and everything goes against you, until it seems as though you could not hold on a minute longer, never give up then, for that is just the time and place that the tide will turn (I wonder if this will be the case to me!)

One can always uncover opportunities by applying persistence to possibilities. Not only Terry and Nancy have shown the possibility but you have also contributed. Emily, what tolerance will you show above? I know you can judge me anyhow you like but please this is the right time to help.

Emily, I have told you that my family is the only thing that ties me to Rwanda and it truly is. I have applied three times hoping to get a visa but this was not the case and I am worried that all I had saved for my young brothers for the second semester of their school fees got used. But, this is not a problem because I will keep my focus on the Vision that I have.

I remember that you sent e-mails to your co-workers saying that as my situation changes, then I am welcome to apply again. I do keep your words.

Terry is coming soon and hopefully we will go together and she will introduce me to Utah and to my sponsor. Once again, Emily, frankly speaking if you can do something, do it on your own because you have already a picture of my case in your hands.

To endure is greater than to dare and the difference between the impossible and possible lies simply in a person's determination. I am not imposing your idea or rejecting your suggestions but this is the reality I hold deep in me.

Please Emily, issue me the Visa. This is the only remaining obstacle for me to behold the wonders!

Thankfully yours,
Louis Gakumba

22 March 2007

Thanks, Terry—

Could you just let me know if you'd be willing for me to put "c/o Terry Tempest Williams" on Louis's student visa?

That would give us an extra level of assurance in the hopefully unlikely event he for some reason does not fulfill the terms of his visa, e.g., his course of study.

Please let me know as soon as you can.

Best,
Emily

26 March 2007

Dearest Terry,

There is a saying in Kinyarwanda which says: "All ways, all roads end at home." This is the end of the road you started and I praise God who has shown his hands all along through this long journey.

If you receive this e-mail, please let me know in time so that I can meet you in Kigali.

Let me promise you one thing: I WILL NOT BE YOUR BURDEN, don't worry about me.

All the best of luck,
Louis

When we arrive at Mama Chakula's House in Gisenyi, Louis is waiting for us. I jump out of the van. We throw our arms around each other.

"I can't believe it. I just can't believe it!" he says.

Brooke and Louis meet for the first time. They shake hands. Louis looks at me and says, "You are my mother." He looks at Brooke, "You are my father."

Brooke and I look at each other.

"And that's the way it's going to be," Louis replies as he takes our hands and walks with us into the house.

The volcano in Gisenyi is glowing. Sparks are exploding like shooting stars in an ebony sky. We have returned: Lily, Alan, Meghan, and I. And we have brought friends. Lily's son, Daniel Traub is here. Brooke is traveling with me. Chris Noble is a photographer from Utah. Chris Landry is a photographer from Philly. Robert Shetterly is an artist who lives in Maine. Eric Reynolds is a social entrepreneur from Colorado. And Dr. James Plumb and his wife, Susan, who were here last year as part of a medical team from Jefferson Jefferson University have also returned. Jim is a physician teaching in the medical school, and Susan is an educator in museum studies, both living in Philadelphia.

We are back at Mama Chakula's House with Medard, the house manager, who has become a dear friend. We sit down for lunch and catch up with the news of the Village.

"The memorial will be dedicated on April 5, 2007," says Jean Bosco. "Wait till you see it. It's very beautiful."

He tells us that over twenty-five houses have been painted in the Village since we were last here.

"You will be interested in knowing that public officials from the surrounding communities believed that the 'painted houses' in the Genocide Survivors Village of Rugerero posed a threat to the security of the residents. By conspicuously 'marking' their homes as belonging to Tutsis," he says, "the survivors put themselves at risk. They strongly advised the Village to cover the images with gray paint. The residents of the Village said, 'No. We will not allow you to destroy what we have created.' "

Dorothée speaks up. "It's true. We told the officials how this project has brought us together. We didn't really know each other before. Now, through the designs of our children, we have worked side by side, painting our houses in bright colors. I told them I asked to have my house painted. The red striped cat above my door and the turquoise and yellow border around our walls, makes me and my children very happy." She looks at Jean Bosco. Mama Emma, the matriarch of the Village, who rarely speaks, said, "It gives us hope."

"There are those within the Village who say it is the public officials who feel threatened by the painted houses," Jean Bosco says.

"Maybe they just want us to remain invisible and gray like the houses they keep us in," Dorothée responds as she looks away.

The memorial rises from the volcanic rubble like a prayer. This is the first time we have seen the physical manifestation of Lily's vision. We walk down the center path of inlaid stones surrounded on either side by lawn. The white undulating wall defines the sacred space. Some of the tallest pinnacles, call them "standing waves," are painted in Rwanda's national colors of turquoise, yellow, and green. A purple band is painted around the base of the white wall, the color of mourning.

We stop and look up from the base of the stairs leading to the blue-roofed pavilion with turquoise-painted pillars. The pavilion houses the altar that will bear the words in glass-jeweled mosaic: *TWIBUKE* (Let Us Remember).

It exceeds our expectations.

Jean Bosco places his hands on his heart. Lily presses her palms together and bows. She climbs up the steps first and greets Siboman Francois, a mosaicist she trained last year. He is overseeing the mosaic work that is embellishing the altar. Lily is pleased and tells him so. Dorothée is completing a mosaic of a red flower with a green stem and leaves that will adorn the right side of the altar. She is wearing a light blue denim jumper with a striped T-shirt and a navy blue bandana on her head. Her eyes are focused on the work at hand.

Consulata is an elder dressed traditionally in a sarong and blouse, with her head wrapped in a red scarf. Her eyes are tired. She sits on an overturned bucket and breaks tile with a small hammer. She then takes the broken pieces of white, beige, and terra-cotta tiles to be used for the mosaic background and tailors them to size with large clippers. I recognize this tool from Ravenna. I sit down beside her. She hands me another set of clippers, and we cut and shape tiles together.

Francois points to the contour of one of the leaves and traces it with his index finger. "This," he says. "You must do." I nod.

The line in mosaic is supreme.

We sit with pieces of tile all around us. Francois shows me with his trowel how to wet the cement and use it as a bed for the tiles. He builds, pats, smooths, and levels the base before he places the tile just so, making certain the surface is even with the other tesserae, then a few taps with the handle of his trowel, and the piece is set. He hands me the trowel and says, "Begin," with a nod of his head.

I do what he says, create the bed of cement, search for the right piece, place it, tap it, make sure it is level with the others, and let it set.

"Good," says Francois.

In 2006, Lily Yeh taught Francois how to make mosaics from beginning to end. This year, when she tried to hire him to do some more work for the memorial, he was too busy and too expensive, having more jobs than he could manage as a mosaicist in Gisenyi.

"Now, the Barefoot Artists work for Francois!" said Lily as she rearranged her schedule around his.

For hours, we work on the mosaic. Cement on trowel, pick a piece of tile, set it, smooth the surface and see that it is level.

A mosaic is like a puzzle. It engages the mind through a sequence of possibilities, trial and error. You look at the broken fragments of tile; your eye assesses the space and searches for a corresponding shape. Piece by piece, you come closer to the desired form and effect.

Consulate and I sit side by side creating a red flower together.

Francois returns and points to the leaf I am working on. He runs his fingers across its uneven surface. "No good." I remove the green tesserae. He demonstrates quickly. His quick placement of new tiles chosen from the pile at my feet creates a much tighter and smoother construction.

With his finger, he points to the line once again, the contour of the outer leaf, and walks away.

Luciana is here in Rwanda.

Consulate holds her grief with each gesture as she rubs the tiles slowly, deliberately, lovingly with a small brown scrap of paper until the mosaic shines.

All of Consulate's children were killed in the genocide. She points to the brick house next door, now collapsed. "My home," she says. The work she is doing at the memorial is for her children. Every day, she mourns them. "Ten years, thirteen years—it was yesterday."

A bank of clouds covers the green canopy of the Congo. The smell of rain is wafting on the wind. It is April, the Rwandan month of remembrance. Purple banners are everywhere and music, explicit and charged with lyrics of loss and lament, fill the streets.

The rain, now falling, a downpour—the past.

The last Saturday of each month is designated a community work day. This one is especially important because it is one week before the National Day of Mourning on April 7, the anniversary of the genocide.

From Mama Chakula's porch, I watch prisoners dressed in pink climbing the gum trees, hacking limbs with machetes. Branches crack, break, and fall to the ground. There must be two dozen or more men at work. A tall, thin woman carrying a baby around her waist stops on her way to town. She cannot get through the roadblock. She waits. She has been here before. Flashback. Trauma. The hacking of bodies not trees.

Diaspora. I think of the people who fled Rwanda before the war, during the war, and after. Diaspora. The word sounds like the definition it holds: *a scattering of language, culture, or people that was formerly concentrated in one place.* The African Diaspora. To disperse. To scatter like seeds. *Scatterlings.*

But what about the people who choose to stay? I want to hear their stories. We need to know their stories, their own unnatural histories of family and place.

We listen to Leá, the daughter of Mama Emma:

My name is Mukangwije Leá. I live in the survivor village of Rugerero. I live with my children and my mother. I have four children who go to school, and when they are on holiday, that's the time we live together.

I am the representative of the genocide survivors in Rugerero sector, and I am in charge of all the activities that our sponsors do for us here in the Village. When I took over the office, I continued what had been previously done.

I can give you day-to-day details of my responsibilities. For example, we have a hygiene project in the village. I work with a group of fourteen people. Each person has four houses that they teach hygiene to—from proper hand-washing techniques to brushing one's teeth. My task is to supervise and make sure each family implements the practices. This has a significant effect on the overall health and well-being of the Village.

I also have a responsibility to listen to different issues and advocate for the survivors in Rugerero sector, which is a heavy load for me.

Before the genocide, I was working for the government, with the health ministry. I had a husband and children. I took care of my family and my job. After the genocide, my husband died, and I had to take care of my children and everything that the war destroyed. Life changed dramatically, but I continued working for the government until 1996. Despite what happened, life continued.

I realized that my mother was growing older and that she needed assistance. I made the choice to leave my job in Kigali and be with her here in the Village.

Ever since my arrival, now almost a year, I have found so many issues unresolved here, especially health issues. I try to support the women, especially the widows. Lily has been a great help to me in organizing the Village around problems of water and jobs. And that's what we are doing for the moment.

My primary concern, however, is still my mother. She is very old and has been through so much. If you look closely, all the people that inhabit this Village are traumatized. She is in this category. She lives in a very deep silence. I try to entertain her, but you realize that she is overloaded with sorrow. The survivors live in a vast loneliness. This is the case with my mother, Mama Emma. Even now, she cannot fully understand what happened.

She lost her children, her brothers, her uncles, her aunties—her whole family was exterminated. And those who were still alive, her brothers, were soldiers who were eventually shot dead. There are only three of us left in a family that counted eighty people. In my father's family, no one survived.

For those of us who survived, the machetes are waiting for us. Each time we bear witness in Gacaca, we are at great risk to be killed by the Hutus we are testifying against.

This worsens the situation. We are fighting every day to live with this pain. We have to help those who are traumatized more than others. I am among those who suffer, but in helping others, it helps me to continue to live. My dream would be that these people can live without bearing mental problems, to sleep without struggling.

We have a long way to go. It is not easy to forgive, but what I can tell you is that we are all trying to understand this process of forgiving. We cannot always be at war, and living with this kind of mental conflict will not bring back our people.

There is a continual knocking on Mama Emma's green wooden door in the heart of the Village. One by one, young women arrive and stand inside her modest room as the meeting is about to begin. We are gathered together to hear what is on their minds. They are the silent ones, the invisible ones, the majority within the Village.

Mama Emma sits on a stool in the back of the room. Leá sits near her mother. Clementine is present. Dorothée sits in the corner with her two young children. Lily and I sit on the couch. Meghan and Jean Bosco sit across from us. Dozens of girls ages eleven to twenty-two are standing, kneeling, and sitting on the cement floor.

Leá welcomes everyone to her mother's home. Jean Bosco laughs and apologizes for not being a woman but explains he is there as our interpreter. Louis is working, and Damas is at school.

Meghan addresses the young women and expresses her respect for what they are going through at this point in their lives. A young woman herself, she talks about the power of emerging women all over the world and the need to organize and support one another. She shares with them what it's like to teach girls their ages in the United Arab Emirites. She talks about the war in Iraq and the two million Iraqi refugees, some of whom are finding sanctuary there. "War is war no matter where it is," says Meghan. "I believe education can open the door to peace and empowerment."

She invites the girls to introduce themselves, beginning with Francine, who is standing by the window.

"My name is Francine, and I wish to be a Catholic nun." Everyone laughs. There is nervousness in the room. Clementine says, "That's good. Let's keep going around the room."

My name is Florence, and I wish to be a minister.
My name is Claudine. I wish to be a minister, as well.
My name is Devota, and I want to study at a university.
My name is Josane. I want to be a member of Parliament.
My name is Therese, and I want to be president.

There is more laughter. The girls' voices become stronger.

My name is Emailance, and I wish to be a teacher.
My name is Monique, and I want to be a doctor.
My name is Innocent, and I want to be a doctor.
My name is Solange, and I want to be tailor.
My name is Sandrine, and I want to be minister.
My name is Console, and I wish to be a minister, too.

The room darkens as the last light of day is filtered through the shutters. The young women continue their litany of dreams.

My name is Colette, and I want to help orphans.

There is a long pause before the next girl speaks.

My name is Ange, and I wish to be a tailor.
My name is Denise, and I want to be president.

Jean Bosco claps his hands and says, "Maybe the two of you who want to be president will run together!" Everyone laughs.

My name is Asiya, and I want to run for Parliament.
My name is Francine, and I want to be a tailor.
My name is Jeanine, and I want to be in Parliament.
My name is Tami, and I want to be a teacher.
My name is Natharie, and I want to study in America.
My name is Chantal, and I want to be a policeman.
My name is Alisa, and I also want to be a teacher.

There is another pause. The room has grown dark, and it is difficult to see who has not spoken. Clementine points to a young woman, "And you?"

My name is Claire, and I want to be a Catholic priest. She nudges the girl next to her. *My name is Claudine, and I want to study in America.*

My name is Delphine, and I wish to be a writer.
My name is Lebeka, and I wish to be a doctor.

There is another long silence.

A young woman's voice comes forward, "I have a dream to be a member of Parliament, but I have no school fees, and without school fees, my dream is only a few words spoken out loud like a game."

Another voice follows. "I want to be a tailor but without a sewing machine . . ."

"We want to talk about HIV and AIDS," interrupted a voice closest to the door.

It was here that a real discussion began. *How do we protect ourselves sexually from contracting AIDS? Can we be tested? We are afraid to be tested. And if some of us are HIV positive, what can we do?*

It was determined that a Young Women's Support Group would be initiated. The primary goals established by the girls themselves would be health, education, and empowerment. Clementine and Leá offered to help organize the young women initially; then the young women said they would determine their own leadership. They asked if an AIDS counselor from Gisenyi could come talk to them and answer their questions.

Jean Bosco said he could make that happen through the Red Cross, alongside reproductive health seminars that could be offered by medical students from Jefferson University when they return in the summer.

There was great excitement in the room with many conversations occurring simultaneously. Silhouettes of women flickered on the walls in candlelight. They agreed to meet on Sunday evenings, twice a month.

When it was time to go, nobody wanted to leave. Mama Emma slowly stood up from her stool and pressed her hands together beneath her chin.

"Here's an example of how things have changed," Amy says. "In every meeting I go to, someone inevitably says, 'What about gender? There are not enough women at this meeting.' You did not hear that in the nineteen seventies and eighties in Rwanda." She amends her comments. "Gender and AIDS are always brought up at every meeting regardless of the topic."

Amy Vedder is back in Rwanda after a hiatus of more than twenty years as a gorilla biologist. We meet for coffee. She is now working for the Global Environmental Authority, helping to create development plans for two national parks. She and her husband, Bill Weber, are the authors of *In the Kingdom of Gorillas,* a book written about their years as scientists working with the mountain gorillas in Virunga National Park.

"Kigali is very different, more progressive, forty percent of the Parliament is women; there is a resurgence of economic development under Paul Kagame's leadership." She pauses. "But when you get into the countryside, it doesn't seem that different to me. The women are still doing the heavy lifting in the fields, there is much poverty, and you certainly see the scars of 1994."

In 1995, Amy returned to Rwanda after having to leave their research camp in the Virungas during the genocide, only to find most of her friends were dead or missing. And many of those individuals were Hutu as well as Tutsi. She rented a car and drove the long, lonely road still burning from the violence into one of the true hotbeds of terror, Ruhengeri, the town at the base of the mountains where she and Dian Fossey did their groundbreaking research on gorilla behavior.

"Today there are approximately three hundred and eighty mountain gorillas in Virunga National Park," she says. "The population was up to four hundred and has been as low as two hundred and fifty. They are still extremely vulnerable to poaching, loss of habitat, and exposure to human disease. The park resides in three countries: Rwanda, Uganda, and Congo. So it's difficult to manage the population in a consistent way."

Amy is tall, thin, tanned, and smart. She and I met twenty years ago in the Adirondacks at a seminar on local governance and conservation. We later served together on the Governing Council of The Wilderness Society.

"You ask me how Rwanda has changed. It's such a difficult question, a complicated question. In many ways, there has been real progress, as I was saying, but there are still real problems. We have a minority government that is becoming more homogeneous, not less. People talk about spies searching out the opposition. And there is still tremendous pressure from the outside in the Congo.

"You see what are being called 'zipper villages.' You can see them from the air, those towns that are reconstructed villages since the genocide that are not circular and organic in structure, but organized on straight roads with houses on either side. Traditionally, Rwandans are not 'village people' but want and like their privacy."

"Why have these villages been designed this way?"

"Security trumps all other concerns. I don't know if this kind of community configuration will continue. But the Rwandan government controls are fierce. Plastic bags are illegal. Family planning is strongly encouraged. Environmental regulations are being put into law. Agricultural practices are being challenged with alternative crops being encouraged for greater diversity. There is a shift from aid to investment, and Kagame is pushing hard for educational reform. This is all part of this administration's plan for reconstruction called 'Agenda 20/20,' the reforms that will be in place by the year 2020. It's ambitious. You have to give President Kagame credit. He's very progressive, dynamic, and forceful. He was, after all, the leadership behind the Rwanda Patriotic Front, the resistance, a brilliant mind and a fearless soldier, determined to return to his home country after being exiled in Uganda as a child."

Dorothée takes my hand and leads me to the Bone Chamber. The last time I was here it was a hole in the ground, still being dug by men with pickaxes and shovels. She has just finished painting the cement floor green and the walls turquoise. The coffins will be brought in tomorrow, covered with purple and white cloth, and placed on the shelves. However, one coffin rests on a wooden platform that is displayed against the wall. It is made of glass with an intact skeleton inside.

"When I am here," she says, "I am not alone. I am here with my family."

Francois's son is working on the memorial today. His name is also Francois. He is fourteen years old. We are working on the same flower. He is creating the leaves on the right side of the stem. I am making mosaic leaves on the left. Each piece fits beautifully. He taps me on the shoulder and raises his eyebrows.

"Beautiful."

Dorothée and Consulate are working on the flower on the opposite side of the altar. Like ours, it measures close to five feet tall.

As we finish, Francois the younger surprises all of us with round jewel stones that Lily had given him. He places them like secrets in the white-tiled mosaic background.

Consulate gets up from her bench, walks around to where Francois is standing to look at his mosaic. She smiles and touches his shoulder and then resumes her work rubbing each stone with the corner of her wet cloth. They take on the countenance of eyes.

I watch and witness their sustaining patience, how beauty is brought into each gesture of the memorial, from cutting the lawn with hand clippers to painting the beams to breaking tile and making flowers. On one hand, it is paid work. On the other hand, it is soul work.

Through the meditation of mosaic, both Hutu and Tutsi, perpetrators and victims, masons and mosaicists, are working toward a unity of expression.

These tiles, now the structure of mosaic, are the fragments of war reimagined.

Robert Shetterly is not painting in Rwanda. He is drawing words. His passion has become "a dictionary project." And wherever he goes, he unearths words.

While others are doing mosaic or painting beams, Rob sits with Emmanuel and Innocent, two street kids, who are leaning over him, their legs dangling over the platform of the memorial. He keeps handing his sketchbook and pen back and forth to them, trading words in English and Kinyarwanda, pointing at their faces, at objects, anything and everything around them—nose/*izuru;* eyes/*amaso;* blue/*ubururu;* leg/*ukuguru;* chicken/*inkoko;* sky/*ikirere;* cloud/*ibicu;* sun/*izuba.*

They are working side by side with words and images, making bridges across the river of silence.

fish/*ifi;* water/*amazi;* mouth/*umunwa;* tongue/*uburimi;* flower/*indabo;* tree/*ibiti;* Earth/*isi.*

Words. Words as fragments. A conversation is its own mosaic.

"Umutima mwiza," Emmanuel says to Rob. The boys take his notebook and draw a heart and point to their chests.

Friend/*inshuti;* love/*urukundo;* thank you/*murakoze;* the same/*kimwe.*

An American photographer, Chris Noble, enters the Village. A young woman is staring at him.

"May I take your photograph?"

She nods and leads him to a square cinder-block house. They enter. His eyes adjust. The room is filled with carrots. She proudly sits on top of them, and he takes a picture.

Inside a concrete room on the edge of the Village, sunflower seeds are being pressed into oil by an elongated green machine that looks like a heron poised for prey. Dark brown oil drips into a plastic bottle. Alan, Eric, and Brooke are trying to figure out with members of the community how to make this piece of simple technology work efficiently. At least thirty people are packed inside, curious to see how this sunflower oil machine works, all wondering if a viable sunflower seed oil cooperative is possible.

Eric is sitting on the desk intensely reading the manual. Brooke is on his back on the floor with a wrench trying to tighten one of the screws to make the press more stable. There is an expected chaos to the whole cooperative experiment created by two languages, too many hands, and the enthusiasm of trial and error. The funnel is loaded with seeds, a large metal handle is brought down that activates a press that squeezes oil from the seeds. The oil flows into a bottle held in place. Eric has figured out that if the seeds are heated, greater productivity occurs. After the first day, four ounces of unfiltered oil is the prize.

The next day, one twelve-ounce bottle of unfiltered sunflower oil emerges. Alan figures this cottage industry could make up to ten thousand U.S. dollars a year for the Village.

"This is going to be hard going in the beginning," Alan says to the group. "The machines take some getting used to, and it's harder than it needs to be right now, but we can figure this out." He has made arrangements with KickStart, the company, located in Kenya, that makes the sunflower presses, to provide professional production and maintenance training.

Outside, half a dozen women are showing children color photographs of yellow sunflowers against a blue sky, explaining the process of squeezing oil out of sunflower seeds. Clementine lets some of the children dip their tiny fingers into the bottle to taste the oil. Fields of sunflowers will be planted in the next few weeks, and there is already speculation about having the seeds harvested by prisoners in Gisenyi.

Full Moon. Smoke. Headlights. Bicycle bells. Women are walking on the side of the road. A child comes to the back of a house, knocks, and waits. A man comes outside. The child hands the man some money. The man goes back inside. The child waits. The child waits for a long time. The child walks to the side of the house and disappears. The child returns and stands beneath the light. The child waits. The child waits for a long time. The door opens. The man hands the child a plastic bag. The door closes. The child disappears with a plastic bag (illegal in Rwanda as a result of environmental legislation). Who knows what is inside the bag? The wind blows. A whistle blows. Women are walking on the side of the road.

Firkovitch and Vicmanotor come to the memorial. They have spent the past two years in secondary school and are eager to practice their English. They are much more confident. We sit on the lawn and catch up.

"We did not tell you everything," Vicmanotor says. "I am Twa. I should not be going to school, that I am must remain a secret."

He tells me his father was a leader among the Batwa. During the genocide, the Interahamwe forced him to kill Tutsis in a nearby village, one of whom was Firkovitch's father. After the killings, the Hutu militia turned around and shot Vicmanotor's father.

"At that moment," says Firkovitch as he turns to Vic, "I knew we were brothers."

They have been inseparable ever since.

An uncle abuses two boys. One is his nephew; the other is his nephew's friend. *Come to me,* the uncle says. *I will protect you. I will protect you,* he says repeatedly as he violates the boys inside the only place they call home. His name is Prosper.

Louis drops off a poem at Mama Chakula's house with a note that says, "Please share this with the Barefoot Artists. Love, Louis."

Rwandans, stand hand in hand
It is time to break the silence
Stand to prove your unity
Play your politic breaking the hearts of secrets
Reveal the truth
Stay united to lift the solidarity
Raise the patriotism to the high hills
Let everyone give you a hand, Rwanda,
Put your strength together
Set the world right, claim your right
France, stop painting us a Red Camel.

We have shed much tears
Rejoice twice for the many deaths
You chopped with machetes—
You drove in running streams of blood
You raped kids and young girls
France, you left no virgin in Rwanda
Blood pleased you
Cries of pain brought you courage
Heaps of dead bodies gave you strength
You killed without choice
You dumped many in the Nyungwe
France, stop painting us a Red Camel.

France, glorious murderer
You needed no water to wash your hands
You swam in blood as if in swimming pools
You drunk our blood to calm your thirst
Never will Rwanda ignore your career
You nourished flies and eagles
Dogs barked to call you
You erupted in Rwanda like a volcano
Burning hills and history
Your hands killed and fed the wild—

The dogs you served human flesh are now groaning
France, stop painting us a Red Camel.

You had no mercy for smiling kids
You had no pity for old people
You had no excuse to pregnant women
France, you killed women with your swords
You and your dogs hunted people
France, why all this?
Is your bravery loading trucks with dead bodies?
Rejoice twice for the reddishness of rivers
Our sorrow is your joy—
France, rejoice for the nightmare in our hearts
You tortured me and left me as a narrator—
You left me a useless man
France, you will remain in my heart
Corrupted France—
France, stop painting us a Red Camel.

France, such a good trainer, you
Use sledgehammers to kill babies
Use spears to pass through pregnant women's wombs
Use javelins to carry cut heads to show your power
Use crossbow to embark those trying to escape,
Use machetes to cut cut cut cut and chop all Tutsis
Stand all together—
Old men and women
Kids and young girls
Support the Hutu team to win
Collect Tutsis from the bush
Be the exemplary for your grandchildren
France, the genocide mastermind,
France, stop painting us a Red Camel.

France, stop painting us a Red Camel.

April 5, 2007. The mosaic work is finished. The jeweled letters are complete.

TWIBUKE

ABACUBAZIZE GENOCIDE 1994

Let Us Remember
Our Beloved Lost to the Genocide

Young women are mopping the mosaic floor of the pavilion. Consulate continues to clean each tile, each letter, with young Francois. A few final paint touches are being made on the turquoise pillars.

The dedication is set for today at 4:00 P.M.

Three mosaic sunflowers stand as guardians above the Bone Chamber, whose yellow doors, newly painted, are locked.

Last night, the purple satin coffin covers edged with white lace had been washed and draped over the trees to dry.

Behind the memorial, dozens of men and women from the Village are hoeing the ground, making it level for the thousands of people to come.

A policeman is standing guard. His club is painted purple and yellow.

Young women, bent over with straight legs, are sweeping the stone pathway to the pavilion with bundles of fine sticks.

Jean Bosco is slowly walking the grounds, his chin raised, smiling. I put my arm through his. "This is a great day in my life," he says.

Louis arrives in his best clothes. Alan teases him. He will be translating the ceremony from Kinyarwanda to English and back to Kinyarwanda. Lily walks with her son, Daniel, to the altar. He leaves her at the steps. Dressed in purple, she walks forward alone, places her hands together and bows.

More policemen arrive with men in military uniforms carrying guns. "For security," Jean Bosco says to Lily. "Just a precaution."

A quarter mile away, on the side of the road, we can see the procession of children walking from the Village led by Clementine, Spacious, and Fabrice. As they approach, we can see they are dressed in gold and white costumes, prepared to dance, their faces sprinkled with glitter. The women dancers from the Village are dressed in yellow chiffon kaftans with gold headbands. They, too, have glitter sprinkled on their faces.

As we all stand outside the memorial entrance watching the dignitaries arrive, from the governor to the mayor to various local officials, extra security gathers anticipating the arrival of Joseph Habineza, the minister of Culture, Youth, and Sports.

Habineza is well known for organizing a volleyball game between the Rwandan Patriot Front (Tutsi) and President Habyarimana's Rwandan Army (Hutu), shortly after the Arusha Peace Accords were signed in August 1993. If the handshake meant something between the warring factions, then why not participate in good sportsmanship on the field. Ten thousand people were packed into the stadium in Kigali to watch.

On January 29, 1994, the day after the volleyball match, Habineza drove home where he saw Hutu extremists waving machetes in front of his home. In a split second, he turned another direction, sought refuge at his neighbor's, where he found his family in hiding. A moderate Hutu who suddenly found himself at risk with many others in the buildup to the genocide, Habineza joined the Rwandan Patriotic Front and fought alongside the Tutsi leader, Paul Kagame, in the bush. As he tells the story, the two men were actually talking about the volleyball game when they received the news on April 6, 1994, that President Habyarimana's plane had been shot down, the event that triggered the war.

In 2000, Paul Kagame became president of Rwanda. He never forgot "Joe Cool" and his daring volleyball match. He appointed him as part of his cabinet.

Over an hour passes in the hot Rwandan sun, as we wait, listening to the music played only during the month of April. Genocide music. Music of remembrance.

A woman scantily dressed, unusual in Rwandan culture, begins dancing wildly in front of the memorial. The photographers raise their cameras to shoot. "Please, no," says Clementine. Leá quickly steps forward and gently takes the woman's arm and walks her back home.

"She is not right," says Clementine. "Ever since the genocide."

The minister's entourage of black SUVs arrives. The crowd backs up.

Joseph Habineza steps out of the black shiny vehicle, dressed in a black well-fitted suit and black patent leather shoes, an impressive man in his early forties. He adjusts his aviator sunglasses and is greeted by the governor of Gisenyi. He is then introduced to Jean Bosco and Lily.

Dorothée, dressed like a Greek goddess in a sleeveless white chiffon gown with a purple sash over one shoulder, holds a silver tray with scissors, at the entrance of the Rugerero Genocide Memorial. She stands stoic and regal. The minister steps forward as Lily is invited to cut the purple ribbon. The ribbon flies open, and the crowd claps.

There are many speeches, many songs, and many tributes to the genocide survivors and those who died and are buried here.

Joseph Habineza delivers his speech in both Kinyarwanda and English. *"May we never forget that the genocide was a result of bad governance. May we never forget the consequences of prejudice. May we never forget our loved ones who are buried here and all over the countryside of Rwanda. May we never forget the power of forgiveness and reconstruction."*

He urges the thousands of people gathered on this occasion to participate in the Gacaca process. *It's how Rwanda can move forward. It is how we are healing ourselves. It takes time. We are telling our stories. We are listening to one another. We are no longer Hutu or Tutsi; we are Rwandans. A united Rwanda is not just our future; it is now.*

Lily stands and walks to the podium. It begins to rain. A woman appears behind Lily with an open umbrella. Jean Bosco whispers to me, "In Rwanda, when it rains, it is a sign of blessings." Lily delivers her speech, one line at a time, followed by Louis's translation in Kinyarwanda.

Dear Friends:
　　We have painted the village. We have created this memorial together. And it is beautiful.
　　We remember. We will never forget. We stand together united.
　　We are building a sustainable village filled with light, imagination, and creative action.
　　It begins with beauty. It moves toward joy. We wish you a peaceful and brilliant future called Hope.
　　We came to Rwanda with the hope of helping. Instead, you have helped us.
　　Thank you.

The dedication ends. Music resumes. Many people walk up the steps of the pavilion to lay bouquets of flowers at the base of the altar. "More of our dead are at peace," Leá says wiping her eyes. "But we will never be."

It would be a beautiful place if the dark things in your heart hadn't happened. But things change. What I would want you to know is this: Please do not close your eyes or ears when you know people are being killed. Because if you close your eyes, I will go out and act on it. While you are sleeping, people are dying. The world was told, 'People are dying.' They closed their eyes. Right now, people aren't sleeping. They regret what they did and did not do.

HABIMANA MARTIN, DIRECTOR OF GOOD GOVERNANCE, GISENYI PROVINCE

The procession: They walk. They walk with the memory of the geno- cide. They walk in remembrance of those who died, their loved ones among them. We walk. We walk with them. It is a river of solemnity winding through the roads of Rwanda.

It is April 7, 2007, the thirteenth anniversary of when Hutu extremists turned simple machetes into sabers of war and filled stadiums with young men whipped into a frenzy, waving their farm tools, crying "cock- roaches" and "snakes." *Machete Season*. April. May. June. The people walk with their memories. Eyes straight ahead covering familiar ground.

We stop. A particular family is remembered. Here. This house. See the burnt foundation. Still. The names are read. A silence is held. We walk. We remember.

The procession of people gathers in size as men and women and chil- dren, the young and the old, enter into the respectful flow of feet walking together to mark the National Day of Mourning. We walk. We stop. We remember. The names are read. The soil is red. A silence is held. We walk and we walk and we walk together. This is storied ground.

The governor of Gisenyi is wearing a black pinstripe suit; his hands are clasped behind his back. The mayor walks next to him. The colonel walks to his right in full uniform with a purple scarf tied around his wrist.

Purple scarves are being worn by most around their necks or arms or wrists.

We cross the river on a wooden bridge. We stop. Stories are recounted. Jean Bosco whispers in my ear that this river ran red, choked with bodies. The bodies created a damn, and the bloody river flooded people's homes.

The procession turns. We pass a graveyard. We walk past a Catholic church. We stop. The story is told that only two people survived the mass killings here. Those two survivors step forward and speak. We listen.

We hold the silence between the names that are read. We walk through the religious grounds that are now graves.

Buzzards and kites follow the procession.

"These are the same birds that followed the Interahamwe," Dieudonne says to me as he looks straight ahead. We walk and we walk. The width of the road is the measure of feet, walking, in front of us, behind us, on either side, all sizes of feet, some in leather shoes, some in sandals, some bare, worn, walking, slowly walking, belonging to the memory of genocide.

"No one asks God who is a Tutsi or a Hutu," the voice from the loudspeaker utters. *"We are all God's children. We only ask God to stop the genocide."*

The procession is a spectrum of colors. The woman in front of me is draped in orange cloth with designs of gold dolphins. Her shoes are black patent leather. Aimee, next to me, is a young woman in her twenties who works at Mama Chakula's house. She lost all her family in the war and is dressed in a black suit with a long narrow skirt; a purple scarf is tied around her neck. She carries a handbag with a photograph inside: a picture of herself kneeling in front of a line of skeletons, identifying her family.

We pass another church, this one made of lava stones. We stop. Another story is told. *The priest and sisters were murdered. They tried to hide Tutsis. Grenades were thrown. Houses were burned. All were killed.* Names are read. Prayers are given. We proceed. We walk. Bits and pieces of broken tiles are everywhere.

A woman hands me a purple scarf, and another woman ties it on my right wrist. Children are running along the side of procession, trying to keep up. Momentum is building. Orphans. Survivors. Neighbors.

Another turn. We walk on a dirt path through green fields, feet traversing over red and black lava stones, uneven ground, the glint of mica. Banana palms are waving in afternoon breezes. Blue sky. Cumulus clouds. The cry of kites. Always, the circling of kites.

Jean Bosco wipes his forehead and then takes my hand as we enter the grounds of a large memorial. We follow the procession inside. Public officials take their seats. Some people stand; others sit on the lawn. Jean Bosco walks to the side and follows the governor of Gisenyi who leads us down to the Bone Chamber. I hesitate. His eyes say, "Come." We follow.

Inside, there are fifteen coffins draped in white cloth appliqued with a purple cross and a wooden cross on top of each of them. Each person is invited to sign the guest book, which we do. The room is small and crowded. As we are leaving, Alan and Meghan are entering. Our eyes meet. Our heads bow.

Brooke and I are now with Aimee. We walk around to the other side of the memorial to find a place to sit. There is another Bone Chamber. Aimee takes our hands and pulls us inside. It is damp. We are the only ones there. Suddenly, as if in a gesture of defiance, Aimee walks up to a coffin, pulls the cloth away and opens it, then just as quickly lets the lid drop and slam shut.

Exposed were small cloth bundles of bones, wrapped bones in the brightly colored, now faded fabric of women's sarongs, holding the remains of their loved ones together in motifs of flowers and birds.

We leave quickly. I am unhinged by what Aimee has done. She says nothing, just walks outside where people are singing and sits down. We sit beside her on the cement steps against the chain-link fence.

Jean Bosco joins us. Lily is sitting with her back against a white cement wall. Her eyes are closed. The midday sun is bearing down on the speakers, on everyone; all of us are dripping wet with sweat. Thousands of people stand behind the fence surrounding the grounds of the memorial, which could not accommodate the crowd.

Various survivors speak, sharing their stories now. Jean Bosco translates one woman's story, quietly whispering, "*She begins her story in 1990, being excluded, discriminated against for being Tutsi; this was all a prelude of hatred and then the war came in 1994. The Interahamwe burned her husband before her eyes. Grenades were thrown inside the priest's house where he was keeping them. They cut her arm, her neck, and left her for dead* (Jean Bosco makes this cutting motion on my own neck to make sure I understand), *this after they made her watch them butcher each one of her three children, her last one asking her for water before he died.* Many women are wailing uncontrollably. Jean Bosco shakes his head. *After two days, her husband found her. He was badly burned but alive. They go to their neighbors to see if they will help them bury their children, but they will not. They go from neighbor to neighbor, badly wounded, almost dead, but can find no help. The killers are coming. They hide in the fields. Friends bring food to them. After two months, the RPF find them and tell her to come back. She and her husband survived. But her children are dead.*

"This woman's name is Ubuhamya," says Jean Bosco. "She is very strong. She calls for unity. Unity. This is what she wants."

At noon, everyone stands in silence.

All over Rwanda, silence. There is no one working in the vertical fields, no cars, no motorbikes, no ringing bells of bicycles; even the birds are quiet.

On our way back, graffiti appears on a collapsed building: STRIP US OF OUR SKIN AND WE ARE ALL THE SAME WITHIN.

At night, bonfires burn across the land.

April 11, 2007
THE NEW TIMES, KIGALI

TWO RWANDESE ARRESTED FOR BELITTLING GENOCIDE *A Rwandan has been charged with belittling the 1994 genocide after tying purple scarves—used to commemorate the slaughter—to his two dogs, police said today.*

The man said he wanted to remember his pets killed during the genocide of 800,000 people by extremists from the ethnic Hutu majority, police spokesman Willy Marcel Higiro said.

Police also arrested his neighbor for publicly supporting the gesture, regarded as an insult by many genocide survivors who recall dogs scouring the Kigali streets during the 100 days of bloodshed, feasting on rotting corpses.

"The two men are being held under our custody and will be charged with harbouring a genocide ideology and belittling the genocide," Higiro said.

He quoted the second man as saying: "If I also had dogs, I would dress them in those scarves and set them on streets to mourn their fellow dogs."

Rwandan law is strict on genocide-related crimes. Suspects found guilty of promoting killings or denying the occurrence of the ethnic slaughter could face life imprisonment.

Survivors were enraged and have urged authorities to prosecute the two suspects without delay.

Damas reads me the story. He folds the paper and puts it under his arm. He shakes his head, clicking his tongue. "These men mock us."

"During the genocide, everywhere you turned, dogs were running in packs, living off the dead bodies of Tutsis. That's how we see them still: Dogs as vultures. For some," he says, "the genocide project will never be over until Tutsis cease to exist."

Looking across Gisenyi to Goma and the vast reaches of the Congo, erupting in conflict, I fear he may be correct.

W e are his biological parents," Louis's father says to Brooke as he takes his hand in his. "Now you are his developmental parents."

Brooke and I catch each other's eyes in a look we have never shared before in three decades of marriage.

Louis has brought his parents, Michel Kinyungu and Kagoyire Annociata, with his older brother Michael to Mama Chakula's house to meet us.

"You must educate him and be devoted to him," his mother says quietly holding Louis's hand with both of hers as she sits next to him. "I cannot express myself. I am sorry. I have not the words."

Brooke and I sit directly across from Mama Odia and Michel with our friends gathered around us. The atmosphere is formal, ceremonial. I am perched somewhere between shock and denial as it slowly dawns on me that they are transferring their son to us. Mama Odia is trusting me with her beloved boy. I am not prepared. There is a butterfly in my heart. *Developmental parents.* We chose not to be parents. We have no children. My eyes flash to Chris Noble, a father twice, one of our oldest friends, who is wearing the biggest coyote grin from the desert. I also see his tears.

Louis's father explains their genealogy. His father was a Congolese king. He was a prince with great land holdings and many cows. They lost everything in the war. Everything. His wife, Louis's mother, is Tutsi. She fled to the Congo in 1959, after the first genocide, and stayed. In 1994, her brother was part of the RPF and helped Mama Odia cross the border back to Rwanda, moving from Masisi in the Congo, from one refugee camp to another, until they finally settled in a small house with their mother in Ruhengeri, one room, all of them. Mama Odia had her seven children with her.

Louis's father turns and speaks to Michael.

Michael says, "My father wants you to know that he stole his wife from another suitor by paying eight cows for her because she was so beautiful."

This was new information to both sons. Mama Odia is indeed lovely, as well as humble and refined. She looks down at her lap. She is one of the most striking women I have ever seen, elegant in her features, great dignity in her carriage.

Her beloved son, the younger son who has supported her family since he was ten, is leaving for America. I cannot imagine her thoughts.

We would later learn that Mama Odia's husband, Michel, abandoned her and their children during the war, that he had two other wives who tried to poison her, that it was her many Hutu friends with whom she had shared her land to cultivate food for their families who ultimately helped her and her family survive. On the night they were to be killed (she had been warned by Hutu women), she gathered her children together and said a prayer. She told them to be kind to every person they met, and then sent each of them in a different direction with the name of a woman who she promised would come find them. Louis survived in the bush for several months, eating spoiled avocados, whatever he could find. And then one day, the woman his mother had told him to watch for at a market spoke his name. Disguised as a Congolese boy instead of a Tutsi, they crossed into Rwanda, where she delivered him safely to his mother. Miraculously, after four months, all of Mama Odia's children were returned to her.

My eyes begin to tear. I look down at my own hands, folded. I cannot look at her; I am wondering if Louis coming to America is the right thing.

Where are we? What is happening? We have a son.

Mama Odia speaks, "My son can be stubborn. He can get angry. Please see that he attends church." She smiles as Louis translates reluctantly.

Louis's father takes off a necklace he is wearing, hidden beneath his shirt. It is an ivory charm on a silver chain, an elephant. He places it in Brooke's hands. "I've worn this around my neck ever since I left the Congo. It belonged to my father and his father." He then pulls out another ivory charm from his pocket, a turtle, and places it in my hand, closing my fingers around its finely etched body. "We believe our ancestors come back to help us." He kisses my cheek three times and whispers the name of his eldest sister into my ear.

Louis and his mother come up beside him. Mama Odia's eyes hold mine. I look to Louis and ask him if he will translate for me.

"Thank you for sharing your beautiful son with us—for trusting us. I promise you, we will watch after him, take care of him, and see that he receives a good education. He will be part of our family. And I believe that when he returns home to you, he will do great things for Rwanda."

She nods, takes my hands, and speaks. Louis listens to his mother and is silent for a few moments. "She says, 'God loves my son more than I do.'"

"I want to tell you a story," says Louis as we sit on Mama Chakula's porch, where we met almost two years ago.

"There is a woman who was married to a pastor. It was a happy family. Some people say they were a family of six; others say they were eleven. The woman was away, and when she returned, she saw how the Interahamwe were butchering her children on the ground along with her husband.

"After the war, the man who murdered her family came back from the Congo, and when Gacaca called him to explain what he had been accused of, he said, 'I accept everything I have been charged with, and from the depth of my heart, I apologize.'

"The woman said, 'I saw everything happen. I know you killed my family. I loved my children and my husband. I am alone. I have nothing, but I now choose to forgive you and take you into my home. You will live with me, and I will do whatever it takes to make you feel like my own son.'

"Can you be in the same shoes with this woman?" Louis asks.

Louis then says, "Rwanda is struggling with peace one person at a time. This is as hard as growing wheat on rock. We are finding our way toward unity and reconciliation on a walkway full of thorns, and we are walking barefoot."

He stands up and walks over to the balcony that overlooks Gisenyi into the Congo where he was born.

"We are trying to forgive, but to forgive is to forget, and we cannot forget. Perhaps there is another word. I am searching for that word."

Once upon a time, we knew the world from birth. Now we have to learn it again, piece by piece, understanding from the name out.

KATHERINE E. STANDEFER

Louis and I are sitting on the shore in Maine looking out toward the shimmering water. All at once, Louis jumps up, "Why is the ocean chasing me?" I had forgotten to mention the tides. And when I try to explain the phenomenon, I fail miserably. To say tides are caused by the gravitational pull of the moon is not helpful to one who has lived his life near the equator, where daily tides were of war, not water.

We take a field trip to the Bay of Fundy, only a few hours downeast. We sit on a granite cliff at a place called Reversing Falls and watch the ocean empty out until only a small pool of perfectly still water remains. Nothing stirs, not even terns overhead. They have vanished. For a sustained moment in time, we witness a pause, an equilibrium, a calm with such force it takes away our words.

And then, as if led by a line of light, the incoming tide rushes in, absorbing the pool back into its liquid body, quickly filling every cove and cranny along the rocky coast. Terns return to their fishing and whirlpools once spiraling clockwise, are now spinning counter. Amber kelp is lifted from the sandy floor, buoyant, and the sea's voice roars; waves are crashing against pink granite cliffs as millions of gallons of saltwater flood the bay.

"This is how I know God," Louis says.

We live our lives looking for that golden thread we can follow to the next clearing of light. It is momentary. We are caught in the recognition that we are not alone but belong to a quivering web of faith.

The play of light is the first principle of mosaic.

To watch the play of light on water, on the prairie, on a bejeweled ceiling or face is to witness the power of illumination. For as long as she lives, Madame Head Wide Apart will be facing the sun at dawn and at dusk on the high plateau of Bryce Canyon. She and her clan of Prayer Dogs will continue to make their stand above ground, carrying the knowledge of their Pleistocene minds forward: To survive one must belong to an ecological mosaic.

I want to stand with them.

Outside. Inside. Aboveground and below. There is a way of being in the world that calls us beyond hope. Mosaic is not simply an art form but a form of integration, a way of not only seeing the world but responding to it.

Simon Rodia, an Italian who immigrated to the United States, bought a piece of land at 1765 East 107 Street in Los Angeles, California. From 1921 to 1955 he constructed what has come to be known as The Watts Towers.

A contractor by day, Rodia traveled through his neighborhood with a wheel-barrow collecting the old, the unwanted and discarded. He embellished his metal sculptures with broken glass, seashells, stones, dishes, and pottery given to him by residents (a study in itself of twentieth-century ceramics), alongside tossed tiles. He improvised. He worked without a map or blue-print. And for years, he labored until his towers were complete. He signed his work with the imprint of his tools in concrete: hammer, chisel, and trowel.

A headless angel stands on top of the towers that rise 99½ feet above the communities of Watts and Compton, neighborhoods of mixed racial tensions and poverty. Shortly after Rodia completed his project, there was a move by concerned citizens to take the towers down. They feared the towers would not endure an earthquake. A stress test revealed uncommon strength and resiliency. Another movement emerged to protect them.

During the 1965 riots in Watts, when everything was being torched, Rodia's mosaics were not touched. Nor were they vandalized, almost three decades later, when the Rodney King uprisings occurred and the Watts neighborhood was burning once more.

"Everybody knows they're off-limits," a resident told me.

Finding beauty in a broken world is creating beauty in the world we find.

Mosaics are created by hand.

Louis Gakumba took my hand, and he is now our son.

From Rwanda, he wrote, "Everywhere you walk in the streets of Africa, you find many different kinds of glass from broken bottles, good colors to see through. Believe me, nice things can be made from these bottles; cups can be made from them, dishes, too. What is broken can produce something new and important for the community.

"Street kids are not considered on the same level as others more fortunate. Sure they are disappointed by life. On the other hand, people always talk that this generation is the one with future leaders inside. For some, yes. For others, no. Those in the street have no hope. No education. They are responsible for themselves. They do not think about what is going to happen. They only think about their daily bread. But they have minds; they think and act. They are dying to be transformed."

We all are.

Shards of glass can cut and wound or magnify a vision. Mosaic celebrates brokenness and the beauty of being brought together.

Our survival, the vitality of the planet depends on mental flexibility and emotional acuity. Hands raised. Hands put to work. We can improvise. We can create without a map. And we don't have to live in isolation. The gift of an attentive life is the ability to recognize patterns and find our way toward a unity built on empathy. Empathy becomes the path that leads us from the margins to the center of concern.

The pattern is the thing.

The beauty made belongs to everyone. We all bow.

Finding beauty in a broken world becomes more than the art of assemblage. It is the work of daring contemplation that inspires action.

Louis Gakumba made me a mother, his mother in America. I didn't see the need; he did. And when he called me "Mum," I struggled, wondering why this name was necessary.

"What are you afraid of?" he asked.

I didn't answer because I didn't know.

"Commitment," he said.

I understand commitment as a wife, a daughter, a sister, and an observer of the natural world. And I have committed myself to the dying and have learned how to bury the dead.

But to commit to a child, even a man-child, is a journey of vulnerability that remains unknown to me. I am learning. I am coming to understand that saying yes to Louis is about engagement, a reconfiguration of everything I have known. He has become a safe harbor I could not have imagined.

What I didn't know is that I would need him much more than he needs me.

DECEMBER 21, 2007: Winter Solstice, darkness moving toward light. Brooke and Louis and I are sitting in front of the fire in a cabin in Jackson Hole, Wyoming. We drink cups of tea, talking, laughing, and questioning how all this came to be. And then we are quiet.

A Christmas tree stands in the corner. It carries our family history. Many of the ornaments hung on my grandmother's tree: an angel with gossamer wings, an owl made of wheat, and white wooden snowflakes whose tips are now bent. My mother's bracelet, a cloisonné circle of flowers, is here, as well as a bird that Steve braided with blue ribbon when we were children. Three stars sprinkled with silver glitter hang in a vertical line. This is a new ornament, alongside the ivory elephant that Louis's father gave to Brooke as a talisman.

There is a blizzard outside, just as there was on Louis's first morning in America, when he awoke and walked outside to experience snow falling for the first time. He looked up and said, "What a beautiful catastrophe!"

"Do you remember?" I ask.

"I do."

NOTES

p. ix   **Interstices:** a space between; a narrow opening; an interval between actions. [Middle English, from Old French, from Latin *interstitium*, from **intersti-tus*, past participle of *intersistere*, to pause, make a break: *inter-*, *inter-* + *sistere*, to cause to stand.]

p. ix   **These fragments I have shored against my ruins:** T. S. Eliot, *The Wasteland*, introduction by Mary Carr (New York: Modern Library, 2002), p. 51. Originally published in 1922, the poet William Carlos Williams described the effect of *The Waste Land* as that of an atom bomb. This 433-line poem is Eliot's monument of words to a fragmented and disparaging world, his own poetic mosaic or collage that celebrates the failure of civilization, the distractive and destructive impulses of the modern era.

p. ix   **The cosmos works by harmony of tensions, like the lyre and bow:** Heraclitus, *Fragments: The Collected Wisdom of Heraclitus*, foreword by James Hillman (New York: Viking, 2001), p. 37.

p. ix   **And so it was I entered the broken world:** Hart Crane, "The Broken Tower," 1932. This was Hart Crane's last and many say his greatest poem. He was influenced by T. S. Eliot and his view of modernity. The tower was a frequent image for Crane. Paul Bowles in his foreword to *O My Land, My Friends: The Selected Letters of Hart Crane*, compares Crane's writing to the way "Romans created their mosaics, choosing, chipping and shaping to make the size and form of each tile precisely what was needed for the space it was to fill."

p. ix   **Turning shadow into transient beauty:** T. S. Eliot, *Four Quartets*, 1943. This line can be seen in relationship to the line that precedes it, "At the still point of the turning world." And then later, "Except for the point, the still point / There would be no dance, and there is only the dance."

p. ix   **Once upon a time, we knew the world from birth:** Katherine E. Standefer, "The Names of Things," written at the Murie Center, Moose, Wyoming, Summer 2006.

p. 4   **Her name is Luciana:** Luciana Notterni is a master mosaicist and a brilliant teacher in the rigorous techniques of Roman and Byzantine mosaics. She has been the president and founder of the Mosaic Art Studio in Ravenna since 1990, and teaches at the School of Mosaic Restoration of Ravenna. She is one of the few mosaicists in the world allowed to restore ancient masterpieces. Her own mosaics have been exhibited internationally. Her colleague, Brunetta Zavatti, is also an instructor at the Mosaic Art Studio. Classes are limited to eight to ten participants. For more information contact: Mosaic Art Studio, Via Francesco Negri 14 - 48100 Ravenna. Tel. +39 3496 014566; fax. +39 0544 67061. E-mail: info@mosaic school.com. Web site: www.mosaicschool.com.

p. 7 **Natascia Festa, Nittola:** Quote given to me by Marco de Luca as he was describing the aesthetic surprise that can be found through the breaking of stone into tesserae and the joy that can be expressed in the reconfiguration of fragments into a unified whole.

p. 8 **Giulu Carlo Argan:** *Mosaico d'amicizia fra i popoli,* Parco Della Pace, Ravenna, Longo Editore, Con il Patrocinio di Parlamento Europeo Consiglio d'Europa, UNESCO, 1988, p. 11. There is a Park of Peace that resides in the heart of Ravenna. It is an outdoor museum of mosaics. "Once the capital city of the empire, Ravenna today wants to be the capital of friendship and peace." Mosaicists from around the world have contributed works of art to this international initiative, "with its chief aim of uniting the many peoples of the world through the universal language of art." The mosaics within the park combine the history of nature to the history of man. One of the mosaicists, Mario Manieri-Elia, says, "Mosaic, in fact, is a technique of assemblage of various materials brought together in a continuous surface that is animated, that comes to life in the liveliness and the variety of their arrangements . . . in a full, rich, and perfect continuity . . . an allegory of peace" (pp. 17–18).

p. 14 **Henry James:** *Italian Hours* (1909; New York: Penguin Classics, 1995), p. 298.

p. 15 **"Remember, mosaic is an art not a craft":** Elaine Scarry, "On Beauty and Being Wrong," in *On Beauty* (Princeton, NJ: Princeton University Press, 1999), p. 11. Scarry asks the question, "What is an instance of an intellectual error you have made in your life?" Or more clearly stated, "Describe an error you have made about beauty." My error in making a judgment about beauty has been mosaic. I saw it as a craft not an art; mosaic was something you made after breaking family dishes and making peace with shards of china on picture frames or flower pots. If mosaic was something other than a crude craft, in my mind, it belonged to the realm of turquoise-tiled swimming pools. I am learning mosaic follows Heidegger's notion of art as "the setting-into-the-work of truth."

p. 16 **I cut and set the lines of gold:** Whenever we worked with gold tesserae in the Mosaic Art Studio, the name Orsoni came up in the conversation. "Gold and Orsoni are one in the same," someone would say, followed by, "Orsoni means bear and Lucio Orsoni is the meanest man in the world."

I became intrigued and made a pilgrimage to Venice to see for myself if this family whose name is synonomous with gold lived up to their reputation. You would never know that the world's largest exporter of gold smalti resides on a humble street off the Grand Canal in Venice. It took me months to secure an appointment with Mr. Lucio Orsoni. I am thirty minutes early and sit outside the compound and wait.

The company of Angelo Orsoni has been manufacturing tiles and dedicated to the art of mosaic for over a century. Angelo Orsoni, a master glassmaker, was born in Venice in 1843 and was part of the revival of mosaic in the nineteenth century.

The story goes like this. In 1840, Lorenzo Radi, from Murano, Italy, rediscovered the lost secrets of glassmaking so vital to Venetian glassmakers in the thirteenth through fifteenth centuries. Mr. Radi was able to create the materials necessary for the restoration of the mosaics in the Basilica of San Marco, badly in need of repair.

Techniques were simplified and improved and, in 1888, Giovanni Facchina entrusted his whole mosaic glass factory to Angelo Orsoni, a master glassmaker who had been working with Radi in the restoration of the art.

Orsoni successfully imitated the Ravenna-style smalti and with new technologies (moving from a wood- to a coal-fired furnace, employing a cylinder-driven machine that created uniform slabs of glass) was able to produce a spectacular array of colors with great subtlety. He then spent enormous energy in perfecting gold, ultimately, transforming the gold smalti into the quality tesserae used in the mosaics in San Marco in Venice.

The Orsoni Workshop is still known today for the elegance of its gold.

The well-guarded "Book of Secrets" so precious to glassmakers through the centuries that holds the recipes of glass pastes, colors, and the raw materials to be used in what formulas, is now in the hands of Angelo Orsoni's great-grandsons, Lucio and Ruggero, passed down to them from their father and their father's father. Ruggero Orsoni runs the furnace, or the "soul," of this factory. He is the *tecnico*, the one who knows the "secrets" of making the compounds required to create the smalti. He is the one who studies and experiments with colors. He is also the one who the workers say "can never be replaced." They say when he goes, the art of making mosaic will go with him.

Ruggero talks about the alchemy of glassmaking using Italian words, *anima* (soul) and *corpo* (body). The souls are previously melted compounds that are added to change a particular color until the right hue is obtained, whereas the bodies are the quantities of crystalline ingredients that are added to make the transparent glass opaque.

Ruggero follows the same body and soul recipes of his great-grandfather. He is the one who will tell you that to create an opaque turquoise according to the Florentine recipe you must use bone ash as the opacifer. Or that yellow smalto is obtained by adding "tartar of wine casks." And that Byzantine red dates back centuries and is one of the most difficult hues to exact, the color depending on the amount of iron added and the size of the red cuprite crystals. He will then refer you to the *Ricettario Darduin*, one of the earliest recipe books belonging to a Venetian glassmaker, compiled by Giovanni Darduin, who lived from 1585 to 1654. Ruggero is the keeper of the flame, literally.

Lucio is a different beast. He is not the artisan but the businessman, who many fear. He is austere, abrupt, fiery, and impatient. He is the realist, the entrepreneur, the one who keeps the other books in order. Lucio Orsoni is in the business of mosaics.

From my journal: I am formally taken into Mr. Orsoni's office. He is sitting behind a shiny black mosaic desk. In fact, I see his entire office as one black reflective mosaic with bands of gold. This is the effect of Lucio Orsoni, who wears an elegant black suit with a black shirt and black tie.

He asks me why I am here and what I want. I tell him I am a student of mosaic, studying with Luciana.

"The development of mosaic is interwoven with the history of Orsoni glass." He pauses. "My family *is* mosaic."

As I listen to him describe his genealogy from Angelo Orsoni (1843–1921) to Giovanni (1873–1935) to his own father, Angelo (1920–1969), I can't help but be distracted by the color chart behind him, the panel the Orsoni Company made for the Paris Universal Expo in 1889. The squares of colored smalti are a work of art in themselves.

Lucio Orsoni tells me he also a mosaicist. He created the famous mosaic wall of gold in Kuwait. "I love gold," he says. "I cannot live without gold. Gold is not a color, it is an experience."

He designed a large mosaic made of gold and silver smalti for the private suite of the emir of Kuwait. Orsoni tells me the Arab countries can afford the best. It is six meters wide, a large symmetrical composition that is a progression of darker and brighter shades of gold and silver, arranged in straight and curved lines, "reminiscent of a fingerprint."

Mr. Orsoni tells me that he created this for calm and contemplation. "The Arabs understand sheer ornamentation creates spirituality." He shows me a photograph. The mosaic is a subtle, brilliant, monochromatic study in color mounted on a large white wall. It reminds me of Josef Albers's work on color. Orsoni's mosaics enter your field of vision as a vibration more than an abstraction.

He speaks about unity, which transcends shape and color. It's what happens when all the elements are working together. Mosaic is like music, each tesserae is a note. I am writing as fast as I can in my notebook, but my hand cannot keep up with Lucio's rapidity of mind.

"If I had to define my mosaic, I would call it a mosaic score. Jazz. Jazz is more near mosaic than any other."

He talks about the renaissance of mosaic one century ago and how his family helped Antonio Gaudí.

"We have all of our correspondence with him, all of the order forms, and we are still working with the artisans who continue to construct his vision."

He asks me if I have been to la Sagrada Familia. I say yes, remembering a conversation I had with one of the craftsmen who had been working on the cathedral as a mosaicist for forty-six years. "I work for Mr. Gaudí," he told me as he was cutting gold smalti into small squares for the ceiling.

"That is the Orsoni family workshop you witnessed in Barcelona," Lucio says.

p. 21   **His name is Marco de Luca:** "The creative rhythm of producing a work of art is a result of the mind talking to the body, and naturally involving emotions in the process . . . The preparation of materials, research into materials, fragmentation and recomposition, are rituals that I cannot disassociate from the works I produce, both in conceptual and in constructive terms."

I want to thank Manuela Farnetti for being our translator and for her uncommon grace in interpreting our conversation.

p. 26   **It was another broken appendage and I wondered what power these fragments held:** How to dissect truth? Eric Miller, in an homage to Roger Tory Peterson (who originated the famed *Peterson's Field Guide to Birds* with his illustrated plates of North American birds that set an entire natural history series in motion), wrote about his desire to understand the color inherent in feathers. He was interested in chromatography, "the analytical technique for the resolution of solutes in which separation is made by differential migration in a porous medium, migration being caused by the flow of solvents."

How to dissect language?

For Miller, deconstructing color from the feathers of birds "amounted to the manipulation of a kitchen blender," white strips of silica gel somewhat longer and broader than a bookmark, and carbon tetrachloride.

His question was simple: *Did different species of birds like flycatchers, kinglets, vireos, and warblers share the same pigments of green and yellow?* From this question, Miller proceeded to pluck the feathers of green and yellow birds. Here is a fragment of his experiment:

> *Feeling medieval in the denudation of my miniature poultry, precisely and barbarically I learned the answers . . . I took the feathers of, say, five red-eyed vireos, dumped them into the blender, added the solvent carbon tetrachloride to the mix, put a lid on the Faustian mess and turned the blender on high. . . . From the chopped feathers, the solvent soon assumed a manifest green or yellow tint. Through a strainer I drained it off, decanted it sparingly into a glass basin and propped a strip of silica gel in this residuum . . .*
>
> *The tinted solvent slowly rose up through and wetted the strip. To witness the whole process of development, you had to lower yourself almost physically, as into a pool, into the time-sense of infancy, of sanatoria and of hospices, a patience without ambition except to move at universal rather than human tempo. . . . This mood, so rare, is the condition of perfect testimonial honesty . . . I now had the excuse of science.*
>
> *Between the plates in Peterson's book and my results I intuited a relationship. After the solution of pigment had sauntered up each strip, it left a spectral spectrum, a pattern of crescents and dots and bars as each element contributing to the colour of the birds' feathers left its signature. The distribution of these shapes revealed the identity and difference among pigments. The strips thus offered a new name for red-eyed vireo, for ruby-crowned kinglet. I had acquired an abstract companion to Peterson's figures, the flag of each species like a human flag. A flycatcher and a warbler might have a dot in common, but vary in their other chromatographic geometry. I could lay side by side the Peterson plates, sonographs of voices, and read-outs of the colours of plumages.*

Miller's conclusion is a reflection on fragmentation and harmony:

> *No one experiences evolution; mutation, cherished change, takes on eternity the instant it occurs. We speak of "constructing" this and "constructing" that, for all the world like eminent architects . . . Peterson displays on the pages of his book precisely what we are constructed from. To call that substance raw material is a terrible slur upon the elegance and mobile consummation of an American redstart or a common flicker. Peterson was indeed a guide, a field guide. His book is far greater than most literature. It led me through routine and personal disaster. On the far side, those plates, that incomparable book of memory, remain—and not for me alone, though I claim them still as exceptionally accurate autobiography.*

Eric Miller, "Birding with Roger Tory Peterson," *BRICK*, 56 (Spring 1997), pp. 31–34. Reprinted gratefully with Mr. Miller's permission.

I met Mr. Peterson shortly before he died. He was still drawing birds. He signed a copy of my *Peterson's Field Guide to Birds*. It was a simple inscription, *"With Joy."*

p. 28　**Who will give up this world**: Kevin Hart, "The Will to Change," *Flame Tree*, (New Castle, UK: Bloodaxe Books, 2003), p. 62.

p. 28　**The catalog of forms is endless**: Italo Calvino, *Italian Cities* (New York: Harvest Books, 1978), p. 139.

p. 28　**No one sees everything**: Mary Midgley, *Animals and Why They Matter* (Athens: University of Georgia, 1984), p. 77.

p. 28　**I am looking for a way**: C. D. Wright, *Cooling Time* (Port Townsend, WA: Copper Canyon Press, 2005), p. 6.

p. 28　**Fragmentation and breaking up**: Natascia Festa, *Nittola*.

p. 28　**no compass**: Michael Ondaatje, *The English Patient* (New York: Alfred A. Knopf, 1992), p. 249.

p. 28　**Memory is redundant**: Italo Calvino, *Invisible Cities* (New York: Harvest Books, 1978), p. 19.

p. 28　**didn't we plant the seeds**: Louise Glick, *Averno* (New York: Farrar, Straus, and Giroux, 2007), p. 6.

p. 28　**There is an old saying**: Gregor Rezzori, *Antedotage* (New York: Farrar, Straus, and Giroux), p. 47.

p. 29　**It's the dismemberment of a territory**: Claude Royet-Journoud, *Theory of Prepositions* (Albany, NY: Fence, 2006), p. 25.

p. 34　**burrowing owls**: Among the Eastern Shoshone, Burrowing Owl is known as Prairie Dog's brother-in-law, "dinzyhahdaysh." (Researched by Manfred Guina Sr. and Beatrice Haukaas, Eastern Shoshone Cultural Center, November 2006.)

p. 38　**Niles Eldredge**: Niles Eldredge, "A Field Guide to the Sixth Extinction," *New York Times Magazine*, December 2, 1999, pp. 144–46. Other species listed included the African black rhino, the African wild dog, the musk ox, the pollack, the Galapagos penguin, black truffles, and mahogany.

p. 42　**Endangered Species Act**: The Endangered Species Act of 1973 is perhaps the most visionary environmental law we have in the United States of America. To honor and take responsibility for the well-being of another species in a country whose constitution champions private property rights is an enormous gesture in empathy from a governing body. It was designed to protect critically imperiled species from extinction as a "consequence of economic growth and development untendered by adequate concern and conservation." In Section 2,(3) the act reads, "The Congress finds and declares that these species of fish, wildlife, and plants are of esthetic, ecological, educational, historical, recreational, and scientific value to the Nation and its people."

p. 46　**Tim W. Clark**: Tim W. Clark, "Ecological Roles of Prairie Dogs" *Wyoming Range Management* 261 (1968).

p. 47　**Report from the Burrow**: Primary Author: Lauren McCain, Ph.D, Desert and Grassland Projects Director, WildEarth Guardians, 2008. This report was released on Prairie Dog Day, February 2, 2008, a variation on Groundhog Day in the American West. Using a potent combination of litigation, scientific analysis, and grassroots organizing, WildEarth Guardians fiercely defends the American West's wild heritage. Web site: www.wildearthguardians.org.

On May 13, 2008, this news of Utah prairie dog poisoning was reported, no doubt lowering Utah's general grade of concern:

CONSERVATION GROUPS CONDEMN UTAH PRAIRIE DOG KILLINGS

Conservationists call on Fish and
Wildlife Service to increase protections

Santa Fe, NM–May 13. The recent illegal poisoning of a dozen Utah prairie dogs in Enoch has sparked an investigation by the Utah Division of Wildlife Resources (UDWR). UDWR and the U.S. Fish and Wildlife Service (FWS) are offering a combined reward of $3,500 for information leading to an arrest, and the Utah Humane Society has offered an additional $5,000. While WildEarth Guardians and Center for Native Ecosystems join in condemning the Enoch prairie dog poisoning, they point out that UDWR and FWS allowed nearly 100 times this number of Utah prairie dogs to be shot or kill-trapped in 2006.

"It's pretty hypocritical for the government to be jumping up and down about the killing of a dozen Utah prairie dogs when they are allowing 100 times that number to be legally killed," stated Nicole Rosmarino of WildEarth Guardians. "We think Utah prairie dogs should be protected from all lethal control."

Under a special rule issued in 1991, FWS allows up to 6,000 Utah prairie dogs to be killed between June 1–December 31 every year. The rationale for the rule is that it would diminish illegal killings. The Enoch poisoning and two similar incidents earlier this year challenge that rationale. When it issued the special lethal control rule, FWS said it would rely on state annual reports on the species to monitor the level of take. But UDWR has not issued an annual report on the Utah prairie dog since 2002.

The latest census count indicates approximately 11,000 adult Utah prairie dogs currently exist. In comments to the press in April 2007, FWS stated that the current rule allowing take of up to 6,000 animals is not "biologically defensible" and it planned to announce a revision of the rule in summer of 2007. But no revision has yet been announced.

"What other endangered species would people stand by and allow to be killed by the hundreds?" said Erin Robertson, Senior Staff Biologist for Center for Native Ecosystems. "Poisoning these dozen Utah prairie dogs was illegal, but the government allowing hundreds to be killed annually is no less criminal."

p. 47 **Julie MacDonald, wrongfully tampered with the white-tailed prairie dog decision:** See Jerry Adler, "The Politics of Endangered Species," *Newsweek*, June 9, 2008, pp. 40–50.

p. 48 **Black-tailed prairie dogs:** Clay Jenkinson, in his book *Message on the*

Wind (Marmarth, ND: Marmarth Press, 2002), calls the Great Plains "the sacred corridor . . . a poetic name for a district that most people would do anything to avoid, a corridor travelers pass through as quickly as possible, with their souls and windows closed." In a conversation in Dickinson, North Dakota, March 10, 2008, Jenkinson explained that the historical range of the black-tailed prairie dog overlays this "sacred corridor."

p. 54 **Constantine Slobdochik:** Con Slobdochik is professor of Biology at Northern Arizona University and president and CEO of Animal communications, Ltd., dedicated to helping people with their animal companions. The following articles were helpful in my understanding of his work on prairie dog communication: C. N. Slobodchikoff, et al. "Semantic Information Distinguishing Individual Predators in the Alarm Calls of Gunnison's Prairie Dogs," *Animal Behavior* 42(5) (1991): 713–19. Con Slobodochik, "The Language of Prairie Dogs," Museum of Northern Arizona, *Plateau Journal*, 6(2) (Fall/Winter, 2002), pp 30–38. R. K. Bangert and C. N. Slobodchikoff, "Prairie Dog Engineering Indirectly Affects Beetle Movement Behavior," *Journal of Arid Environments* 56(1) (January 2004), pp. 83–94.

I want to thank Dr. Slobodchikoff for permission to publish his April 18, 2008, letter to me.

p. 58 **Natasha B. Katliar:** Bruce W. Baker and April D. Whicker, "A Critical Review of Assumption About the Prairie Dog as a Keystone Species," *Environmental Management* 24, pp. 177–92, 199.

p. 58 **William S. Cooper's:** William S. Cooper, "The Climax Forest of Isle Royale, Lake Superior, and Its Development," *Botanical Gazette*, January 13, 1913.

p. 58 **Richard T. T. Forman:** Richard T. T. Forman and M. Godron, *Landscape Ecology* (New York: Wiley, 1986). For more on the idea of disturbance as "a major natural process of landscape development" and how the type, intensity, and frequency of disturbance creates patch dynamics and patterns of mosaics within the natural world, see S. T. Pickett, and P. S. White, eds., *Ecology of Natural Disturbances* (Academic Press, 1985).

p. 59 **E. A. Johnson's:** E. A. Johnson, "Wildfires in the Western Canadian Boreal Forest: Landscape Patterns and Ecosystem Management," *Journal of Vegetation Science* (1998).

p. 59 **M. G. Turner and D. B. Turner:** M. G. Turner and D. B. Turner, "Effects of a Fire-created Landscape Mosaic on Ecosystem Processes in Yellowstone National Park, Wyoming," August 6–10, 2000. Paper given at the Ecological Society of America Annual Meeting at Snowbird, Utah.

p. 60 **Jean Baudrillard:** Jean Baudrillard, *Transparencies of Evil: Essays on Extreme Phenomena* (New York: Verso, 1993), p. 77. On June 21, 2007, I received this letter from Teresa Cohn, an imaginative geographer receiving her Ph.D from Montana State University. We had just finished teaching a class together called "The Ecology of Residency" at The Murie Center in Moose, Wyoming. She writes,

I am a lover of metaphor, Terry. Of the fibers of wool, water, and story. Do you see how these are the same thing? I've never told anyone this, but for a long time in college, when I decided that I believed in a god again, but couldn't figure out what god was, I said only one short prayer every night: Let me be a part of what brings things together, not what pulls them apart.

I don't think we understand metaphor. We don't understand topography. Maybe in one way, time and space are whole and in another way they're broken. Maybe time doesn't matter at all, except in this world, in this perception. Sunsets are broken light.

I don't think there's any way to maintain that initial sphere of wholeness, not if we plan to really participate in the world. Hearts break; pots break; frog cells break; the future breaks into days so we can walk through them, stories break into words, light to color, sound to notes. Just look at a tree. My Lord, all those pieces: form breaks into branches, which break into leaves with broken veins, and then it seeds.

I don't have the kind of hope that believes we won't destroy our world. I have hope in two streams of water, becoming rhythm. I have hope in the blue sky of scattered light. I have a lot of hope in the power of metaphor, carefully made pots, in good stories and my friends. I have a lot of concern, not for fragments or wholes, but for grace.

We can break and stay broken in our separate pieces, or we break into greater complexity and relationship. This, again, is choice. This is the how of grace.

p. 66   **Varmint:** Conservative radio shock jock Michael Savage has repeatedly called liberals "vermin," including *New York Times* columnist Verlyn Klinkenborg after he wrote a piece on reconciliation between neighbors.

p. 66   **Julie Jargon . . . bears witness:** I want to acknowledge and thank Julie Jargon for permission to both quote and draw from her deeply moving article, "Dog Eat Dog," which appeared on www.westword.com on March 25, 1999. The full essay reports on the complex relationships among shooters', lawmakers', and environmentalists' responses to prairie dogs in Colorado. I also want to thank Westword's editor, Patricia Calhoun, for her permission to use this material.

p. 67   **It's a free-for-all for hunters:** Long-range varmint shooting has a loyal following known as the Red Mist Society. Web site www.seekersofthered mist.com. *Red Mist* refers to the spray of blood a prairie dog is reduced to when shot by members of this club, using high-powered rifles from as far away as 400 yards. The challenge is to find the smallest a target from the longest distance with maximum devastation. Shooters delight in the "explosive action" rendered by a Savage 12 Series Varmint Model, a gun weighing ten pounds (costing close to $1,000.00), where you need a shooting bench with a rifle rest, for optimum accuracy.

Niki Saint Phalle (1930–2002) was a French painter, sculptor, and mosaicist. She created a mosaic park called Il Giardino dei Tarocchi (the Tarot Garden) in Garavicchio, Italy. Begun in 1979 and completed in 1998, it is an assemblage of mosaics built around the Major Arcana of the Tarot deck (Web site: www.nikisaintphalle.com). As wild and eccentric as her mosaics are within the park including the Falling Tower made of broken mirrors, I was struck by her history as a painter. In 1961, she became known worldwide for her Shooting Paintings. Her obsession with "the violent gesture" became her invitation to the public to participate. Constructing an interactive canvas, she filled polythene bags with paint and embedded them within layers of plastic against a wooden board. Spectators were invited to shoot at the paintings where the paint would explode like blood. "The moment of action and an emphasis on chance were as important as the finished work." Niki Saint Phalle stopped making these paintings because, in her own words, "I had become addicted to shooting, like one becomes addicted to a drug."

p. 67   **J. J. Rousseau:** Jean Jacques Rousseau, *A Discourse upon the Origin and Foundation of the Inequality Among Mankind* (Paris, 1755; London, 1761).

p. 69   **Aldo Leopold:** Aldo Leopold, *A Sand County Almanac with Essays on Conservation from Round River* (New York: Ballantine Books, 1966), pp. 237–43.

p. 70   **One day a shovel unearths a day of its own:** Peter Richards, "On the Conditions Presently Needed," *Obliette* (Verse Press, 2001), p. 61.

p. 70   **A terrible beauty is born:** William Butler Yeats, "Easter 1916," *Easter 1916 and Other Poems* (New York: Dover Publications, 1997).

p. 70   **Everything that happens to us:** Javier Marias, *All Souls* (New York: New Directions), p. 140.

p. 70   **At night, putting your ear to the ground:** Italo Calvino, *Invisible Cities* (New York: Harvest Books, 1978), p. 126.

p. 70   **How many millions lost their homes to clear the ground?:** Alasdair Gray, *Five Letters from an Eastern Empire* (London: Penguin, 1984), p. 8.

p. 70   **How many homeless/wandering, improvisatory:** John Ashbery, "Litany," *As We Know* (New York: Penguin Classics, 1979).

p. 70   **The sight made us all very silent:** Alasdair Gray, *Five Letters from an Eastern Empire* (London: Penguin, 1984), p. 3.

p. 70   **We've got to go underground therefore, like seed:** Henry Miller, *Nexus* (New York: Grove Press, 1994), p. 31.

p. 70   **Night-season. I think that is a lovely phrase:** Zadie Smith, *White Teeth* (New York: Random House, 2000), p. 415.

p. 71   **Niles Eldredge:** Niles Eldredge, "A Field Guide to the Sixth Extinction," *New York Times Magazine*, December 2, 1999, pp. 144–46.

p. 71   **Jane Goodall:** Jane Goodall, "An Evening of Conscience," Lyceum II Lecture, March 4, 2008, Symphony Hall, Salt Lake City, Utah, sponsored by the Environmental Humanities Graduate Program, University of Utah.

p. 73   **Jacob:** Jacob Smith is former executive director of the Center for Native Ecosystems located in Boulder, Colorado, whose goal, aside from saving threatened and endangered species in the American West, was to create enough legitimate ruckus that Secretary of the Interior Gale Norton would know him by name. She did. He is currently mayor of Golden, Colorado. I sent him this letter on February 7, 2002, after our road trip to southeastern Colorado.

p. 73   **To a God Unknown:** John Steinbeck, (New York: Penguin Books, 1995).

p. 76   **a small group of friends:** Nicole Rosmarino, Danny Robinson, Robert Alsobrooke, Rich Reading, and Lauren McCain accompanied Jake and me on this outing. They founded the Southern Plains Land Trust (SPLT) whose mission is to create a short-grass prairie reserve network that enables native plant and animal communities to once again thrive, with minimal human intervention. In November 1998, SPLT purchased a 1,280 acre parcel of short-grass prairie in Baca County, Colorado, three miles north of the Comanche National Grassland. They call this preserve, which was secured in response to a generalized loss of prairie and lack of prairie dog habitat, Fresh Tracks. With a strategy of land acquisition and restoration coupled with a strong outreach program, these conservationists are signifying a new path toward land management. There are currently 3,200 acres of protected lands within the Southern Plains Land Trust. Web site: www.southernplains.org.

p. 87 **"If you kill all the prairie dogs"**: Barre Toelken, "Prairie Dogs Cry for Rain," *Quest* (September–October, 1978), p. 115. I had the privilege of meeting Barre Toelken at Utah State University in 1983, where he told me this story in person. It has always stayed with me. When Navajo elders to this day speak of prairie dogs, it sounds as if they are saying "Paradox." Ranchers in southern Utah, when speaking with their accent and inflection, sound as if they are calling prairie dogs, "prayer dogs."

p. 89 **I offer my own opinion**: Terry Tempest Williams, "In the Shadow of Extinction," *New York Times*, February 2, 2003. I would like to thank my editor, David Shipley.

p. 89 **The Lives of Animals**: J. M. Coetzee, *Elizabeth Costello* (New York: Viking, 2003), p. 110. "The Lives of Animals" was delivered by J. M. Coetzee as a series of lectures at Princeton University as part of the 1997–98 Tanner Lectures. It became part of Coetzee's novel *Elizabeth Costello*.

p. 90 **a connection between racism and specism**: Mary Midgley writes provocatively about this relationship of discrimination: "The term racism combines unthinkingly three distinct ideas—the triviality of the distinction drawn, group selfishness, and the perpetuation of an existing power hierarchy . . . speciesism corresponds to the most extreme form of racism." *Animals and Why They Matter* (Athens: University of Georgia, 1984), pp. 100–1. And then there is Kant, "He who is cruel to animals becomes hard also in his dealings with men."

p. 90 **scala naturæ**: Aristotle introduced the idea of *scala naturæ*, or "the ladder of nature," believing God created a succession of life forms beginning from the most lowly formless matter to rocks, plants, lower animals, then higher animals, with human beings eventually developing into divine beings, next to God. This idea of "The Great Chain of Being" in which every organism was "related to every other in a continuously graded scale" persisted through the Middle Ages until the scientific revolution of the seventeenth and eighteenth centuries. One could argue this led us to the scientific understanding of the phylogenetic order of things or evolution. However, one could also argue that it has kept us in an anthropocentric state of mind where hierarchical thinking has contributed to our own arrogance and isolation. Arthur O. Lovejoy's book, *The Great Chain of Being—A Study of the History of an Idea* (Cambridge: Harvard University Press, 1976), provides a brilliant analysis of this progression of thought.

p. 90 **"Anyone who says life matters"**: Coetzee, *Elizabeth Costello*, p. 110.

p. 91 **19 May 2004**: I want to thank John Hoogland for permission to print this letter. April 19, 2008.

p. 109 **a dream of creating a labyrinth**: On December 24, 2007, on what would have been Steve Tempest's fiftieth birthday, a labyrinth was dedicated in his name at the Intermountain Medical Center, 5121 South Cottonwood Street, Murray, Utah. The labyrinth was lovingly funded through the generous support of family and friends.

p. 134 **Tomahawk**: The word "tomahawk" (not a trap but a tool) evokes the poem about prairie dogs by Hart Crane.

The little voices of prairie dogs
Are tireless . . .
They will give three hurrahs
Alike to stage, equestrian, and pullman,
And all unstintingly as to the moon.

And Fifi's bows and poodle ease
Whirl by them centred in the lap
Of Lottie Honeydew, movie queen,
Toward lawyers and Nevada.

And how much more they cannot see!
Alas, there is so little time,
The world moves by so fast these days!
Burrowing in silk is not their way—
And yet they know the tomahawk.

Indeed, old memories come back to life;
Pathetic yelps have sometimes greeted
Noses pressed against the glass.

Gargoyle, *vol. 3, no. 2 (August 1922).*

p. 140　**The real act of anthropomorphism:** I would like to alert readers to the French document, *The Universal Declaration of Animal Rights—Comments and Intentions,* edited by Georges Chapouthier and Jean-Claude Nouet (Paris: Ligue Francaise des Droits de l'Animal, 1998). *"The Universal Declaration of Animal Rights was solemnly proclaimed in Paris on October 1978 . . . The intention of the Universal Declaration of Animal Rights is to establish an egalitarian right to life, no matter what the species be."* This code of ethics, call it "a rational biocentrism or extended humanity" based on a reverence for life, puts into practice what Albert Schweitzer dreamed. The authors write, "Let us hope this new moral concept leads to greater wisdom after so many thousands of years of wars and atrocitites."

p. 142　**would I lose all credibility:** Many of us within the conservation community worry about this when speaking from a place of instinct and intuition verses scientific fact. Stephan Harding, who holds a doctorate in ecology from the University of Oxford and is the coordinator of the master's degree in Holistic Science at Schumacher College in Devon, England, writes, "I ask you . . . to consider yourself a conspirator in the effort to find a new language for breathing life back into our experience of the Earth, who for the last 400 years has been treated as if she were a dead lump of rock with a few insignificant and rather irksome life forms and traditional cultures clinging to her ragged surface." Stephan Harding, *Animate Earth—Science, Intuition and Gaia* (White River Jct., VT: Chelsea Green Publications, 2008), p. 39.

Removing the masks from our animal faces is a task that has hardly begun. . . .
Other animals do not need a purpose in life. A contradiction to itself, the human
animal cannot do without one. Can we not think of the aim of life as being simply
to see?

John Gray, Straw Dogs, *Granta Publications, 2002, p. 38, 199*

p. 142 **Robert Rauschenberg:** An American artist (1925–2008) who was particularly known for his Combines, where nontraditional materials were used to create collage-like constructions. He often picked up trash and other found objects on the streets of New York City to incorporate into his work. Rauschenberg participated with Jasper Johns in many of Niki Saint Phalle's Shooting Paintings in the 1960s. I thank David Rosane for the gift of Rauschenberg's print, and his shared love of birds.

p. 152 **Insight sees the insignificant:** Lao Tzu, *Tao Te Ching*, A New English Version by Ursula LeGuin (Shambhala Publications, 1997), p. 67.

p. 154 **There are no bounds:** Coetzee, *Elizabeth Costello*, p. 80.

p. 154 **"I believe in what does not bother to believe in me":** Ibid., p. 218. This is the last sentence to a beautiful interrogation of belief.

p. 155 **Never postpone gratitude:** Albert Schweitzer (1875–1965) received the Nobel Peace Prize in 1952. His philosophy and phrase "reverence for life" has become bedrock in my own thinking of how we try to embody an ethical stance toward life. He was an early advocate against nuclear weapons and proliferation:

> *I am life which wills to live, in the midst of life which wills to live. As in my own will-to-live there is a longing for wider life and pleasure, with dread of annihilation and pain; so is it also in the will-to-live all around me, whether it can express itself before me or remains dumb. The will-to-live is everywhere present, even as in me. If I am a thinking being, I must regard life other than my own with equal reverence, for I shall know that it longs for fullness and development as deeply as I do myself. Therefore, I see that evil is what annihilates, hampers, or hinders life. And this holds true whether I regard it physically or spiritually. Goodness, by the same token, is the saving or helping of life, the enabling of whatever life I can to attain its highest development.*

Dr. Schweitzer's FBI files are still closed to the public. Werner Picht, *Albert Schweitzer: The Man and His Work* (London: Allen & Unwin, 1964). Also published under the title *The Life and Thought of Albert Schweitzer* (New York: Harper & Row, 1964).

p. 157 **Words come from ancestry:** Lao Tzu, *Tao Te Ching*, p. 90.

p. 164 **A rhizome ceaselessly establishes connections:** Gilles Deleuze and Felix Guattari, *A Thousand Plateaus—Capitalism and Schizophrenia* (Minneapolis: University of Minnesota Press, 1987), pp. 3–25. The chapter "Rhizomes," on the idea of assemblage, has a strong correspondence to Gregory Bateson's notion of metaphor and relational patterns. "A rhizome has no beginning or end; it is always in the middle, between things, interbeing, intermezzo . . . alliance" (p. 25). I thank Adele Bealer for her help and inspiration regarding these semblances of form.

p. 170 **Heaven and Earth aren't humane:** Lao Tzu, *Tao Te Ching*, p. 8.

p. 174 **So the unwanting soul:** Ibid., p. 3.

p. 178 **Animals have only their silence left with which to confront us:** Coetzee, *Elizabeth Costello*, p. 52.

p. 180 **Kiki Smith:** "I think there's a spiritual power in repetition, a devotional quality, like saying rosaries" (1998). "Kiki Smith: Prints, Books, and Things," a first-time collection of this sculptor's works in the world of printed art was exhibited at the Museum of Modern Art in Queens, New York, December 2003–March 2004. I was particularly struck by her engravings of small rodents entitled White Mammals, inspired by study skins at the Carnegie Museum of Natural History. These were inspired by a vision she had of creating "Noah's Ark as a death barge." One of her sculptures, *Born,* is a woman emerging from a deer. Two figures become one. When asked about this merging of species and form, Smith said, "I just got into thinking about the figures in their relationships to nature and animals. First I started making animals, then I made the human figures, then I thought, 'Oh what would happen if I combine the two?' The place where these collide with one another is myth and fairy tale and religion." Interview by Phong Bui and Susan Harris, *The Brooklyn Rail,* December 2006/2007. Lastly, Smith says, "I found this anthropomorphism of animals interesting, the human attributes we give to animals and the animal attributes we take on as humans to construct our identity . . . this relationship between nature and human nature."

p. 184   The root of the noble is in the common: Lao Tzu, *Tao Te Ching,* p. 54.

p. 190   "The Voyage": Eduardo Galeano, "The Voyage," *Parabola* 31:2 (Summer 2006).

p. 191   "Time tells": Ibid.

p. 196   The faith and the love: T. S. Eliot, *Four Quartets* (New York: Harcourt Brace and Company, 1943), p. 15.

p. 196   Where is the Life we have lost in living?: T. S. Eliot, opening stanza from the choruses from "The Rock," 1934 (New York: Harvest HBJ Books, 1967).

p. 198   Faith McNulty: Faith McNulty, *Must They Die? The Strange Case of the Prairie Dog and the Black-Footed Ferret* (Garden City, NY: Doubleday, 1971), p. v.

p. 199   What was it like?: Coetzee, *Elizabeth Costello,* p. 187.

p. 199   Being Different: Lao Tzu, *Tao Te Ching,* p. 28.

p. 200   "Bewilderness": This line comes from Ursula LeGuin's comments on the *Tao Te Ching,* #20 on "Being Different." For further exploration of this idea, see "anarcho-primitivist" John Moore's essay, "Bewilderness" from his pamphlet, *Anarchy and Ecstacy, Visions of Halcyon Days.* He says, "The amalgamation of 'bewilder' and 'wilderness' in this new term possesses the advantage of restoring the emphasis on the wild component of the former term. But the addition of 'ness' to 'bewilder' also remains appropriate . . . the suffix 'ness,' in addition to expressing a particular state (e.g., sweetness, tiredness), originally denoted a 'land' or 'place.' " Hence, as a term "bewilderness" reunites the two separated aspects of "bewilder" as geographical dislocation and as a spiritual condition. Available through www.beatingheartspress.com.

p. 202   "When some portion of the biosphere": Midgley, *Animals and Why They Matter,* p. 145.

p. 202   The Way bears them": Lao Tzu, *Tao Te Ching,* p. 66.

p. 203   Our press on the planet: Ecocide, "ecological suicide," an early reference in 1969 described it as "Ecocide—the murder of the environment—is everybody's business." For further insights into ecocide, read Tom Turnipseed's essay "Ecocide" at www.commondreams.org, July 22, 2005, and "Post-Humanism and Ecocide in William Gibson's *Neuromancer* and Ridley Scott's *Blade Runner*" by Tama Leaver (1997). Ms. Leaver wrote this piece while studying ecotexts at the University of Western Australia.

p. 203   Fazil Iskander: Fazil Iskander, *In the Grip of Strange Thoughts* (Zephyr Press, 2000), p. 77.

p. 208 **We do not serve the weak:** Rachel Naomi Remen, MD, *My Grandfather's Blessings* (New York: Riverhead Books, 2001). "We serve life not because it is broken, but because it is holy." My brother Steve had the privilege of working with Rachel Remen at Commonweal, where he attended the Commonweal Cancer Health Program in January 2004. Alongside the healing grace of Dr. Remen, Steve benefited from the practical and spiritual wisdom of Michael Lerner, Lenore Lefer, Waz Thomas, and the friendship of Jenepher Stowell. All made an extraordinary difference in how he lived with his illness and found an inner peace beyond cure. For more information on this week-long residency, see their Web site at www.commonweal.org

"In the 14th century, the physician Maimonides offered a prayer," says Rachel Naomi Remen, MD, who trains physicians in the art of caring. " 'Inspire me with love for all of thy creatures. May I see in all who suffer only a fellow human being.' "

p. 208 **A pine box built by his neighbor:** Doug Larson, at Steve's request, crafted "a traveling box" for him out of native white pine from the Wasatch Mountains.

p. 218 **A piece of driftwood:** This piece appeared in a slightly different form as the Meridel LeSueur essay "Lightkeepers," in *Stone Water Review* 8 (2005). I want to thank Mary Francois Rockcastle for her editorial care.

p. 220 **Ted Toombs:** For more information on Ted Toombs and work on other Safe Harbor Agreements contact the Environmental Defense Fund at www.edf.org.

p. 222 **Prairie Dog Day:** *Utah Prairie Dog Update.* In February 2007, the U.S. Fish and Wildlife Service made a negative ninety-day finding on a petition to upgrade the Utah prairie dog's status from a threatened species to an endangered one, filed by WildEarth Guardians, Center for Native Ecosystems and Terry Tempest Williams. See Negative 90-day Finding: 72FR 7843 7852. February 21, 2007.

A new Utah Prairie Dog Recovery Plan is being promised by USFWS to be published in the fall of 2008. The last Utah Prairie Dog Recovery Plan was written in 1991. The Fish and Wildlife Service has also announced that they intend to do a five-year review for the Utah Prairie Dog.

Translation: The U.S. Fish and Wildlife Service has denied increasing the protections for Utah prairie dogs and continues to allow the killing of hundreds of this imperiled species.

The future of the Utah prairie dog, alongside the White-tailed prairie dog and the Gunnison prairie dog, remains uncertain at best. Emotions continue to run high. On May 31, 2008, Gerald R. Sherrat, the mayor of Cedar City, Utah, wrote in an editorial appearing in the *Salt Lake Tribune:*

> *Our nation's founders fought the Revolutionary War to preserve property rights, and made a big point of the principle in the Constitution. But evidently prairie dogs trump the Constitution, because they can take a piece of valuable property (into which some might have poured their life savings) and make it worthless overnight, merely by establishing a colony on it and then calling on their allies . . . and the federal government to rule that the land is theirs and any attempt to remove them will result in a heavy fine or a jail sentence. What the British couldn't do, prairie dogs are doing with ease.*

"Judge Refuses to Stop Removal of Prairie Dogs"

An effort to stop the removal of a colony of Utah prairie dogs from a Cedar City golf course has fallen short.

A request for an injunction against a plan to trap prairie dogs at the Cedar Ridge Public golf course was denied in the U.S. 10th Circuit Court of Appeals this week.

That means critters living on the golf course could face extermination, spurring renewed concern from wildlife conservation organizations, which earlier this year filed a law suit in an attempt to save the prairie dogs.

Under a federal plan, prairie dog trapping at the Cedar Ridge public golf course resumed July. At the end of August, course employees would be allowed to set spring-loaded traps to kill the animals and fill their burrows.

The federal plan calls for moving animals trapped on the golf course to Berry Springs, on Forest Service land north of Highway 12 and Ruby's Inn [very near Bryce Canyon National Park].

"Even if federal biologists take the animals to a relocation area, they are likely to die in their new surroundings," said Nicole Rosmarino, senior biologist for Wild Earth Guardians.

In a blog appearing after this article, a reader writes, "Round them up and feed them to the homeless."

Edward O. Wilson writes, "The next century will see the closing of the Cenozoic Era (the Age of Mammals) and a new one characterized not by new life forms but by biological impoverishment. It might be appropriately called the 'Eremozoic Era,' the Age of Loneliness." Consilience: The Unity of Knowledge *(New York: Alfred A. Knopf, 1998)*

p. 224   **Village of Arts and Humanities:** This dynamic community project founded by Lily Yeh in 1986 is located in Germantown, Pennsylvania. For more information visit their Web site, www.villagearts.org.

p. 225   **Barefoot Artists:** For more information on this organization and The Rwanda Healing Project, with photographs of the Rugerero Genocide Survivors Village, visit www.barefootartists.org. Photographer and filmmaker Chris Landry has made a beautiful twenty-three minute documentary entitled *Twibuke* with interviews of members of the Rugerero Genocide Survivors Village, also available through Barefoot Artists. For an in-depth look at Lily Yeh's methodology using art to transform and build community read, "Warrior Angel: The Work of Lily Yeh" by Bill Moskin and Jill Jackson, available for download at this same Web site.

p. 226   **a ghost here on Earth:** "The Rwandanese call them the *Bapfuye Buhagazi*, the 'walking dead.'" Gérard Prunier, *The Rwanda Crisis* (New York: Columbia University Press, 1995), p. 358.

p. 237   **Nyiragongo:** The volcano erupted on Thursday, January 17, 2002, at 5:00 p.m. Over 400,000 people were displaced in Goma and fled to Gisenyi. One third of the city was on fire. The last time Nyiragongo had erupted was in 1977 when 2,000 people were killed. Louis Gakumba tells of carrying his mother across the lava fields and how the soles of his shoes were melting.

p. 238   **The word "genocide":** Raphael Lemkin, *Axis Rule in Occupied Europe: Laws of Occupation—Analysis of Government Proposals for Redress* (Washington, DC: Carnegie Endowment for International Peace, 1944). In 1941, Winston Churchill called it "the crime without a name."

p. 238   **internationally accepted definition of genocide:** Article 2 of the Convention on the Prevention and Punishment of the Crime of Genocide defines genocide as

> any of the following acts committed with intent to destroy, in whole or in part, a national, ethnical, racial or religious group, as such:
> (a) Killing members of the group; (b) Causing serious bodily or mental harm to members of the group; (c) Deliberately inflicting on the group conditions of life calculated to bring about its physical destruction in whole or in part; (d) Imposing measures intended to prevent births within the group; (e) Forcibly transferring children of the group to another group.

p. 240   **Rosamond Halsey Carr:** Rosamund Halsey Carr and Ann Howard Halsey. *Land of a Thousand Hills* (New York: Viking Penguin, 1999). Madame Carr passed away on September 29, 2006, almost a year to the day we met her in 2005. She was a very close friend of Dian Fossey; they met in 1967. Their friendship is celebrated in the film *Gorillas in the Mist*.

p. 241   **Hotel Rwanda:** The film about Paul Rusesabagina, who was the hotel manager of the Mille Collines in Kigali during the genocide (2004). Other films made about the Rwandan genocide include *Sometimes in April* (2005), *Beyond the Gates* (2007), and *Shake Hands with the Devil* (2005), a powerful documentary about Roméo Dallaire, the former head of the UN peacekeeping mission in Rwanda, on genocide and the failure of humanity.

p. 245   **F.A.R.G.:** Fonds National pour l'Assistance aux Rescapés du Génocide (FARG/Victims of Genocide Fund).

p. 248   **William Coffin's:** William Sloan Coffin was a clergyman and social activist, 1924–2006. To view Robert Shetterly's portrait of William Sloan Coffin go to www.americanswhotellthetruth.com

p. 254   **The new Rwandan flag:** A new flag was initiated in 2002 to symbolize an era of hope and restoration in Rwanda. The colors red, reminiscent of blood spilled, and black, associated with grief and mourning, are no longer used. The previous flag, created in 1961, was comprised of three vertical bands, from the hoist red-yellow-green, with a big black letter *R* in the middle of the yellow band.

p. 257   **"You have a humanitarian heart":** You often hear Rwandans say, "*Ufite umutima mwiza,*" which translates to "You have a good heart."

p. 260   **Ingabire Fedele:** Her story is told in National Genocide Museum in Kigali.

p. 261   **Dian Fossey:** Dian Fossey, *Gorillas in the Mist* (New York: Mariner Books, 1983), p. 239.

p. 267   **I am touching only surfaces:** At Dartmouth College, I was invited to have breakfast with Calestous Juma, professor of the Practice of International Development at the Kennedy School of Government at Harvard. Born in Kenya, he is a charismatic leader in the pioneering fields of biodiplomacy and ecological jurisprudence, where he has helped forge linkages between sound scientific knowledge and international relationships, particularly in conservation and private property rights in Africa. I asked him what he thought the most important thing we can do as Americans to help support these issues of sustainability and development on the continent. He let out a hearty laugh. "Get a brain transplant!" And then his eyes narrowed. "I'm serious."

p. 284   **Dr. Paul Farmer:** On March 30, 2005, Dr. Paul Farmer, medical anthropologist, physician, and humanitarian, gave the University of Utah Tanner Lecture on Human Values, titled "Can Human Rights Survive? Reflections on Inequality and Modernity." Farmer is the subject of *Mountains Beyond Mountains: The Quest of Dr. Paul Farmer, A Man Who Would Cure the World* (New York: Random House, 2003), by Pulitzer Prize–winning author Tracy Kidder. To learn more about Partners in Health and their first pilot project, launched in Africa in 2005 at the Rwinkwavu Hospital in Rwanda, go to their Web site, www.pih.org. Speaking personally, meeting Dr. Farmer was a life-changing experience.

p. 284   **If I look at the mass:** Paul Slovik, " 'If I look at the mass I will never act': Psychic Numbing and Genocide," *Judgment and Decision Making* 2(2) (April 2007), pp. 79–95.

p. 285   **Frantz Fanon:** Frantz Fanon, *The Wretched of the Earth* (Paris: Francois Maspero, 1963), p. 3. This is a highly influential book on the psychology of the oppressed and the path toward liberation that impacted the thinking of both Malcolm X and Martin Luther King. "Decolonization is always a violent event." For a contemporary look at Fanon and his relevancy today, I recommend John Edgar Wideman's novel *Fanon* (New York: Houghton Mifflin, 2008).

p. 290   **Lake Kivu in twilight:** The view of Lake Kivu may be changing. Three hundred meters below its surface there is an estimated 55 billion cubic meters of methane gas. The Rwandan government has signed an $80 million deal with an international company, Dane Associates, to start developing the methane. The goal is to double Rwanda's electricity supply within two years. Long-term potential is tremendous, with methane increasing Rwanda's energy production by more than twenty times the capacity in 2008.

p. 292   **Rape:** Award-winning filmmaker Lisa F. Jackson looks at the plight of Rwandan and Congolese women in her film *The Greatest Silence: Rape in the Congo*. It is a stunning portrait of violence and healing through the voices of women. For more information, go to www.info@thegreatestsilence.org.

p. 305   **Nineteenth-century colonialism:** For an in-depth look at the effects of colonialism, I recommend Gérard Prunier, *The Rwanda Crisis* (New York: Columbia University Press, 1995), particularly the chapter, "Rwandese Society and the Colonial Impact: The Making of a Cultural Mythology (1894–1959)."

p. 305   **"the new progressive missionaries"** Omer Bartov, *In God's Name: Genocide and Religion in the Twentieth Century* (New York: Berghahn Books, 2001).

p. 305   **Tom Ndahiro:** Tom Ndahiro, "The Church's Blind Eye to Genocide in Rwanda," *Genocide in Rwanda—Complicity of the Churches?*, edited by Carol Rittner, John K. Roth, and Wendy Whitworth (St. Paul, MN: Paragon House, 2004), p. 231.

p. 307   **"Genocide depends on raising voices":** John Roth, "Raising Voices," *Genocide in Rwanda*, p. 25.

p. 308   **"It was easier than farming"**: Jean Hatzfeld, *Machete Season—the Killers in Rwanda Speak* (New York: Farrar, Straus and Giroux, 2005). This is perhaps one of the most disturbing book I have ever read: the accounts of those who committed the murders, devastating in their matter-of-factness.

p. 308   **Erosion   the other genocide**: Rwanda is roughly the size of the state of Maryland. According to government reports, Rwanda's population of 8.7 million is set to double to 16 million by 2020 at its current growth rate of 3.2 percent per year. Rwanda's population density is the highest in Africa and has risen from 183 per sq km in 1981 to 345 per sq km in 2000. Rural population per square kilometer of arable land was around 901 in 1999, one of the highest in Africa.

In comparison to social indicators of other sub-Saharan countries, Rwanda has the highest level of poverty—70 percent live below the poverty line, up from 53 percent prior to the 1994 genocide. An astute rendering of population density, war, and land can be found again in Gérard Prunier's book *The Rwanda Crisis*. "The decision to kill was of course made by politicians, for political reasons. But at least part of the reason why it was carried out so thoroughly by the ordinary rank-and-file peasants . . . was feeling that there were too many people on too little land, and that with a reduction in their numbers, there would be more for the survivors" (p. 4).

p. 309   **Jean Paul Samputu**: His CD *Testimony from Rwanda* was released in 2004. He is a revered musician in Africa and recognized as one of the most versatile vocal artists in the world, singing in six different languages. In 2007, Samputu was recognized as an Ambassador of Peace by the Interreligious and International Federation for World Peace.

p. 319   **Gacaca**: One of the most insightful books I read on this process is *Justice on the Grass* by Dina Temple-Raston (New York: Free Press, 2005). All over Rwanda you see billboards advertising Gacaca that say *"Ukurikurakiz,"* which translates to "Truth heals."

p. 336   **Paul Kagame's leadership**: For an insightful look at Paul Kagame, taken from over thirty hours of interviews, from 2006 to 2007, foreign correspondent Steven Kinzer has written a fascinating book, *A Thousand Hills*, John Wiley & Sons, 2008, on this charismatic leader's story and how a war-torn nation can re-create itself.

p. 358   **". . . how things have changed"**: Amy Vedder and her husband, Bill Weber, cofounded the Mountain Gorilla Project, heralded for its success in both saving the species and providing economic benefits for a poor nation. They are the authors of *In the Kingdom of Gorillas: Fragile Species in a Dangerous Land* (New York: Simon and Schuster, 2001).

Dr. Vedder worked for the Wildlife Conservation Society from 1990 to 2006, directing various international programs. Since January 2007, she has been the senior technical advisor for the United Nations Development Program's Protected Areas Biodiversity Project. In May 2008 she became vice president of research at The Wilderness Society in Washington, DC, overseeing public lands and natural resources policies.

p. 358   **Virunga National Park**: to read about what is happening to the mountain gorillas in a war zone on the border of Rwanda and the Congo, as of 2008, turn to *National Geographic*'s cover story, "Who Murdered the Mountain Gorillas," by Mark Jenkins, July, 2008, pp. 34–65. A heartbreaking example of how conservation, conflict, and poverty are all interconnected to a devastating end.

p. 362   **sunflower oil:** In January 2008, Alan Jacobson, Eric Reynolds, and Meghan Morris returned to the Village along with Engineers Without Borders. Great progress was made in the sunflower oil enterprise. The brown oil of 2007 is now being replaced with beautiful golden oil and production has been greatly enhanced. More sunflower oil presses have been purchased and the Village of Rugerero is surrounded by acres of towering sunflowers nodding toward a growing cottage industry producing enough seeds to keep production flowing. Over twenty people are being trained in this business venture.

Another project in the Village now underway is the installation of a rainwater harvesting system for one hundred families with gutters and water storage tanks so that they will have clean and safe water, which will improve the overall health situation in the Village of Rugerero. Barefoot Artists are working with other NGOs such as Population Services International. The Compton Foundation has provided support for the water project.

And the Jefferson Medical School is continuing its health program with their research on humanistic medicine. They helped to set up a ten-member Rwandan health team to monitor hygiene practices in the Village. The team members created some lovely paintings, translating health lessons into pictures, readily translatable to other villagers, particularly the children.

p. 369   **The dedication ends:** Dr. Jim Plumb and Susan Plumb, a museum curator, had organized a photography exhibit showing the stages of construction of the Genocide Memorial in an outdoor museum next to the memorial for all the visitors to see. The photographs became windows into the work of the community and there was great interest among the villagers as they found themselves in the pictures and witnessed once again the sequence of events that created this sanctuary for their loved ones who had been killed.

p. 377   **"the genocide project will never be over":** Many Rwandans, especially Tutsi, fear that although Rwanda appears to be at peace, there is "a quiet war" that continues to boil right below the surface.

In March 2008, Rwandan lawmakers voted in a new law that will tackle cases of "genocide ideology." *The New Times*, Rwanda's national paper, reported: "The Bill is introduced months after damning revelations that showed cases in which school children demonstrated predisposition to the genocide ideology. The Senate had also found rampant genocide ideology in families, schools, and some individuals, which sparked the House to react immediately to stop the vice.

Under the new law, children under twelve years found guilty will be sent to rehabilitation centers for up to a year. According to the law, anybody who kills another for ethnic reasons will be jailed for life. There will be no pardon or reduction of sentences for those found guilty. "Hatred is hard to kill," said a young man in Gisenyi.

p. 382   **Once upon a time:** Permission granted by Katherine E. Standefer, "The Names of Things," Murie Ranch, (Summer 2006).

p. 384   **The Watts Towers:** I want to thank my brother Dan Tempest and his wife, Thalo Porter Tempest, for accompanying me to see Simon Rodia's work on September 9, 2006. The Watts Towers are one of nine folk art sites listed on the National Register of Historic Places and were designated a National Historic Landmark in 1990.

p. 385   **The pattern is the thing:** Gregory Bateson, *Steps to an Ecology of Mind* (San Francisco: Chandler Publishing, 1972). The chapter "Redundancy and Coding" provides a provocative discussion on "the idea that communication is the creation of redundancy or patterning." Redundancy is not valued within modernity. We praise innovation and growth, not stability and equilibrium. We are coming to an understanding of ecological and cultural sustainability by necessity. "Meaning, pattern, redundancy depends upon where we sit." Bateson believes "nature maintains wisdom" (p. 147). Art also maintains wisdom. "Love can survive only if wisdom has an effective voice."

p. oo   **The beauty made belongs to everyone. We all bow:** "The beautiful thing about mosaic is that you can't do it alone," Lily Yeh says, "you need other people's help." Mosaic can be viewed as "outsider art," art that is created by those on the margins of the traditional institutions and boundaries of "culture" such as art schools, galleries, museums. The Web site www.rawvision.com is devoted to this exploration of folk art. Mosaic has become "outsider art" that walked away from the religiosity of churches into the common currency of the masses.

A wonderful example of an artist who defies categorization is the untutored Indian sculptor and mosaicist, Nek Chand (1924–), who constructed the Rock Garden of Chandigarh. It is a forty-acre sculpture garden in the city of Chandigarh, India, created to assuage the losses of the 1947 Partition, in which Pakistan was created, displacing 17.9 million people. Of these, only 14.5 million arrived, suggesting that 3.4 million went "missing." He has reconstructed a lost community with the help of a community. I highly recommend the book *Nek Chand's Outsider Art, the Rock Garden of Chandigarh* by Lucienne Peiry and Philippe Lespinasse (Paris: Flammarion, 2005).

Ironically, Nek Chand's whimsical re-creation of places and people and animals made over five decades was being built during the same time in the same city that one of the great architects of the twentieth century, Le Corbusier, was designing the "new India" on a grid.

Indeed, we can all bow to an art form that has evolved from Roman floors to celestial ceilings to Antoni Gaudi's mosaic towers in Barcelona that read "Hosanna" at La Sagrada Familia to the bejeweled altar that reads "Twibuke" designed by Lily Yeh in the Genocide Survivors Village of Rugerero in Rwanda. *We remember.*

In the foyer of the United Nations in New York City, there is a dove made of mosaic carrying an olive leaf. It was made in Ravenna. A gift. A prayer for peace, ongoing.

p. 386   **first morning in America:** April 17, 2007.

In the depths of our darkness there is no one place for Beauty.
The whole place is for Beauty.

RENÉ CHAR, Leaves of Hypnos

SELECTED BIBLIOGRAPHY

MOSAIC

Bendazzi, Wladimiro, and Riccardo Ricci. *Ravenna: Mosaics, Art History, Archeology, Monuments, Museums.* Ravenna: Edizioni Sirri, 1993.

Borsook, Eve, Fiorella Gioffredi Superbi, and Giovanni Pagliarulo, eds. *Medieval Mosaics: Light, Color, Materials.* The Harvard University Center for Italian Renaissance Studies at Villa Tatti. Silvana Editoriale, 2000.

Bovini, Giuseppe. *Ravenna: Its Mosaics and Monuments.* 1956. O.P.

Brown, Peter. *The World of Late Antiquity.* New York: Norton, 1989.

Cameron, Averil. *The Later Roman Empire, AD 284–430.* London and New York: Harvard University Press. Routledge. 1993.

———. *The Mediterranean World in Late Antiquity, AD 395–600.* London: Routledge, 1993.

Dunbabin, Katherine M. D. *Mosaics of the Greek and Roman World.* Cambridge: Cambridge University Press, 1999.

Farneti, Manuela. *Glossario Tecnico-Storico del Mosaico.* Ravenna: Longo Editore, 1993.

Fischer, Peter. *Lucio Orsoni, Mosaici.* Ponzano Veneto: Vianello Libri, 2000.

Goodwin, Elaine. *Encyclopedia of Mosaic.* North Pomfret, VT: Trafalgar Square, 2003.

Goodwin, Elaine M., ed. *Classic Mosaic: Designs and Projects Inspired by 6,000 Years of Mosaic Art.* London: Quintet Books. Apple Press, 2000.

Ling, Roger. *Ancient Mosaics.* Princeton, NJ: Princeton University Press, 1998.

Marco De Luca. *Opera Musiv,* Catalogo. Galleria "La Mosaique." Ravenna, Italy. 1996.

Moldi, Christiana, ed. *I colori della luce.* Venice: Marsilo, 1996.

Pace, Parco Della. *Mosaico d'amicizia fra i popoli.* Ravenna: Longo Editore, 1988.

Read, Herbert. *The Grass Roots of Art.* London: Faber and Faber, 1955.

Rocuzzi, Isotta Fiorentini, and Elisabetta Fiorentini. *Mosaic: Materials, Techniques and History.* Ravenna: MW EV Editions, 2002.

Scarry, Elaine. *On Beauty and Being Just.* Princeton, NJ: Princeton University Press, 1999.

Bateson, Gregory. *Steps to an Ecology of Mind.* San Francisco, CA: Chandler Publications, 1972.

Bekoff, Marc. *Minding Animals: Awareness, Emotions, and Heart.* New York: Oxford University Press, 2002.

Chapouthier, Georges, and Jean-Claude Nouet, eds. *The Universal Declaration of Animal Rights: Comments and Intentions.* Paris: Ligue Francaise des Droits de l'Animal, 1998.

Coetzee, J. M. *Elizabeth Costello.* New York: Viking Penguin, 2004.

Forest Guardians et al. Comments on Utah Prairie Dog five-year review submitted to the Utah Ecological Services Field Office, U.S. Fish and Wildlife Service.

Gray, John. *Straw Dogs: Thoughts on Humans and Other Animals.* London: Granta Books, 2002.

Harding, Stephan. *Animate Earth—Science, Intuition and Gaia.* White River Junction, VT: Chelsea Green Publications, 2008.

Hengesbaugh, Mark Gerard. *Creatures of Habitat.* Logan: Utah State University Press, 2001.

Hoogland, John L. *The Black-Tailed Prairie Dog: Social Life of a Burrowing Mammal.* Chicago: University of Chicago Press, 1995.

Jamison, Dale, ed. *Singer and His Critics.* Malden, MA: Blackwell Publishers, 1999.

Jenkinson, Clay S. *Message on the Wind: A Spiritual Odyssey on the Northern Plains.* Marmarth, ND: Marmarth Press, 2002.

Johnsgard, Paul A. *Prairie Dog Empire: A Saga of the Shortgrass Prairie.* Lincoln: University of Nebraska Press, 2005.

Leopold, Aldo. *A Sand County Almanac.* New York: Ballantine Books, 1986.

McCain, Lauren. *Report from the Burrow: Forecast for the Prairie Dog.* Santa Fe, NM: WildEarth Guardians, 2008.

McNulty, Faith. *Must They Die? The Strange Case of the Prairie Dog and the Black-Footed Ferret.* New York: Doubleday, 1970.

Midgley, Mary. *Animals and Why They Matter.* Athens: University of Georgia Press, 1983.

Miller, Brian, Richard P. Reading, and Steve Forrest. *Prairie Night—Black-Footed Ferrets and the Recovery of Endangered Species.* Washington, DC: Smithsonian, 1996.

Scully, Matthew. *Dominion: The Power of Man, the Suffering of Animals, and the Call to Mercy.* New York: St. Martin's Press, 2002.

Shepard, Paul. *The Others.* Washington, DC: Island Press, 1997.

———. *Thinking Animals.* Athens: University of Georgia Press, 1998.

Singer, Peter. *Animal Liberation.* New York: New York Review of Books, 1990.

———. *One World: The Ethics of Globalization.* New Haven and London: Yale University Press, 2002.

Slobodchikoff, C. N., et al. "Semantic Information Distinguishing Individual Predators in the Alarm Calls of Gunnison's Prairie Dogs." *Animal Behavior* 42(5): 713–19.

U.S. Fish and Wildlife Service Recovery Plan. Utah Prairie Dog Recovery Plan. Denver, CO: U.S. Fish and Wildlife Service, 1991.
Utah Prairie Dog Negative 90-day Finding: 72FR 7843 7852. February 21, 2007.
Utah Prairie Dog Status Review. *Federal Register,* Vol. 73, No. 88, Tuesday, May 6, 2008. Washington, DC: Department of the Interior/ Fish and Wildlife Service.
Wise, Steven M. *Rattling the Cage: Toward Legal Rights for Animals.* New York: Perseus Books, 2000.

RWANDA

Arendt, Hannah. *The Origins of Totalitarianism.* New York: Schocken, 2004.
Carr, Rosamond Halsey, and Ann Howard Halsey. *Land of a Thousand Hills.* New York: Viking Penguin, 1999.
Cheadle, Don, and John Prendergast. *Not on Our Watch: The Mission to End Genocide in Darfur and Beyond.* New York: Hyperion, 2007.
Coffin, William Sloan. *Credo.* Louisville, KY: Westminster John Knox Press, 2004.
Conrad, Joseph. *Heart of Darkness.* Los Angeles: Green Integer, 2003.
Courtemanche, Gil. *Sunday at the Pool in Kigali.* New York: Vintage, 2004.
Dalliare, Roméo. *Shake Hands with the Devil: The Failure of Humanity in Rwanda.* New York: Carroll and Graf, 2004.
Des Forge, Alison. *Leave None to Tell the Story.* New York: Human Rights Watch, 1999.
Diamond, Jared. *Collapse.* New York: Viking, 2005.
Fanon, Frantz. *The Wretched of the Earth.* New York: Grove Press, 2005.
Farmer, Paul, *Pathologies of Power—Health, Human Rights, and the New War on the Poor.* Berkeley: University of California Press, 2005.
Fossey, Dian. *Gorillas in the Mist.* New York: Houghton Mifflin, 1983.
Franck, Frederick, Janis Roze, and Richard Connolly, eds. *What Does It Mean to Be Human?* New York: St. Martin's Press, 2000.
Gioseffi, Daniela. *On Prejudice—A Global Perspective.* New York: Anchor Books Doubleday, 1993.
Gourevitch, Philip. *We Wish to Inform You That Tomorrow We Will Be Killed with Our Families.* New York: Picador, 1999.
Gross, Jan T. *Neighbors.* Princeton, NJ: Princeton University Press, 2001.
Hatzfeld, Jean. *Machete Season—the Killers in Rwanda Speak.* New York: Farrar, Straus and Giroux, 2005.
———. "La Stratégie des Antilopes" ["The Strategy of Antelopes"]. Paris, France, 2007.
Hochschild, Adam. *King Leopold's Ghost.* New York: Houghton Mifflin, 1998.
Illibagiza, Immaculee, *Left to Tell: Discovering God Amidst the Rwandan Holocaust.* Carlsbad, CA: Hay House, 2007.
Keane, Fergal. *Season of Blood: A Rwandan Journey.* New York: Penguin, 1995.
Kidder, Tracy. *Mountains Beyond Mountains.* New York: Random House, 2003.
Kinzer, Stephen, *A Thousand Hills: Rwanda's Rebirth and the Man Who Dreamed It,* Hoboken, NJ: John Wiley & Sons, 2008.

Koff, Clea. *The Bone Woman.* New York: Random House, 2004.

Loomba, Ania, eds. *Postcolonial Studies and Beyond.* Durham, SC: Duke University Press, 2005.

Mamdami, Mahmood, *When Victims Become Killers: Colonialism, Nativism and Genocide in Rwanda,* London: James Curry, 2001.

Melvern, Linda. *Conspiracy to Murder: The Rwandan Genocide.* New York: Verso, 2004.

———. *A People Betrayed: The Role of the West in Rwanda's Genocide.* London: Zed Books, 2000.

Neuffer, Elizabeth. *The Key to My Neighbor's House: Seeking Justice in Bosnia and Rwanda.* New York: Picador, 2001.

Power, Samantha. *A Problem from Hell: America and the Age of Genocide.* New York: Basic Books, 2002.

Prunier, Gérard. *The Rwanda Crisis: History of a Genocide.* New York: Columbia University Press, 1997.

Rieff, Philip. *Charisma.* New York: Pantheon, 2007.

Rittner, Carol, John K. Roth, and Wendy Witworth, eds. *Genocide in Rwanda: Complicity of the Churches?* St. Paul, MN: Paragon House, 2004.

Rusesabagina, Paul. *An Ordinary Man.* New York: Viking, 2006.

Said, Edward W. *Culture and Imperialism.* New York: Vintage, 1994.

Salzberg, Sharon. *Faith: Trusting Your Own Deepest Experience.* New York: Riverhead Books, 2002.

Schaller, George. *The Mountain Gorilla.* Chicago: University of Chicago Press, 1963.

Schweitzer, Albert. *Out of My Life and Thought.* New York: New American Library, 1953.

Schweitzer, Albert, ed. *A Place for Revelation: Sermons on Reverence for Life.* New York: Macmillian Publishing Company, 1988.

Seaver, George. *Albert Schweitzer: The Man and His Mind.* New York: Harper Brothers, 1947.

Temple-Taston, Dina. *Justice on the Grass.* New York: Free Press, 2005.

Vedder, Amy, and Bill Webber. *Kingdom of the Gorillas: Fragile Species in a Dangerous Land.* New York: Simon and Schuster, 2001.

Young, Robert J. C. *Postcolonialism.* London: Oxford University Press, 2003.

ACKNOWLEDGMENTS

First and last, Brooke. Always, Brooke. This acknowledgment with love. Especially for his support and insights through this eight-year inquiry of how one finds beauty in the midst of war. Without Brooke, there would never be Maine or Italy or a long view of prairie dogs or a pilgrimage to Rwanda. Without Brooke, our family would not include Louis. Without Brooke, the doors to the wider world would not be open. Without Brooke, no voice.

My father. John Tempest. Henry James said he preferred "tough-minded people with tender hearts." He would have liked my father. He understands work and the power of physical labor. He believes in the dignity of dirt. He believes in the landscape of books and nature and taught me how to read both. He has dared to change and has. My father: tough and tender, smart and honest. Generous.

My brothers. Steve. His spirit. Dan. His mind. Hank. His heart. All three embody an intelligence born of the body in relationship to place. This place. Utah. Family. Home. It is my brothers who have taught me *"Today the cry of the laborer is the cry of the Earth" (Nikos Kazantzkis).*

ITALY: The Mosaic Art Studio in Ravenna. My teacher, Luciana Notterni, who taught me the rules of mosaic; who showed me the power of Byzantium red, how color is the key and expression is the gift; how Byzantine people used mosaic to tell both a spiritual and political story; how mosaic is the medium of the people. Marco de Luca, who took me into his studio and exposed his radical heart through art; who showed me how three red tesserae next to three green tesserae create the gray line of shadow on a face of mosaic; that part of the nature of man is to recompose a unity that has been broken. Manuela Farneti, my guide and translator through the mosaics of Ravenna. Lucio Orsoni in Venice. Jorie Graham, who sent me to Cattedrale Di Santa Maria Assunta on the island of Torcello where I witnessed the mosaic of Universal Judgment resting on the shoulders of Mary. Beatrice Monti della Corte von Rezzori at Santa Maddalena in Tuscany, who provided me a room in the Tower, rich conversations around a dinner table, and much writing material. Wade Davis, who sent me the invitation. My housemates in Donnini for their inspiration: Anna Pavord, Divan Abeydayo, and Tomáz Salamun, especially for his line *"I grew tired of the image of my tribe and moved out" (Four Questions).* Marco Cantoni and a hundred lit candles at dinner. Massimo Sottani, the former mayor of Reggello, who introduced me to Masacchio in Cascia. Giuppe Pietromarch, who brought me into the grace of her garden and the mosaic park of artist Niki Saint Phalle in Garavicchio; and a brief, magical conversation with Ivan Illich in Firenze. Lee Kogan at the American Museum of Folk Art in New York provided rigorous insight into mosaics and "outsider art," especially the work of Indian mosaicist Nek Chand. And Bill Resor, a scholar of Roman history and a rancher in Teton County, Wyoming, helped me tremendously through his astute understanding of Rome.

PRAIRIE DOGS: Dr. John L. Hoogland is my prairie dog guru. His landmark text, *The Black-tailed Prairie Dog: Social Life of a Burrowing Mammal,* remains the gold standard in prairie dog research. His forthcoming book on his ten-year study of Utah prairie dogs is eagerly anticipated. Through his personal commitment, joyful engagement, and meticulous science on behalf of the genus *Cynomys,* we are all the beneficiaries of his integrity. I am in his debt for both allowing me to participate as one of his field assistants, with the good company of Alyssa Taylor, Sarah Druy, and Theo Manno, at Bryce Canyon National Park, as well as his thorough reading and precise editorial help on this manuscript. Nicole Rosmarino, PhD, who directs the animal wildlife program of WildEarth Guardians, has been my guardian angel and general heroine through education, example, and the endless queries she answered throughout the writing of this book. Her critical reading and fact-checking of all materials made an extraordinary difference. If the Utah prairie dog survives the onslaught of development and cruelty in this century, it will largely be because of the vigilance, understanding, and fierce love of scientists and advocates like her. Jacob Smith and Erin Robertson of the Center for Native Ecosystem (CNE) are among those heroes. It was Jake who first mapped out the ecological and political landscape of prairie dogs for me. Through his leadership as executive director of CNE, the prairie dogs are being given the stature they deserve. It was the tenacity of biologist Erin Robertson that helped break the story of corruption within the United States Fish and Wildlife Service, exposing Julie A. MacDonald (a Bush appointee), the deputy secretary for Fish and Wildlife and Parks, for undermining and manipulating scientific data on endangered species for the benefit of industry. The Department of Interior in 2007 admitted MacDonald had "inappropriately influenced" eight endangered species decisions, the white-tailed prairie dog among them. I thank both Jake and Erin for their careful reading and vital suggestions. Con Slobodchikoff is a visionary ecologist, for whom I am deeply grateful for the use of his research on prairie dog communication. Dave Crawford of the Rocky Mountain Defense Fund has been a leader in prairie dog awareness and action in Boulder County, Colorado. Lynne Hull continues to inspire a conversation on the ground between art and animals, sculpture and habitat. Ted Toombs is a compassionate conservationist. His brave work in establishing Safe Harbor Agreements through Environmental Defense shows us what ecological diplomacy can become. Ted Owens and Elise Boeke at U.S. Fish and Wildlife Service in Salt Lake City have been very helpful and accommodating in answering my questions on Utah prairie dogs. Their jobs as field biologists have not been easy in these last eight years. Bless them for staying.

The work of Albert Schweitzer, Gregory Bateson, Paul Shepard, Peter Singer,

J. M. Coetzee, Mary Midgley, Jack Turner, Michael Soulé, Jane Goodall, and Marc Beckoff have been central to my thinking and understanding of our relationships with animals; the American Museum of Natural History in New York and the Field Museum of Natural History in Chicago have been very generous in allowing me to work with their collections of *Cynomys*. Isabel Sterling, research librarian at UCLA, has been enormously helpful in identifying "mosaic" as an ecological concept and idea as described within scientific literature; also Curt Meine; I thank Ursula LeGuin for her revelatory translation of the *Tao Te Ching;* Julie Jargon, for her article, "Dog Eat Dog" that appeared on www.westword.com and for her permission in letting me draw from her experience.

Our family thanks Commonweal, where Michael Lerner, Rachel Naomi Remen, Lenore Lefer, Raz Thomas, and Jenepher Stowell in particular, gave so much of themselves to Steve during his residency at the Cancer Health Program retreat. Their influence became part of his healing path of transformation.

RWANDA: I met Lily Yeh on March 12, 2003. My life changed on that day. She is an artist who is truly changing the world, one person at a time. When Lily spoke in her office at the Village of Arts and Humanities about seeking "a luminous place," "a place where [she] could locate the sacred in the mundane," never could I have imagined that two years later, we would be standing together in a place called Rwanda, locating another kind of numinosity. For allowing me to be her scribe and to share this story, my deepest bows. Together, with Alan Jacobson and Meghan Morris, we forged a new sense of family. I love them dearly in the name of all we have shared—spoken and unspoken. Rukirande Musana Jean Bosco of the Rwandan Red Cross is a remarkable leader whose ability to inspire and act has transformed the Rugerero Genocide Survivors Village and all of us who have had the opportunity to work with him and the community within Gisenyi. In truth, without Jean Bosco, this project would not have happened. We also acknowledge the support of the secretary general of the Red Cross in Rwanda, Mr. Karamaga Appolinaire. I thank fully our family in Rwanda: Ndebwohe Damas, Nyirambangutse Donatila, Harerimana Medard, Mujawiyera Aimée, Habumugisha Michel, Munyarubega Jolie, Buseruka Brown, Didien Yutti, Safari Kazindu Patrick, Barengayabo Ramadhan, Mabete Niyonzima Dieudonné, Gapasi Desmtes, Mugensa Joshua, Umurerwa Liberata, Bwanakweli Ildephonse, Uwanyirigira Roselyne, Uwamariya Rosette, Habumugisha Wilson, Kabayiza Eric, Twagiramungu Husein, Mutabazi Fabrice, and Mutumwinka Clementine. I want to acknowledge all those within the Rugerero Genocide Survivors Village itself, particularly Nyiraminan Emma, Mukangwije Leá, Nyiranshuti Dorotheé, Sharamanzi Thadeyo, and Nukobatango Sipesiyoss (whom I call Spacious), for their generosity of spirit. And Riberakurora Vicmanotor and Isabane Dieudonne Firkovitch, bless them, for their strength and friendship. Jean Claude, Patrick, and Emmanuel, too. My debt is large for the ways each of them has opened their heart to us. *Murakozee.* I loved working with Sibomana Francois and Mugorewindekwe Consulate on the mosaics of the memorial for which I am grateful. And to the children of the Village, all of them, blessings, may peace protect their sweet and strong presences. My fellow travelers, Chris Noble, Eric Reynolds, Robert Shetterly, Chris Landry, Daniel Yeh Traub, the Reverend

Carol DeMicco Pobanz, and Dr. James and Susan Plumb, have my love, my loyalty, and deepest respect. I also want to thank Amy Vedder, whose work in Rwanda has spanned decades and has been a point of illumination for both countries, as she and her husband, Bill Weber, have slowly and consistently built the bridge of understanding between conservation and communities. Rwandan Minister of Culture, Youth, and Sports Joseph Habineza is a charismatic leader with eloquence and passion. I appreciate his sharing of stories. Solange Katarebe, Paul Farmer, and Wangari Maathai have contributed to my thinking about Africa, in general, and Rwanda, in particular, regarding health, justice and the politics of reconstruction. The work of Alison Des Forges at Human Rights Watch, Samantha Power, Philip Gourevitch, Gérard Prunier, Jean Hatzfield, Jared Diamond, and Roméo Dallaire has been central to my immersion in Rwandan history and the genocide. Emily Shaffer, the consulate at the American Embassy in Rwanda was nothing short of a miracle worker in securing Louis Gakumba's visa. Thank you. Cynthia Bioteau, B. Murphy, and Nancy Filat, in particular, were instrumental in finding a place for Louis Gakumba and enrolling him as a student at the Salt Lake Community College; Geralyn Dreyfous has been a source of emotional support for him at the Salt Lake Film Center. So has the leadership of Rocky Anderson at High Road for Human Rights inspiring education and action. The librarians at the Map Room at the United States Library of Congress helped me to understand the ground beneath my feet through hundreds of maps, historical, geological, and cultural. Frances Pollak, in her wise and intuitive generosity, opened the doors for the Young Woman's Support Group in Rugerero. Betty L. Farrell, CNM, at Engenderhealth helped to educate me on issues of HIV and reproductive health, specifically in Sub-Saharan Africa. Laura Simms, my sister in storytelling, continues to show me what is possible through compassion on the page and in the world. Her insights have been central to this book's evolution. Ishmael Beah navigated us through the process of visas and what it means to come home to America as an African who has experienced war. Peter Matthiessen always sets the bar for me as a writer skilled in and mindful of all the ways that nature and culture meet.

Louis Gakumba: My immeasurable gratitude for being my eyes and ears and voice in Rwanda; for the power of his perceptions; for his help with this manuscript and permission to publish his poems; for bringing us into a new configuration of family; for tolerance and patience with my endless questions; for Mama Odia and Michel and his entire family, their faith. Because of him, I believe in miracles. Because of him, I believe in the capacity to heal and forgive. And especially, because of him, I believe in the power of one wild word.

HOME: Graham Greene wrote that each time a writer picks up a pen, he betrays someone. Even so, I have tried to honor my family. To Ann Tempest, Callie and Andrew Jones, Sara and Diane Tempest, no words, only my love. There were so many neighbors and friends of Steve and Ann who were remarkable during his illness: Dr. Nelson and Nancy Wright; Dr. Bill and Brenda Nibley; Dr. David Thorne; Heidi and Chris Nielson; Julie and Bill Prince; Chris and Clark Ivory; Alayne Peterson; Laurie and Ben Hathaway; Holly and Kevin Glade; Ann and Ken

Bullock; Kathy and Alan Stallings; Mark Jones; Doug Hill; Doug Larson; Kath and Bob Nilsen; Carolyn Nilsen Crawford; Kathleen and Dave Miner; Linda and Mike Dunn. I want to especially thank my family, Lynne Tempest and Steve Earl and their children, Ruby, Mason, and Hayden; Liz and Bob Tempest; Debbie and Mike Tempest; Stephanie Grimme and Matt Tempest; David Tempest; Ruth and Richard Tempest; the Dixon clan; the Williams clan, especially Shirley and Rex Williams; Becky Williams Thomas has been an ongoing source of support and strength. As has Thalo Porter Tempest and Jan Sloan.

In deep friendship: Lyn Dalebout, Dana and Jack Turner, Story Clark, Bill Resor, and their daughters, Avery and Felicia, have provided depth and optimism in the midst of doubts. Lee Carlman Riddell and Ed Riddell have been aunt and uncle to Louis; Susan Carlman, Beth McIntosh and Phil Rounds, Florence Krall Shepard, Teresa Cohn, Daryn Melvin, Katy Standefer, Jeff Foott, Charlie Craighead, Sophie Craighead, Malinda Chouinard, Joanne Dornan, Leslie Petersen and Hank Phibbs, Marcia Kunstel and Joe Albright, Fred Margolis, Marly and Dan Merrill, Andrea and Bill Broyles, Karen Skaggs, and especially Bob Schuster, whose capacity to listen deeply and guide us during a particular trying time, have made all the difference; Christopher Merrill, William Merwin, Cort Conley, Rose Moonwater, Peter Lewis, Diana Blank, Steve Tatum, Mark Bergstrom, Heidi Camp, Merrilyne Lundahl, Leo Treitler and Mary Frank, Sue Halpern and Bill McKibben, Rita and John Elder, Sonya and Tom Campion, Cindy Shogan and Brooks Yeager, Robert and Vicky Newman, Elizabeth and Rick Bass, Andrea and Doug Peacock, Trent Alvey and Dennis Sizemore, Lisa and Chris Peterson, Annette and Ian Cummins, Anne and John Milliken—each one of these friends is extended family.

In Castle Valley, Eleanor Bliss and Bill Hedden have been bedrock with their daughters, Chloe and Sarah; Laura Kamala, Vigali Hamilton, and Mary O'Brien with Deanna Harris have held their doors open for us. In Maine, Mariah Hughes and Nick Sichterman have been compass points. Their shop, Blue Hill Books, is one of the finest in this country; Susan Longaker opened her land to us; Susan and Ray McDonald allowed us to stay; Ann and Bill Backer, Susan Hands Shetterly, Jetsun Penkalski, Hugh Curran, Terry Mason, Ellen Best, Jim Dow, and Gail Page provided neighborliness; Kim Ridley and Tom Curry, insight; Christine Leith, beauty; Deb Soule, grace; Missy Greene and Eric Ziner, comfort; Peter Blaze Corcoran, his spirit, the sea.

My gratitude to Andy Friedland at Darmouth College for his influence and support alongside Carol Folt, Michael Dorsey, Jennifer Peacock, Doug Bolger, Terry Osborne, and Susan Wright, who made the Montgomery Fellowship possible in the spring of 2006. This was a rich time of thought regarding post-colonialism and environmental justice. It was here I was also able to have crucial conversations with Deogratias (Deo) Niyizonkiza, a medical student from Burundi, and Calestous Juma, who both challenged my thinking and shaped it.

To those members of the Next Generation Project from Moose, Wyoming, to Oracle, Arizona, may we continue to honor the unlearned moments through story.

I want to acknowledge the extraordinary care of Steven Barclay and Eliza Fischer, and all the ways they support my work, from protecting freedom of speech to gifts of bouquets of lavender in times of need. Through it all, it is their humor I appreciate most.

Monette Clark, my literary assistant, is a blessing of patience, professionalism, and, delightfully, a trustworthy companion in work and friendship. Her editorial help on this book was early and frequent, astute and appreciated.

READERS: Jan Sloan gave me the courage to continue with this book and not apologize as a writer; Lyn Dalebout provided her earthbound insights and love; Linda Asher gave me her expansive thinking and questions, always. Betsy Burton shared her perceptions and support both as a friend and as an independent bookseller at the King's English. Jennifer Sahn, my editor at *Orion* magazine, is as sensitive to language as anyone I know. Laurie Graham edited "Prayer Dogs" for a special issue of *Creative Nonfiction*, Diversity Dialogues, 19 (2002). Her influence remains singular. And a special glass raised to Alexandra Fuller, who has been the godmother of this book and saved my sanity repeatedly.

Pantheon Books: Heartfelt thanks to Fran Bigman for her gentle nudgings, general care, and excellent editorial judgment; Brian Barth, for his cover; Kristen Bearse; Victoria Pearson; Hannah Oberman-Briendel; Carol Rutan; Katie Freeman; Michiko Clark; Altie Karper; and a special thanks to Janice Goldklang, in particular, for the history we share. Sonny Mehta, my highest respect.

Dan Frank is my collaborator in every sense of the word. And his work as my editor for twenty years at Pantheon Books has been impeccable. He is an editor of ideas. He is fearless in his capacity to take creative risks. The shape of his mind has shaped my manuscripts again and again. But more valuable than his brilliance as a visionary publisher and lover of words is his engaging and enduring friendship.

Carl Brandt has been the backbone of my writing life for twenty-five years. Chekhov has said that the two qualities a writer needs most are faith and stamina. When I lack both, Carl has held these qualities for me. I am so grateful for his integrity, his sound judgment, and for caring enough to be critical. He is my mentor, my confidant, my reader, and my advocate. This book is dedicated to him.

Beauty . . . comes to us with no work of our own; then leaves us prepared to undergo a great labor.

ELAINE SCARRY, *On Beauty and Being Just*

ABOUT THE AUTHOR

TERRY TEMPEST WILLIAMS is the Annie Clark Tanner Scholar in Environmental Humanities at the University of Utah. Her previous books include *The Open Space of Democracy, Red, Leap,* and *Refuge,* and her writing appears frequently in journals and newspapers worldwide. She is the recipient of Lannan and Guggenheim fellowships in literary nonfiction. She divides her time between Utah and Wyoming.

A NOTE ON THE TYPE

The text of this book was set in Ehrhardt, a typeface based on the specimens of "Dutch" types found at the Ehrhardt foundry in Leipzig. The original design of the face was the work of Nicholas Kis, a Hungarian punch cutter known to have worked in Amsterdam from 1680 to 1689. The modern version of Ehrhardt was cut by the Monotype Corporation of London in 1937.

Composed by Creative Graphics
Allentown, Pennsylvania

Printed and bound by Berryville Graphics
Berryville, Virginia

Designed by M. Kristen Bearse